JOHNNY HIRO

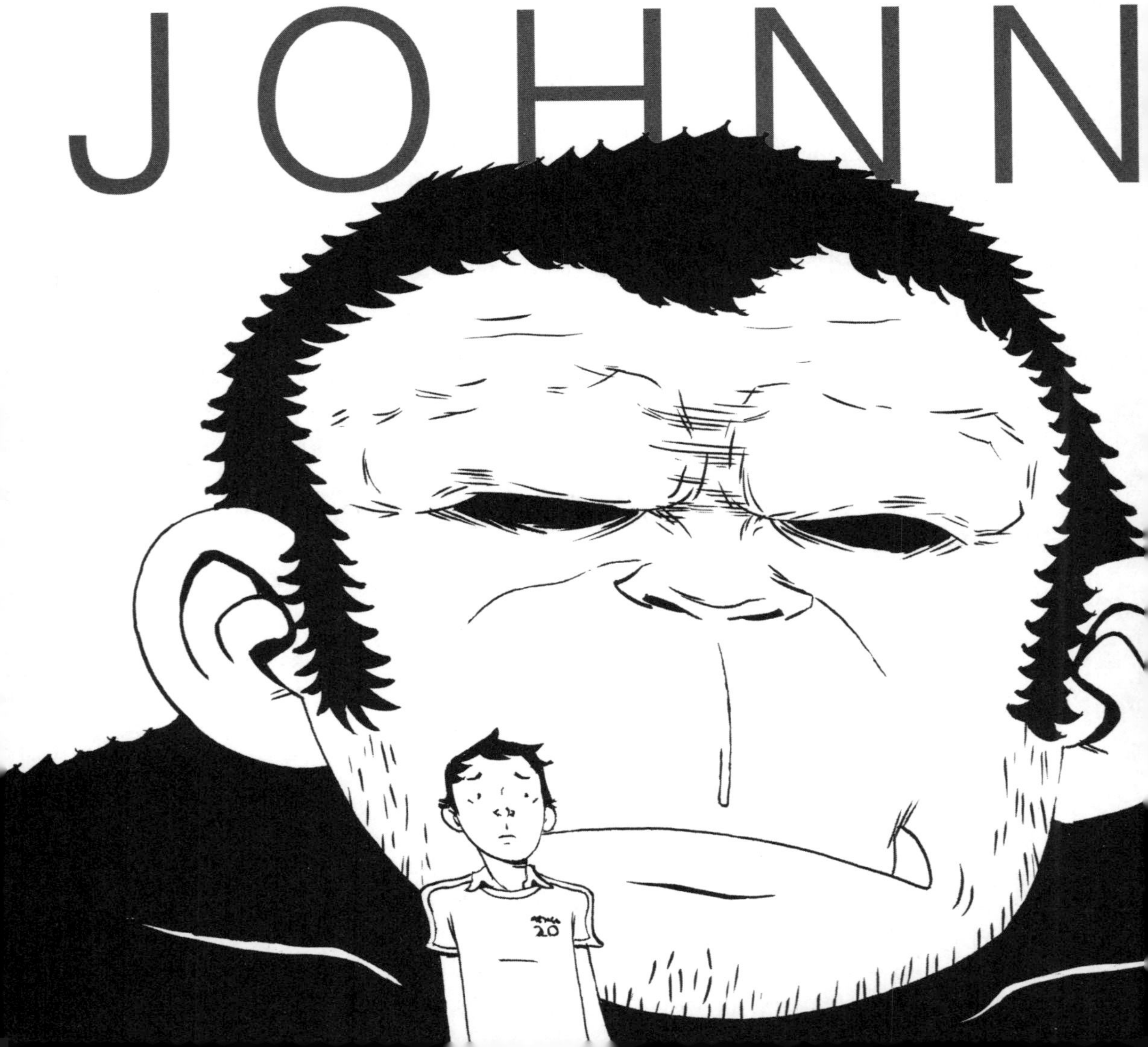
JOHNN

Y HIRO

{ The Skills to Pay the Bills }

Fred Chao

letters by David C. Hopkins

TOR®

A Tom Doherty Associates Book
New York

This is a work of fiction. All of the characters, organizations, and events portrayed in this novel are either products of the author's imagination or are used fictitiously.

JOHNNY HIRO: THE SKILLS TO PAY THE BILLS

A Tor Book
Published by Tom Doherty Associates, LLC
175 Fifth Avenue
New York, NY 10010

www.tor-forge.com

Tor® is a registered trademark of Tom Doherty Associates, LLC.

The Library of Congress Cataloging-in-Publication Data is available upon request.

ISBN 978-0-7653-2938-7

Tor books may be purchased for educational, business, or promotional use. For information on bulk purchases, please contact Macmillan Corporate and Premium Sales Department at 1-800-221-7945, extension 5442, or write specialmarkets@macmillan.com.

First Edition: October 2013

Printed in the United States of America

0 9 8 7 6 5 4 3 2 1

For Ethan, Mikey, Seth, Jeff, Peter, Scott, Opus, Beth

I couldn't imagine a better crew
to have my back.

One of the themes of my earlier life, as I recall it now, is that I was forever projecting myself forward and backward at the same time, negating the present moment, changing my mind with alarming frequency. . . . I couldn't name my longing, and yet it was there, always driving me away from the place where I stood.

—Michael Paterniti, *Driving Mr. Albert*

I got that head nod shit that make you break your neck.
Woo hah! I got you all in check.

—Busta Rhymes, "Woo Hah!! Got You All in Check"

おとこ、おんな、ゴリラ

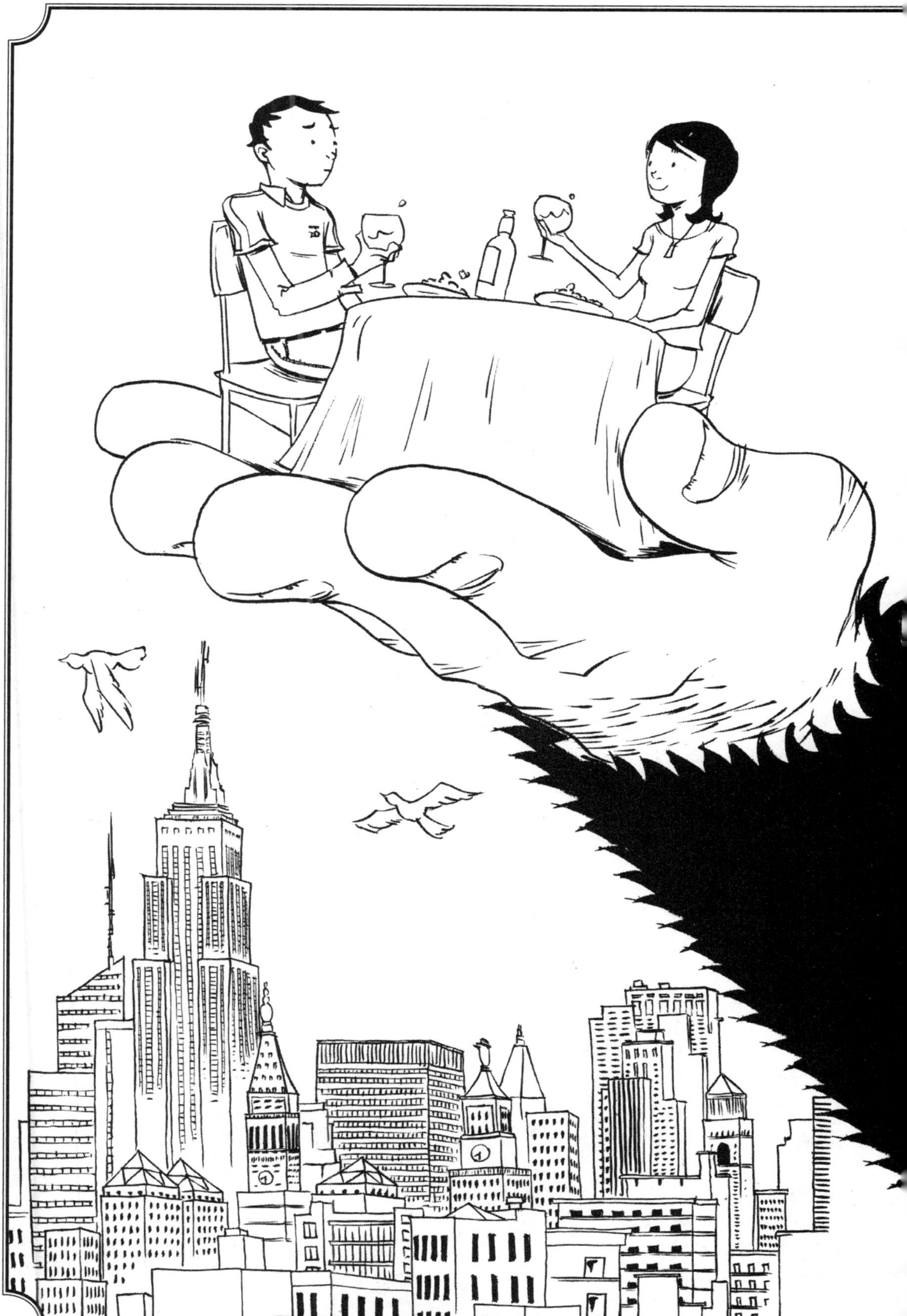

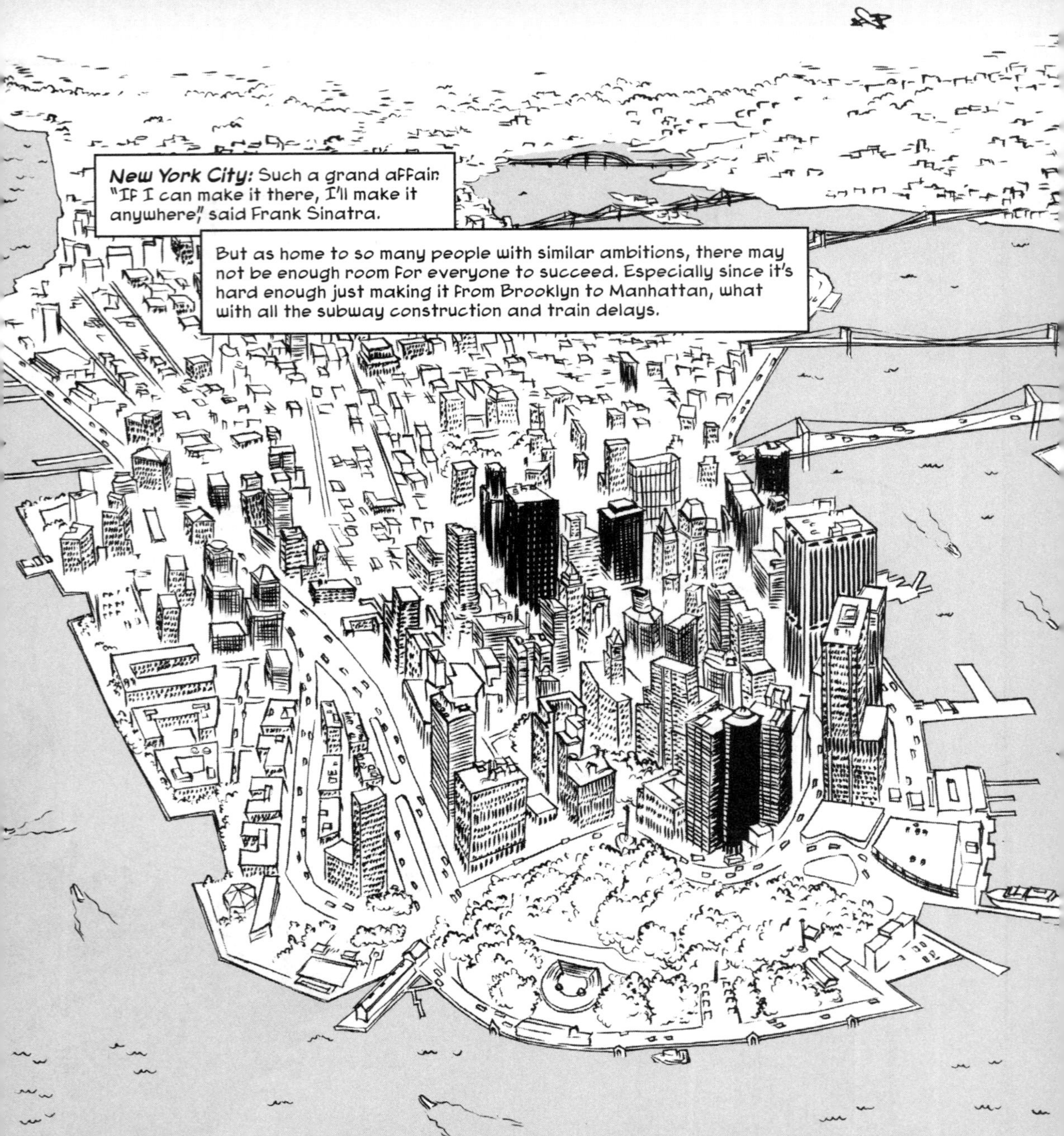
New York City: Such a grand affair. "If I can make it there, I'll make it anywhere," said Frank Sinatra.
But as home to so many people with similar ambitions, there may not be enough room for everyone to succeed. Especially since it's hard enough just making it from Brooklyn to Manhattan, what with all the subway construction and train delays.

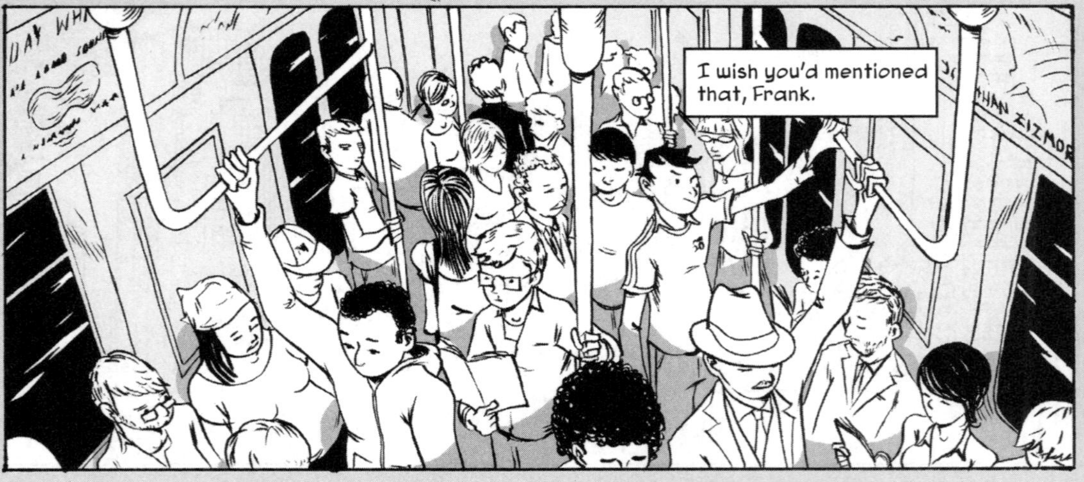
I wish you'd mentioned that, Frank.

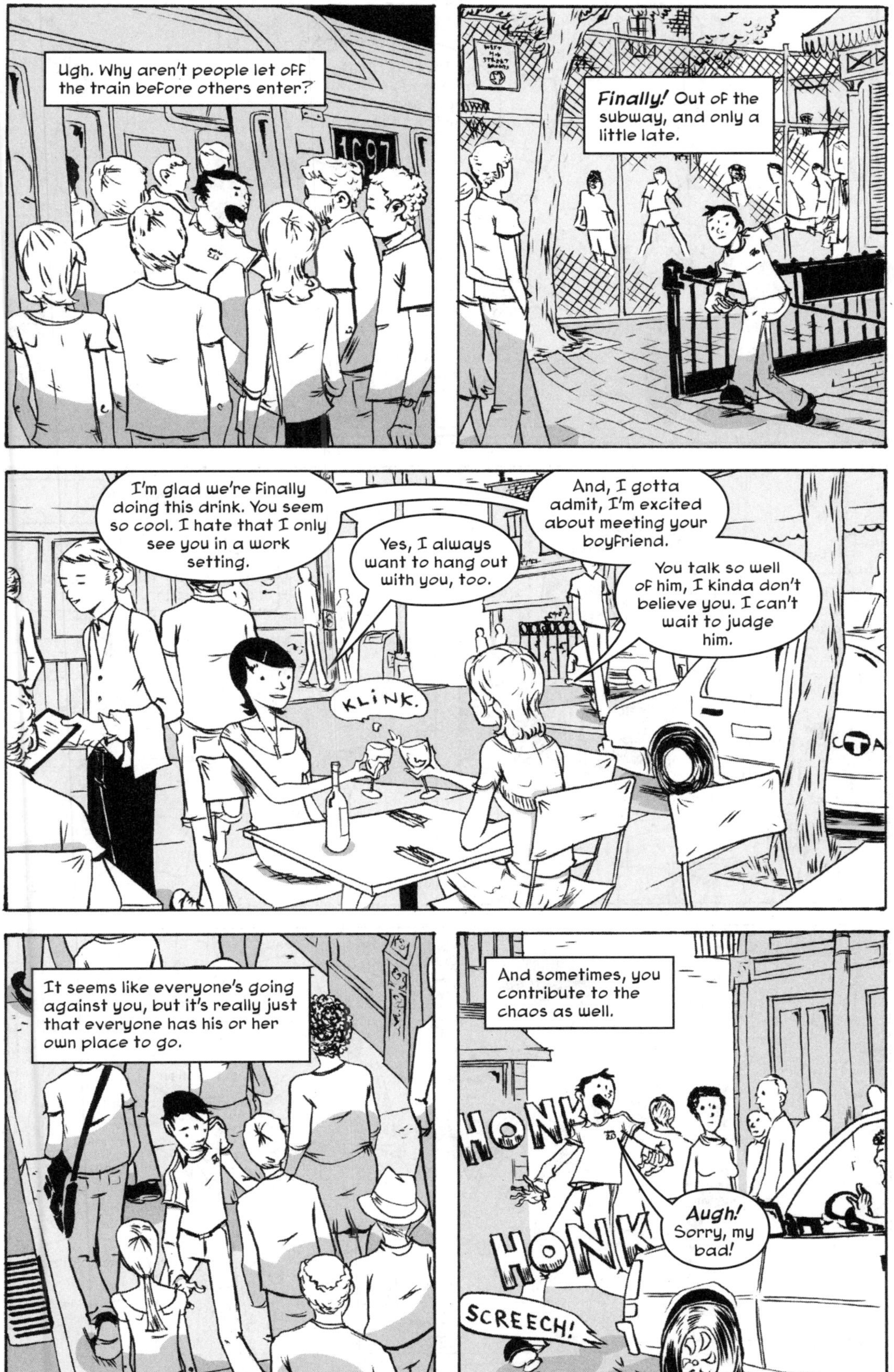
Ugh. Why aren't people let off the train before others enter?
1C97
Finally! Out of the subway, and only a little late.
I'm glad we're finally doing this drink. You seem so cool. I hate that I only see you in a work setting.
Yes, I always want to hang out with you, too.
And, I gotta admit, I'm excited about meeting your boyfriend.
You talk so well of him, I kinda don't believe you. I can't wait to judge him.
KLINK.
It seems like everyone's going against you, but it's really just that everyone has his or her own place to go.
And sometimes, you contribute to the chaos as well.
HONK
HONK
Augh! Sorry, my bad!
SCREECH!

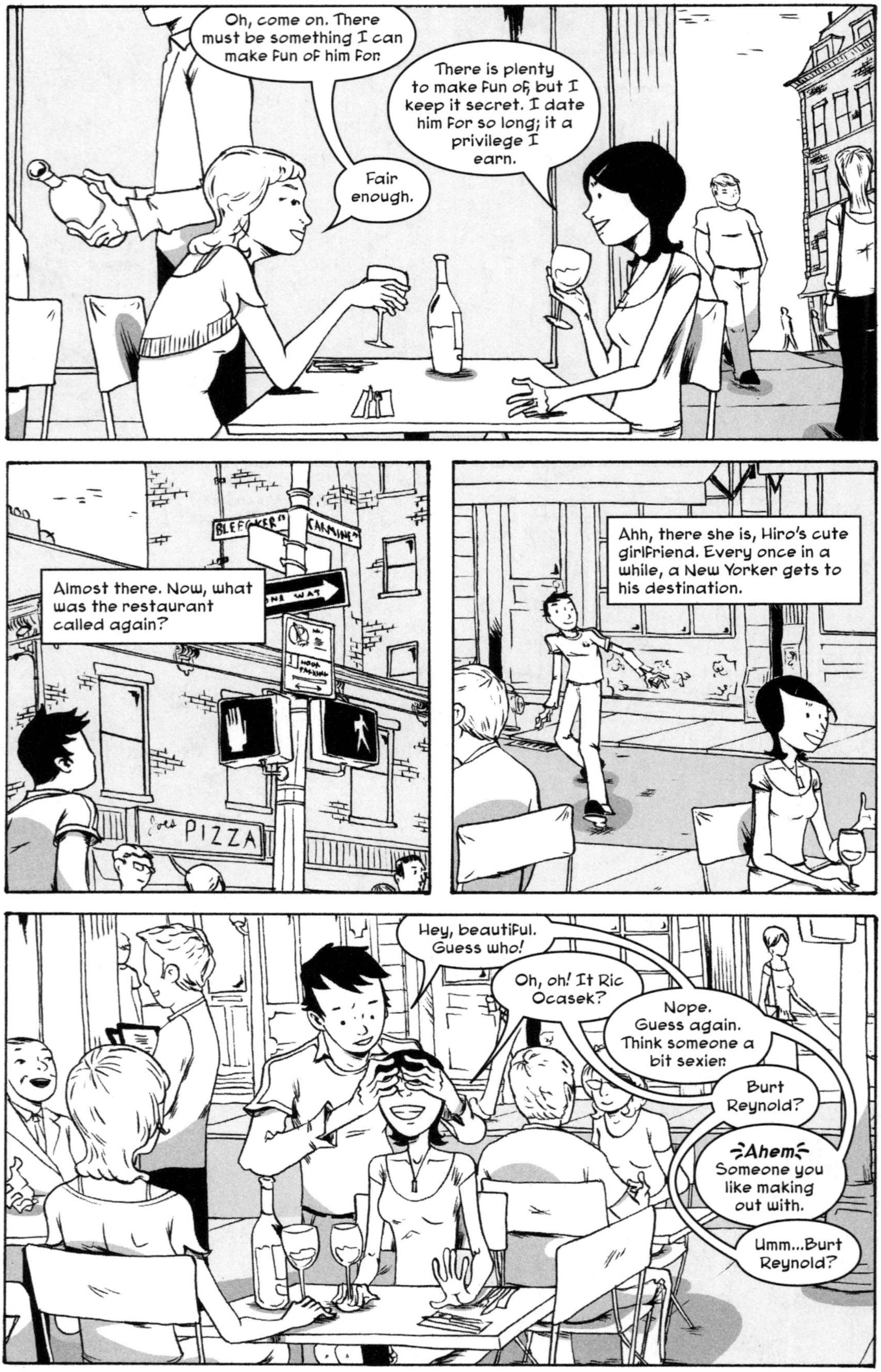
Oh, come on. There must be something I can make fun of him for.
There is plenty to make fun of, but I keep it secret. I date him for so long; it a privilege I earn.
Fair enough.
Almost there. Now, what was the restaurant called again?
PIZZA
Ahh, there she is, Hiro's cute girlfriend. Every once in a while, a New Yorker gets to his destination.
Hey, beautiful. Guess who!
Oh, oh! It Ric Ocasek?
Nope. Guess again. Think someone a bit sexier.
Burt Reynold?
Ahem
Someone you like making out with.
Umm...Burt Reynold?

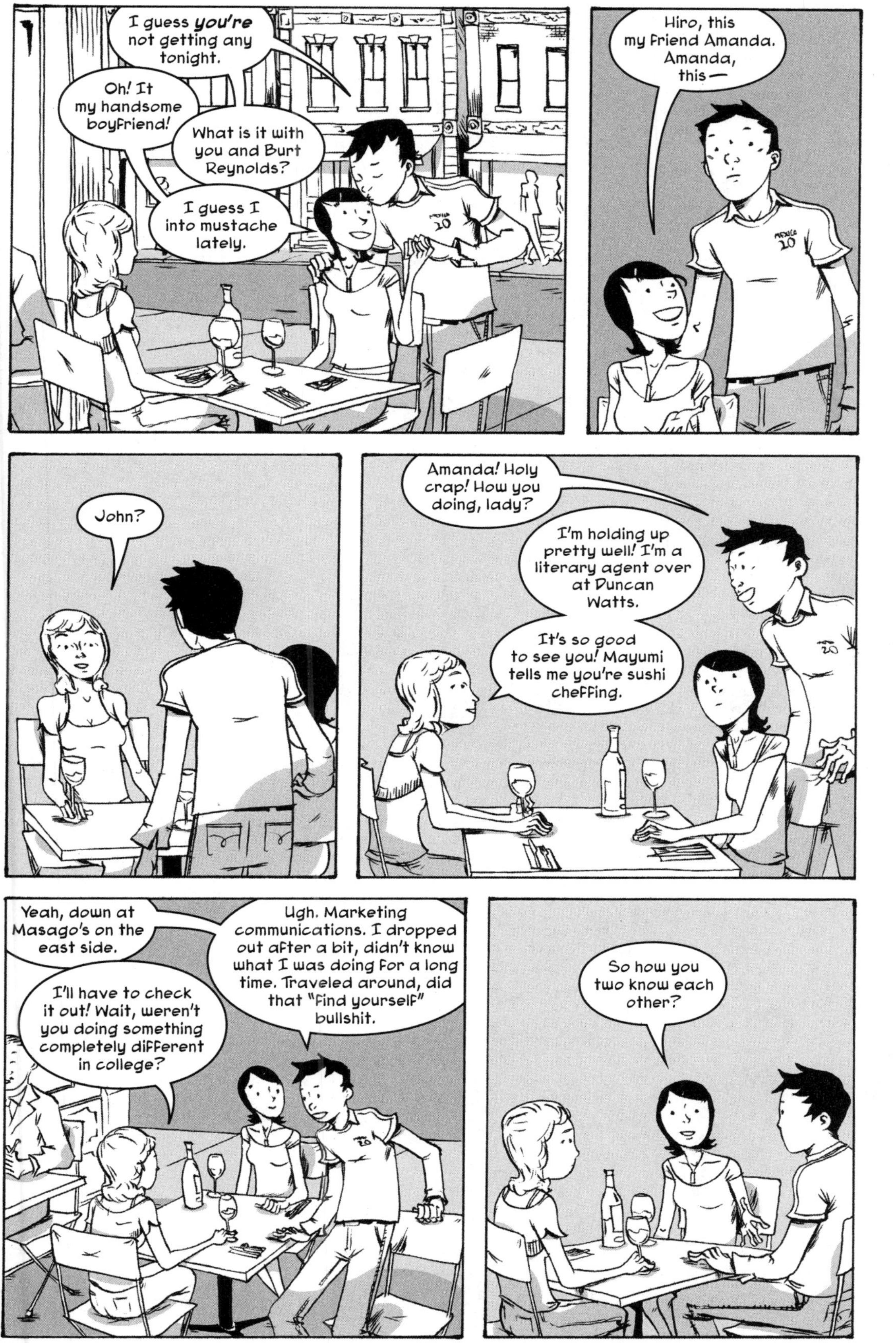
Oh! It my handsome boyfriend!
I guess *you're* not getting any tonight.
What is it with you and Burt Reynolds?
I guess I into mustache lately.
Hiro, this my friend Amanda. Amanda, this—
John?
Amanda! Holy crap! How you doing, lady?
I'm holding up pretty well! I'm a literary agent over at Duncan Watts.
It's so good to see you! Mayumi tells me you're sushi cheffing.
Yeah, down at Masago's on the east side.
I'll have to check it out! Wait, weren't you doing something completely different in college?
Ugh. Marketing communications. I dropped out after a bit, didn't know what I was doing for a long time. Traveled around, did that "find yourself" bullshit.
So how you two know each other?

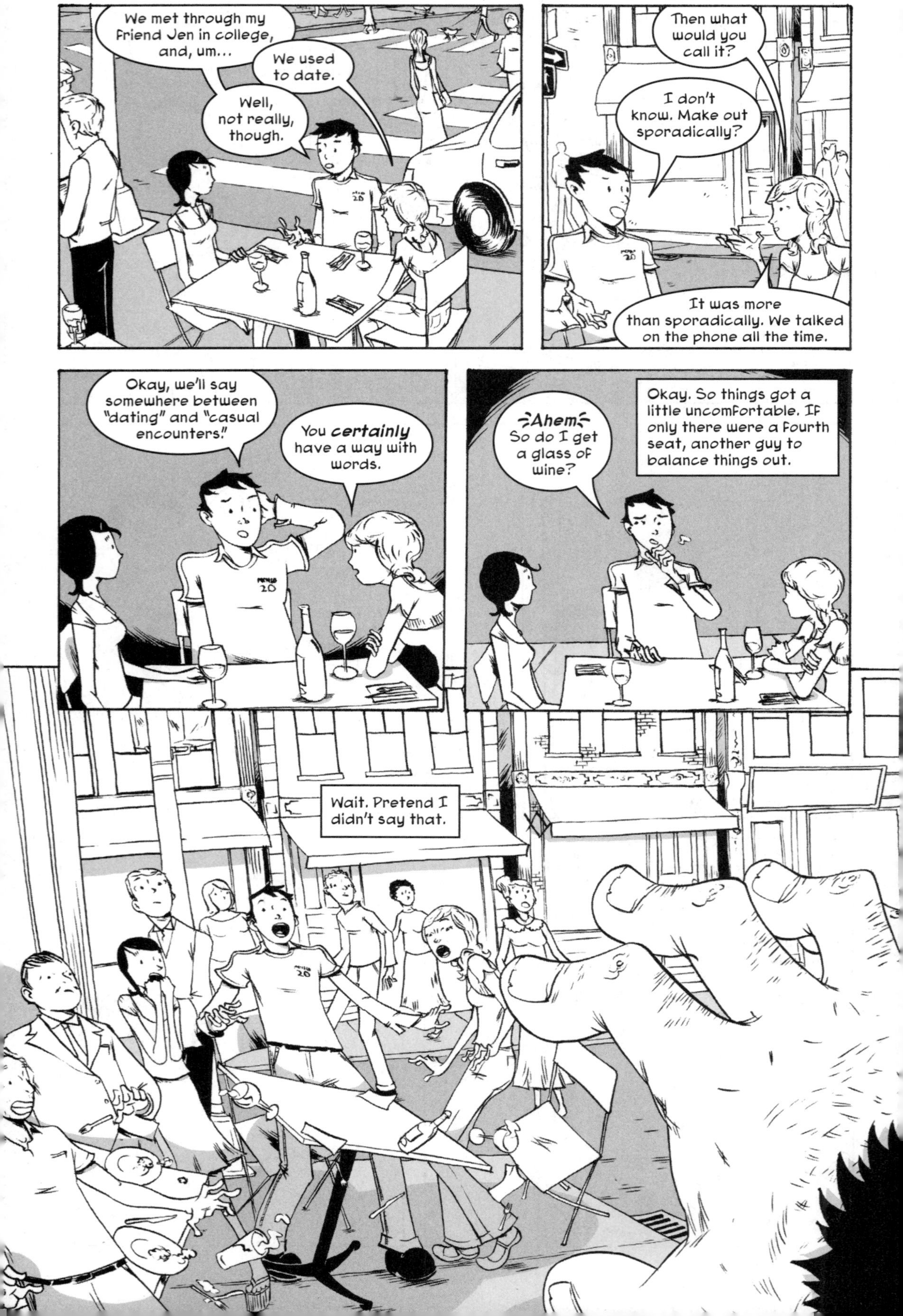
We met through my friend Jen in college, and, um…
We used to date.
Well, not really, though.
Then what would you call it?
I don't know. Make out sporadically?
It was more than sporadically. We talked on the phone all the time.
Okay, we'll say somewhere between "dating" and "casual encounters."
You *certainly* have a way with words.
Ahem
So do I get a glass of wine?
Okay. So things got a little uncomfortable. If only there were a fourth seat, another guy to balance things out.
Wait. Pretend I didn't say that.

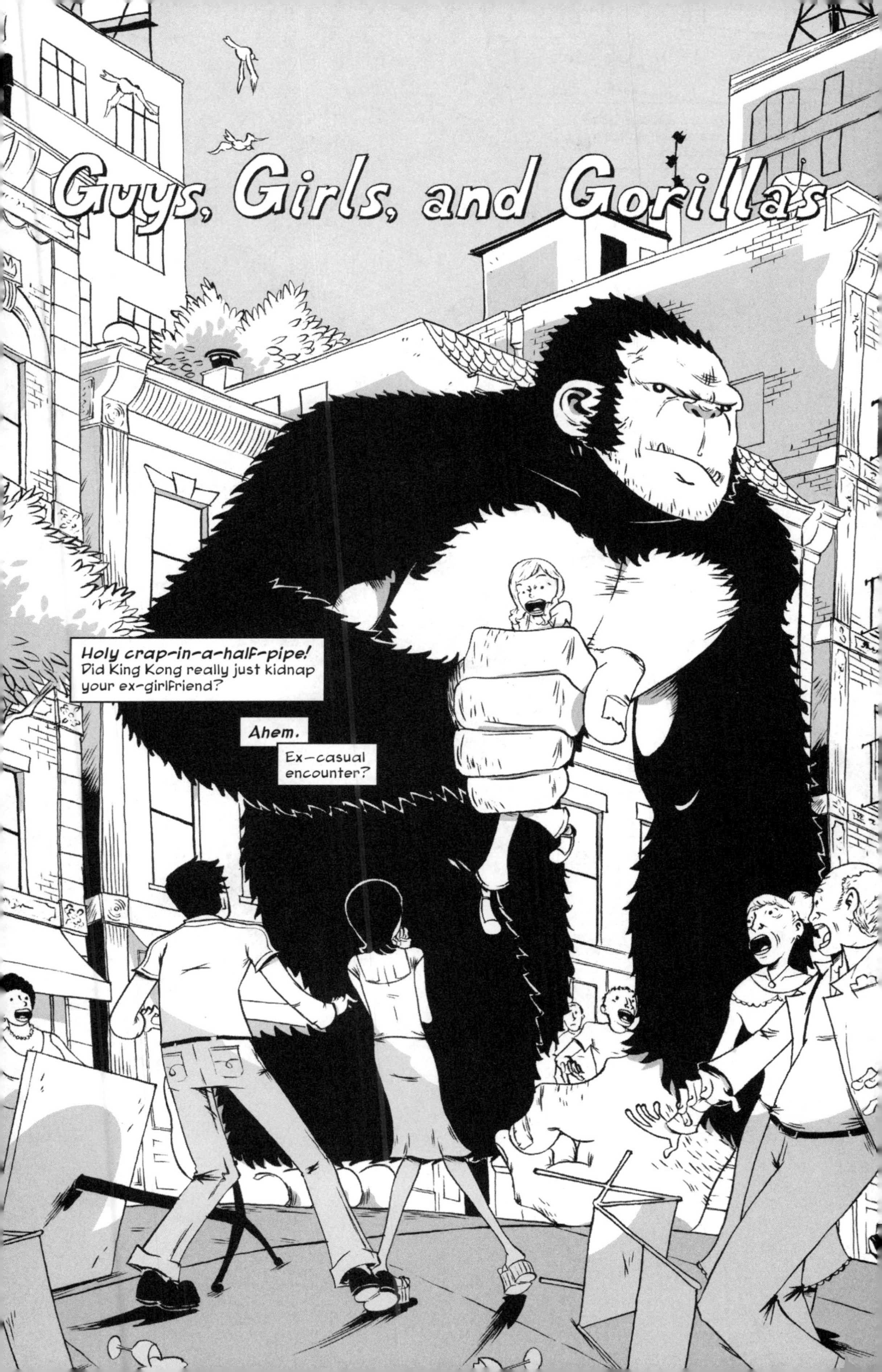
Guys, Girls, and Gorillas
Holy crap-in-a-half-pipe! Did King Kong really just kidnap your ex-girlfriend?
Ahem.
Ex-casual encounter?

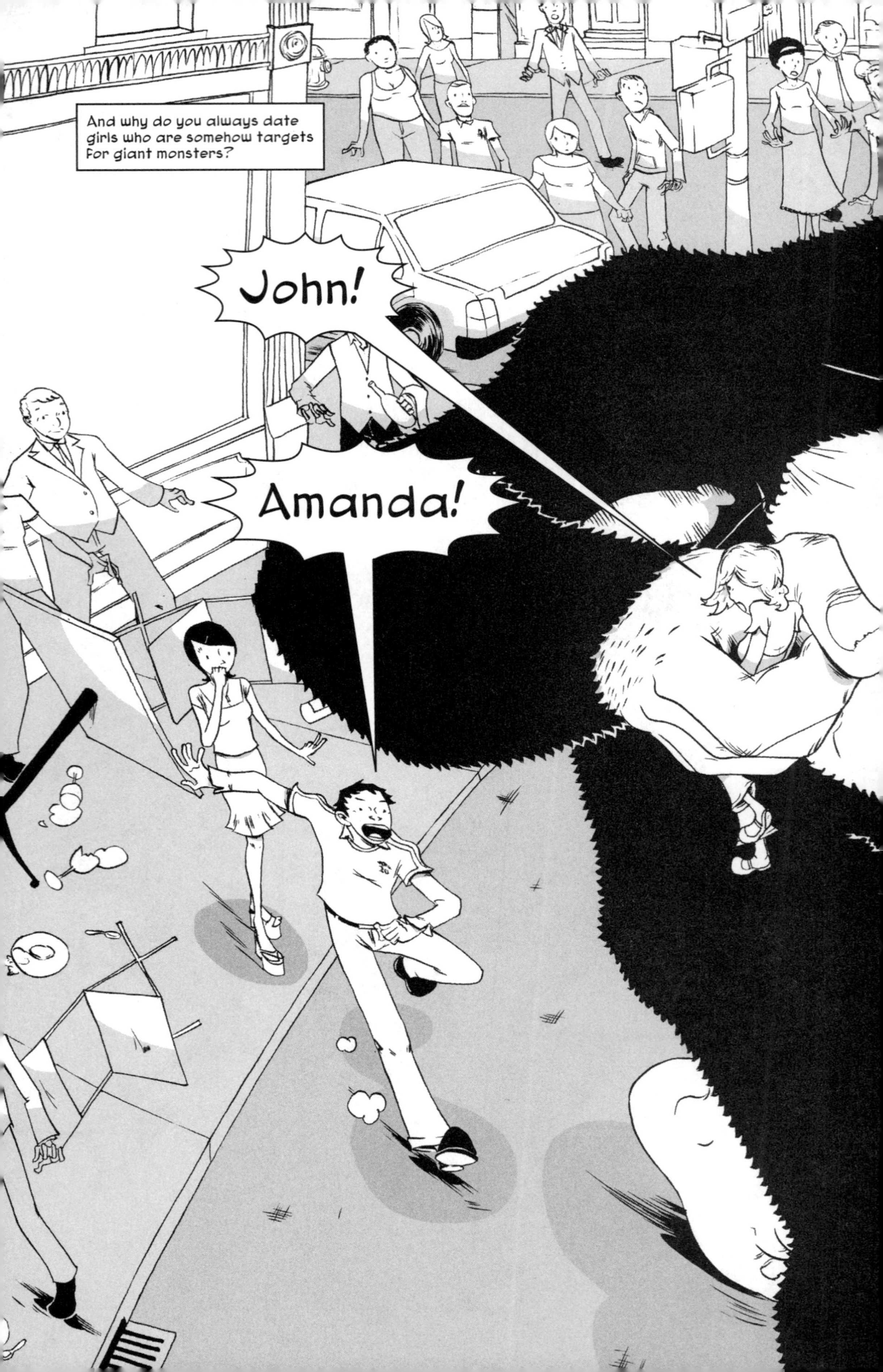
And why do you always date girls who are somehow targets for giant monsters?
John!
Amanda!

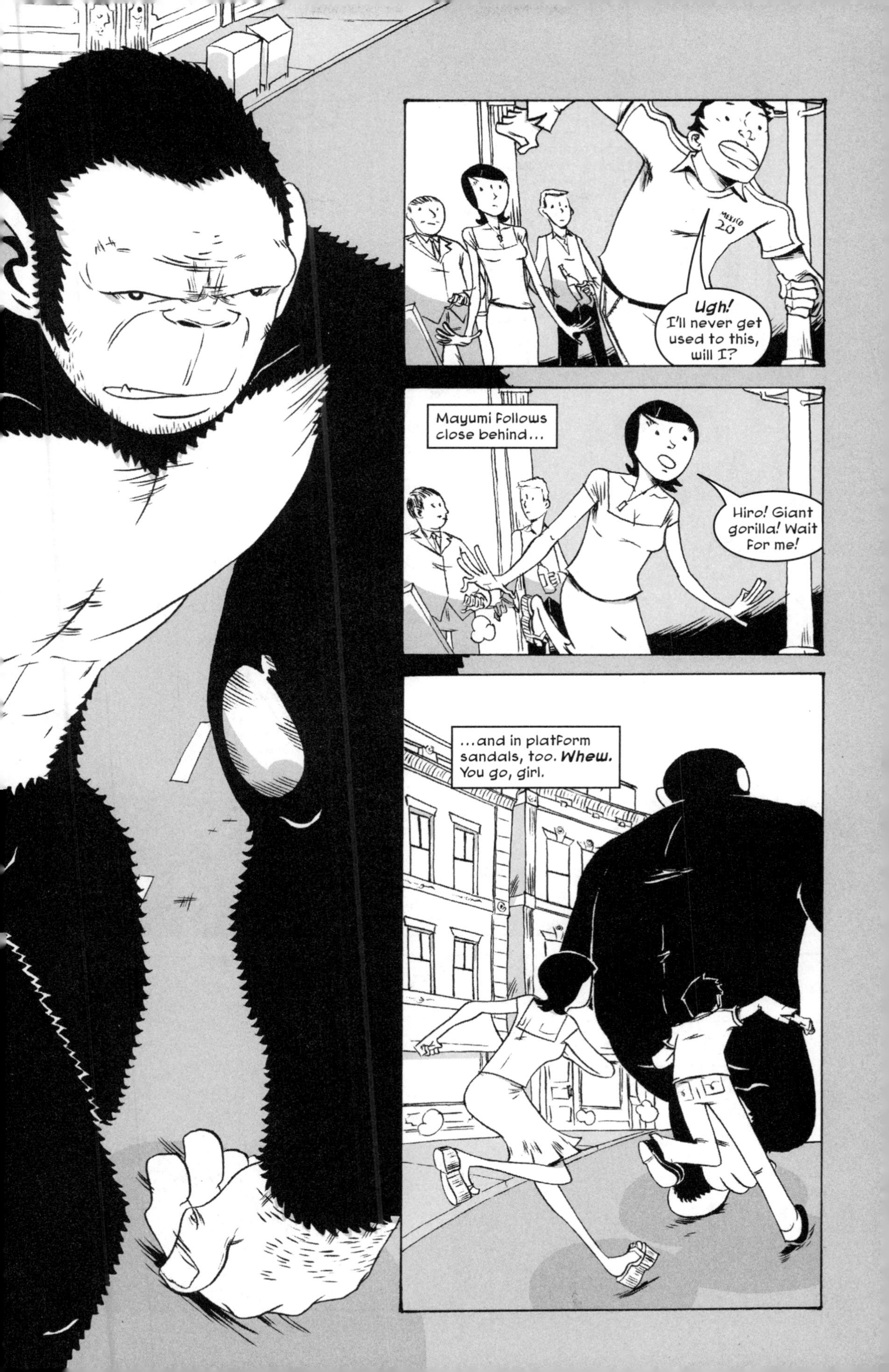
Ugh! I'll never get used to this, will I?
Mayumi follows close behind...
Hiro! Giant gorilla! Wait for me!
...and in platform sandals, too. Whew. You go, girl.

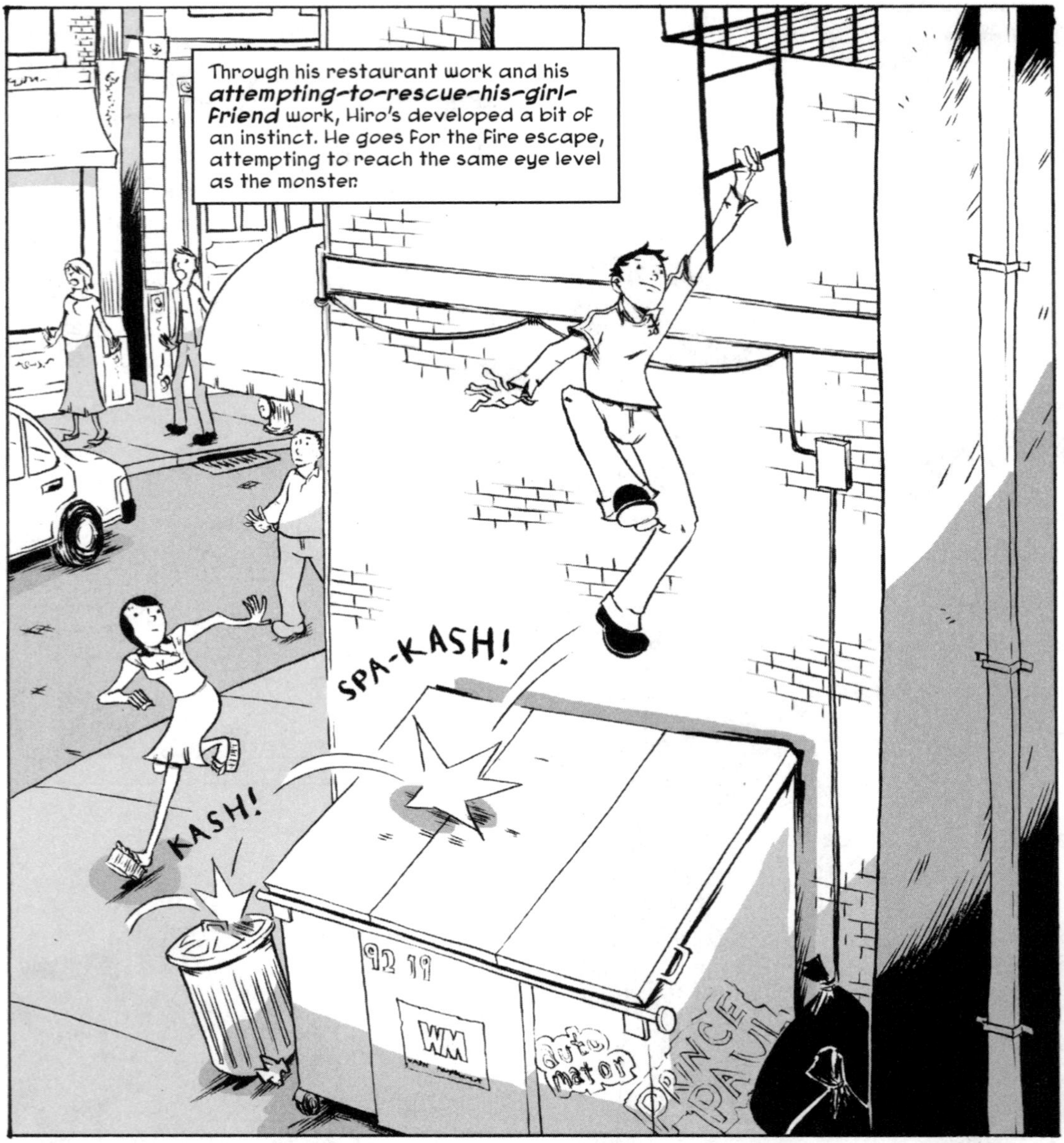
Through his restaurant work and his ***attempting-to-rescue-his-girl-friend*** work, Hiro's developed a bit of an instinct. He goes for the fire escape, attempting to reach the same eye level as the monster.
SPA-KASH!
KASH!
92 19
WM
auto mator
PRINCE PAUL

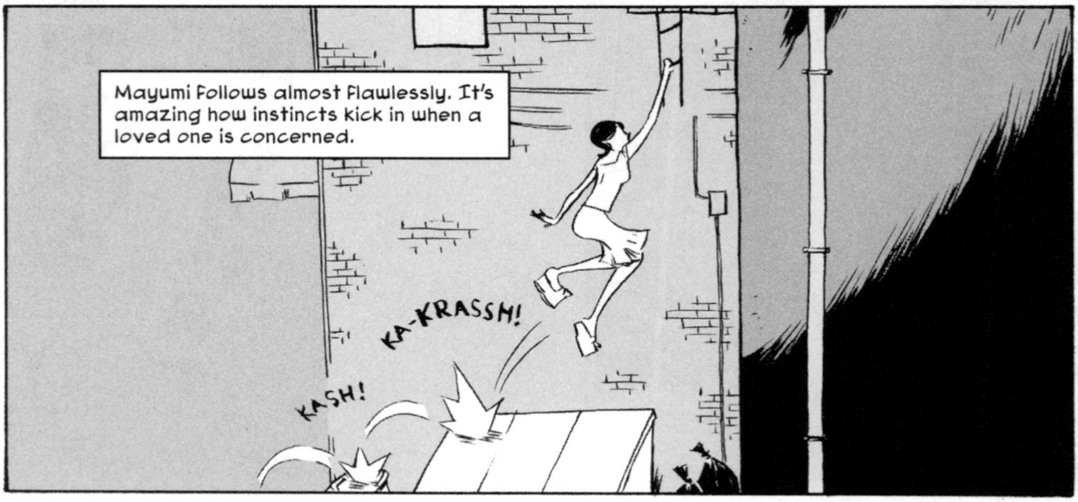
Mayumi follows almost flawlessly. It's amazing how instincts kick in when a loved one is concerned.
KA-KRASSH!
KASH!

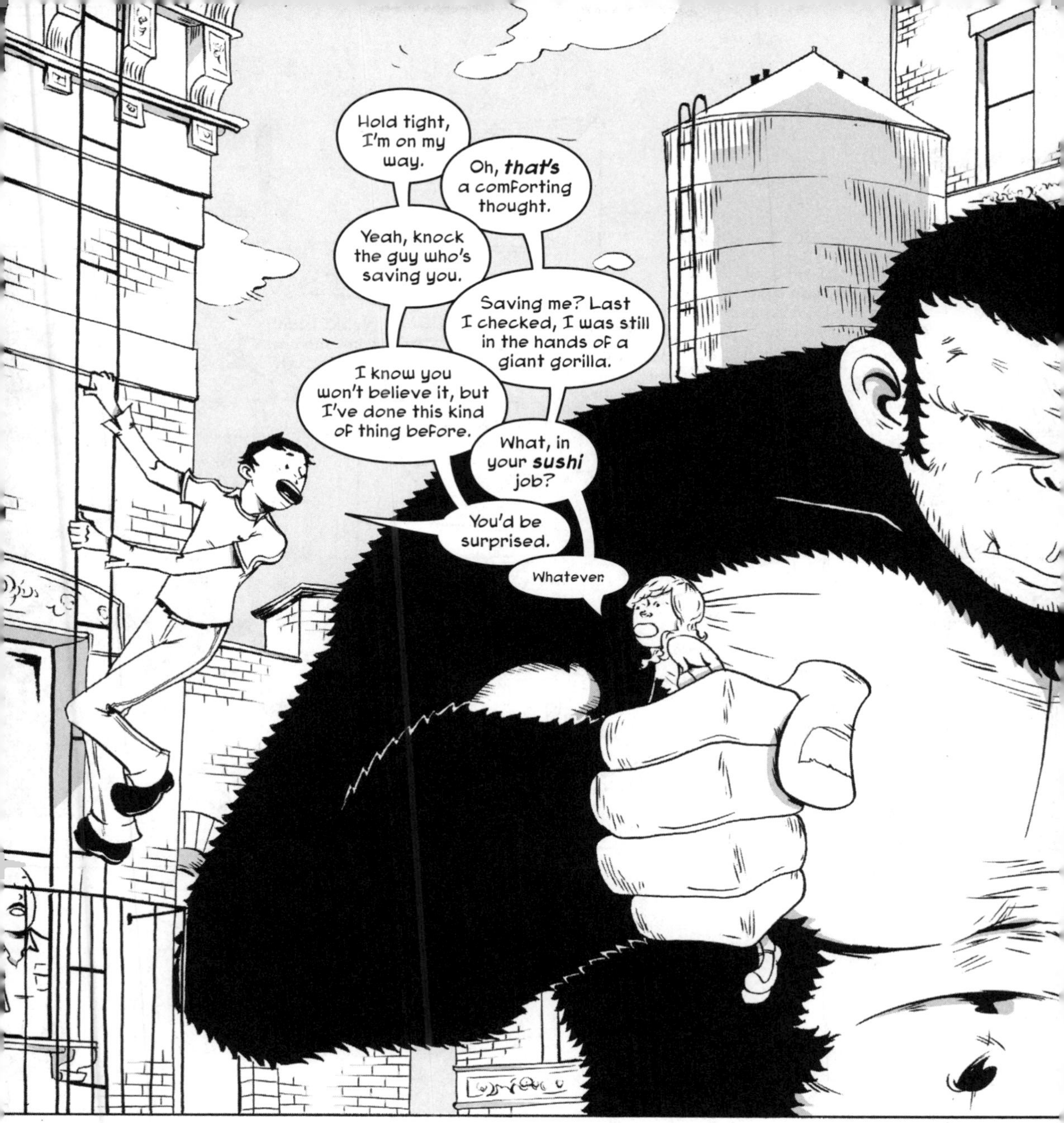
Hold tight, I'm on my way.
Oh, *that's* a comforting thought.
Yeah, knock the guy who's saving you.
Saving me? Last I checked, I was still in the hands of a giant gorilla.
I know you won't believe it, but I've done this kind of thing before.
What, in your *sushi* job?
You'd be surprised.
Whatever.

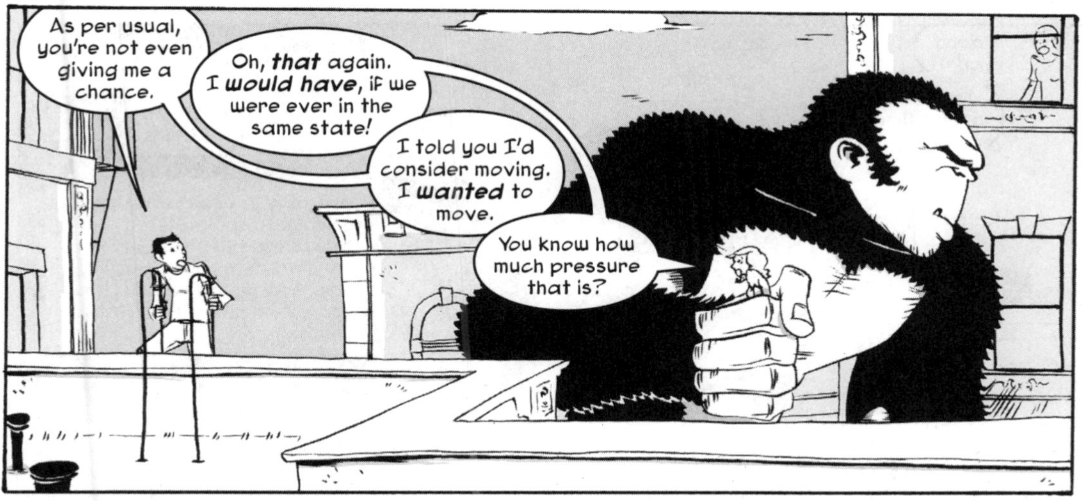
As per usual, you're not even giving me a chance.
Oh, *that* again. I *would have*, if we were ever in the same state!
I told you I'd consider moving. I *wanted* to move.
You know how much pressure that is?

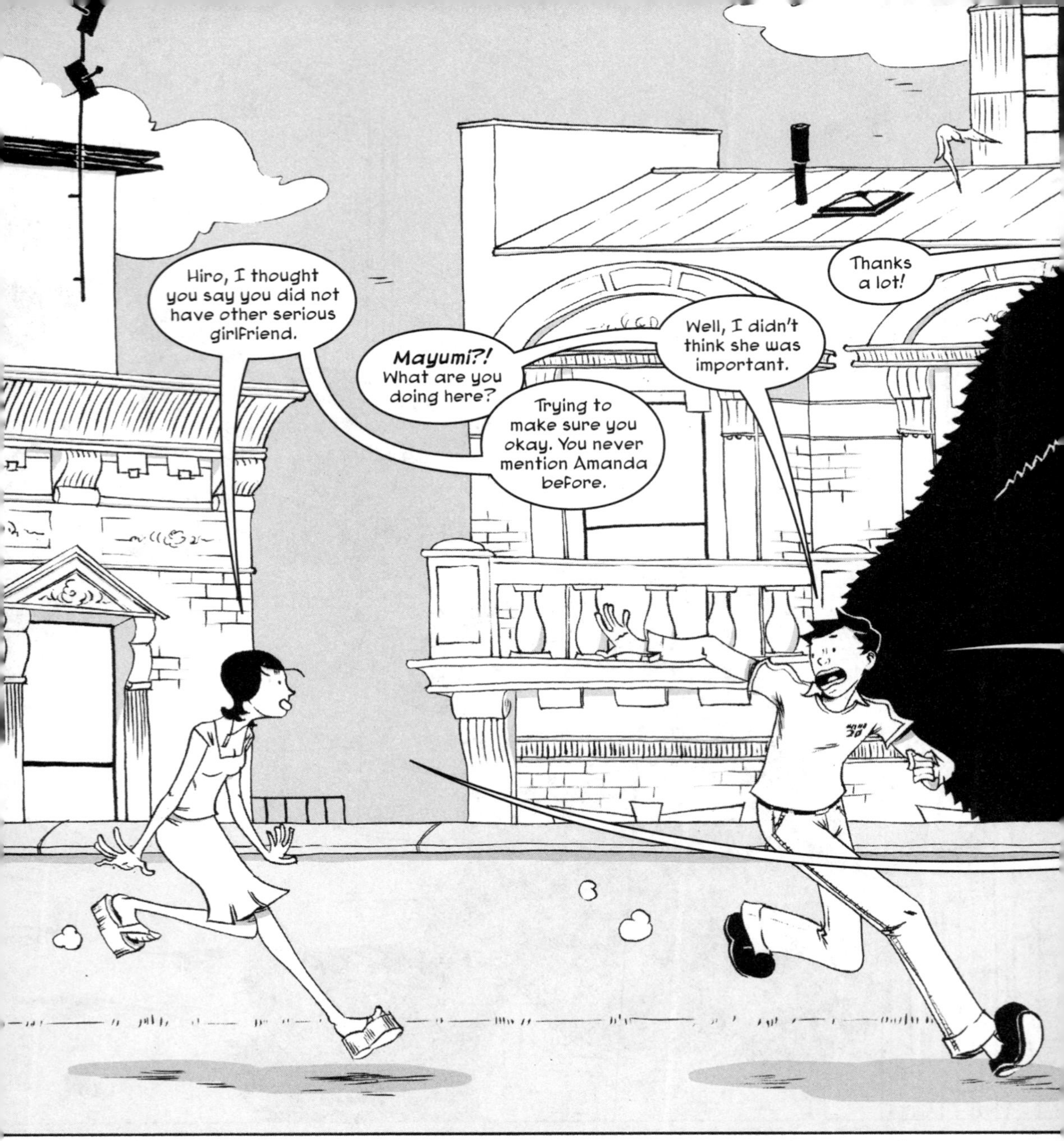
Thanks a lot!
Hiro, I thought you say you did not have other serious girlfriend.
Mayumi?! What are you doing here?
Well, I didn't think she was important.
Trying to make sure you okay. You never mention Amanda before.
MEXICO 20

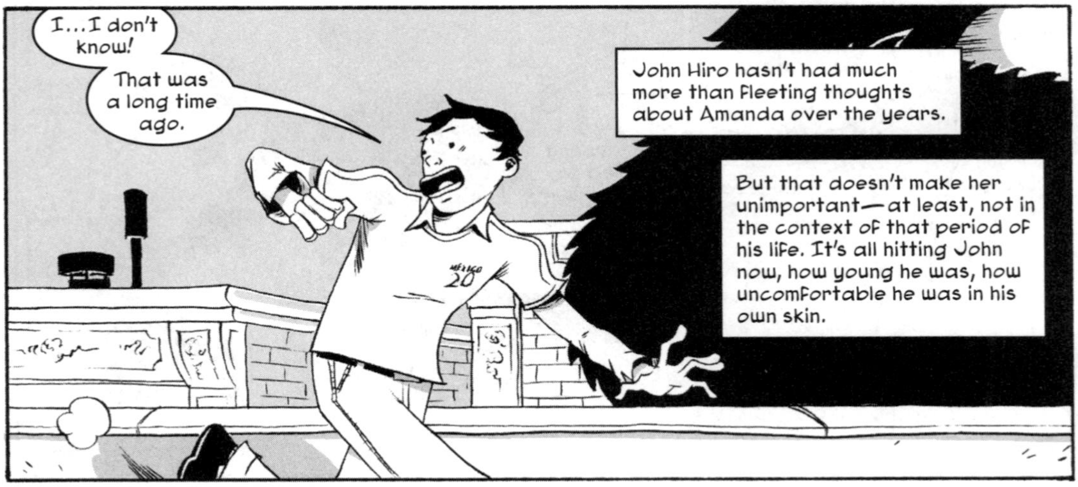
I...I don't know!
That was a long time ago.
John Hiro hasn't had much more than fleeting thoughts about Amanda over the years.
But that doesn't make her unimportant—at least, not in the context of that period of his life. It's all hitting John now, how young he was, how uncomfortable he was in his own skin.
MEXICO 20

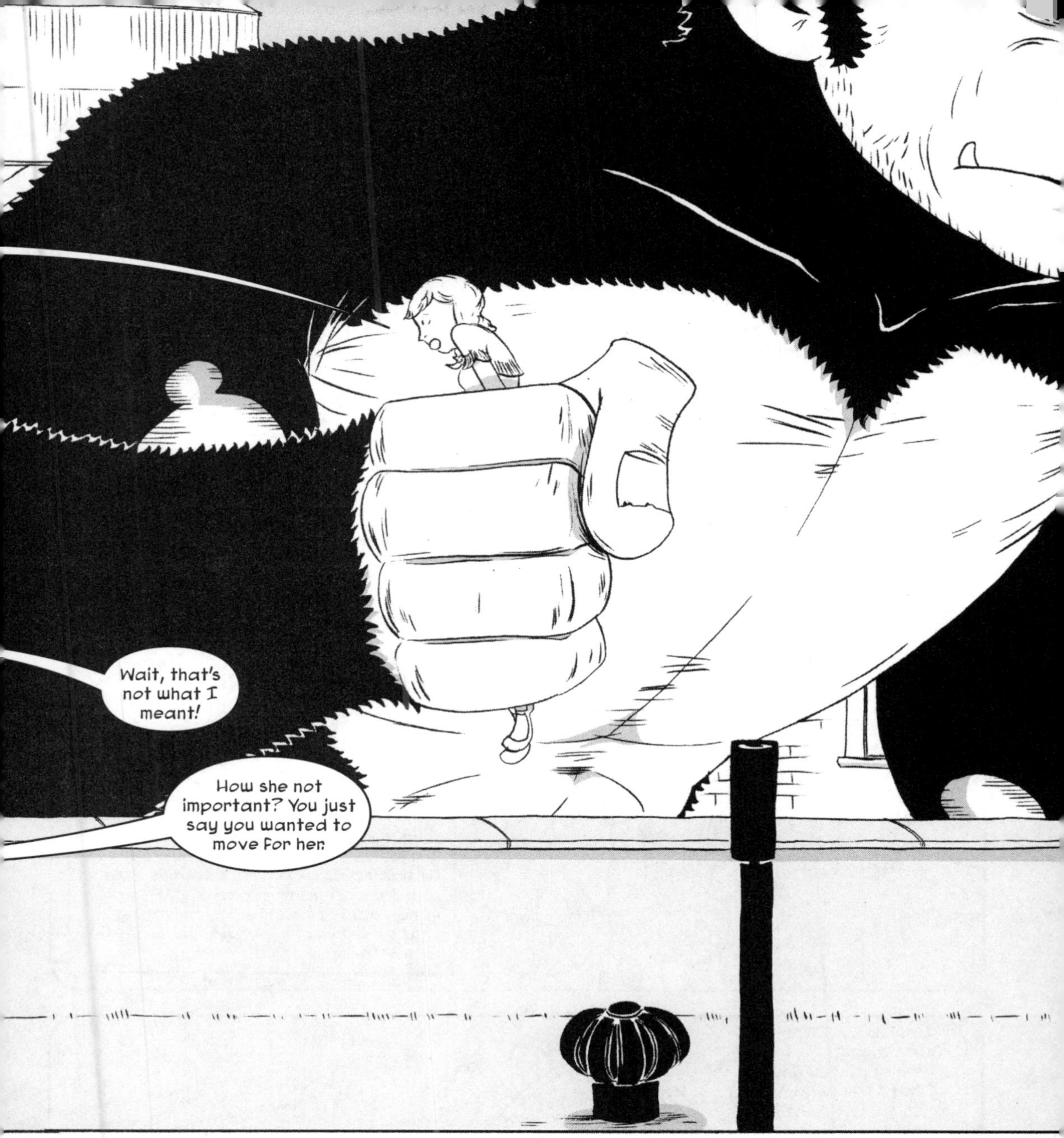

Wait, that's not what I meant!
How she not important? You just say you wanted to move for her.

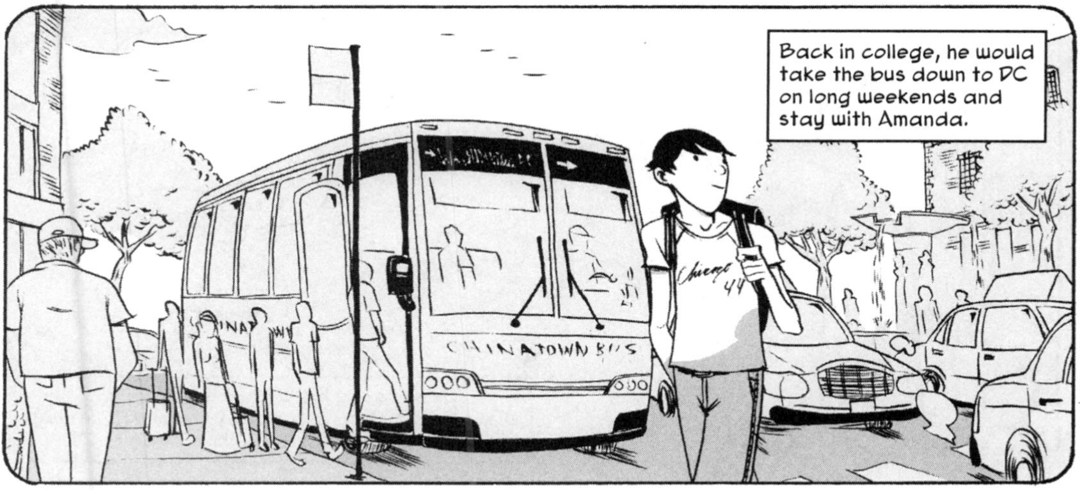

Back in college, he would take the bus down to DC on long weekends and stay with Amanda.
CHINATOWN BUS

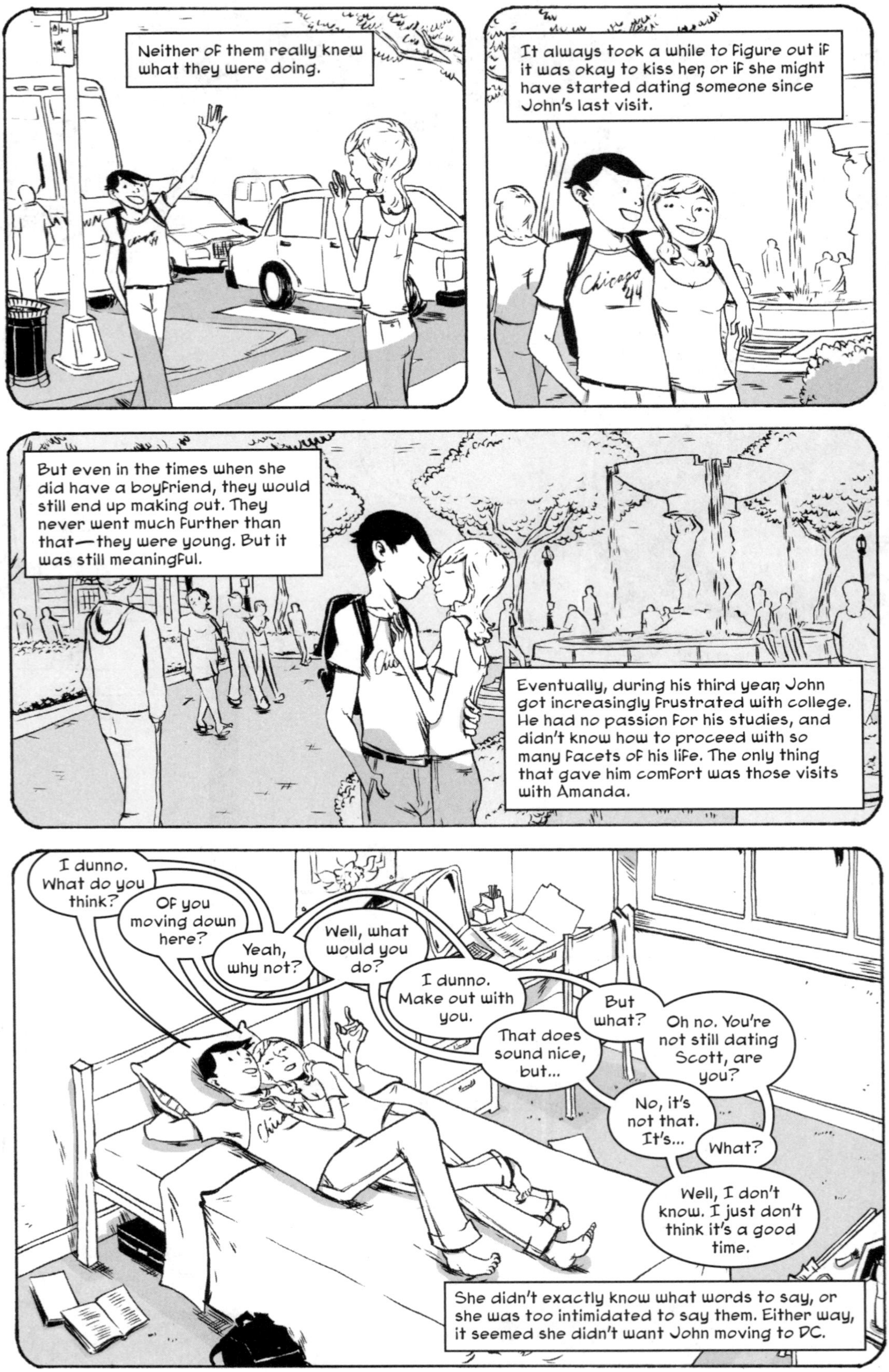
Neither of them really knew what they were doing.
It always took a while to figure out if it was okay to kiss her, or if she might have started dating someone since John's last visit.
But even in the times when she did have a boyfriend, they would still end up making out. They never went much further than that—they were young. But it was still meaningful.
Eventually, during his third year, John got increasingly frustrated with college. He had no passion for his studies, and didn't know how to proceed with so many facets of his life. The only thing that gave him comfort was those visits with Amanda.
I dunno. What do you think?
Of you moving down here?
Yeah, why not?
Well, what would you do?
I dunno. Make out with you.
That does sound nice, but...
But what?
Oh no. You're not still dating Scott, are you?
No, it's not that. It's...
What?
Well, I don't know. I just don't think it's a good time.
She didn't exactly know what words to say, or she was too intimidated to say them. Either way, it seemed she didn't want John moving to DC.

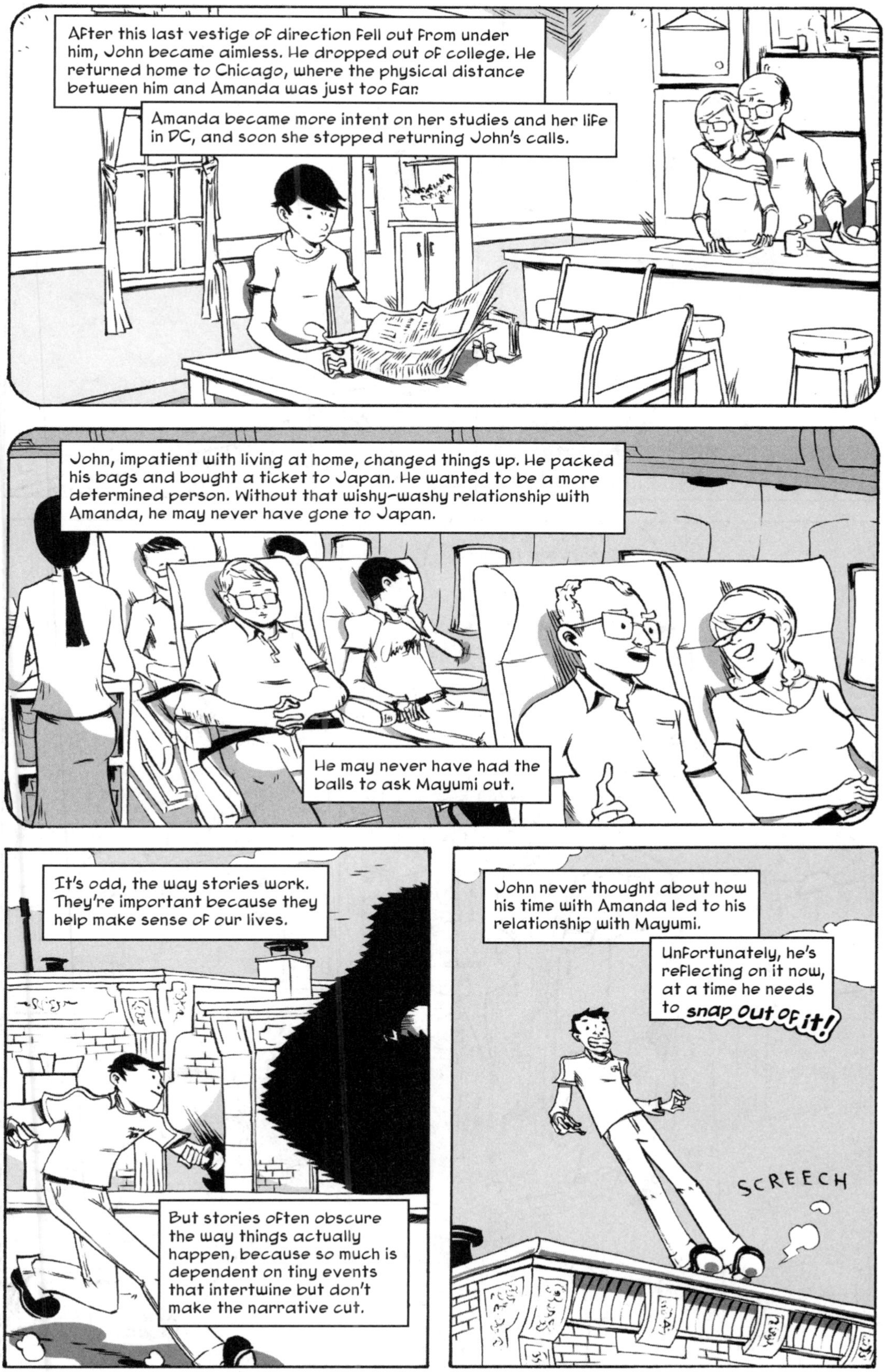
After this last vestige of direction fell out from under him, John became aimless. He dropped out of college. He returned home to Chicago, where the physical distance between him and Amanda was just too far.
Amanda became more intent on her studies and her life in DC, and soon she stopped returning John's calls.
John, impatient with living at home, changed things up. He packed his bags and bought a ticket to Japan. He wanted to be a more determined person. Without that wishy-washy relationship with Amanda, he may never have gone to Japan.
He may never have had the balls to ask Mayumi out.
It's odd, the way stories work. They're important because they help make sense of our lives.
But stories often obscure the way things actually happen, because so much is dependent on tiny events that intertwine but don't make the narrative cut.
John never thought about how his time with Amanda led to his relationship with Mayumi.
Unfortunately, he's reflecting on it now, at a time he needs to snap out of it!
SCREECH

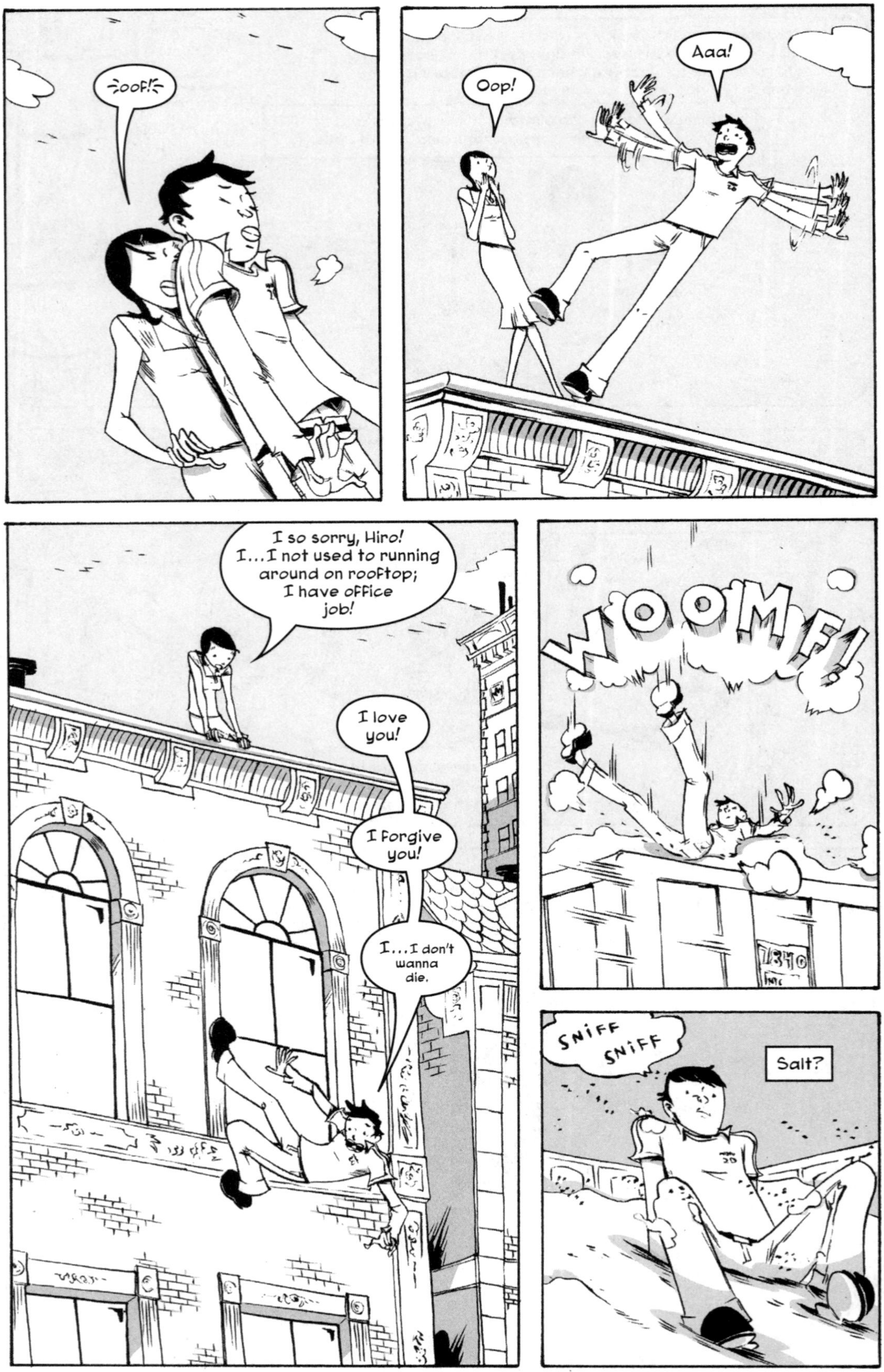
oof!
Oop!
Aaa!
I so sorry, Hiro! I...I not used to running around on rooftop; I have office job!
I love you!
I forgive you!
I...I don't wanna die.
WOOMF!
SNIFF SNIFF
Salt?

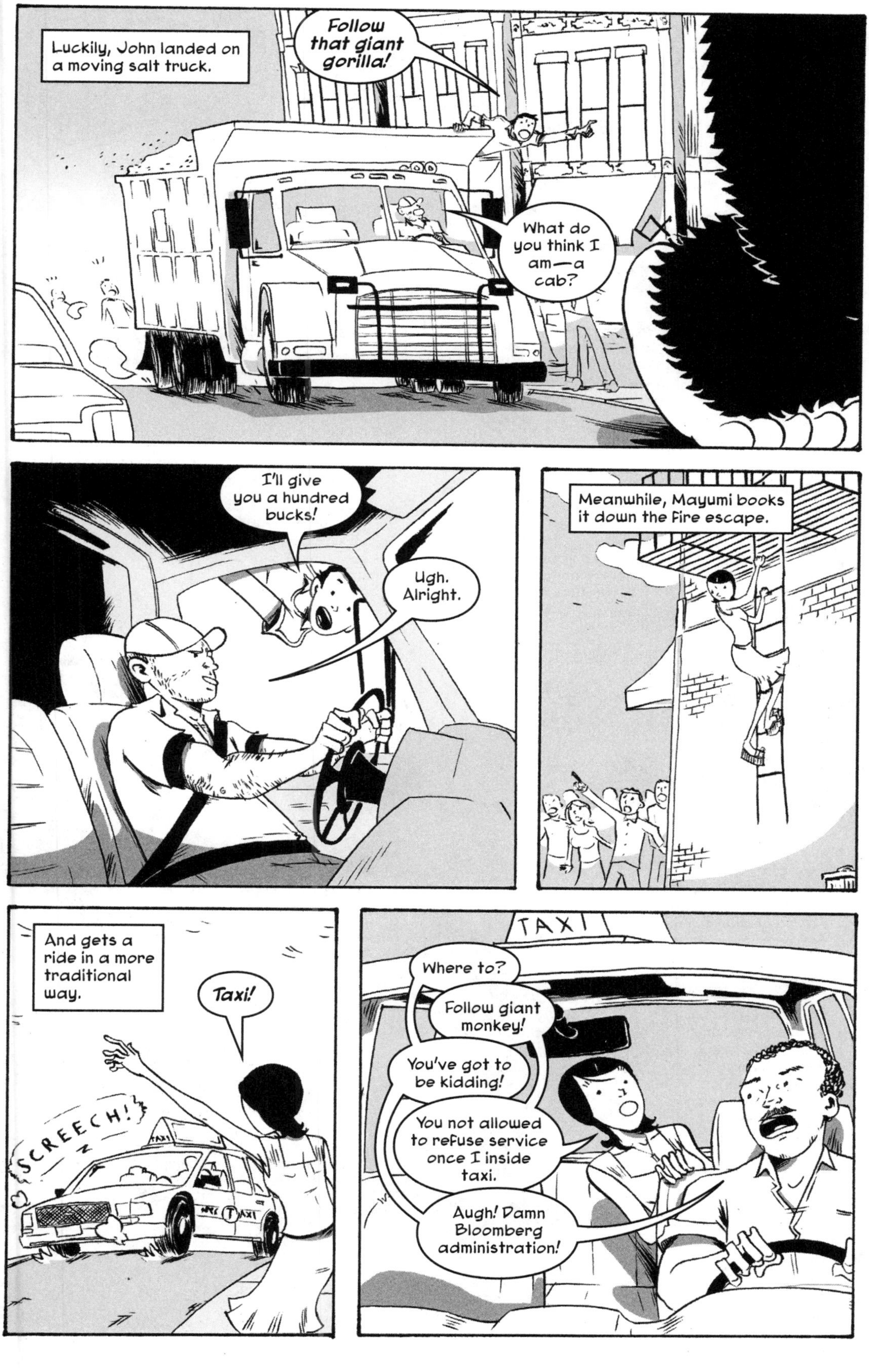
Luckily, John landed on a moving salt truck.
Follow that giant gorilla!
What do you think I am—a cab?
I'll give you a hundred bucks!
Ugh. Alright.
Meanwhile, Mayumi books it down the fire escape.
And gets a ride in a more traditional way.
Taxi!
SCREECH!
TAXI
Where to?
Follow giant monkey!
You've got to be kidding!
You not allowed to refuse service once I inside taxi.
Augh! Damn Bloomberg administration!

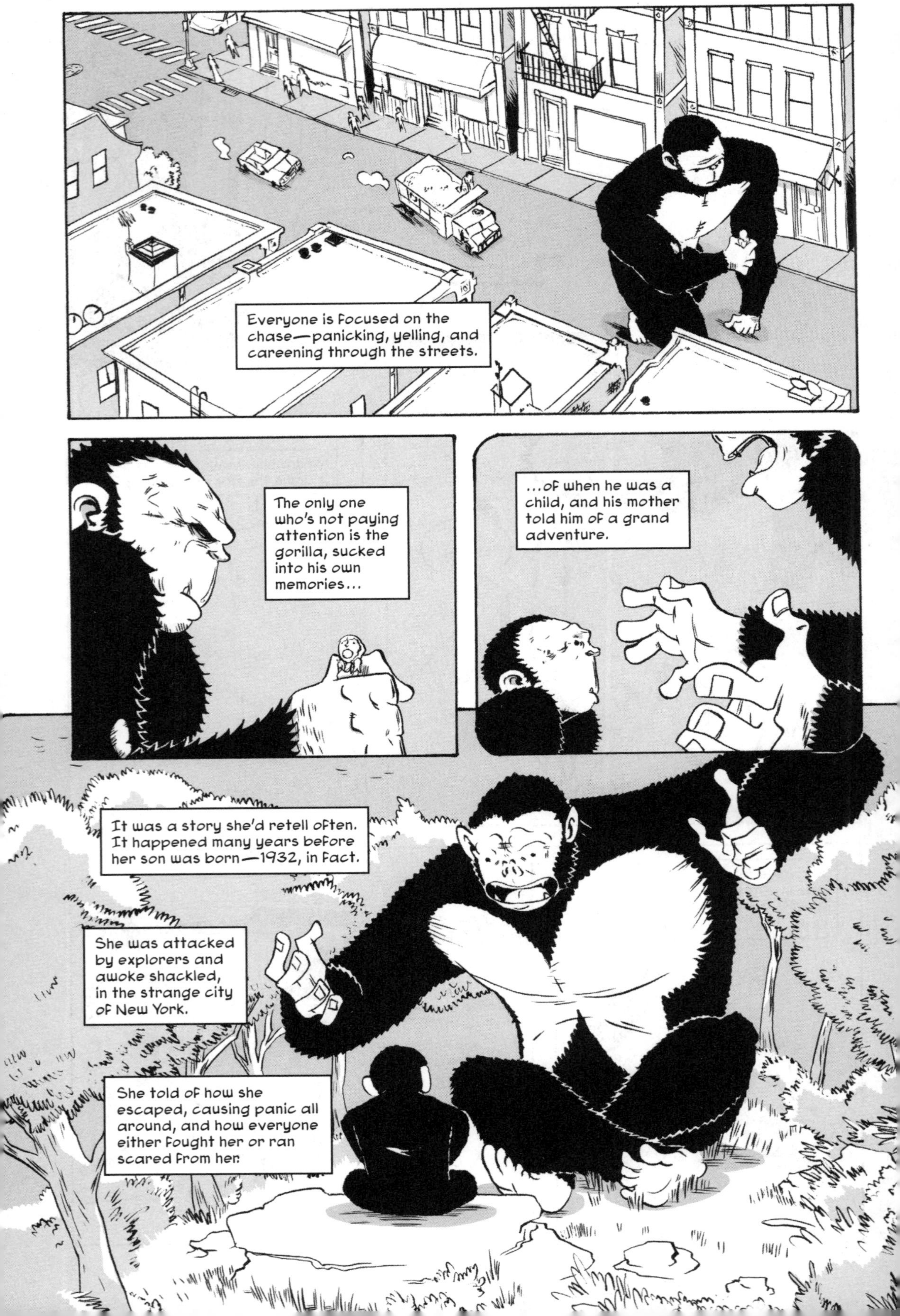
Everyone is focused on the chase—panicking, yelling, and careening through the streets.
The only one who's not paying attention is the gorilla, sucked into his own memories...
...of when he was a child, and his mother told him of a grand adventure.
It was a story she'd retell often. It happened many years before her son was born—1932, in fact.
She was attacked by explorers and awoke shackled, in the strange city of New York.
She told of how she escaped, causing panic all around, and how everyone either fought her or ran scared from her.

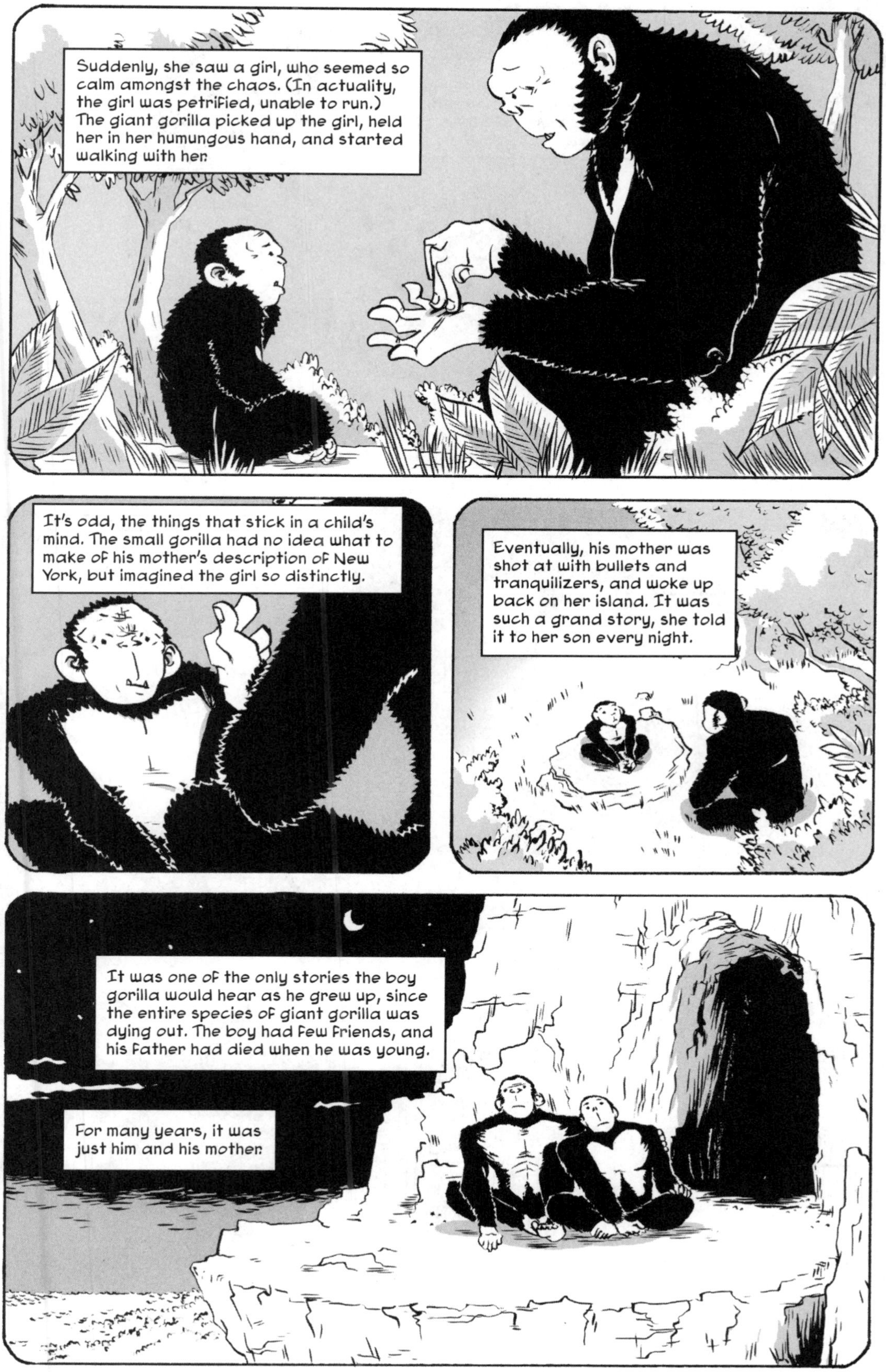
Suddenly, she saw a girl, who seemed so calm amongst the chaos. (In actuality, the girl was petrified, unable to run.) The giant gorilla picked up the girl, held her in her humungous hand, and started walking with her.
It's odd, the things that stick in a child's mind. The small gorilla had no idea what to make of his mother's description of New York, but imagined the girl so distinctly.
Eventually, his mother was shot at with bullets and tranquilizers, and woke up back on her island. It was such a grand story, she told it to her son every night.
It was one of the only stories the boy gorilla would hear as he grew up, since the entire species of giant gorilla was dying out. The boy had few friends, and his father had died when he was young.
For many years, it was just him and his mother.

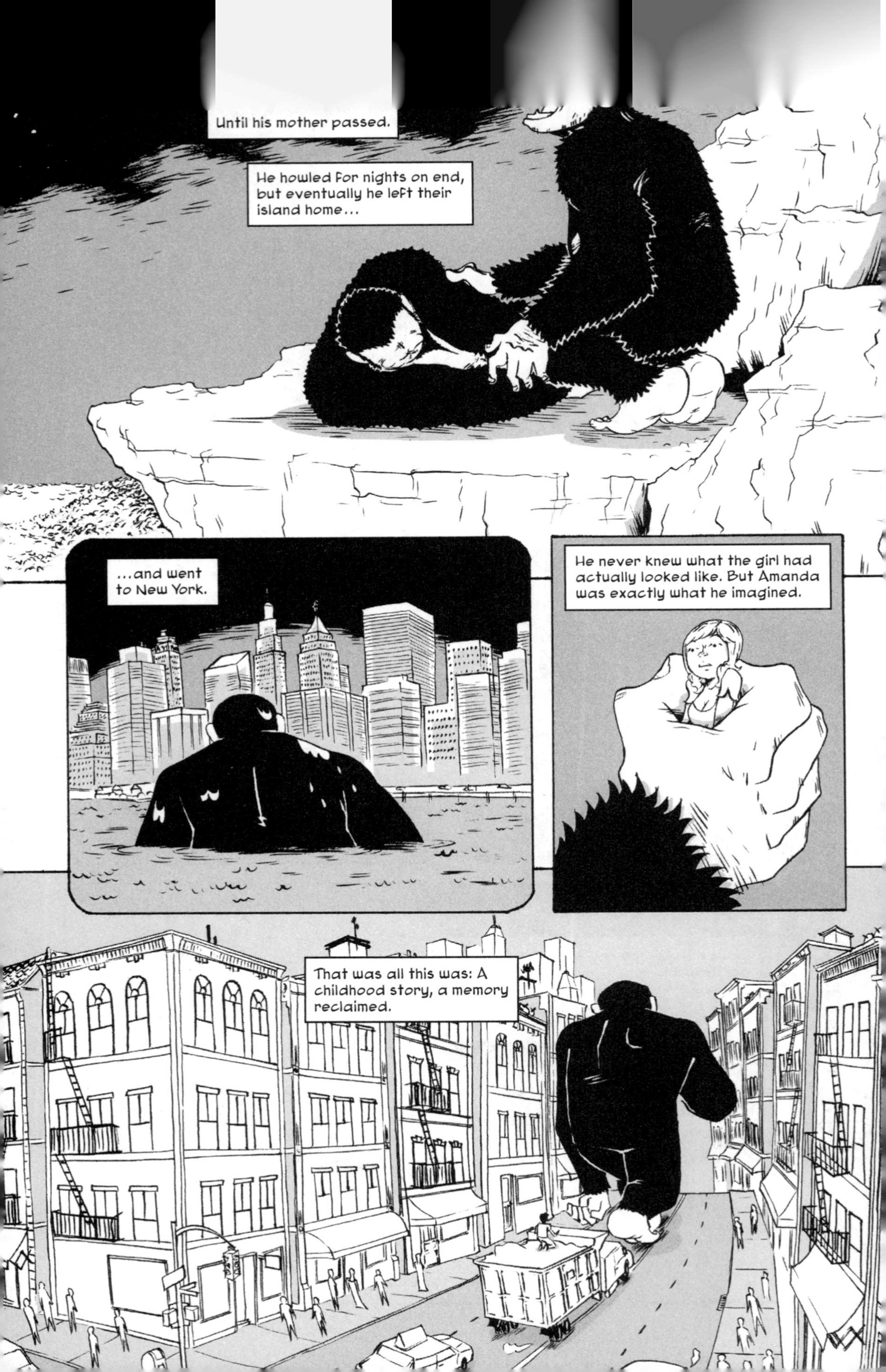
Until his mother passed.
He howled for nights on end, but eventually he left their island home...
...and went to New York.
He never knew what the girl had actually looked like. But Amanda was exactly what he imagined.
That was all this was: A childhood story, a memory reclaimed.

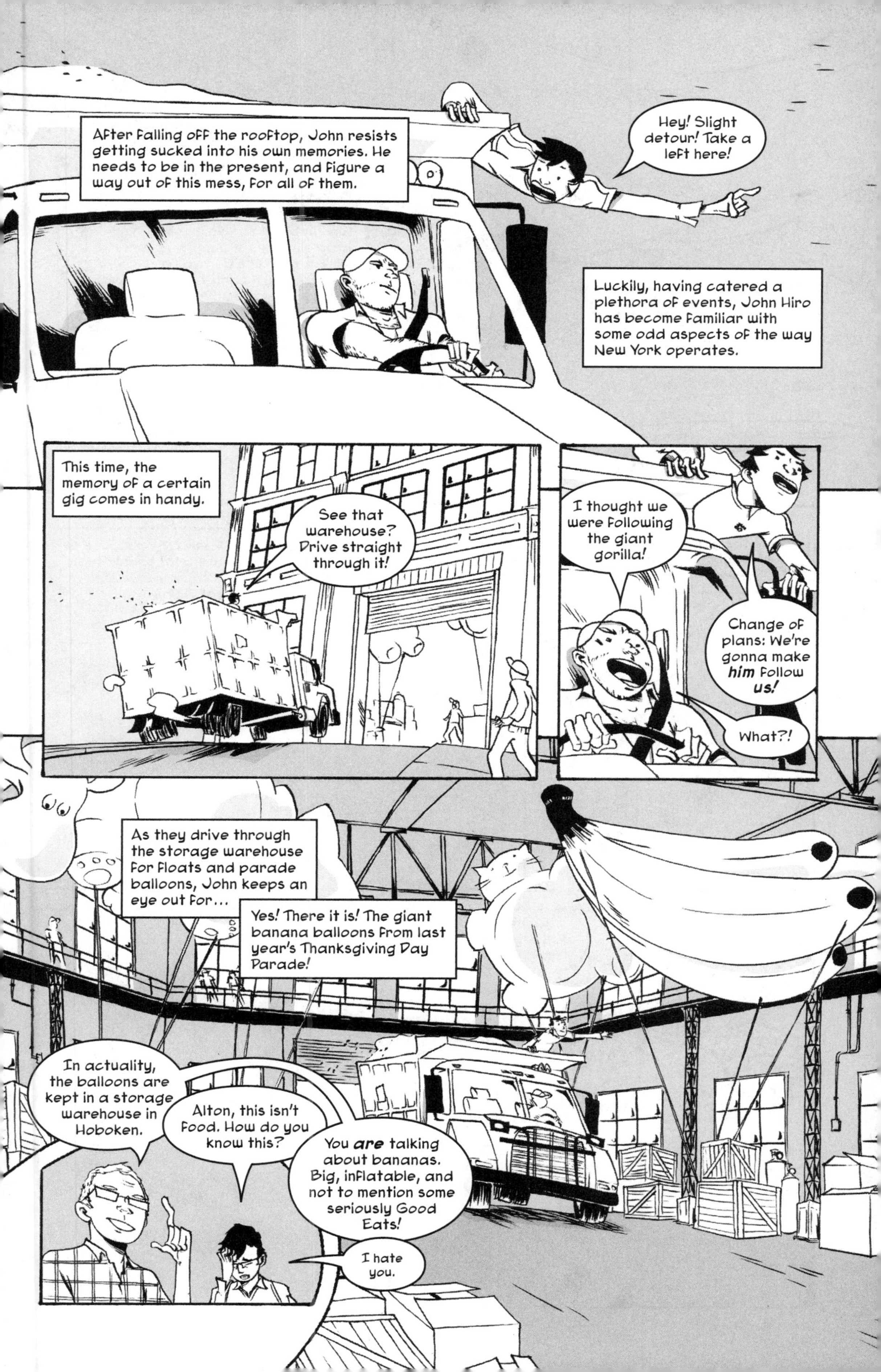
After falling off the rooftop, John resists getting sucked into his own memories. He needs to be in the present, and figure a way out of this mess, for all of them.
Hey! Slight detour! Take a left here!
Luckily, having catered a plethora of events, John Hiro has become familiar with some odd aspects of the way New York operates.
This time, the memory of a certain gig comes in handy.
See that warehouse? Drive straight through it!
I thought we were following the giant gorilla!
Change of plans: We're gonna make *him* follow *us!*
What?!
As they drive through the storage warehouse for floats and parade balloons, John keeps an eye out for…
Yes! There it is! The giant banana balloons from last year's Thanksgiving Day Parade!
In actuality, the balloons are kept in a storage warehouse in Hoboken.
Alton, this isn't food. How do you know this?
You *are* talking about bananas. Big, inflatable, and not to mention some seriously Good Eats!
I hate you.

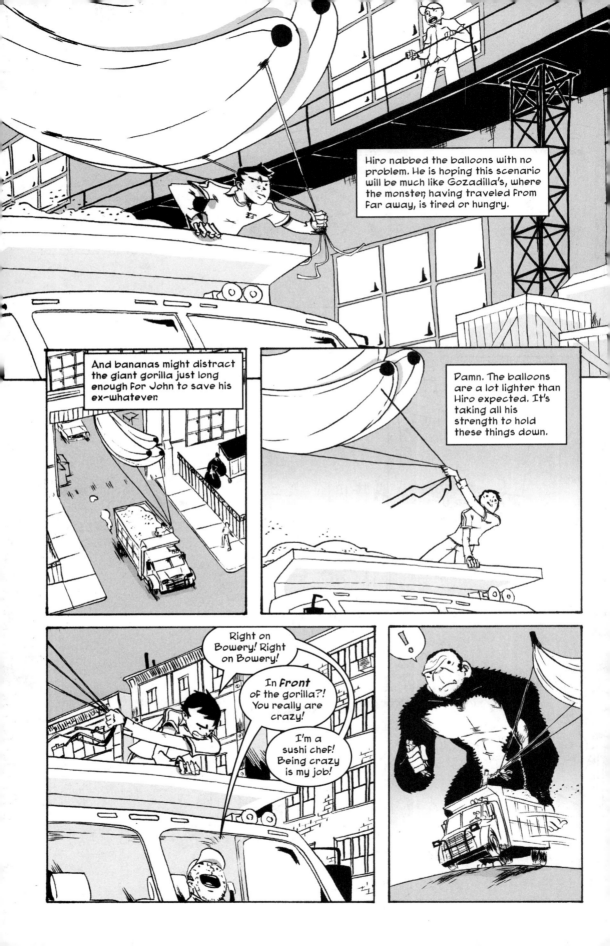

Hiro nabbed the balloons with no problem. He is hoping this scenario will be much like Gozadilla's, where the monster, having traveled from far away, is tired or hungry.

And bananas might distract the giant gorilla just long enough for John to save his ex-whatever.

Damn. The balloons are a lot lighter than Hiro expected. It's taking all his strength to hold these things down.

Right on Bowery! Right on Bowery!

In *Front* of the gorilla?! You really are crazy!

I'm a sushi chef! Being crazy is my job!

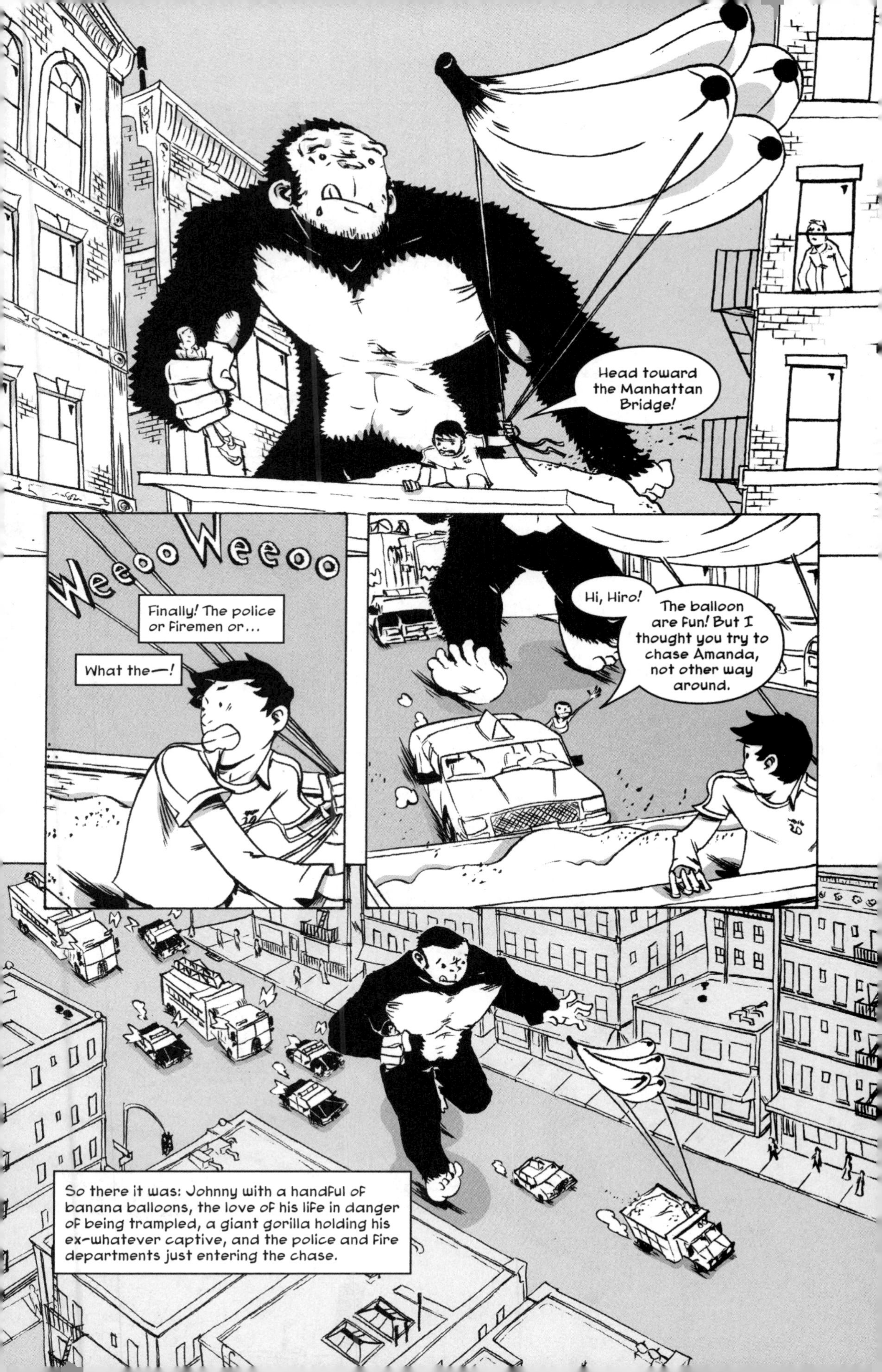
Head toward the Manhattan Bridge!
Weeoo Weeoo
Finally! The police or firemen or…
What the—!
Hi, Hiro!
The balloon are fun! But I thought you try to chase Amanda, not other way around.
So there it was: Johnny with a handful of banana balloons, the love of his life in danger of being trampled, a giant gorilla holding his ex-whatever captive, and the police and fire departments just entering the chase.

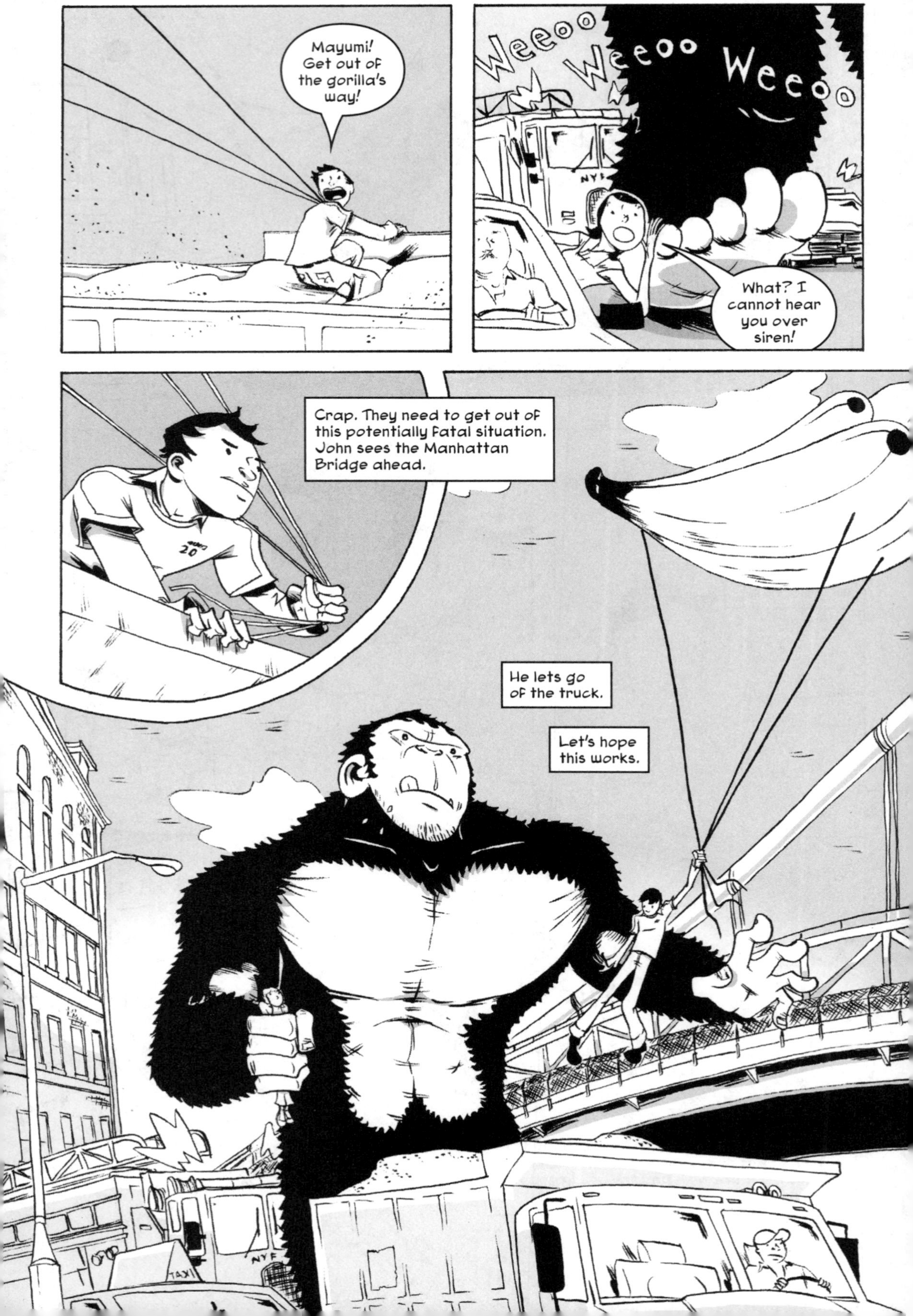
Mayumi! Get out of the gorilla's way!
Weeoo Weeoo Weeoo
What? I cannot hear you over siren!
Crap. They need to get out of this potentially fatal situation. John sees the Manhattan Bridge ahead.
He lets go of the truck.
Let's hope this works.

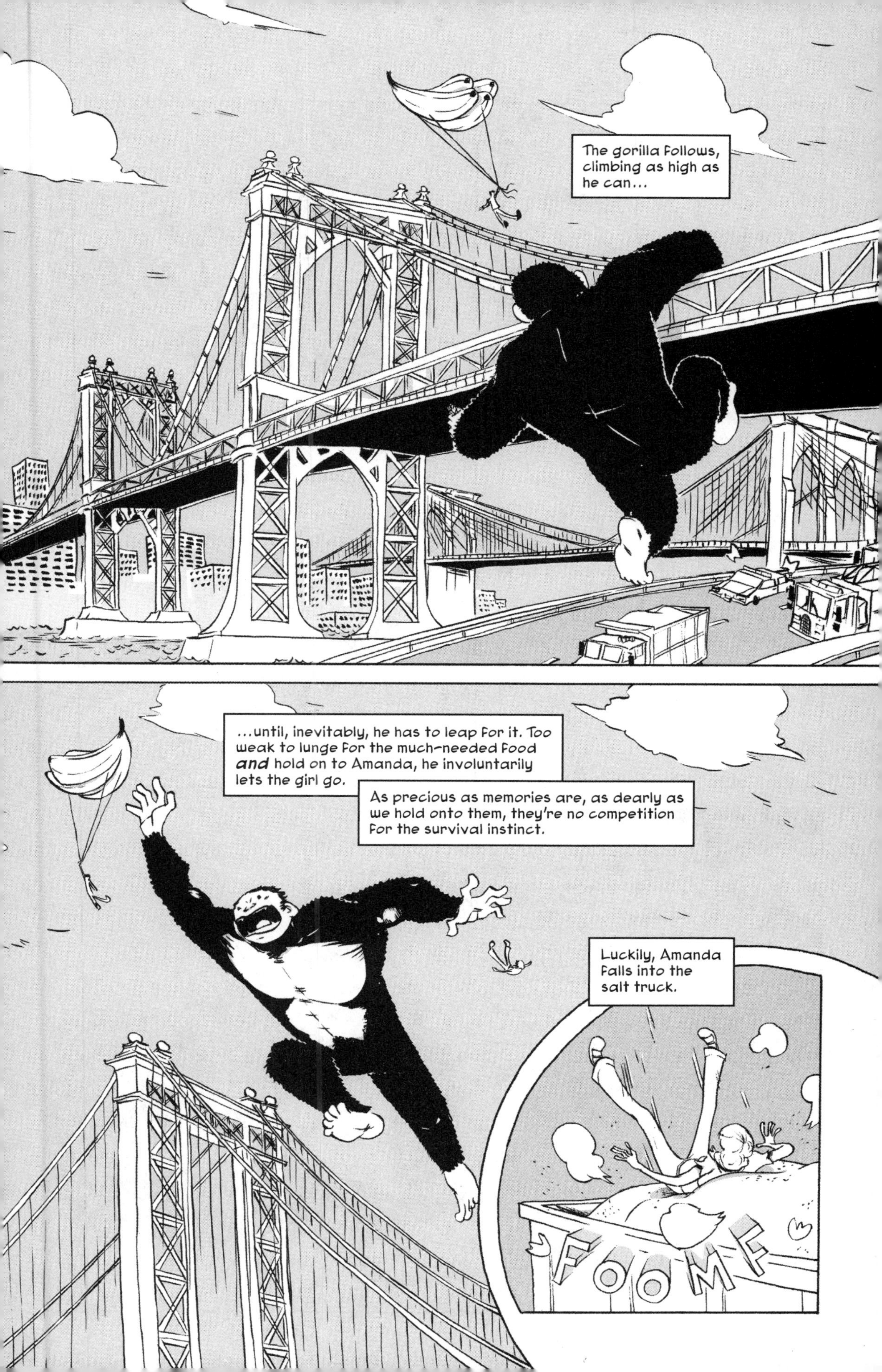
The gorilla follows, climbing as high as he can...
...until, inevitably, he has to leap for it. Too weak to lunge for the much-needed food *and* hold on to Amanda, he involuntarily lets the girl go.
As precious as memories are, as dearly as we hold onto them, they're no competition for the survival instinct.
Luckily, Amanda falls into the salt truck.
FOOMF

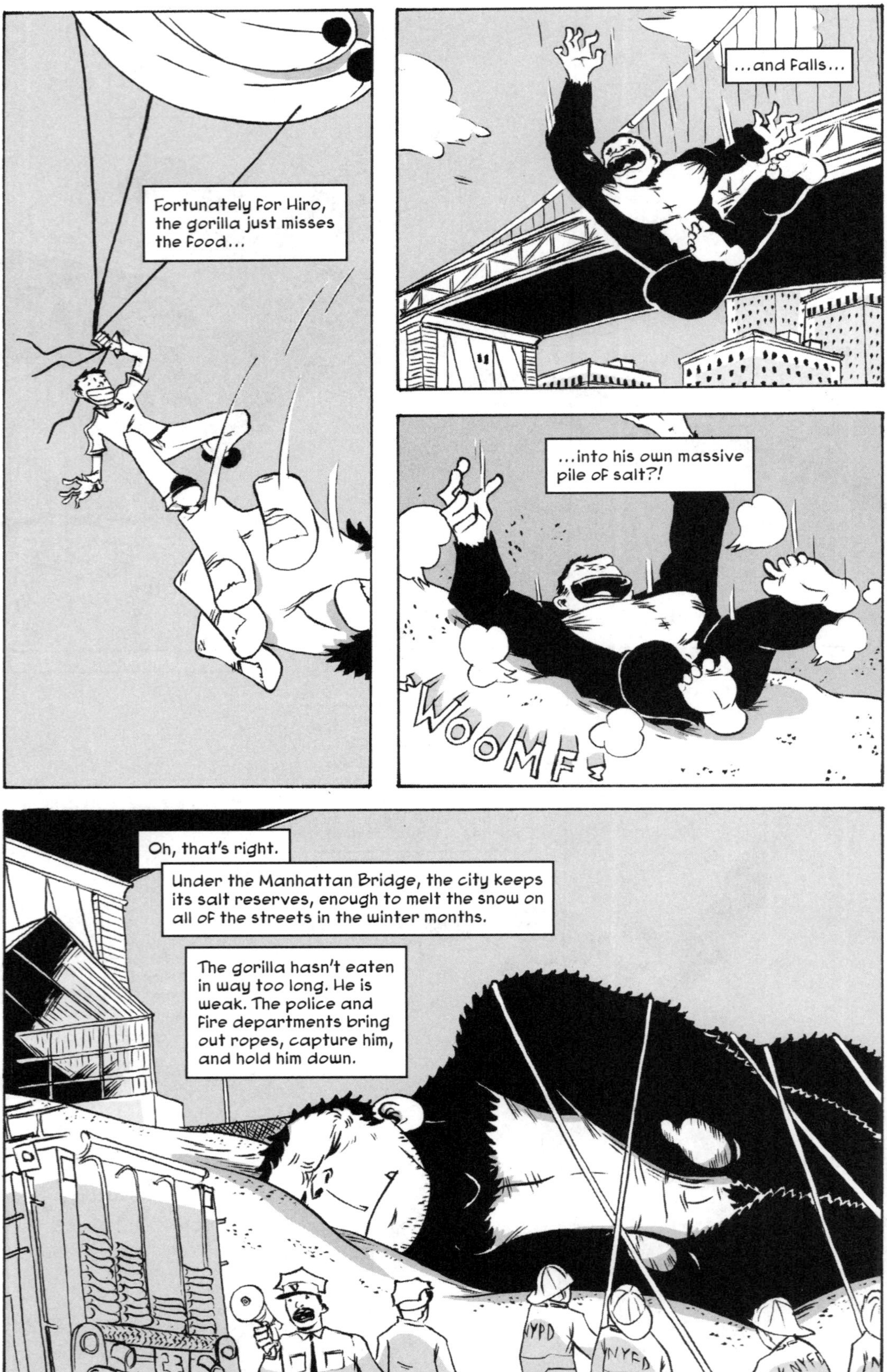
Fortunately for Hiro, the gorilla just misses the food...
...and falls...
...into his own massive pile of salt?!
WOOMF!
Oh, that's right.
Under the Manhattan Bridge, the city keeps its salt reserves, enough to melt the snow on all of the streets in the winter months.
The gorilla hasn't eaten in way too long. He is weak. The police and fire departments bring out ropes, capture him, and hold him down.
23
NYPD
NYFD
NYFD

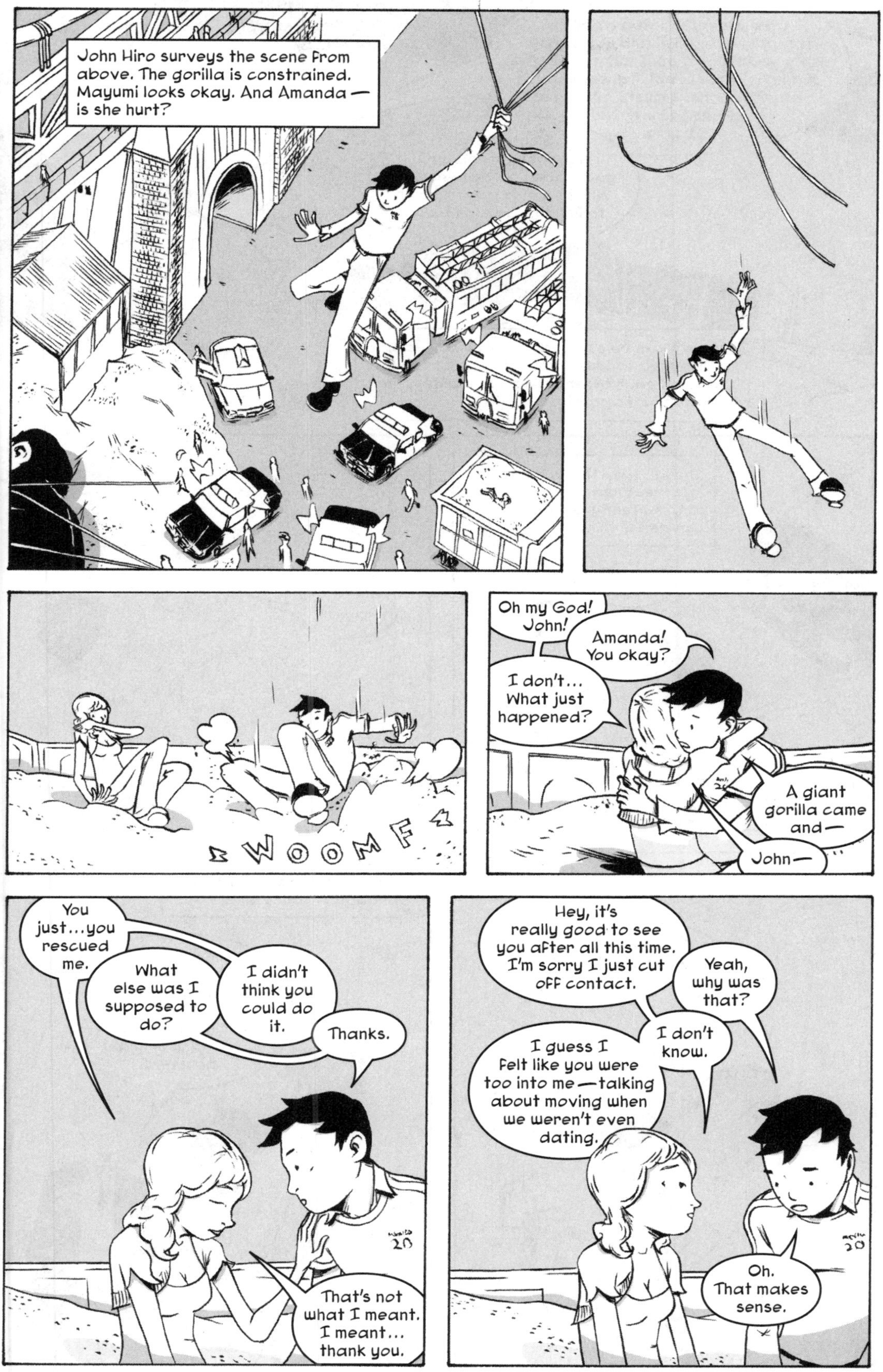
John Hiro surveys the scene from above. The gorilla is constrained. Mayumi looks okay. And Amanda — is she hurt?
WOOMF
Oh my God! John!
Amanda! You okay?
I don't... What just happened?
A giant gorilla came and—
John—
You just...you rescued me.
What else was I supposed to do?
I didn't think you could do it.
Thanks.
That's not what I meant. I meant... thank you.
Hey, it's really good to see you after all this time. I'm sorry I just cut off contact.
Yeah, why was that?
I don't know.
I guess I felt like you were too into me—talking about moving when we weren't even dating.
Oh. That makes sense.

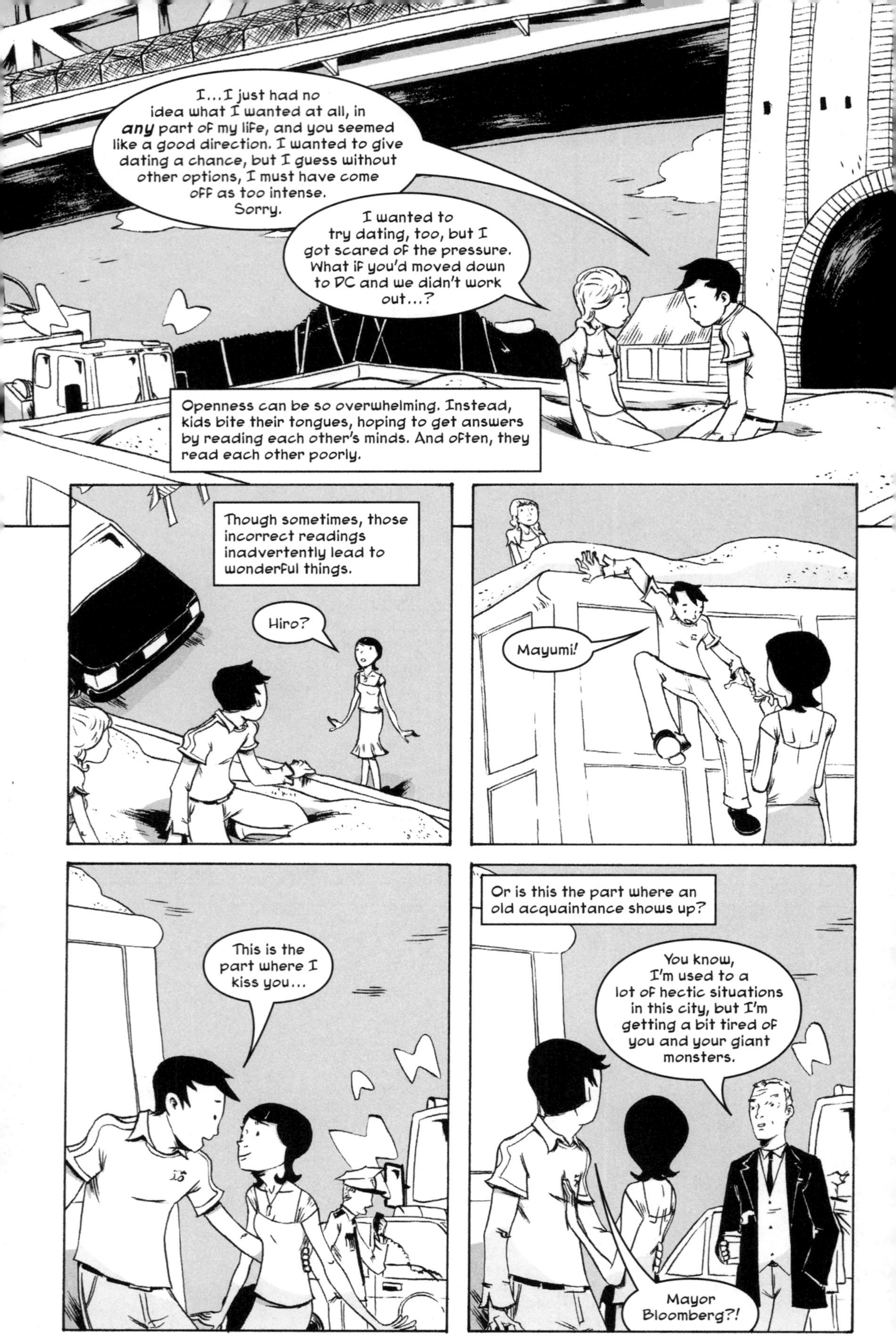
I...I just had no idea what I wanted at all, in any part of my life, and you seemed like a good direction. I wanted to give dating a chance, but I guess without other options, I must have come off as too intense. Sorry.
I wanted to try dating, too, but I got scared of the pressure. What if you'd moved down to DC and we didn't work out...?
Openness can be so overwhelming. Instead, kids bite their tongues, hoping to get answers by reading each other's minds. And often, they read each other poorly.
Though sometimes, those incorrect readings inadvertently lead to wonderful things.
Hiro?
Mayumi!
This is the part where I kiss you...
Or is this the part where an old acquaintance shows up?
You know, I'm used to a lot of hectic situations in this city, but I'm getting a bit tired of you and your giant monsters.
Mayor Bloomberg?!

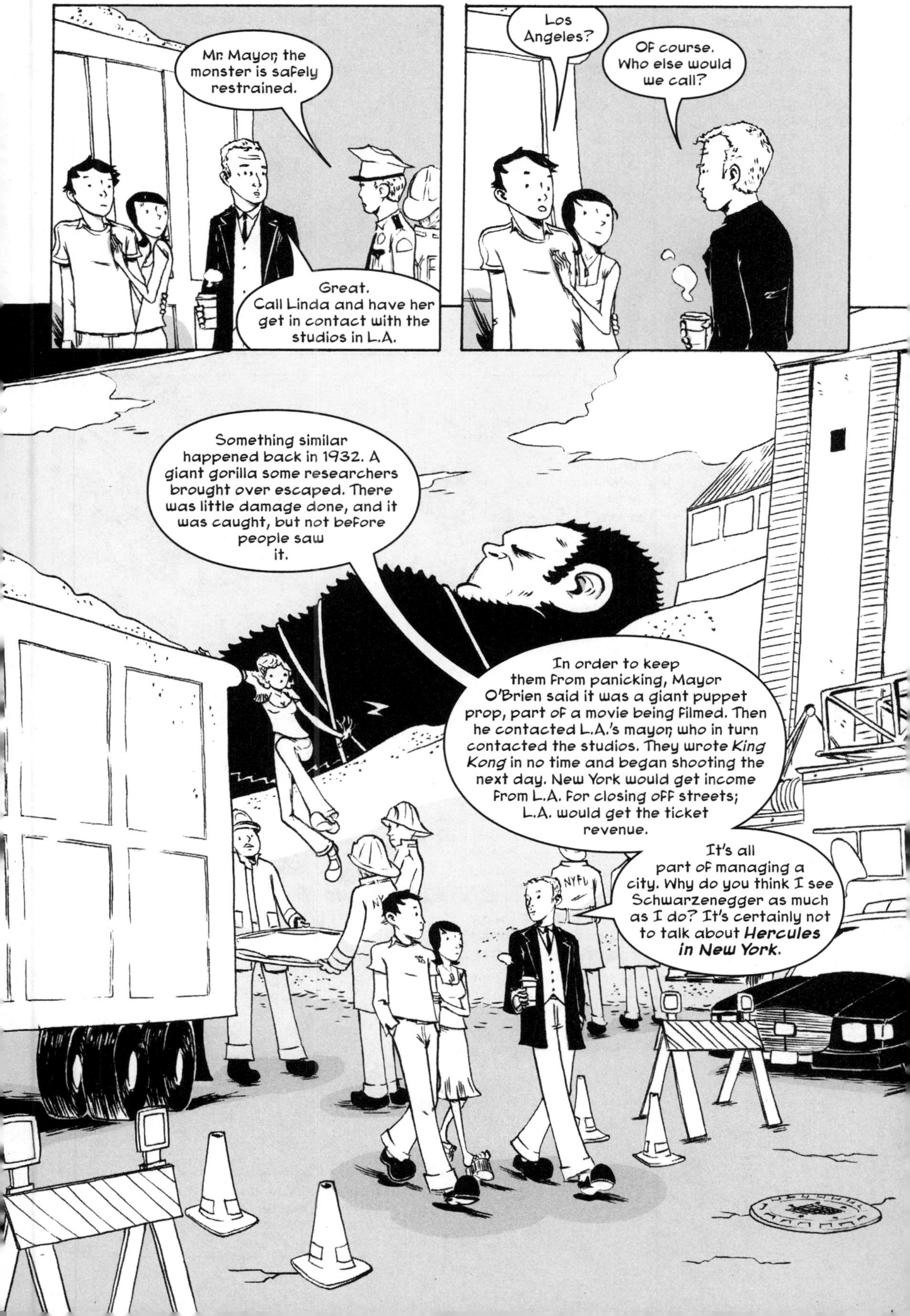
Mr. Mayor, the monster is safely restrained.
Great. Call Linda and have her get in contact with the studios in L.A.
Los Angeles?
Of course. Who else would we call?
Something similar happened back in 1932. A giant gorilla some researchers brought over escaped. There was little damage done, and it was caught, but not before people saw it.
In order to keep them from panicking, Mayor O'Brien said it was a giant puppet prop, part of a movie being filmed. Then he contacted L.A.'s mayor, who in turn contacted the studios. They wrote *King Kong* in no time and began shooting the next day. New York would get income from L.A. for closing off streets; L.A. would get the ticket revenue.
It's all part of managing a city. Why do you think I see Schwarzenegger as much as I do? It's certainly not to talk about ***Hercules in New York***.
NYFD

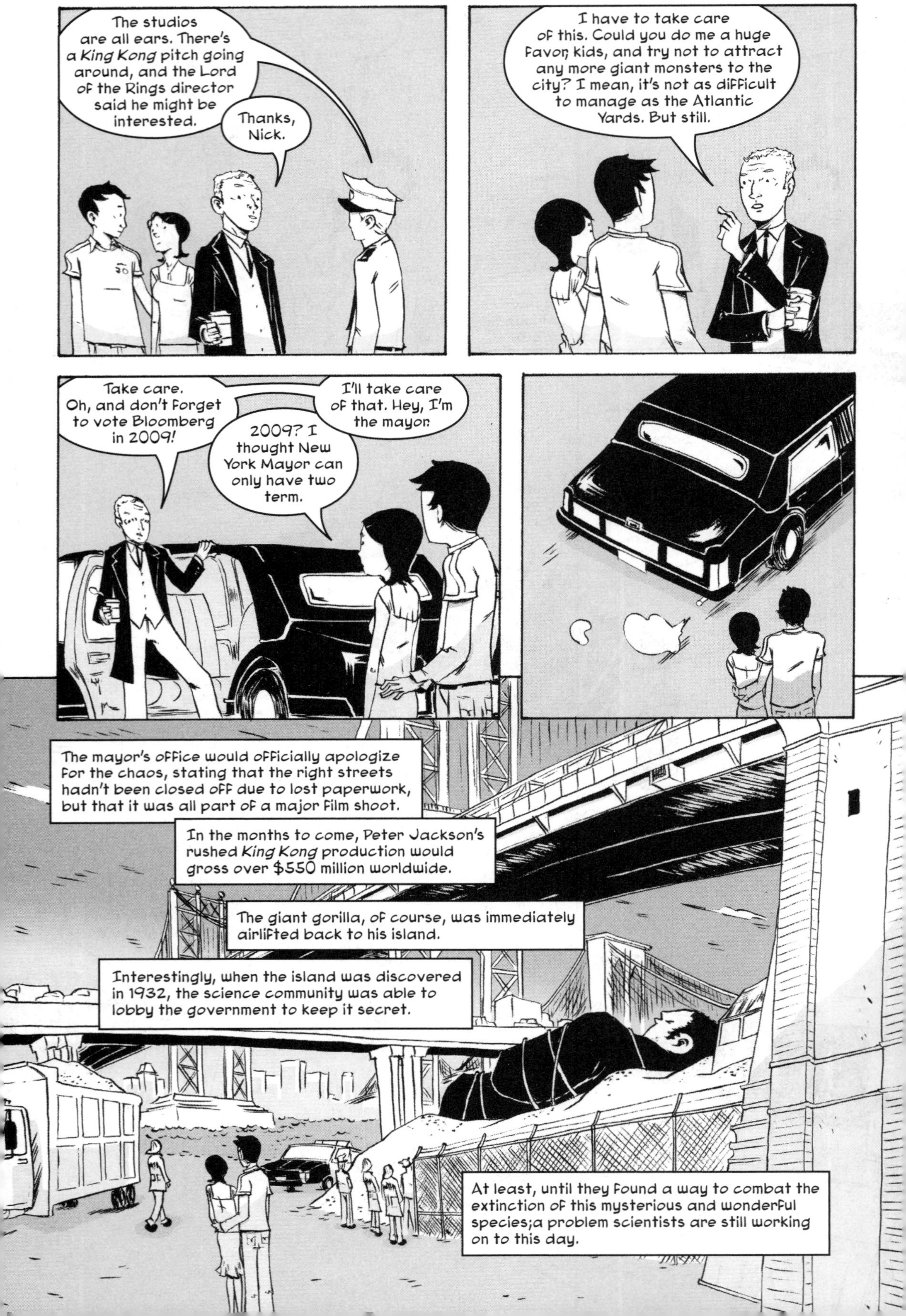
The studios are all ears. There's a *King Kong* pitch going around, and the Lord of the Rings director said he might be interested.
Thanks, Nick.
I have to take care of this. Could you do me a huge favor, kids, and try not to attract any more giant monsters to the city? I mean, it's not as difficult to manage as the Atlantic Yards. But still.
Take care. Oh, and don't forget to vote Bloomberg in 2009!
I'll take care of that. Hey, I'm the mayor.
2009? I thought New York Mayor can only have two term.
The mayor's office would officially apologize for the chaos, stating that the right streets hadn't been closed off due to lost paperwork, but that it was all part of a major film shoot.
In the months to come, Peter Jackson's rushed *King Kong* production would gross over $550 million worldwide.
The giant gorilla, of course, was immediately airlifted back to his island.
Interestingly, when the island was discovered in 1932, the science community was able to lobby the government to keep it secret.
At least, until they found a way to combat the extinction of this mysterious and wonderful species;a problem scientists are still working on to this day.

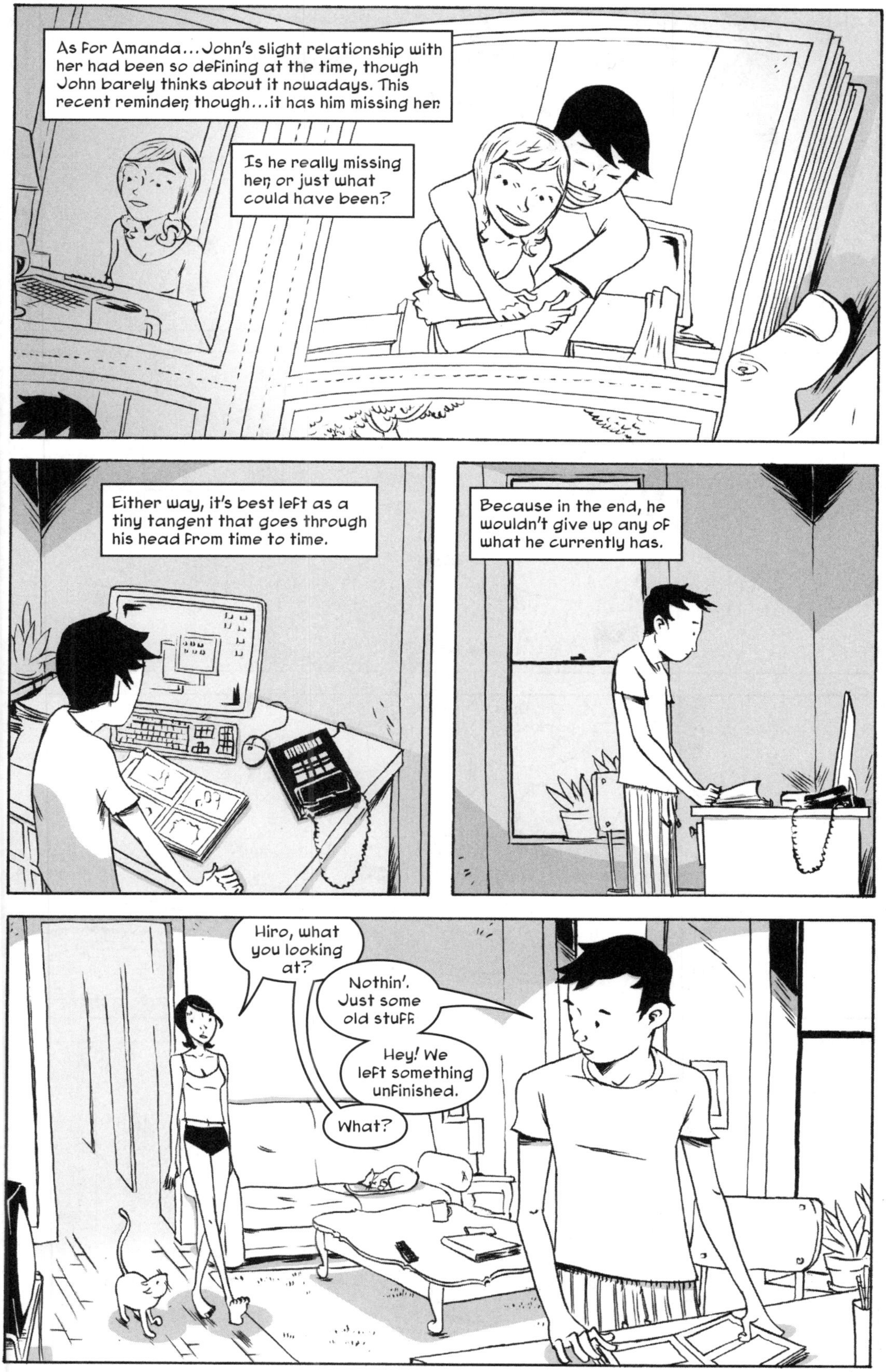
As for Amanda... John's slight relationship with her had been so defining at the time, though John barely thinks about it nowadays. This recent reminder, though... it has him missing her.
Is he really missing her, or just what could have been?
Either way, it's best left as a tiny tangent that goes through his head from time to time.
Because in the end, he wouldn't give up any of what he currently has.
Hiro, what you looking at?
Nothin'. Just some old stuff.
Hey! We left something unfinished.
What?

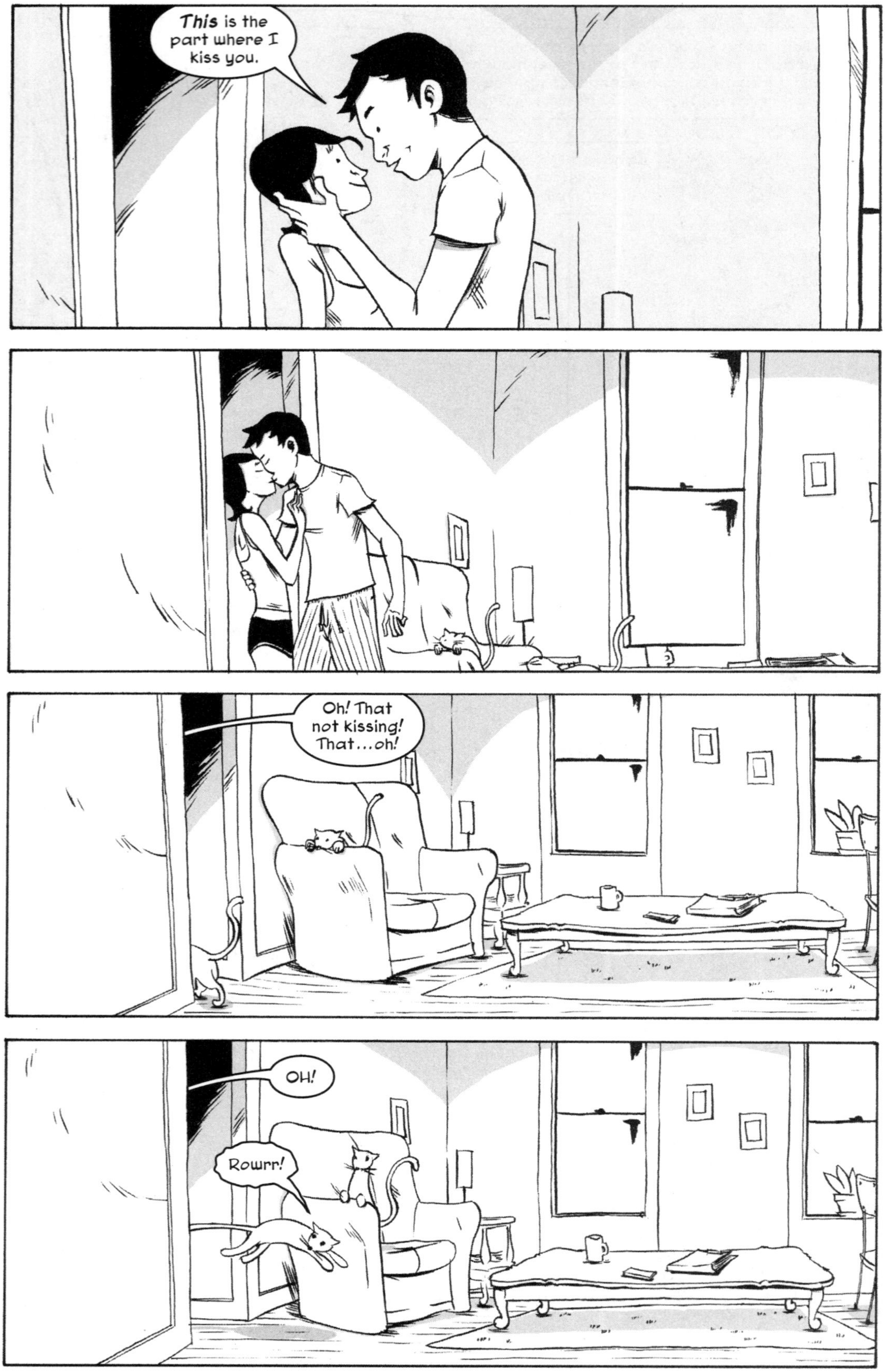
This is the part where I kiss you.
Oh! That not kissing! That...oh!
OH!
Rowrr!

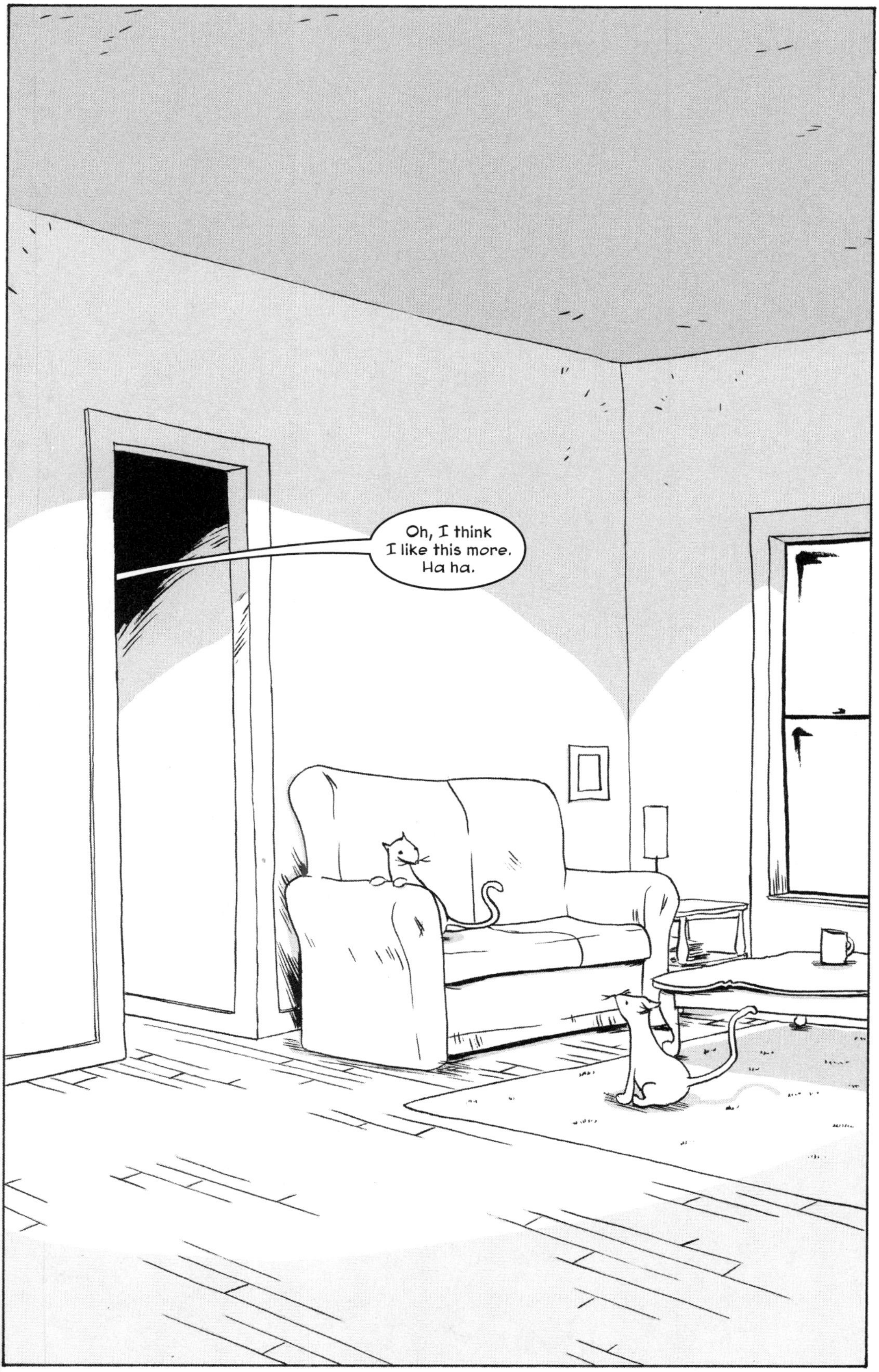
Oh, I think I like this more. Ha ha.

こきゅうけい1

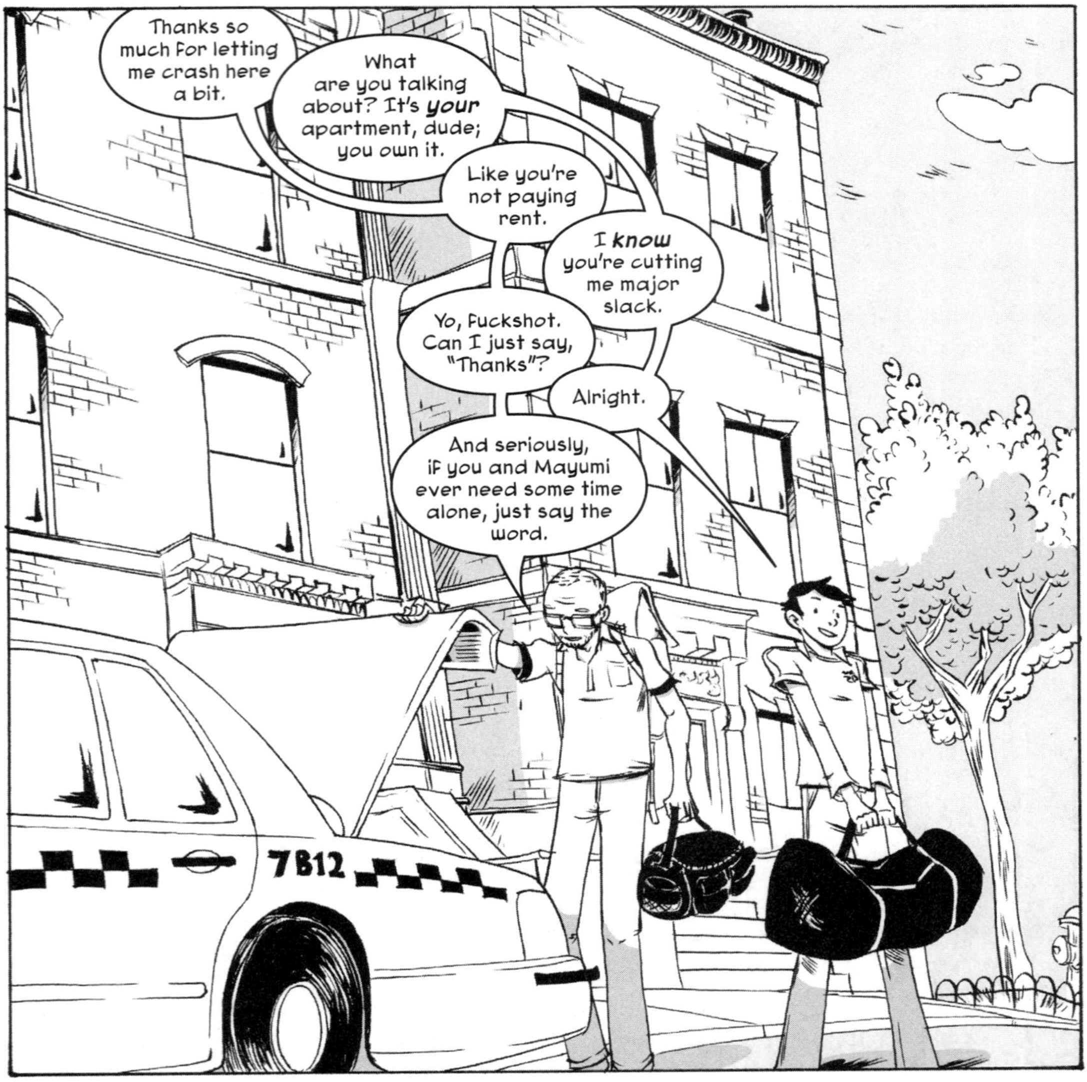
Thanks so much for letting me crash here a bit.
What are you talking about? It's your apartment, dude; you own it.
Like you're not paying rent.
I know you're cutting me major slack.
Yo, Fuckshot. Can I just say, "Thanks"?
Alright.
And seriously, if you and Mayumi ever need some time alone, just say the word.
7B12

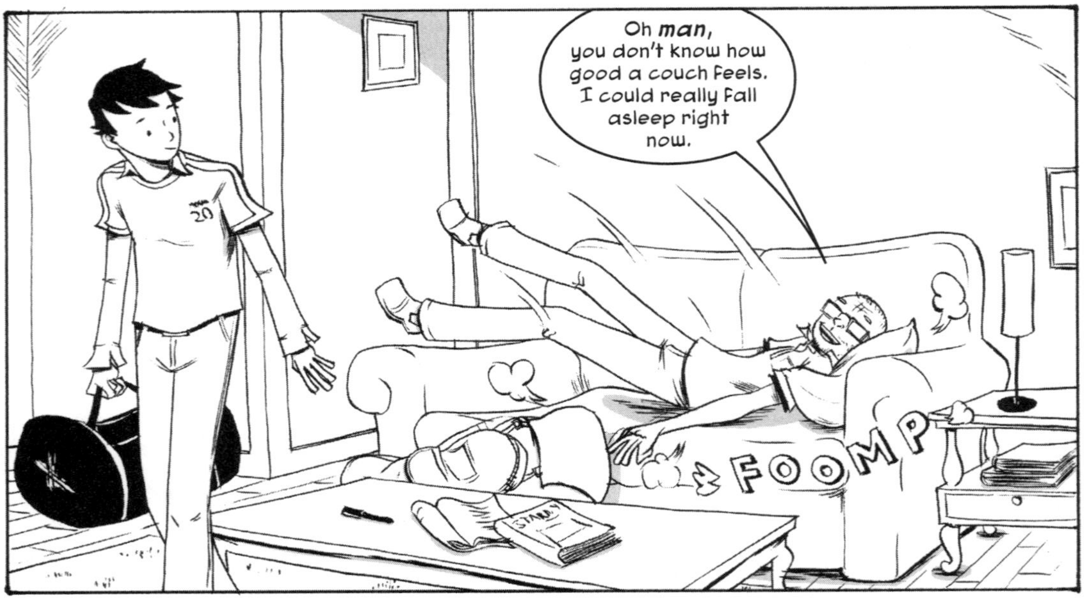
Oh man, you don't know how good a couch feels. I could really fall asleep right now.
FOOMP

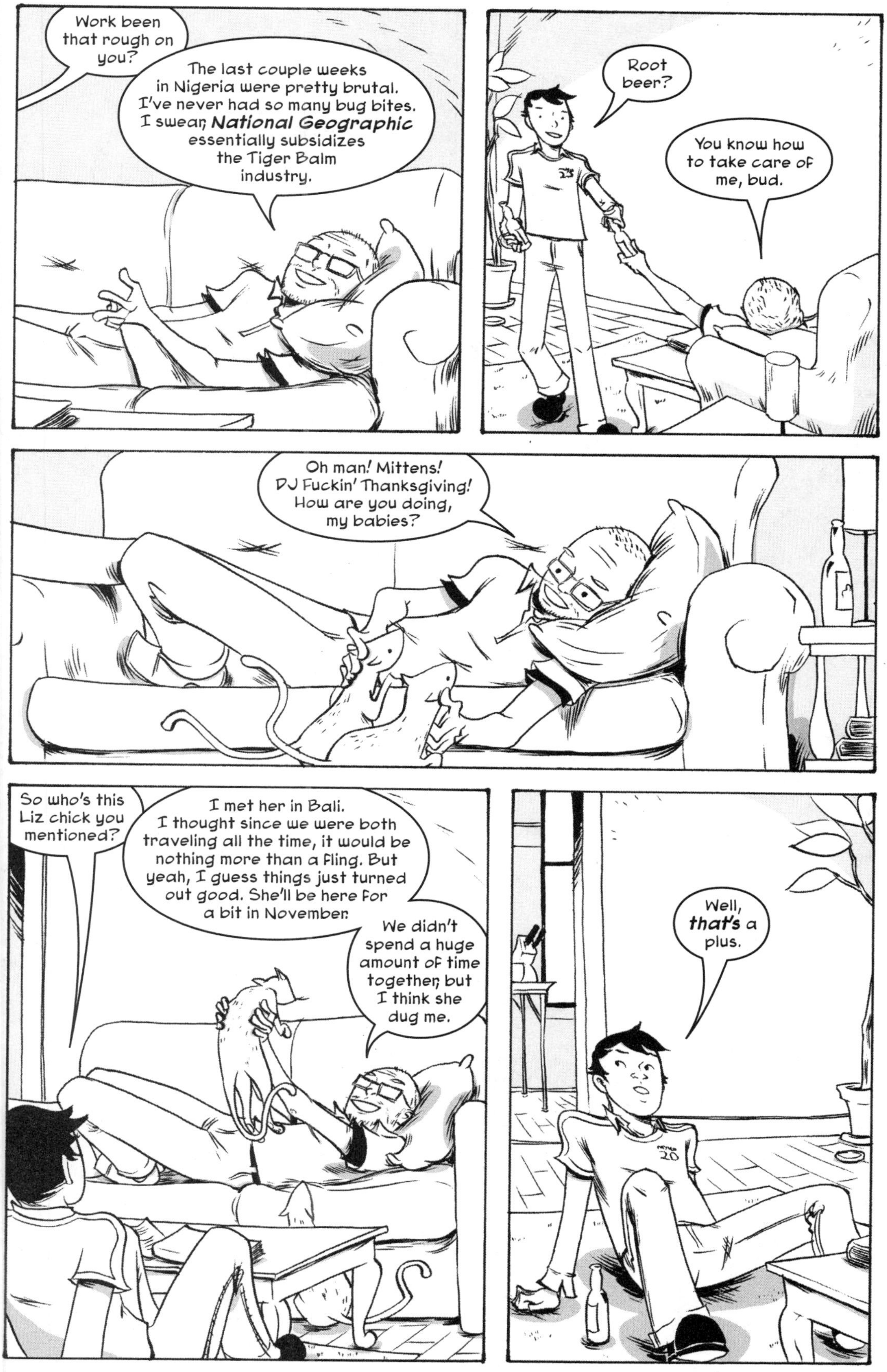
Work been that rough on you?
The last couple weeks in Nigeria were pretty brutal. I've never had so many bug bites. I swear, **National Geographic** essentially subsidizes the Tiger Balm industry.
Root beer?
You know how to take care of me, bud.
Oh man! Mittens! DJ Fuckin' Thanksgiving! How are you doing, my babies?
So who's this Liz chick you mentioned?
I met her in Bali. I thought since we were both traveling all the time, it would be nothing more than a fling. But yeah, I guess things just turned out good. She'll be here for a bit in November.
We didn't spend a huge amount of time together, but I think she dug me.
Well, ***that's*** a plus.

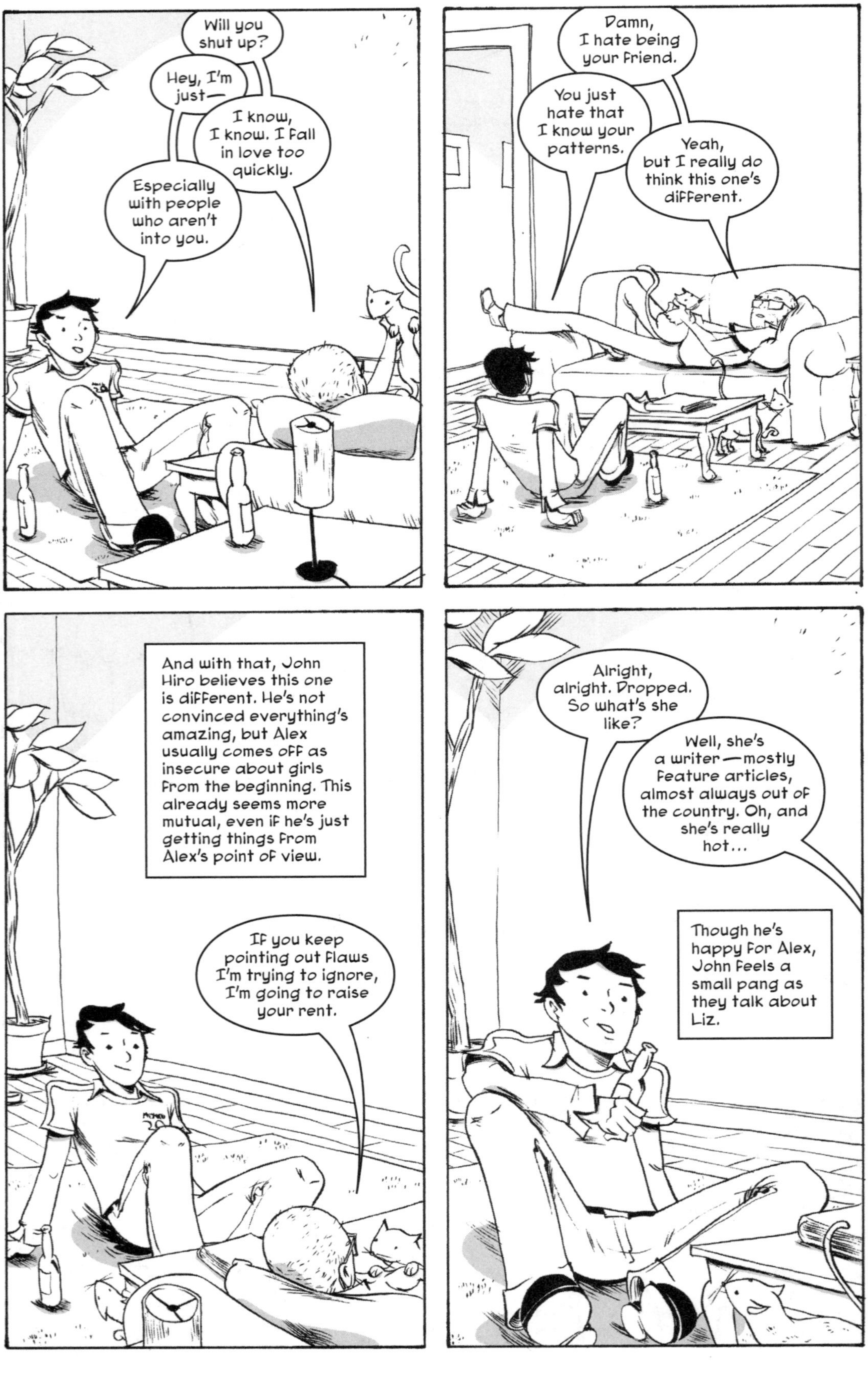
Will you shut up?
Hey, I'm just—
I know, I know. I fall in love too quickly.
Especially with people who aren't into you.
Damn, I hate being your friend.
You just hate that I know your patterns.
Yeah, but I really do think this one's different.
And with that, John Hiro believes this one is different. He's not convinced everything's amazing, but Alex usually comes off as insecure about girls from the beginning. This already seems more mutual, even if he's just getting things from Alex's point of view.
If you keep pointing out flaws I'm trying to ignore, I'm going to raise your rent.
Alright, alright. Dropped. So what's she like?
Well, she's a writer—mostly feature articles, almost always out of the country. Oh, and she's really hot...
Though he's happy for Alex, John feels a small pang as they talk about Liz.

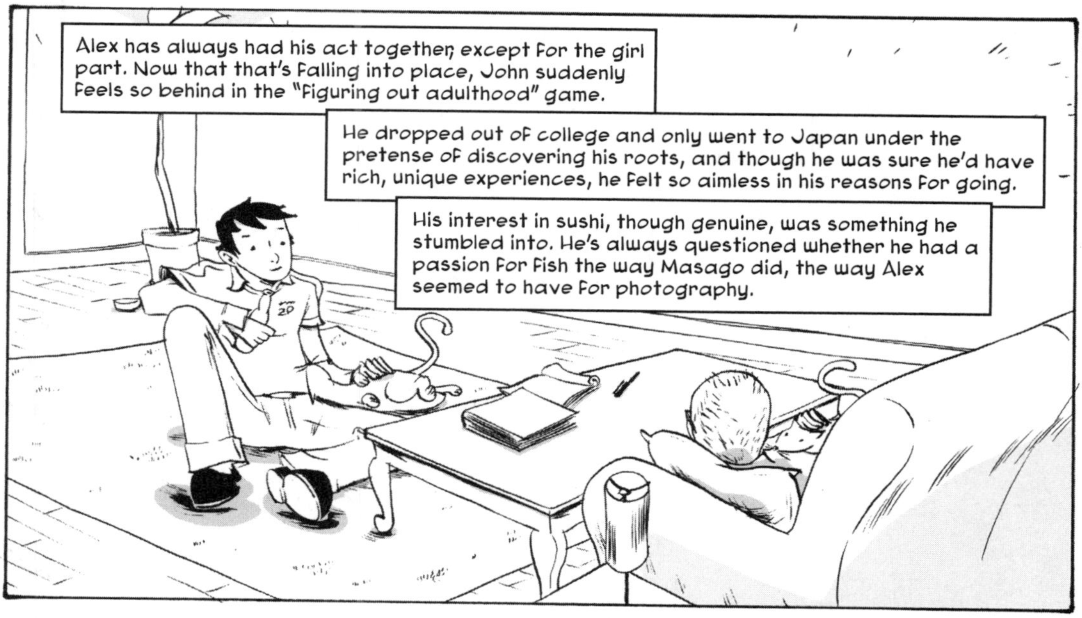
Alex has always had his act together, except for the girl part. Now that that's falling into place, John suddenly feels so behind in the "figuring out adulthood" game.
He dropped out of college and only went to Japan under the pretense of discovering his roots, and though he was sure he'd have rich, unique experiences, he felt so aimless in his reasons for going.
His interest in sushi, though genuine, was something he stumbled into. He's always questioned whether he had a passion for fish the way Masago did, the way Alex seemed to have for photography.

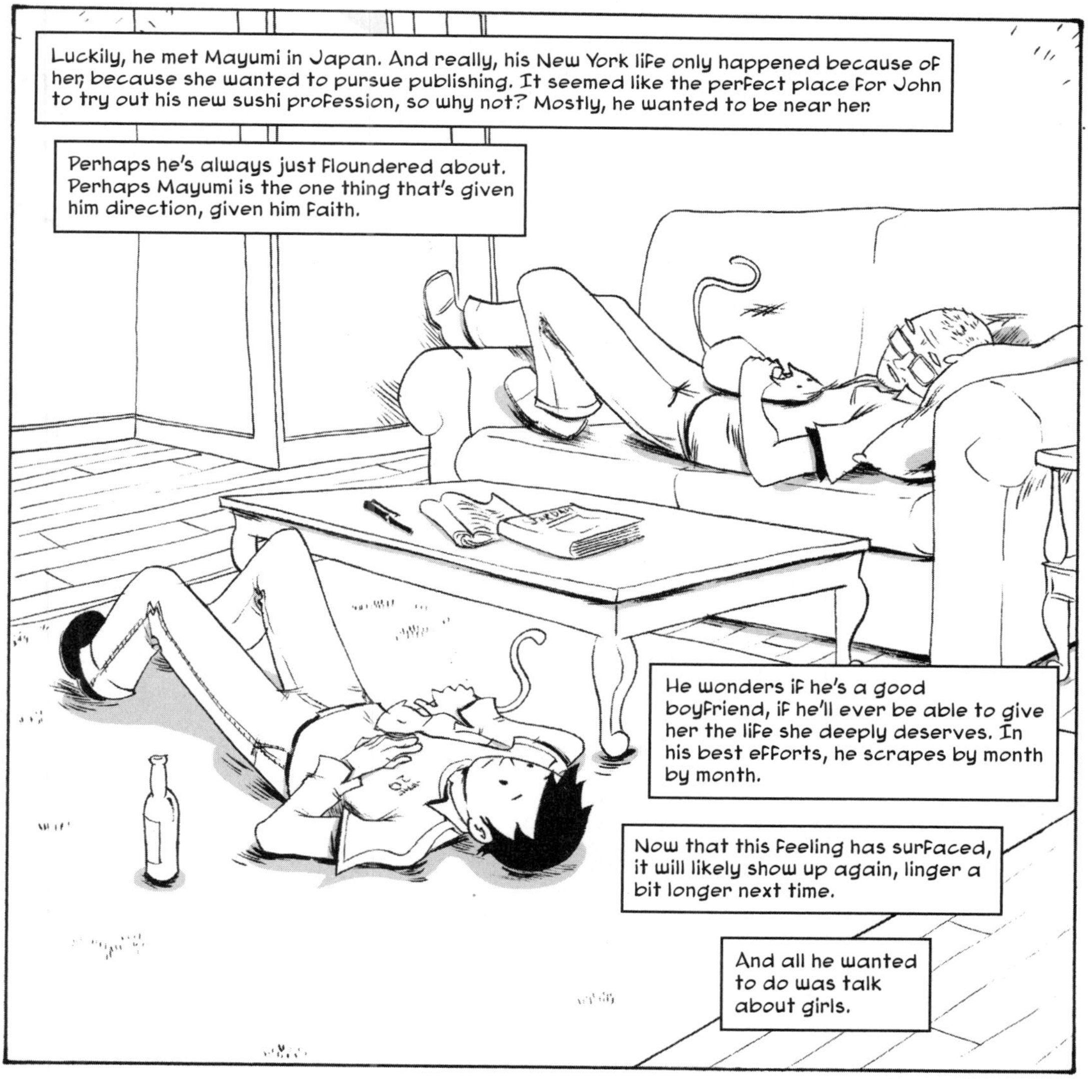
Luckily, he met Mayumi in Japan. And really, his New York life only happened because of her, because she wanted to pursue publishing. It seemed like the perfect place for John to try out his new sushi profession, so why not? Mostly, he wanted to be near her.
Perhaps he's always just floundered about. Perhaps Mayumi is the one thing that's given him direction, given him faith.
He wonders if he's a good boyfriend, if he'll ever be able to give her the life she deeply deserves. In his best efforts, he scrapes by month by month.
Now that this feeling has surfaced, it will likely show up again, linger a bit longer next time.
And all he wanted to do was talk about girls.

ビッグ イン ジャパン

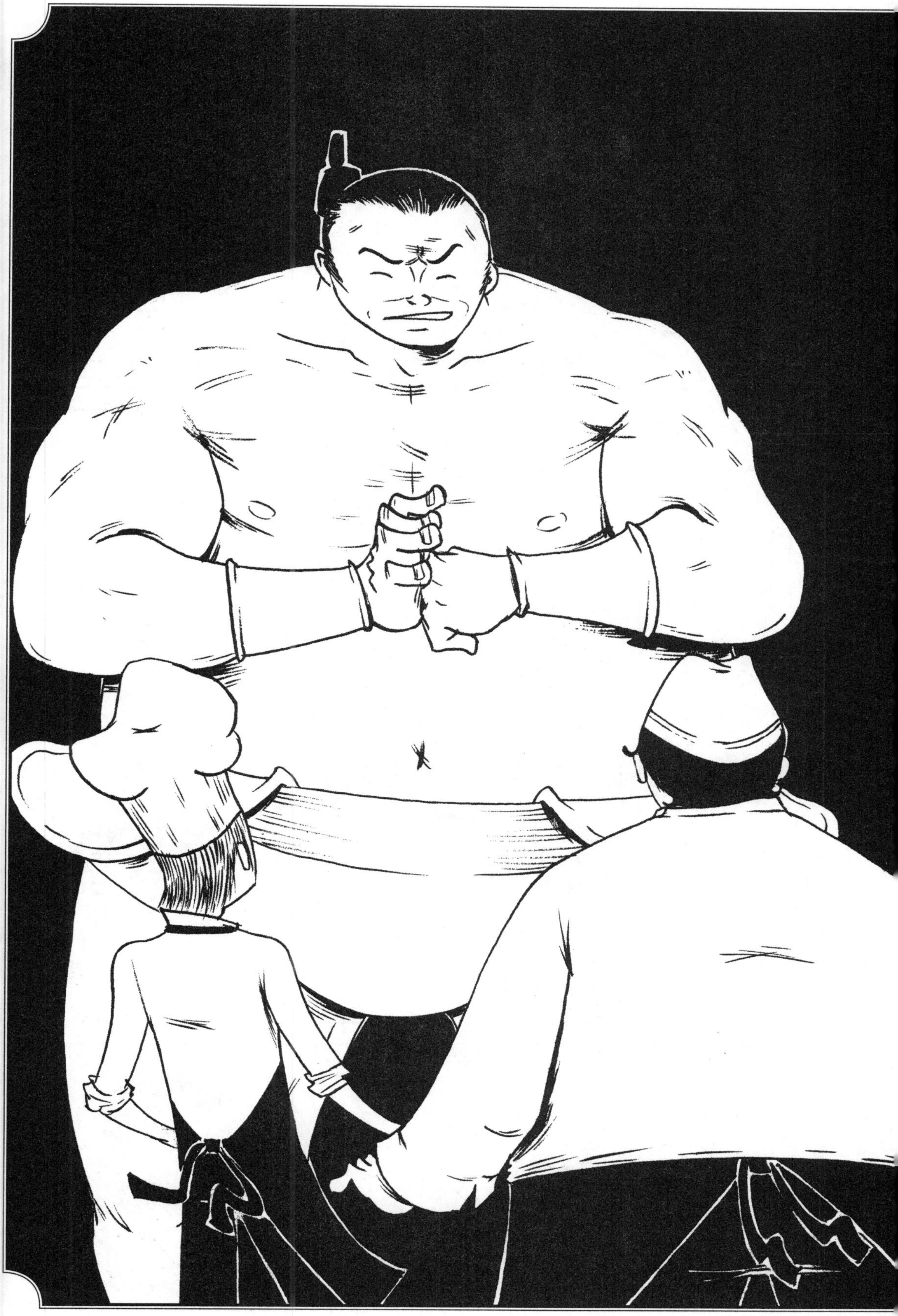

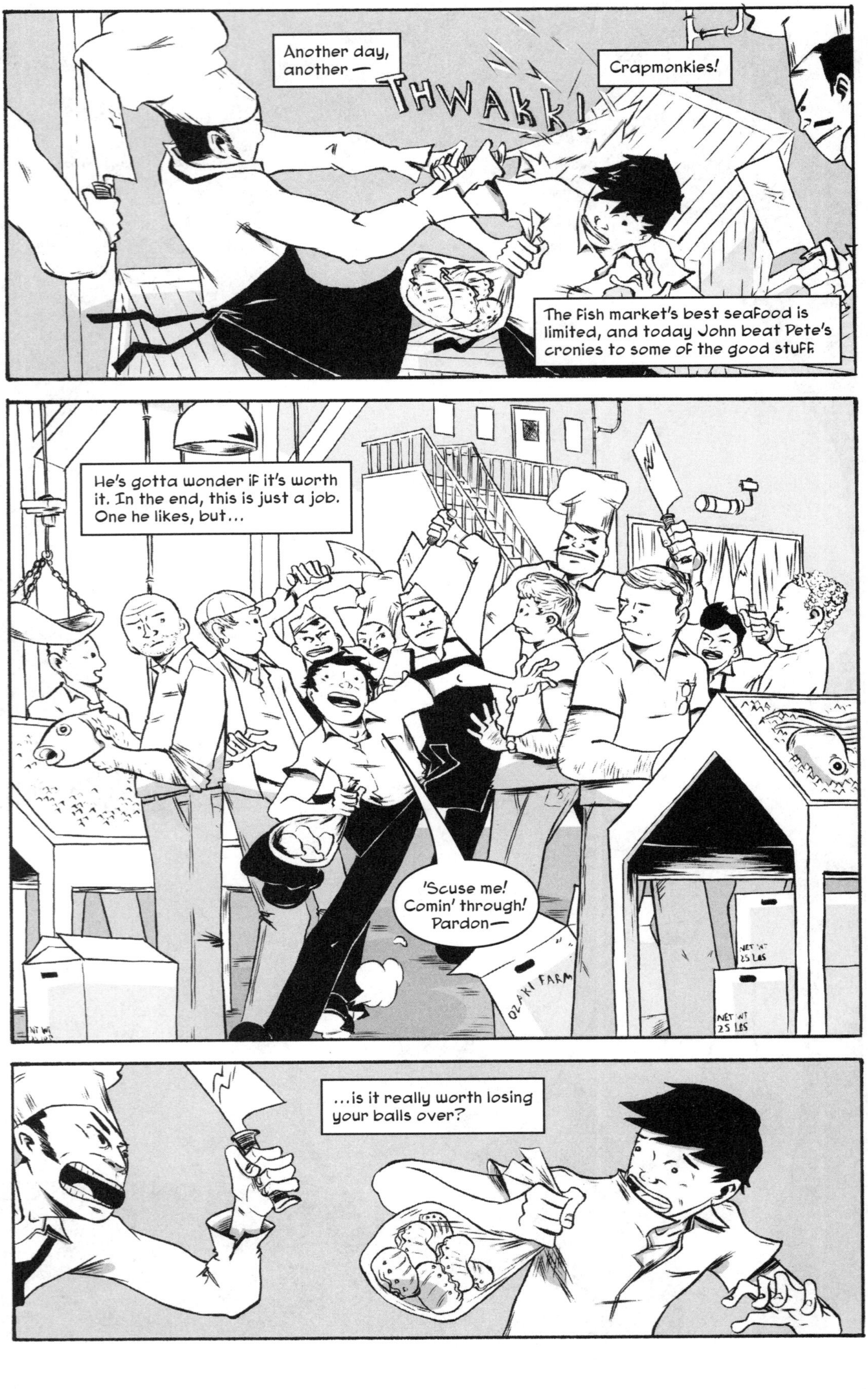
Another day, another —
THWAKK!
Crapmonkies!
The fish market's best seafood is limited, and today John beat Pete's cronies to some of the good stuff.
He's gotta wonder if it's worth it. In the end, this is just a job. One he likes, but...
'Scuse me! Comin' through! Pardon—
OZAKI FARM
NET WT 25 LBS
NET WT 25 LBS
...is it really worth losing your balls over?

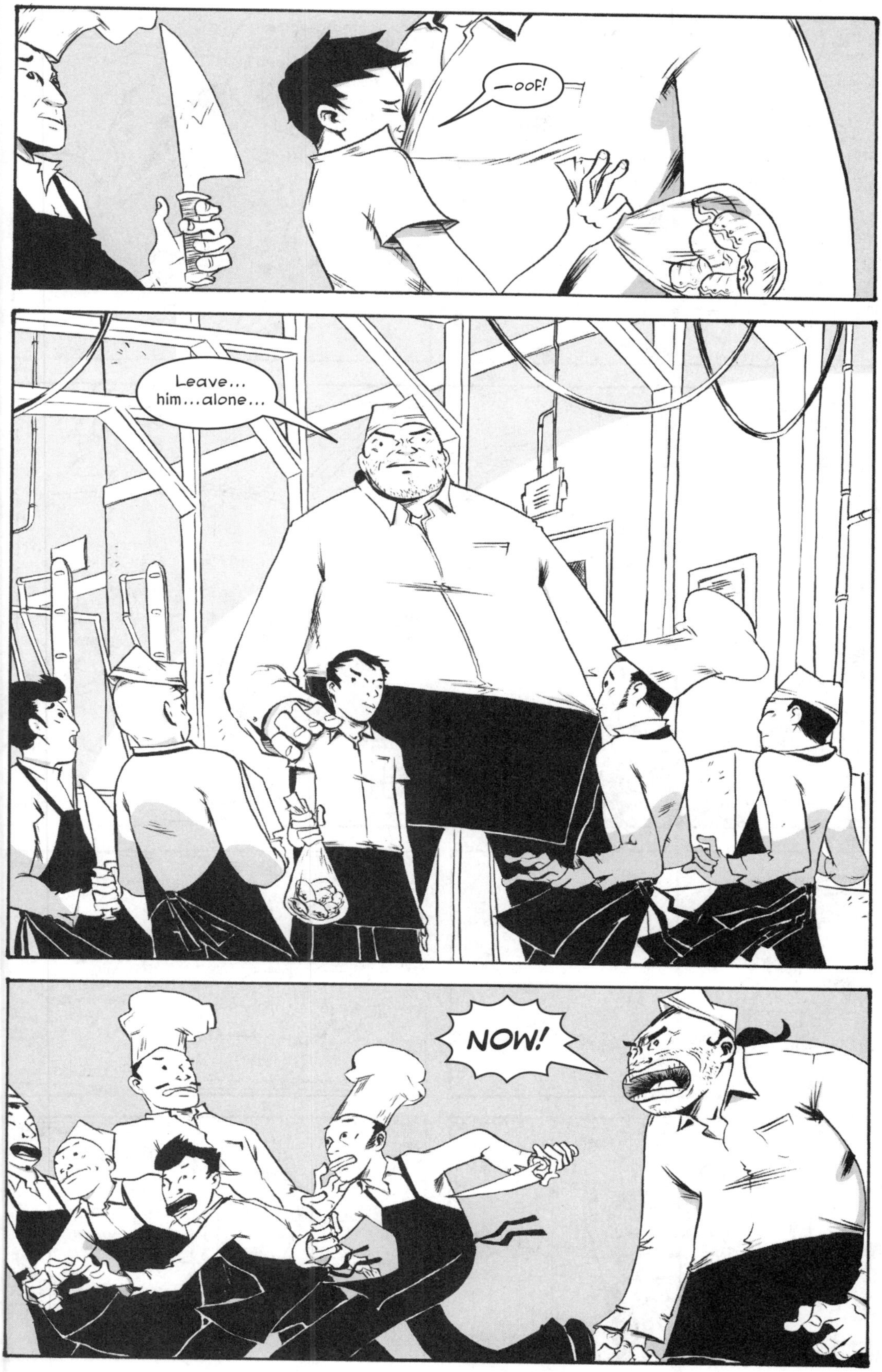
—oof!
Leave... him...alone...
NOW!

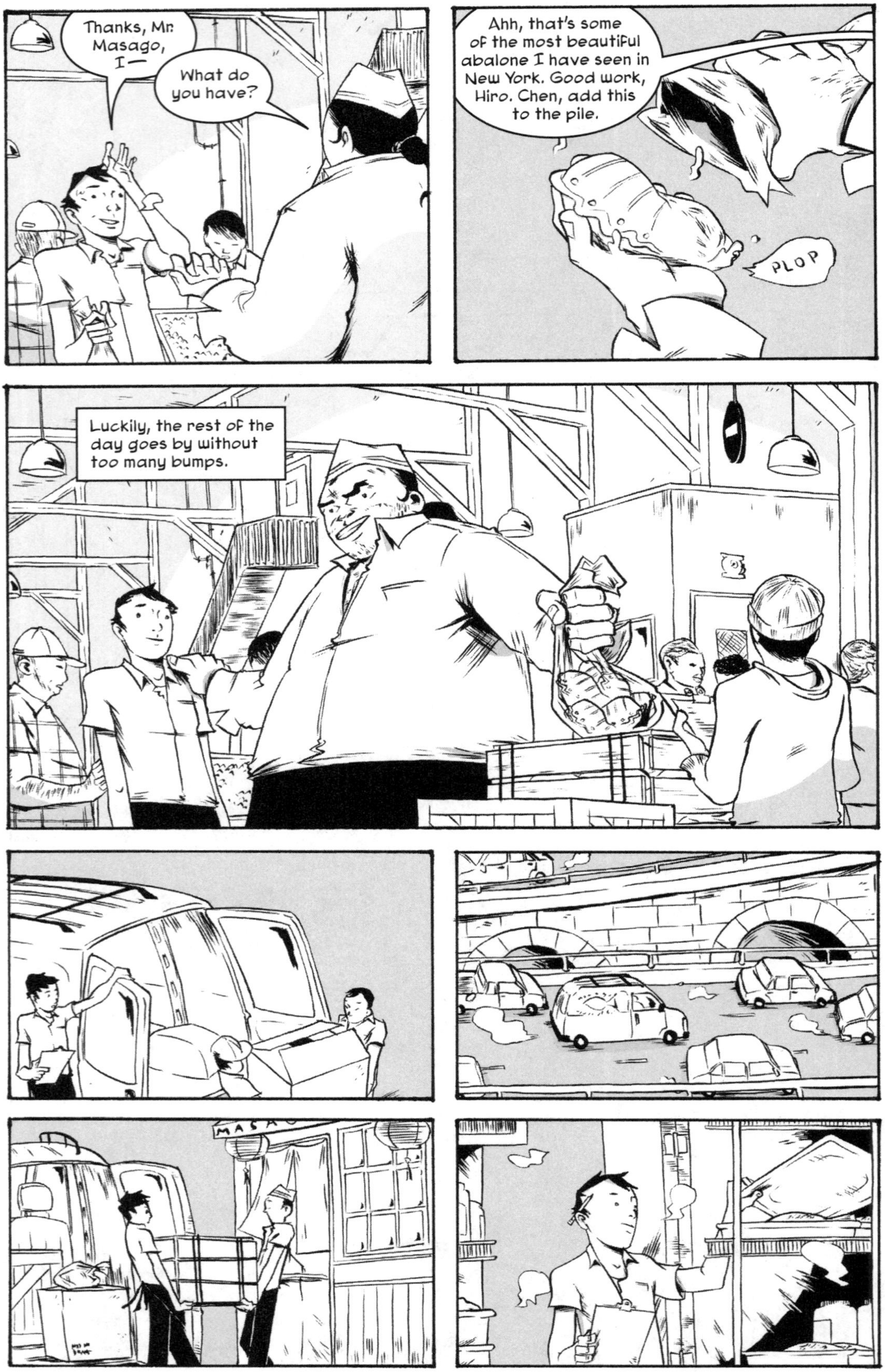
Thanks, Mr. Masago, I—
What do you have?
Ahh, that's some of the most beautiful abalone I have seen in New York. Good work, Hiro. Chen, add this to the pile.
PLOP
Luckily, the rest of the day goes by without too many bumps.

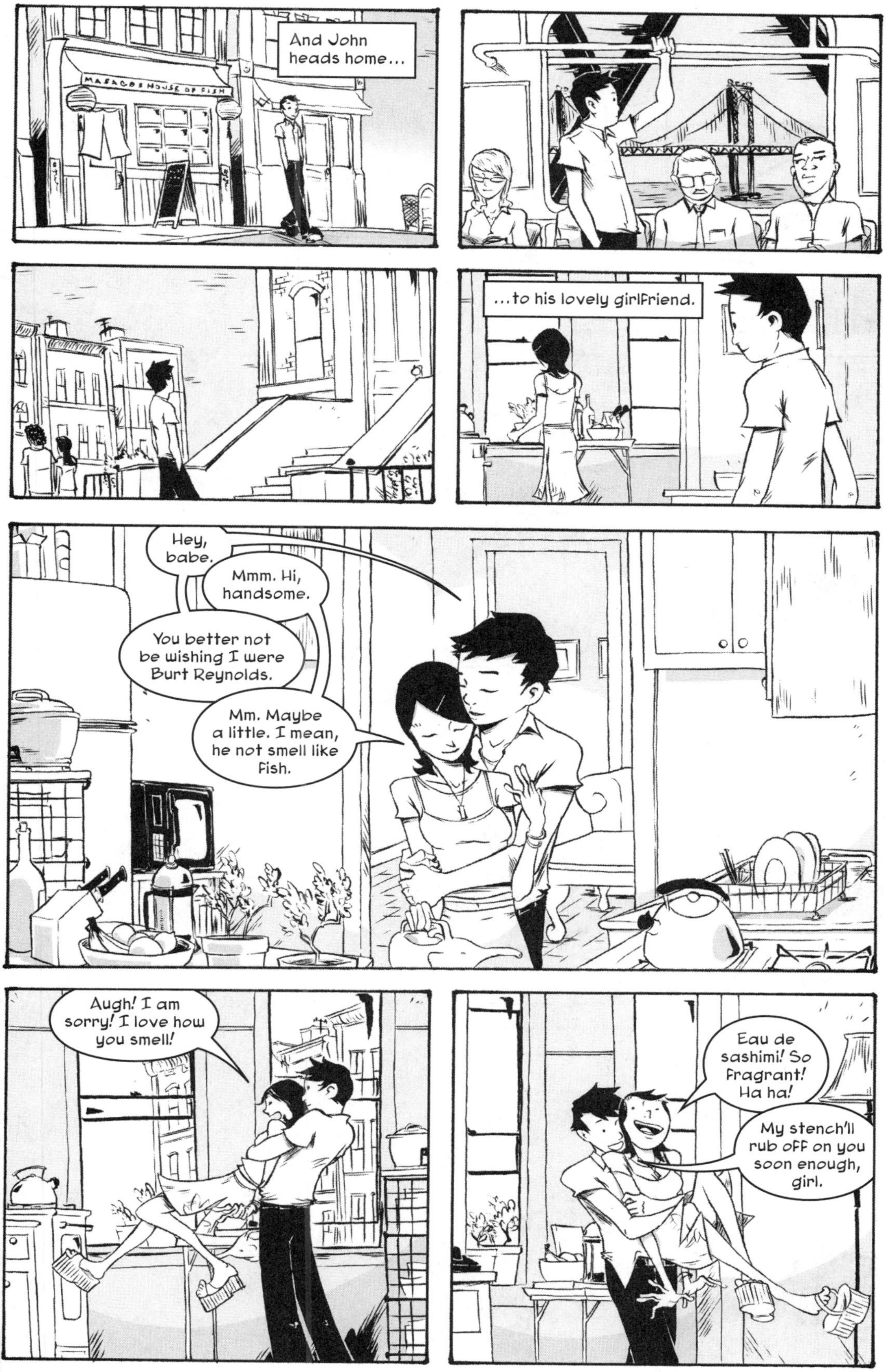
And John heads home...
MASAGOS HOUSE OF FISH
...to his lovely girlfriend.
Hey, babe.
Mmm. Hi, handsome.
You better not be wishing I were Burt Reynolds.
Mm. Maybe a little. I mean, he not smell like fish.
Augh! I am sorry! I love how you smell!
Eau de sashimi! So fragrant! Ha ha!
My stench'll rub off on you soon enough, girl.

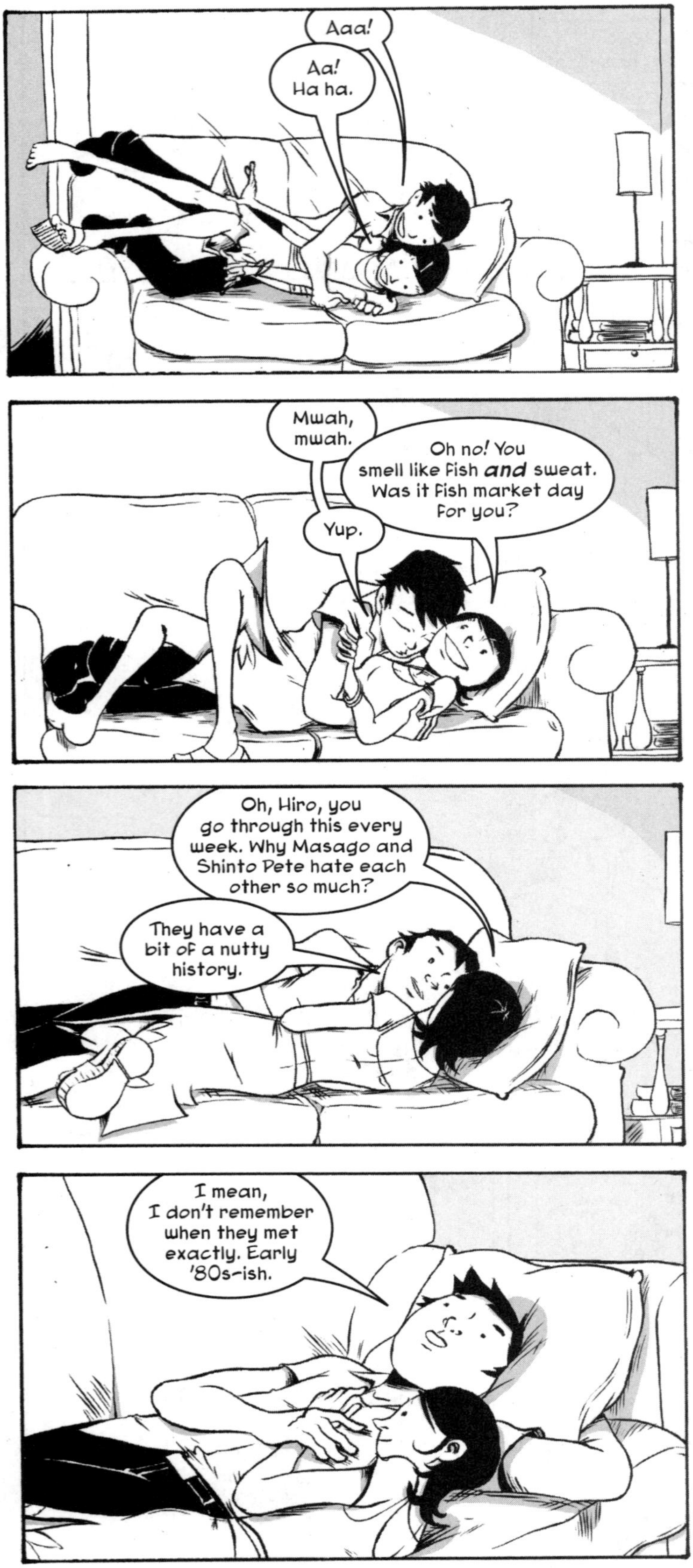
Aaa!
Aa! Ha ha.
Mwah, mwah.
Oh no! You smell like fish ***and*** sweat. Was it fish market day for you?
Yup.
Oh, Hiro, you go through this every week. Why Masago and Shinto Pete hate each other so much?
They have a bit of a nutty history.
I mean, I don't remember when they met exactly. Early '80s-ish.

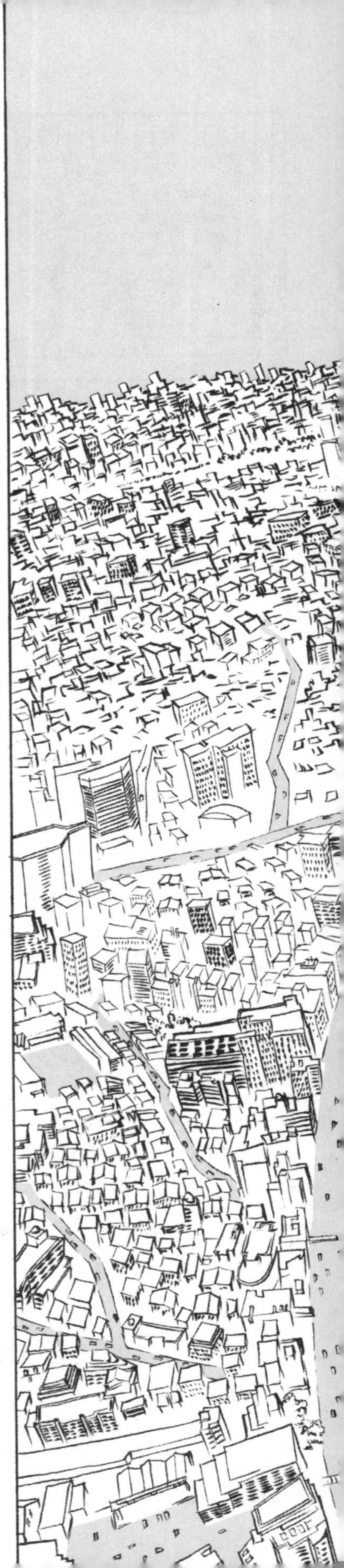

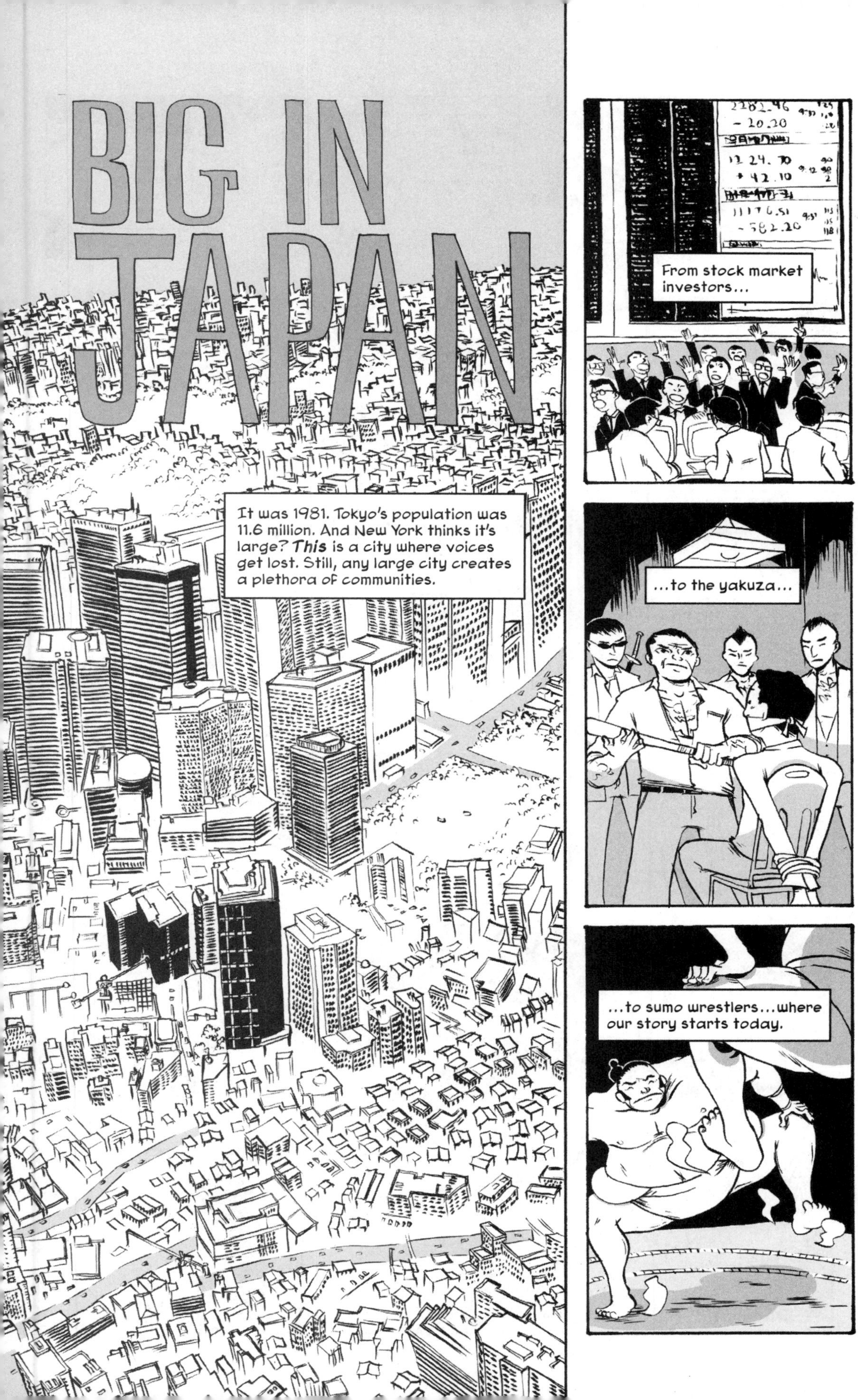
BIG IN JAPAN
It was 1981. Tokyo's population was 11.6 million. And New York thinks it's large? *This* is a city where voices get lost. Still, any large city creates a plethora of communities.
From stock market investors...
...to the yakuza...
...to sumo wrestlers...where our story starts today.

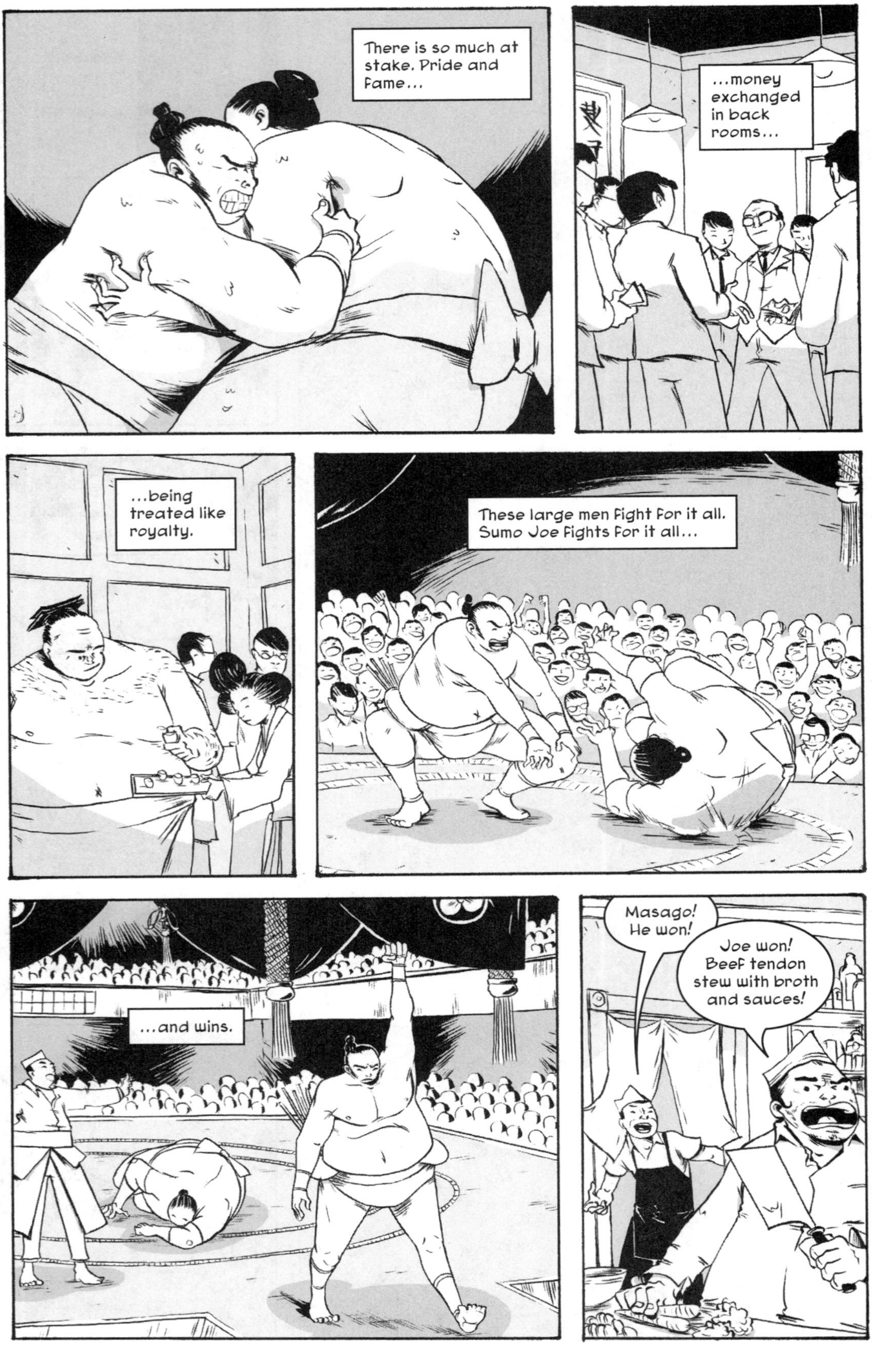
There is so much at stake. Pride and fame...
...money exchanged in back rooms...
...being treated like royalty.
These large men fight for it all. Sumo Joe fights for it all...
...and wins.
Masago! He won!
Joe won! Beef tendon stew with broth and sauces!

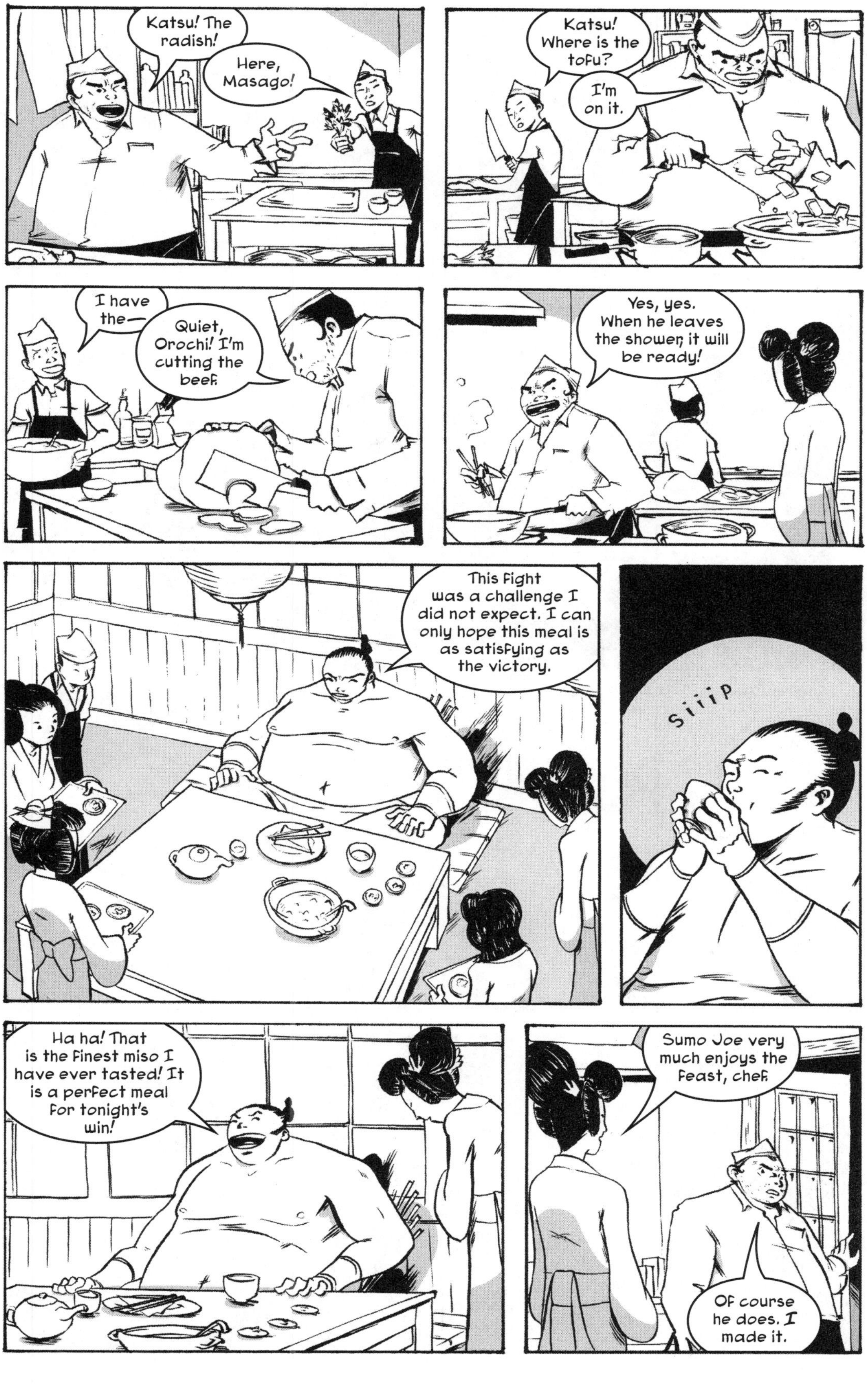
Katsu! The radish!
Here, Masago!
Katsu! Where is the tofu?
I'm on it.
I have the—
Quiet, Orochi! I'm cutting the beef.
Yes, yes. When he leaves the shower, it will be ready!
This fight was a challenge I did not expect. I can only hope this meal is as satisfying as the victory.
Siiip
Ha ha! That is the finest miso I have ever tasted! It is a perfect meal for tonight's win!
Sumo Joe very much enjoys the feast, chef.
Of course he does. I made it.

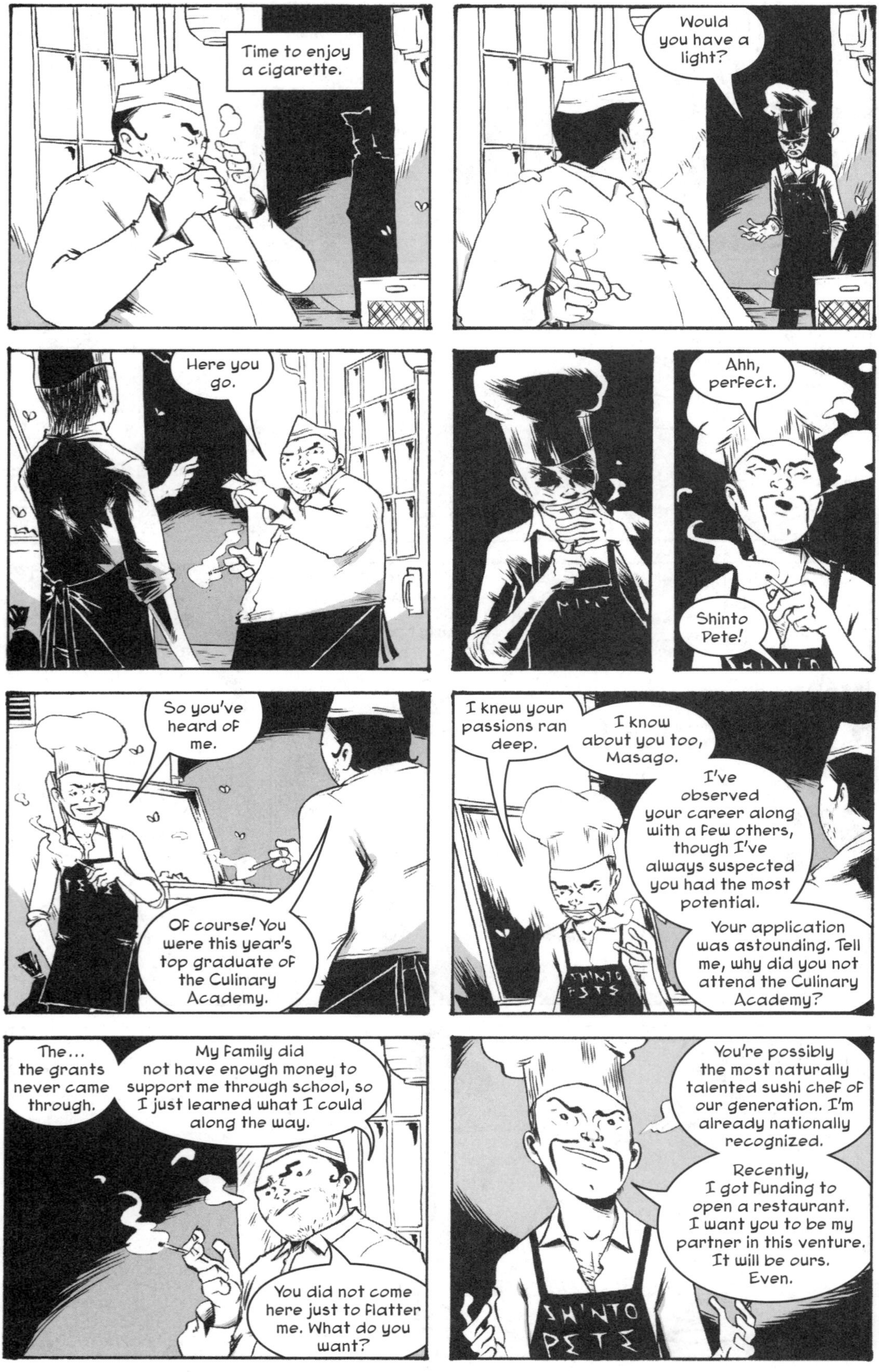
Time to enjoy a cigarette.
Would you have a light?
Here you go.
Ahh, perfect.
Shinto Pete!
So you've heard of me.
Of course! You were this year's top graduate of the Culinary Academy.
I knew your passions ran deep.
I know about you too, Masago.
I've observed your career along with a few others, though I've always suspected you had the most potential.
Your application was astounding. Tell me, why did you not attend the Culinary Academy?
The... the grants never came through.
My family did not have enough money to support me through school, so I just learned what I could along the way.
You did not come here just to flatter me. What do you want?
You're possibly the most naturally talented sushi chef of our generation. I'm already nationally recognized.
Recently, I got funding to open a restaurant. I want you to be my partner in this venture. It will be ours. Even.

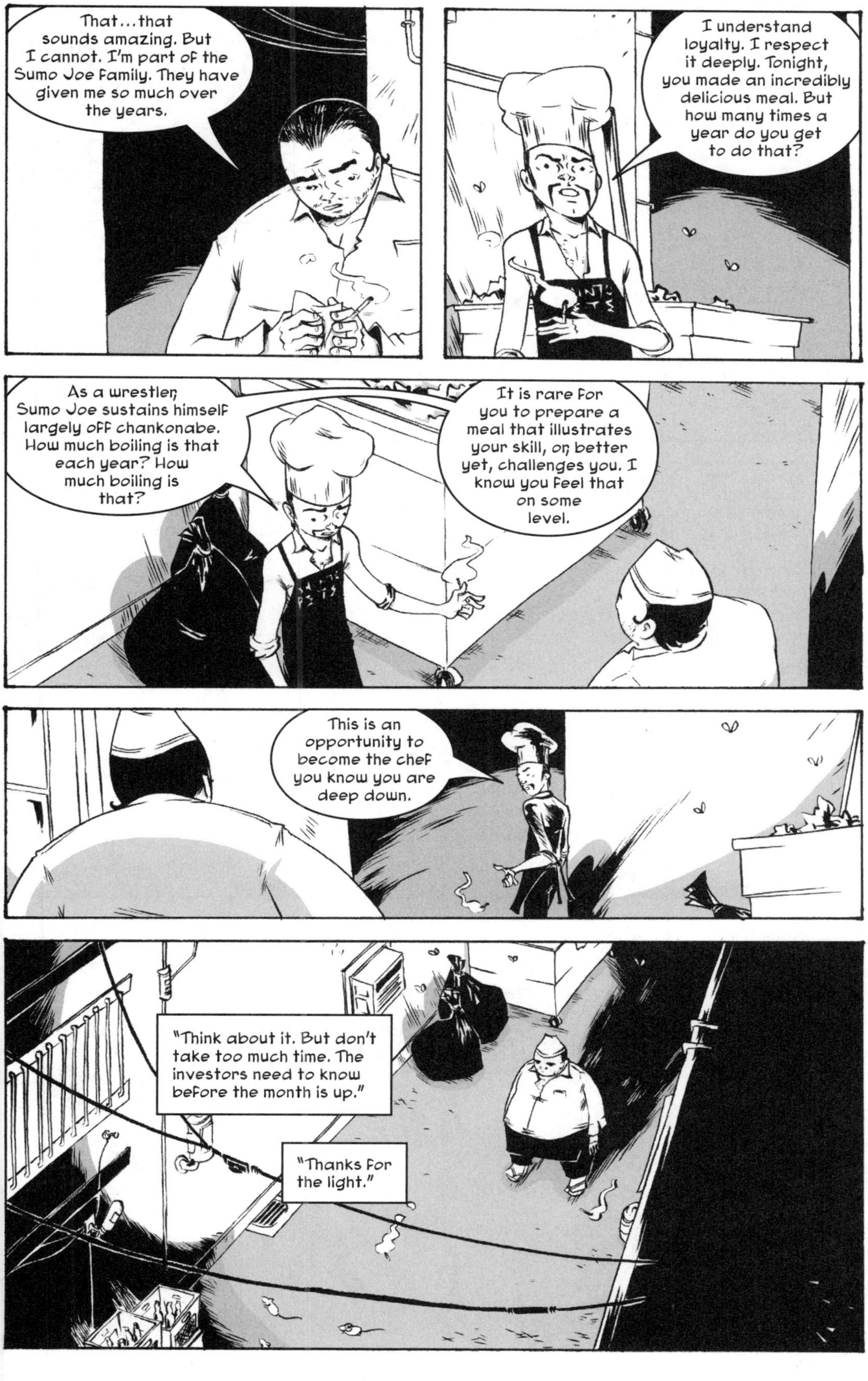
That...that sounds amazing. But I cannot. I'm part of the Sumo Joe family. They have given me so much over the years.
I understand loyalty. I respect it deeply. Tonight, you made an incredibly delicious meal. But how many times a year do you get to do that?
As a wrestler, Sumo Joe sustains himself largely off chankonabe. How much boiling is that each year? How much boiling is that?
It is rare for you to prepare a meal that illustrates your skill, or, better yet, challenges you. I know you feel that on some level.
This is an opportunity to become the chef you know you are deep down.
"Think about it. But don't take too much time. The investors need to know before the month is up."
"Thanks for the light."

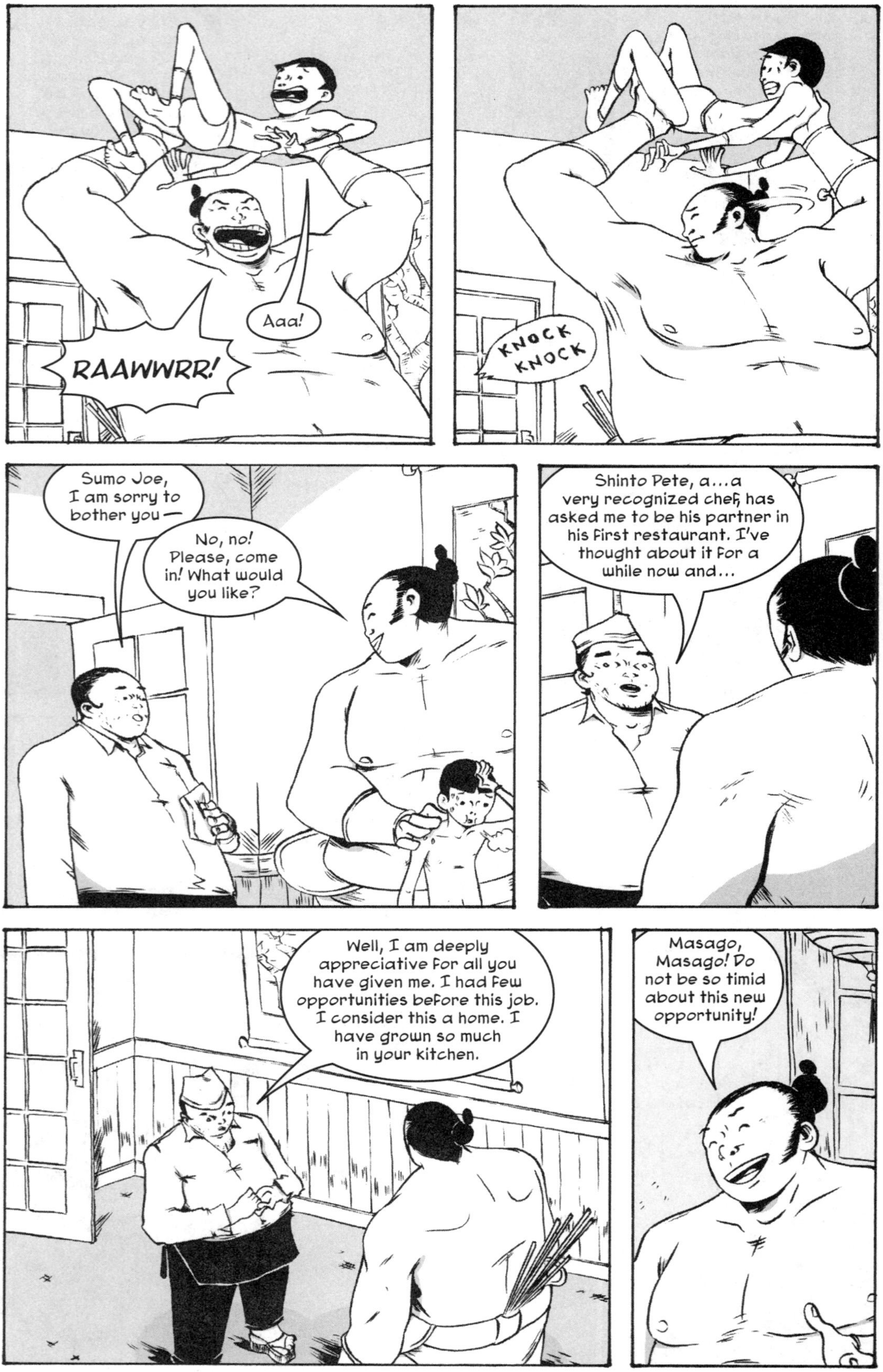
RAAWWRR!
Aaa!
KNOCK KNOCK
Sumo Joe, I am sorry to bother you—
No, no! Please, come in! What would you like?
Shinto Pete, a…a very recognized chef, has asked me to be his partner in his first restaurant. I've thought about it for a while now and…
Well, I am deeply appreciative for all you have given me. I had few opportunities before this job. I consider this a home. I have grown so much in your kitchen.
Masago, Masago! Do not be so timid about this new opportunity!

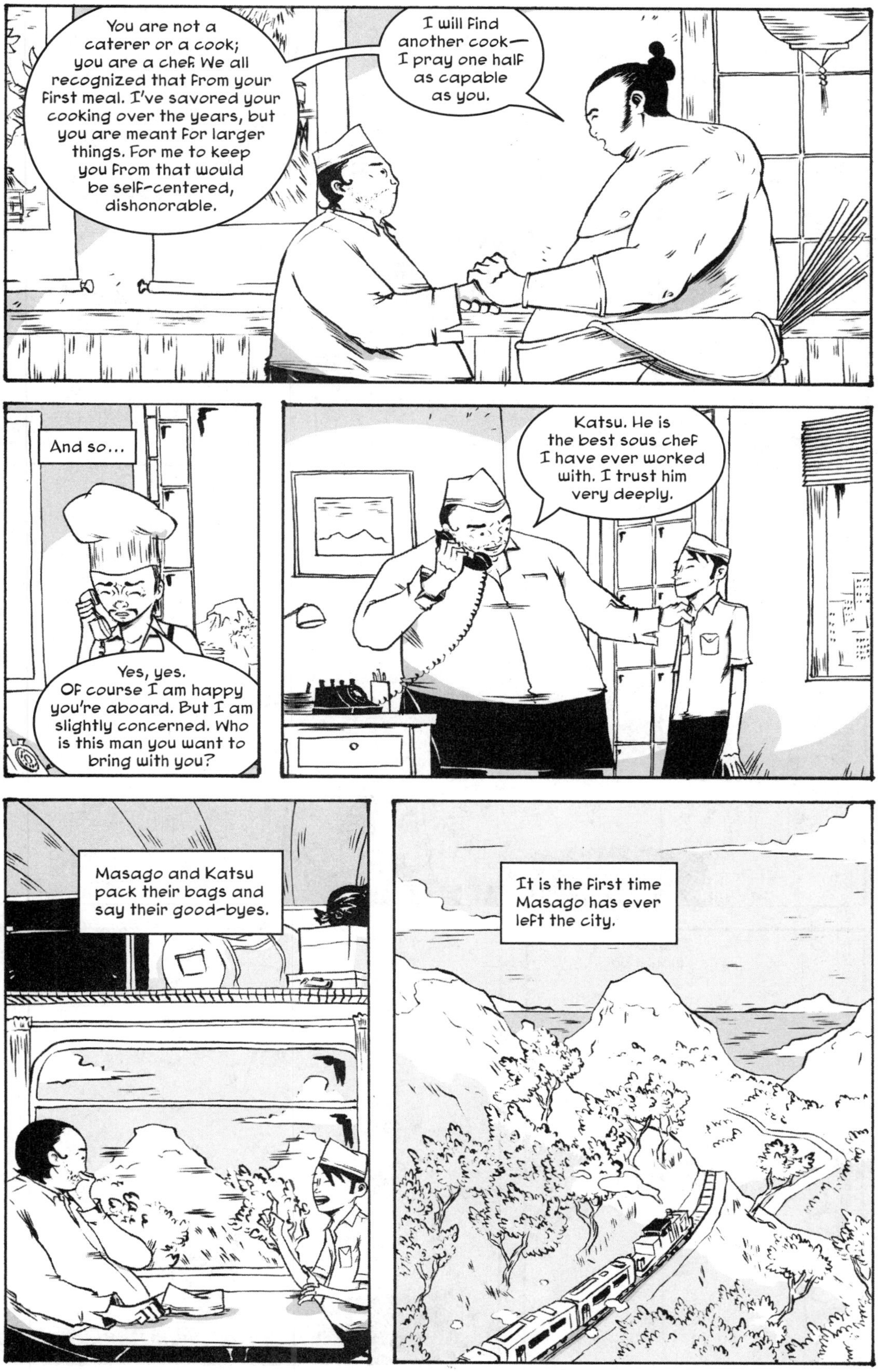
You are not a caterer or a cook; you are a chef. We all recognized that from your first meal. I've savored your cooking over the years, but you are meant for larger things. For me to keep you from that would be self-centered, dishonorable.
I will find another cook— I pray one half as capable as you.
And so…
Yes, yes. Of course I am happy you're aboard. But I am slightly concerned. Who is this man you want to bring with you?
Katsu. He is the best sous chef I have ever worked with. I trust him very deeply.
Masago and Katsu pack their bags and say their good-byes.
It is the first time Masago has ever left the city.

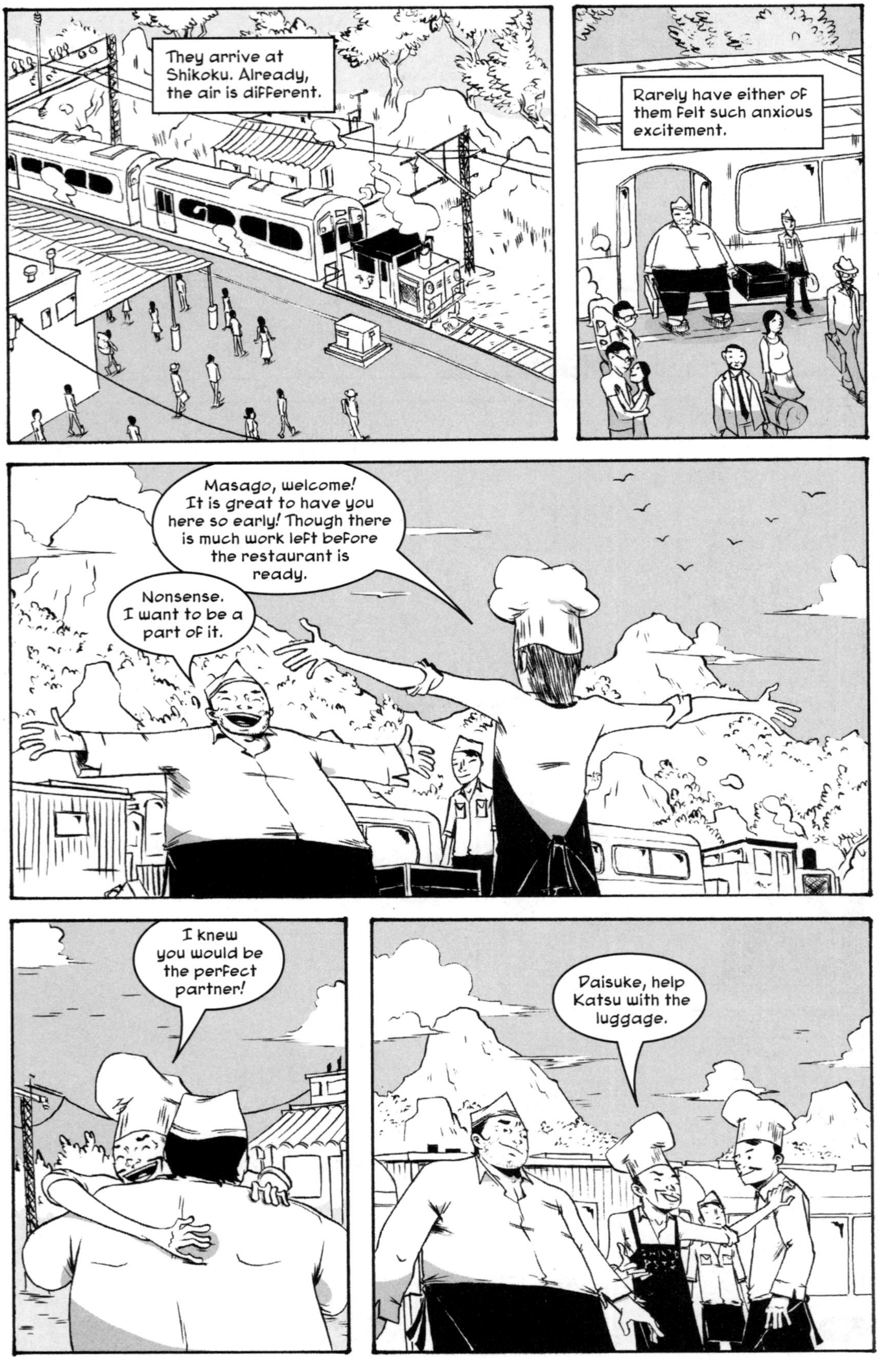
They arrive at Shikoku. Already, the air is different.
Rarely have either of them felt such anxious excitement.
Masago, welcome! It is great to have you here so early! Though there is much work left before the restaurant is ready.
Nonsense. I want to be a part of it.
I knew you would be the perfect partner!
Daisuke, help Katsu with the luggage.

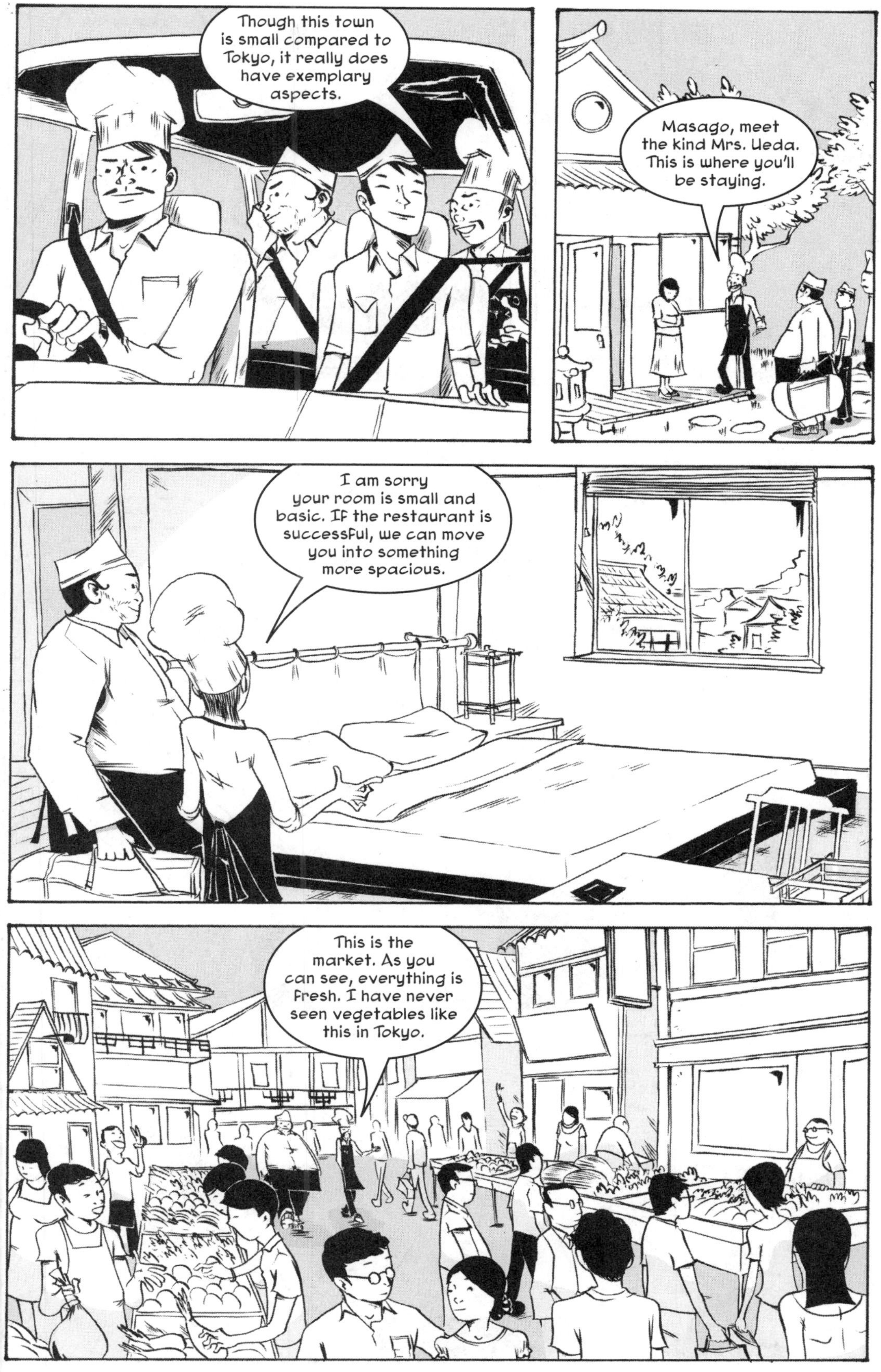
Though this town is small compared to Tokyo, it really does have exemplary aspects.
Masago, meet the kind Mrs. Ueda. This is where you'll be staying.
I am sorry your room is small and basic. If the restaurant is successful, we can move you into something more spacious.
This is the market. As you can see, everything is fresh. I have never seen vegetables like this in Tokyo.

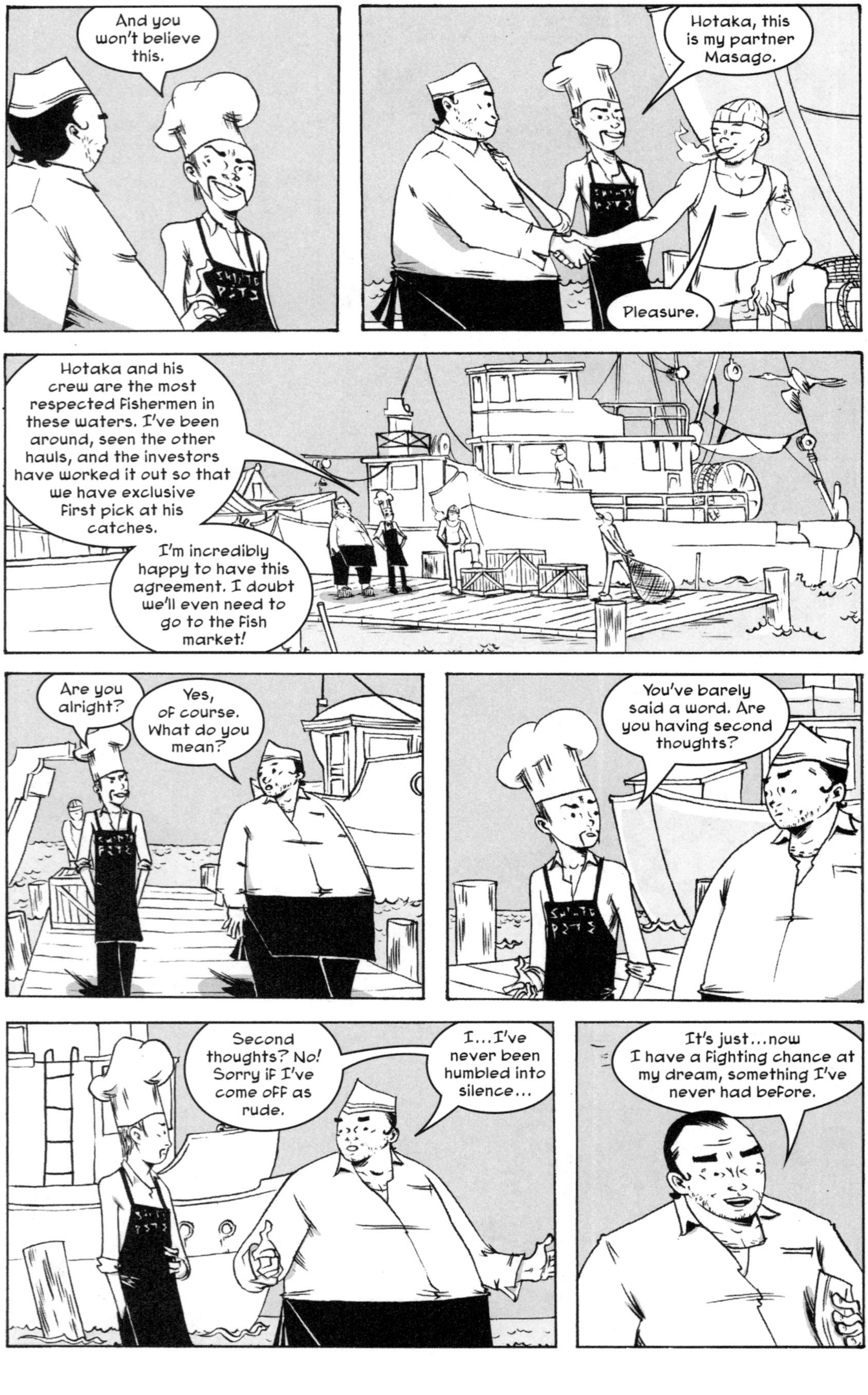
And you won't believe this.
Hotaka, this is my partner Masago.
Pleasure.
Hotaka and his crew are the most respected fishermen in these waters. I've been around, seen the other hauls, and the investors have worked it out so that we have exclusive first pick at his catches.
I'm incredibly happy to have this agreement. I doubt we'll even need to go to the fish market!
Are you alright?
Yes, of course. What do you mean?
You've barely said a word. Are you having second thoughts?
Second thoughts? No! Sorry if I've come off as rude.
I... I've never been humbled into silence...
It's just... now I have a fighting chance at my dream, something I've never had before.

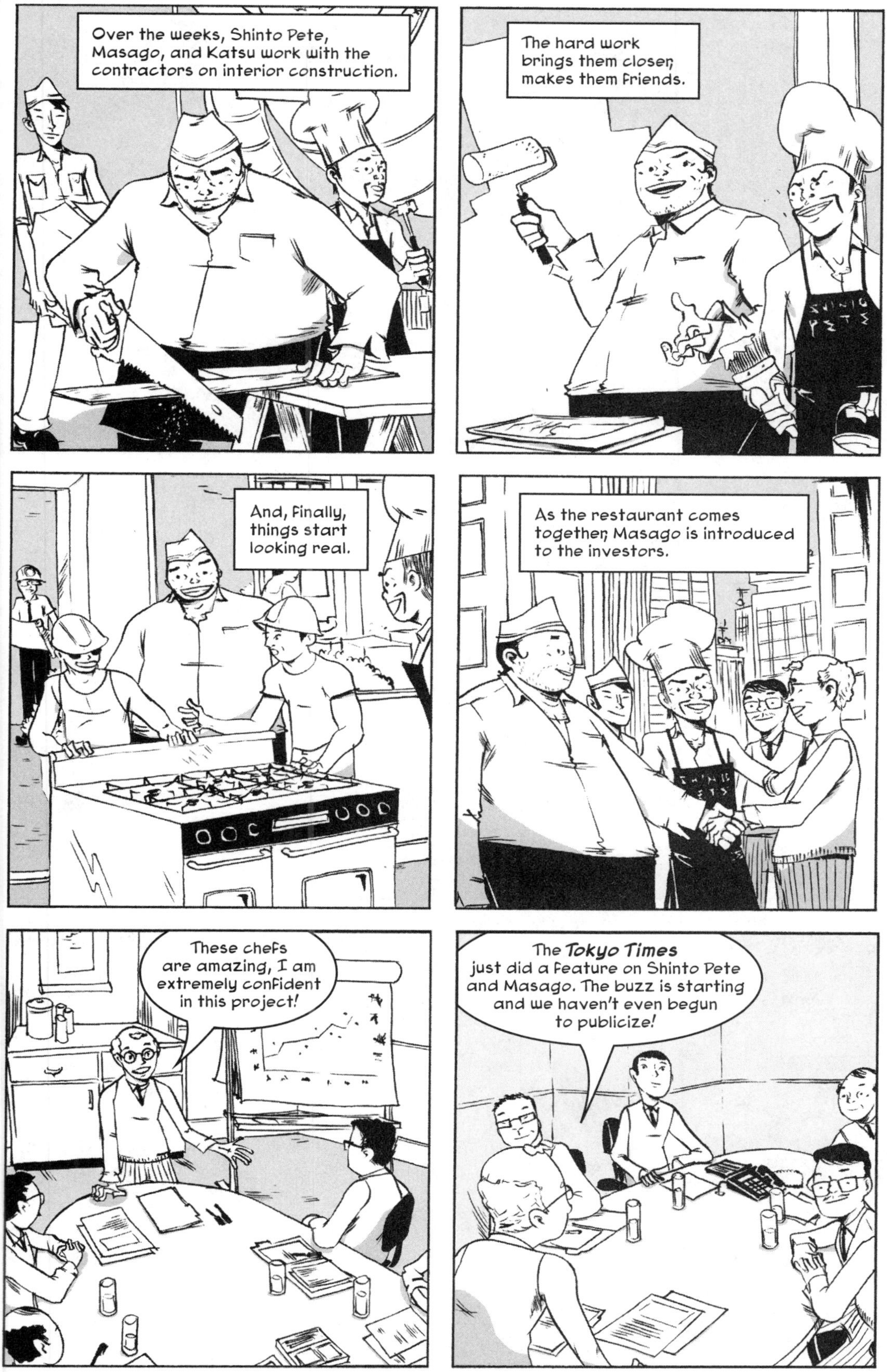
Over the weeks, Shinto Pete, Masago, and Katsu work with the contractors on interior construction.
The hard work brings them closer, makes them friends.
And, finally, things start looking real.
As the restaurant comes together, Masago is introduced to the investors.
These chefs are amazing, I am extremely confident in this project!
The Tokyo Times just did a feature on Shinto Pete and Masago. The buzz is starting and we haven't even begun to publicize!

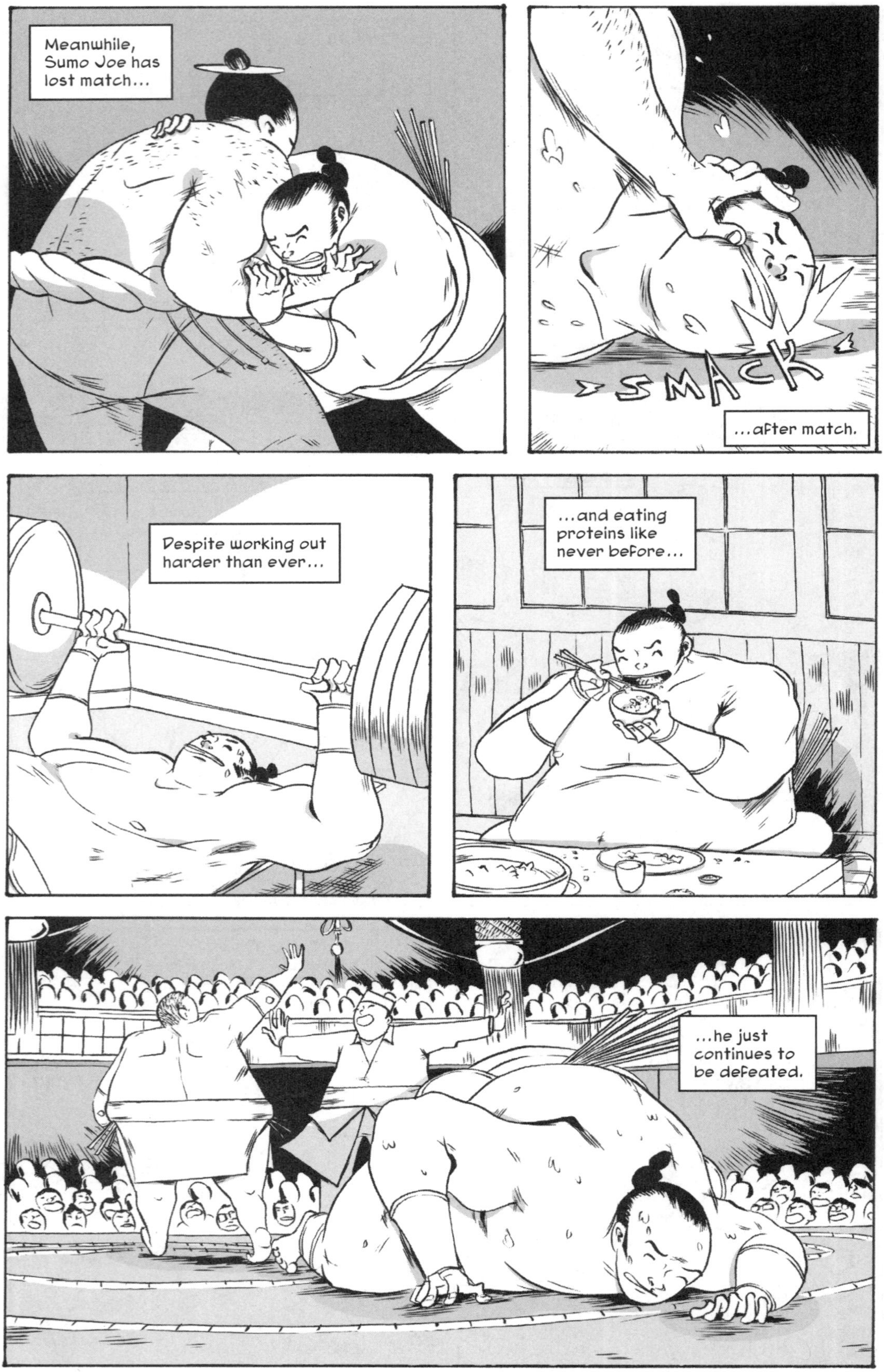
Meanwhile, Sumo Joe has lost match...
SMACK
...after match.
Despite working out harder than ever...
...and eating proteins like never before...
...he just continues to be defeated.

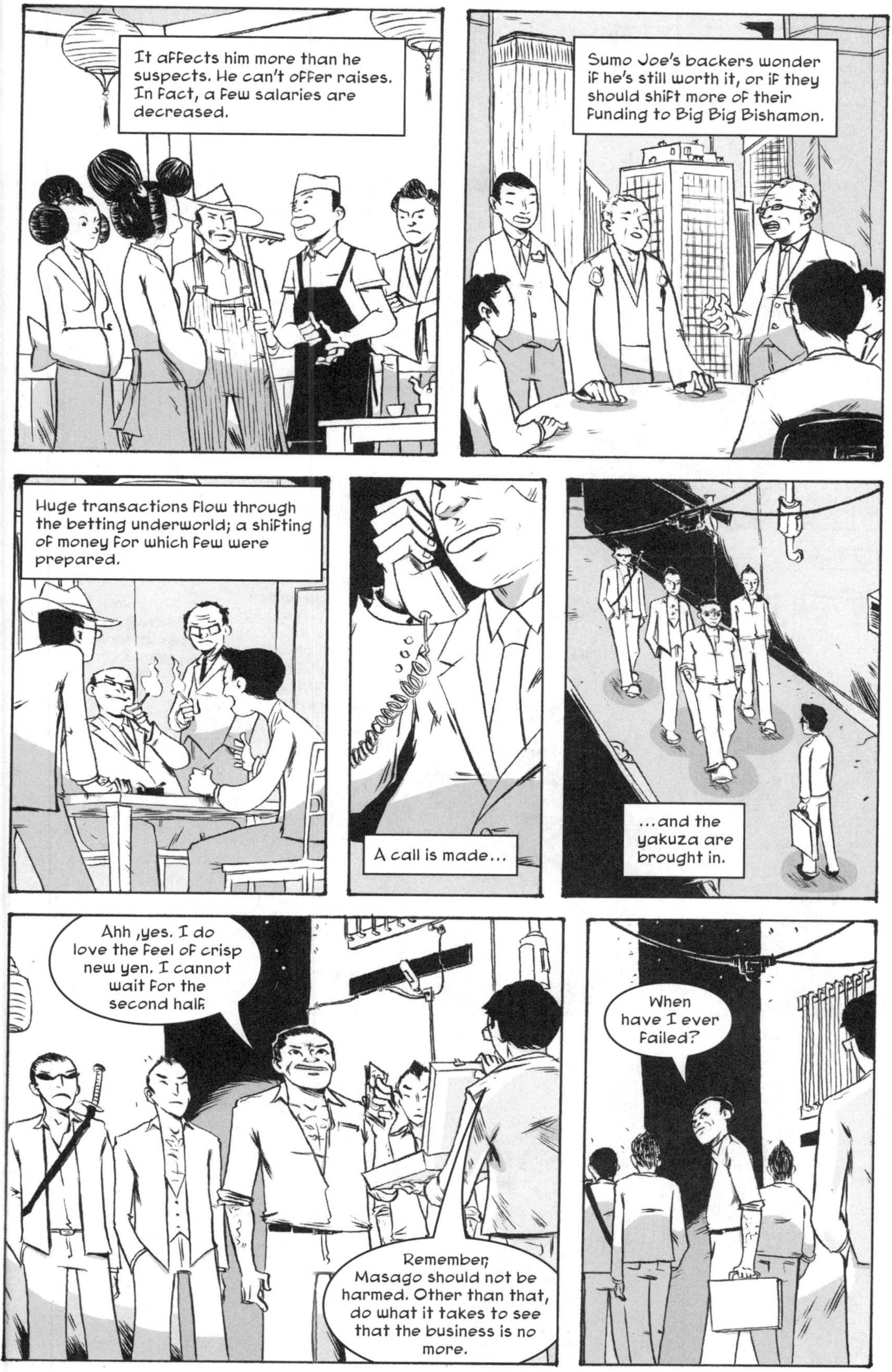
It affects him more than he suspects. He can't offer raises. In fact, a few salaries are decreased.
Sumo Joe's backers wonder if he's still worth it, or if they should shift more of their funding to Big Big Bishamon.
Huge transactions flow through the betting underworld; a shifting of money for which few were prepared.
A call is made...
...and the yakuza are brought in.
Ahh ,yes. I do love the feel of crisp new yen. I cannot wait for the second half.
Remember, Masago should not be harmed. Other than that, do what it takes to see that the business is no more.
When have I ever failed?

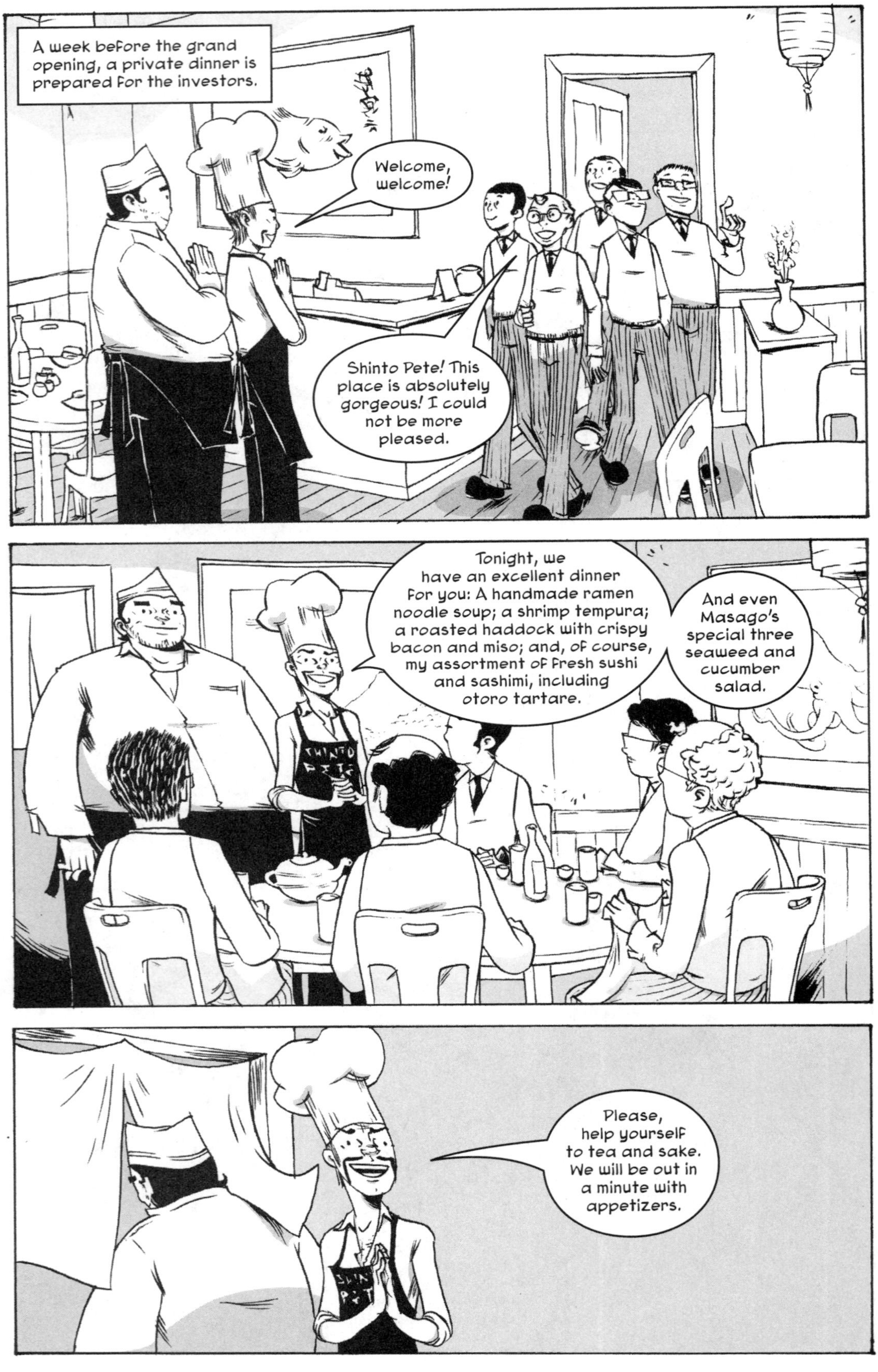
A week before the grand opening, a private dinner is prepared for the investors.
Welcome, welcome!
Shinto Pete! This place is absolutely gorgeous! I could not be more pleased.
Tonight, we have an excellent dinner for you: A handmade ramen noodle soup; a shrimp tempura; a roasted haddock with crispy bacon and miso; and, of course, my assortment of fresh sushi and sashimi, including otoro tartare.
And even Masago's special three seaweed and cucumber salad.
Please, help yourself to tea and sake. We will be out in a minute with appetizers.

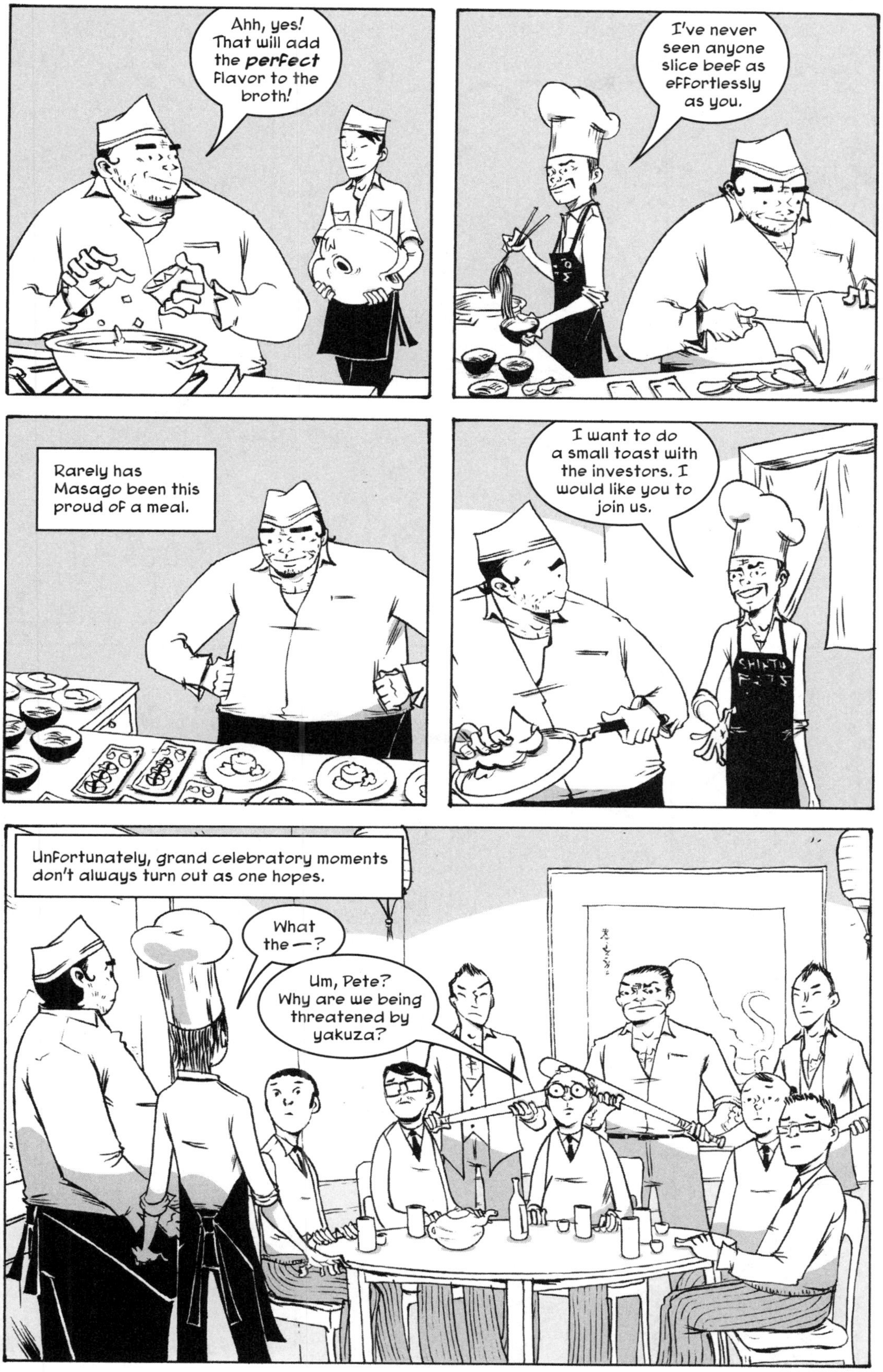
Ahh, yes! That will add the **perfect** flavor to the broth!
I've never seen anyone slice beef as effortlessly as you.
Rarely has Masago been this proud of a meal.
I want to do a small toast with the investors. I would like you to join us.
Unfortunately, grand celebratory moments don't always turn out as one hopes.
What the—?
Um, Pete? Why are we being threatened by yakuza?

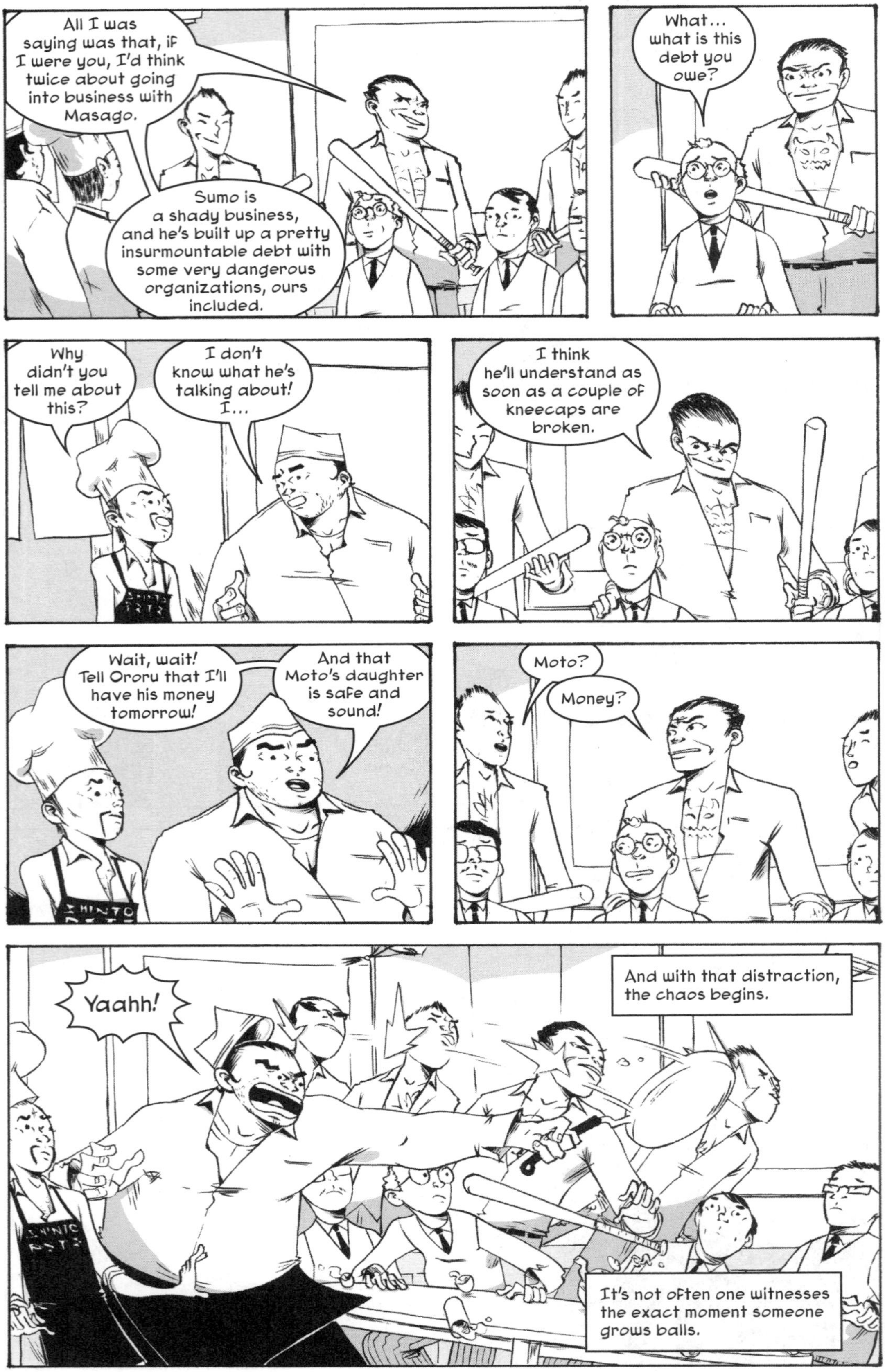
All I was saying was that, if I were you, I'd think twice about going into business with Masago.
Sumo is a shady business, and he's built up a pretty insurmountable debt with some very dangerous organizations, ours included.
What... what is this debt you owe?
Why didn't you tell me about this?
I don't know what he's talking about! I...
I think he'll understand as soon as a couple of kneecaps are broken.
Wait, wait! Tell Ororu that I'll have his money tomorrow!
And that Moto's daughter is safe and sound!
Moto?
Money?
Yaahh!
And with that distraction, the chaos begins.
It's not often one witnesses the exact moment someone grows balls.

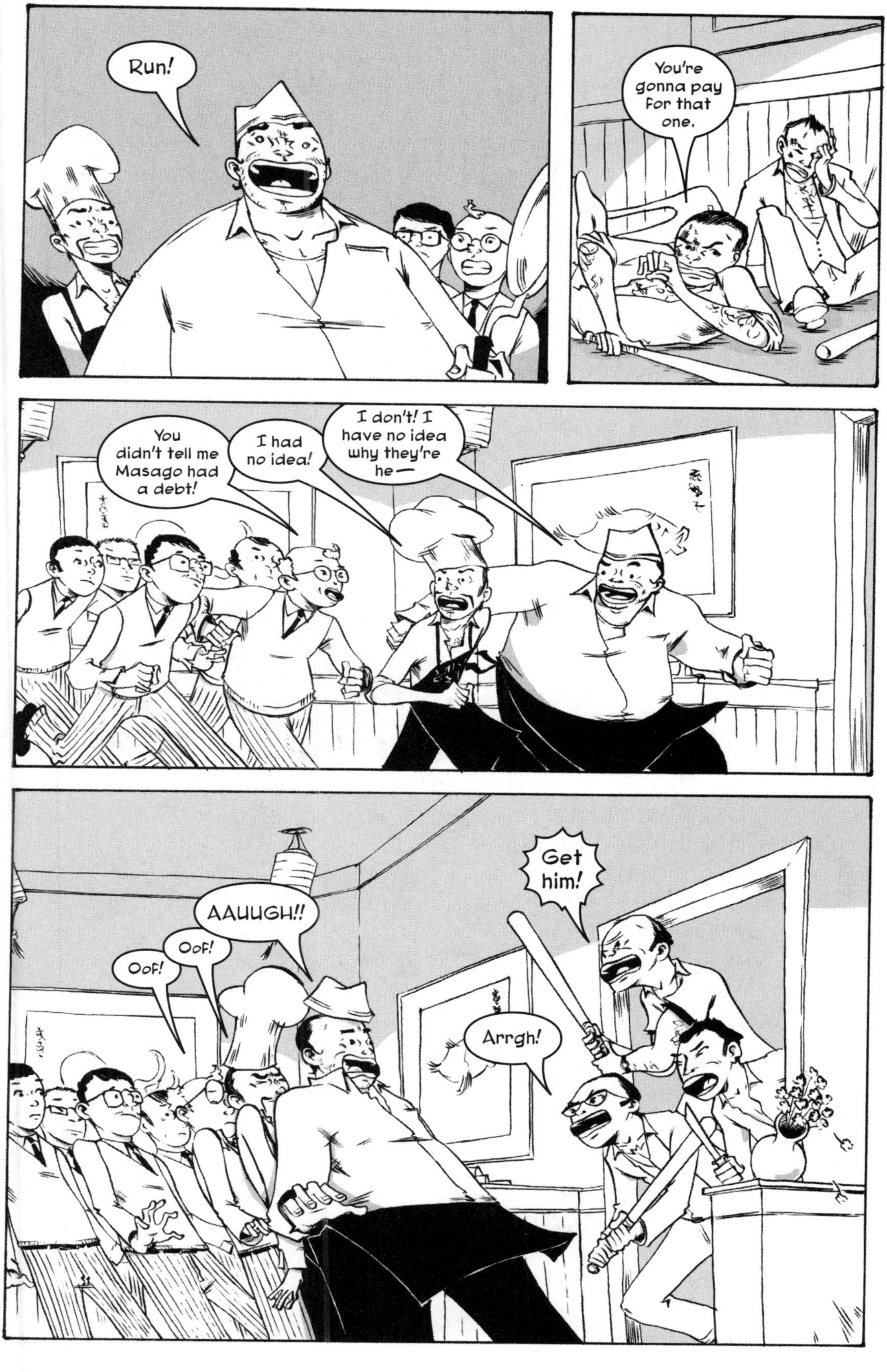
Run!
You're gonna pay for that one.
You didn't tell me Masago had a debt!
I had no idea!
I don't! I have no idea why they're he—
Get him!
AAUUGH!!
Oof!
Oof!
Arrgh!

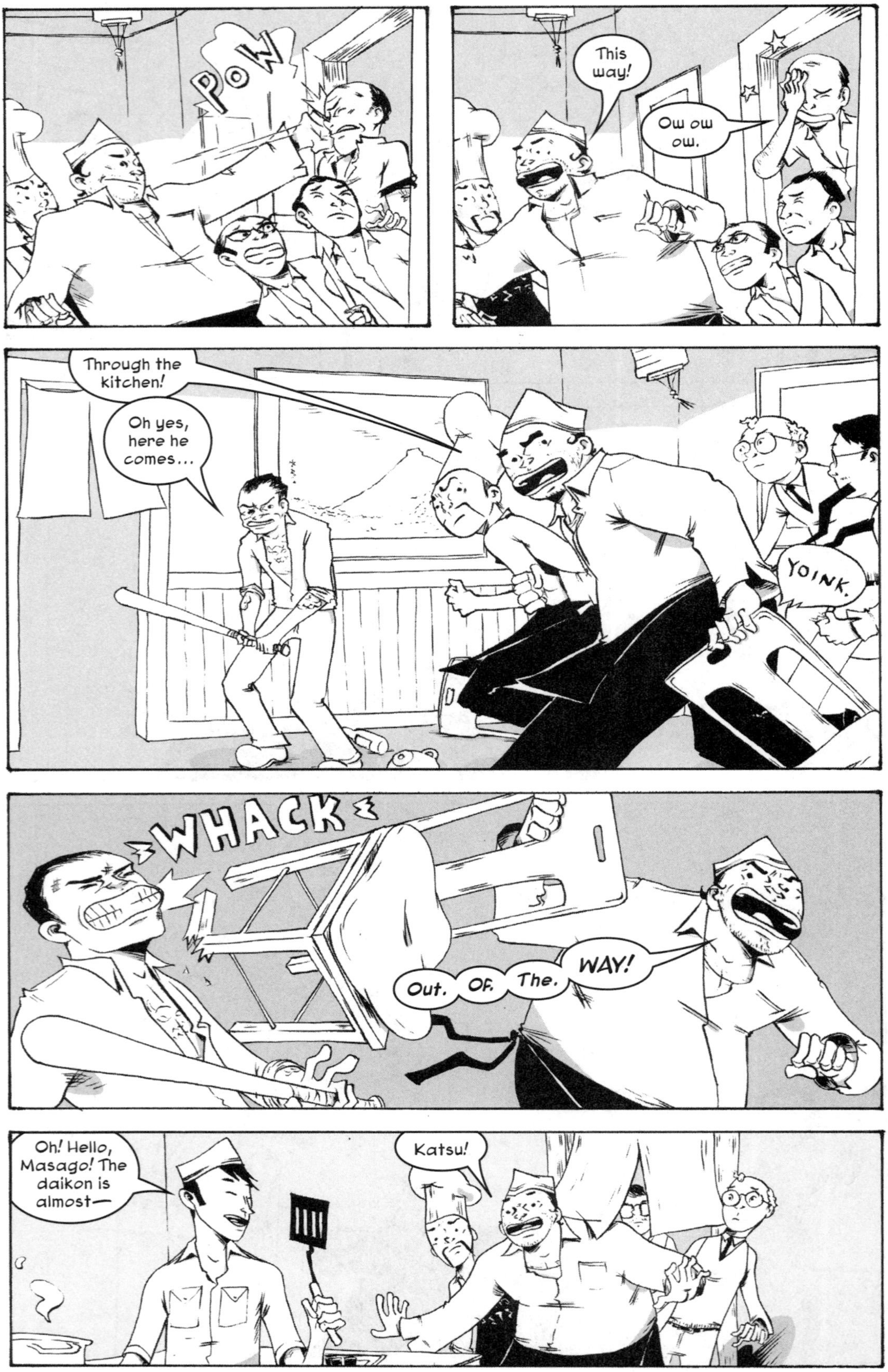
POW
This way!
Ow ow ow.
Through the kitchen!
Oh yes, here he comes...
YOINK.
WHACK
Out. Of. The. WAY!
Oh! Hello, Masago! The daikon is almost—
Katsu!

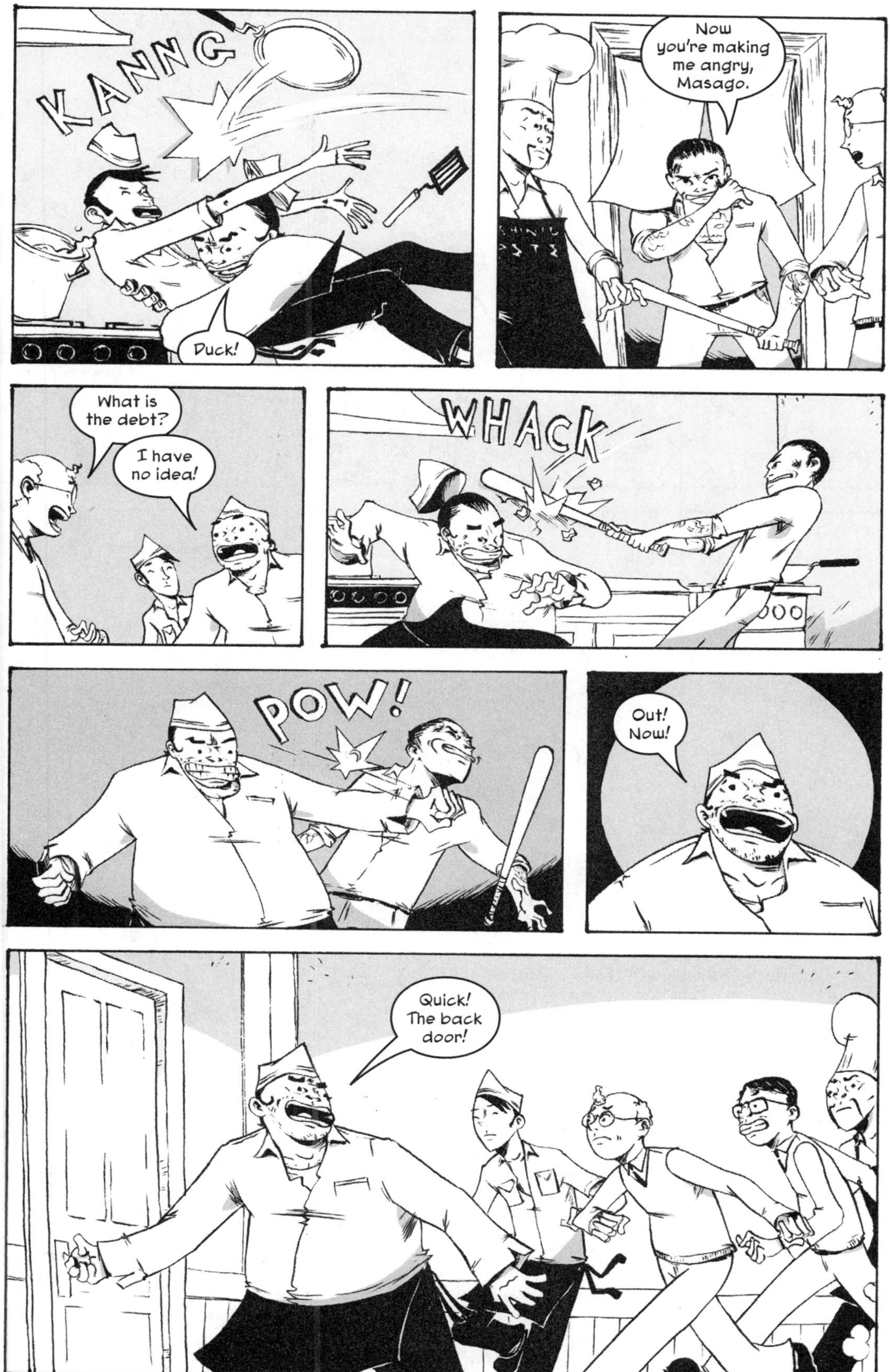
KANNG
Duck!
Now you're making me angry, Masago.
What is the debt?
I have no idea!
WHACK
POW!
Out! Now!
Quick! The back door!

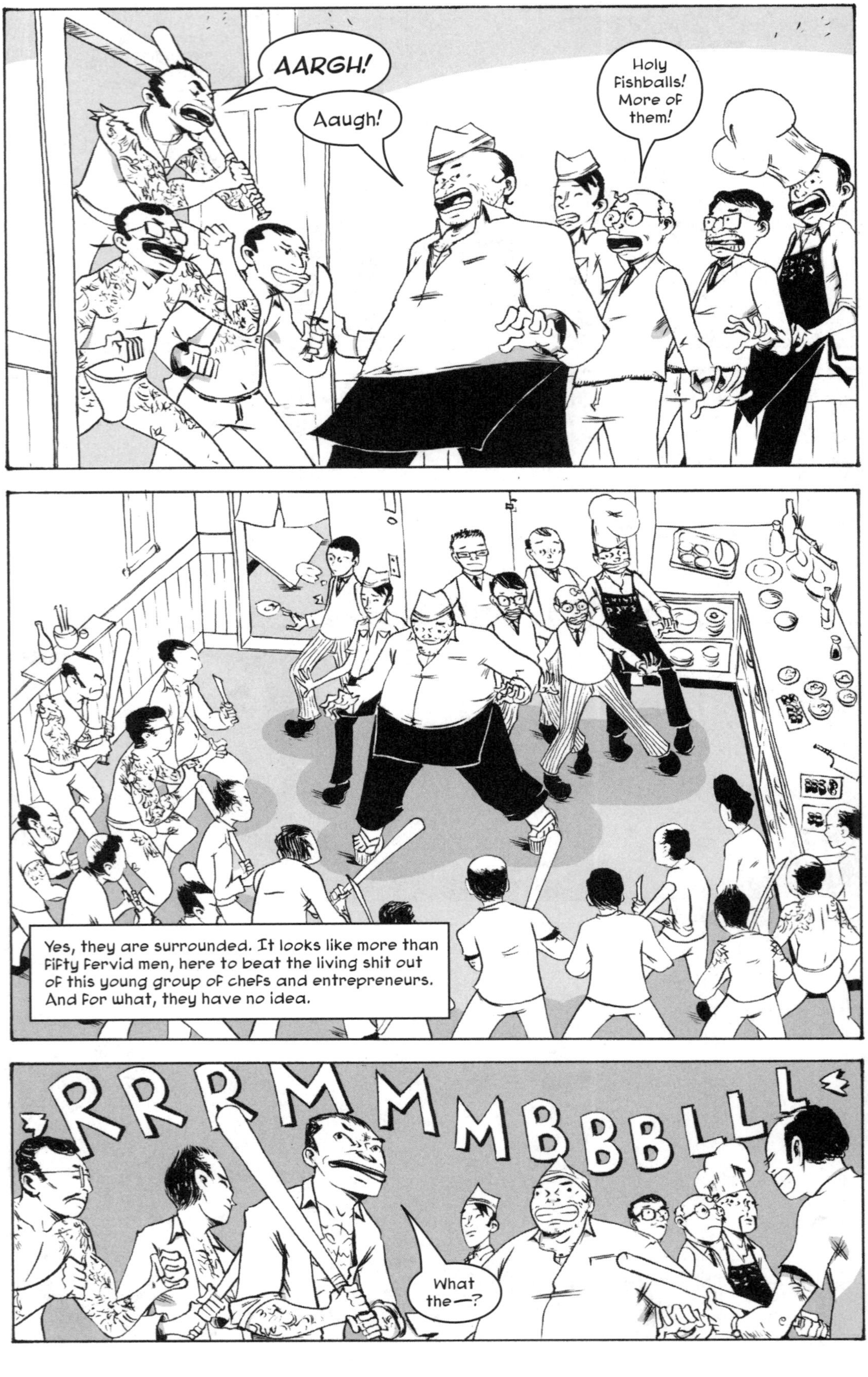
AARGH!
Aaugh!
Holy Fishballs! More of them!
Yes, they are surrounded. It looks like more than fifty fervid men, here to beat the living shit out of this young group of chefs and entrepreneurs. And for what, they have no idea.
RRRMMMBBBLLL
What the—?

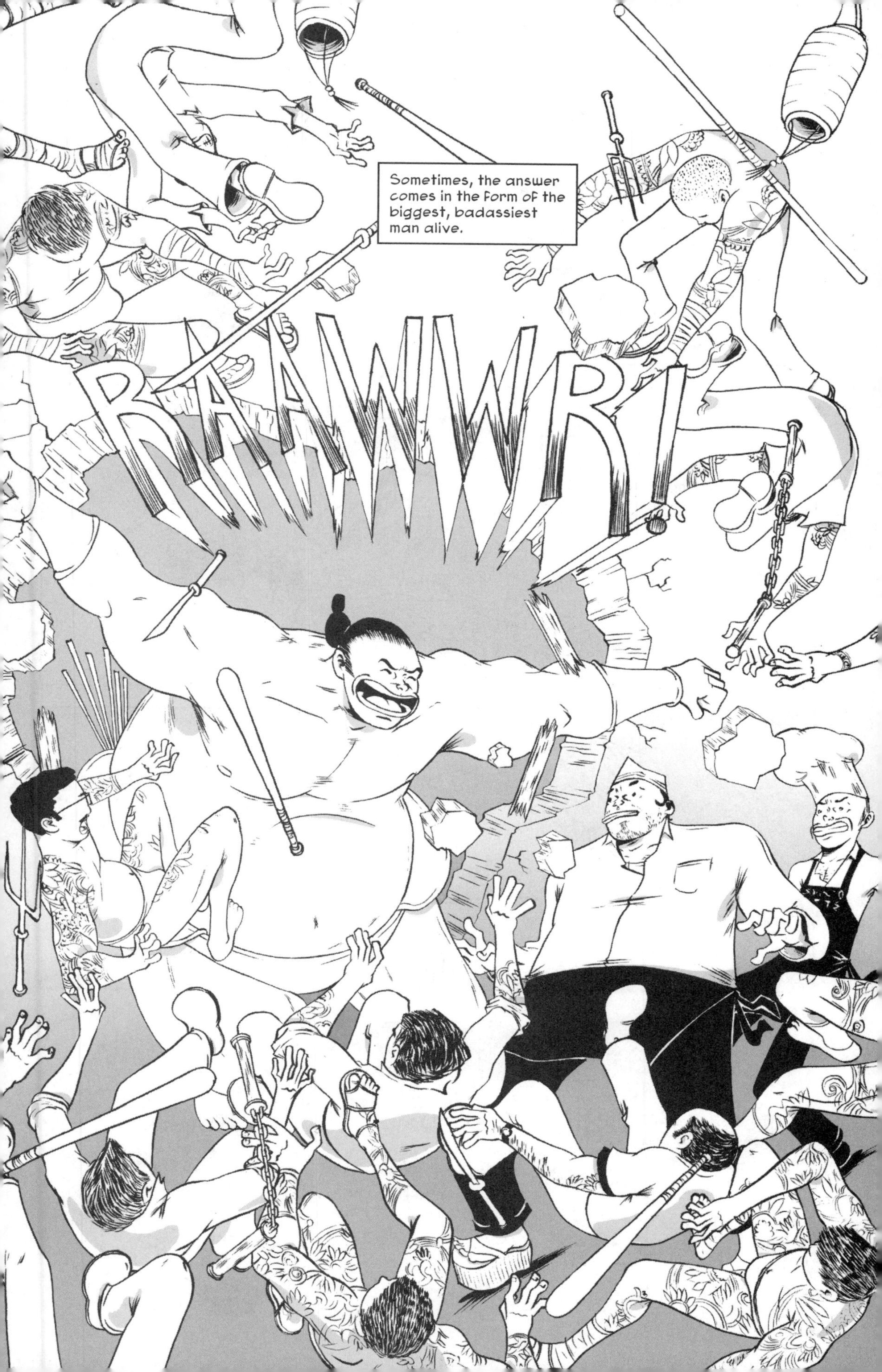
Sometimes, the answer comes in the form of the biggest, badassiest man alive.
RAAWWR!

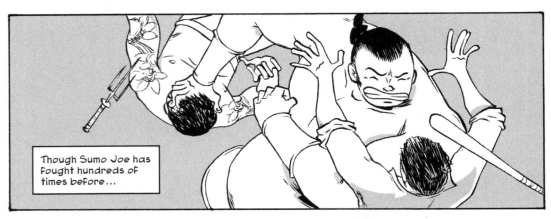

Though Sumo Joe has fought hundreds of times before...

...it's obvious he's fighting harder than he ever has in the ring...

...as he takes out every last one of them.

Masago watches this grand battle, taking it all in.

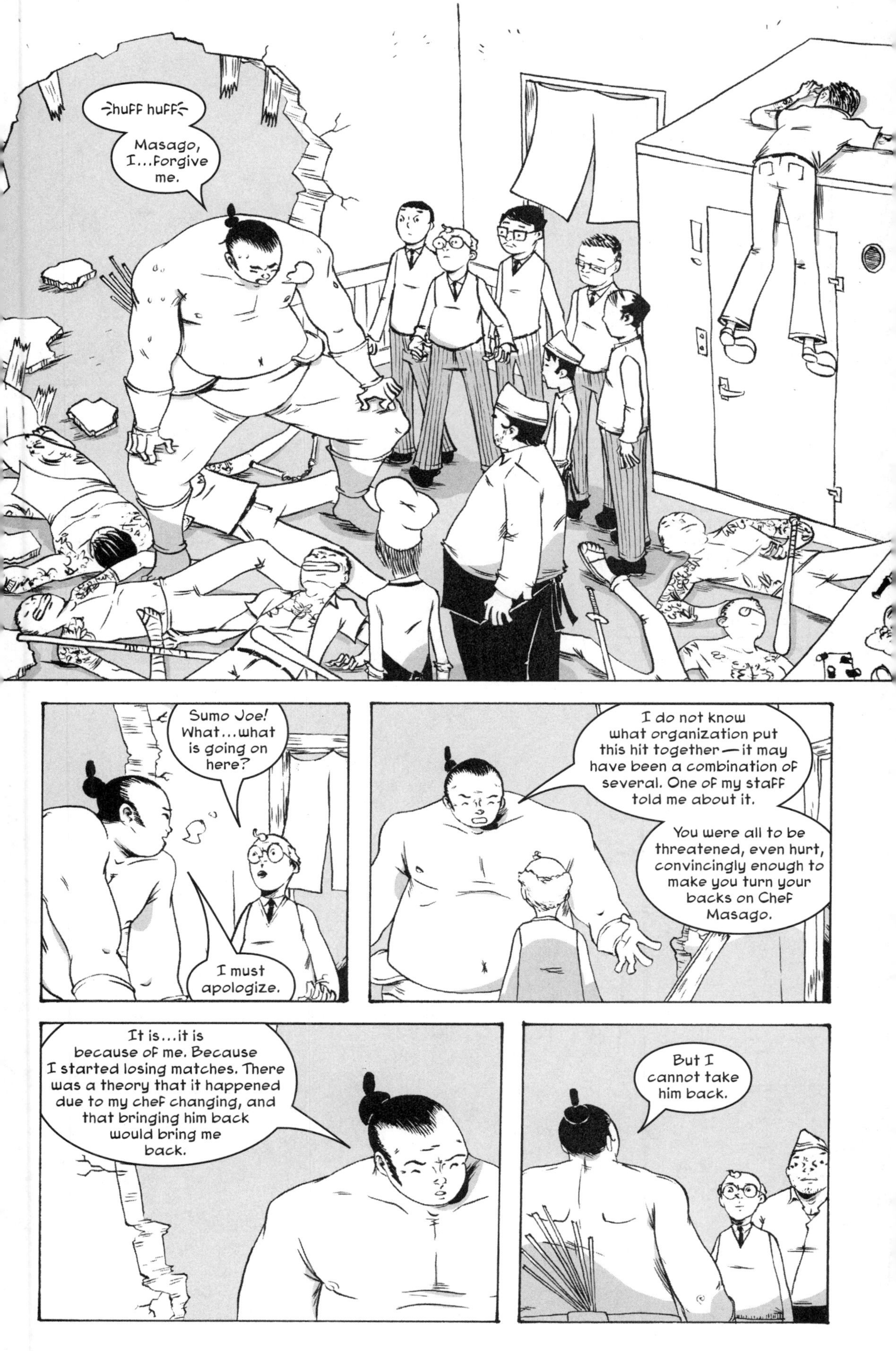

huff huff
Masago, I...forgive me.
Sumo Joe! What...what is going on here?
I must apologize.
I do not know what organization put this hit together—it may have been a combination of several. One of my staff told me about it.
You were all to be threatened, even hurt, convincingly enough to make you turn your backs on Chef Masago.
It is...it is because of me. Because I started losing matches. There was a theory that it happened due to my chef changing, and that bringing him back would bring me back.
But I cannot take him back.

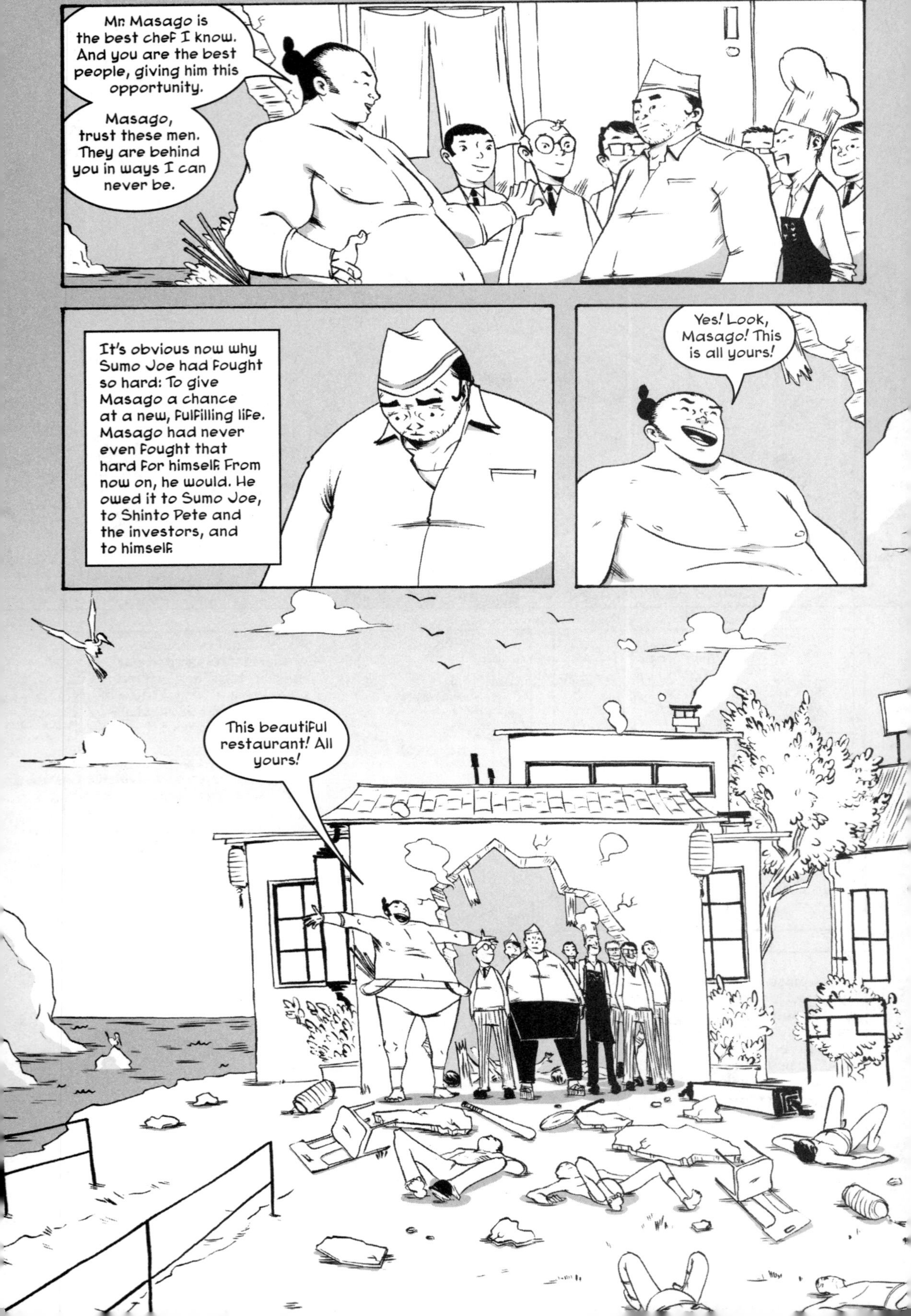
Mr. Masago is the best chef I know. And you are the best people, giving him this opportunity.
Masago, trust these men. They are behind you in ways I can never be.
It's obvious now why Sumo Joe had fought so hard: To give Masago a chance at a new, fulfilling life. Masago had never even fought that hard for himself. From now on, he would. He owed it to Sumo Joe, to Shinto Pete and the investors, and to himself.
Yes! Look, Masago! This is all yours!
This beautiful restaurant! All yours!

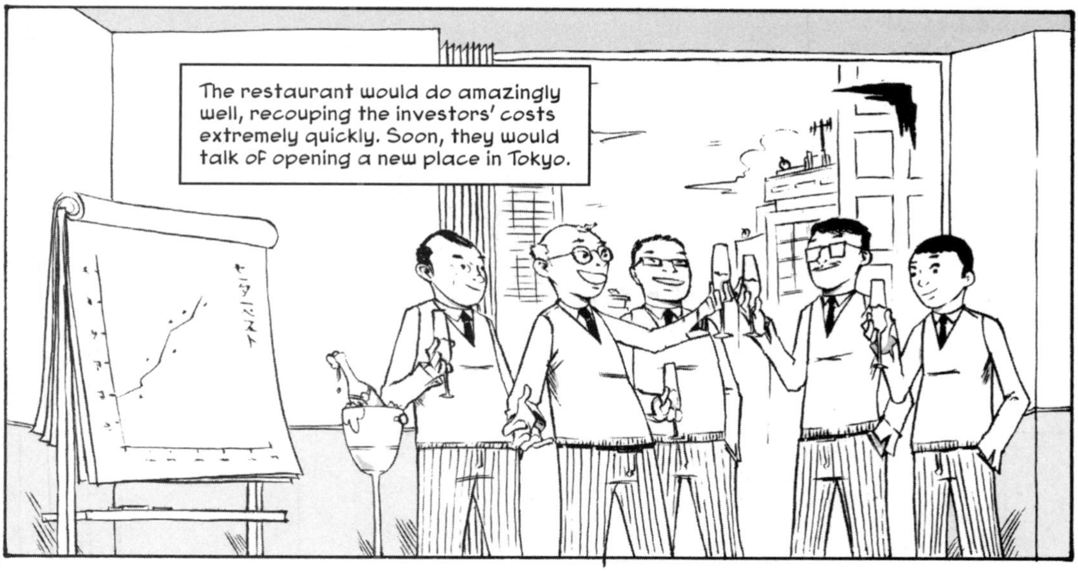
The restaurant would do amazingly well, recouping the investors' costs extremely quickly. Soon, they would talk of opening a new place in Tokyo.

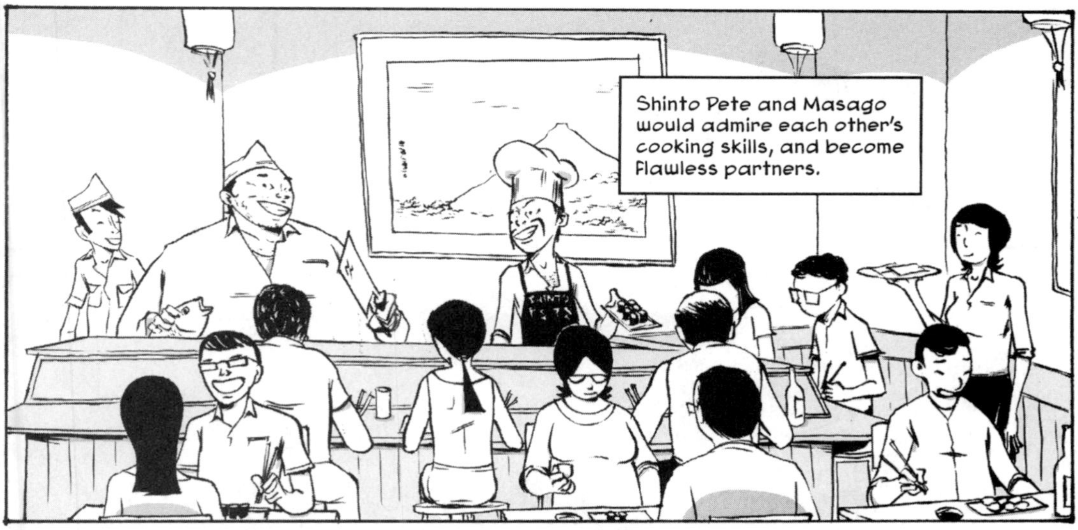
Shinto Pete and Masago would admire each other's cooking skills, and become flawless partners.

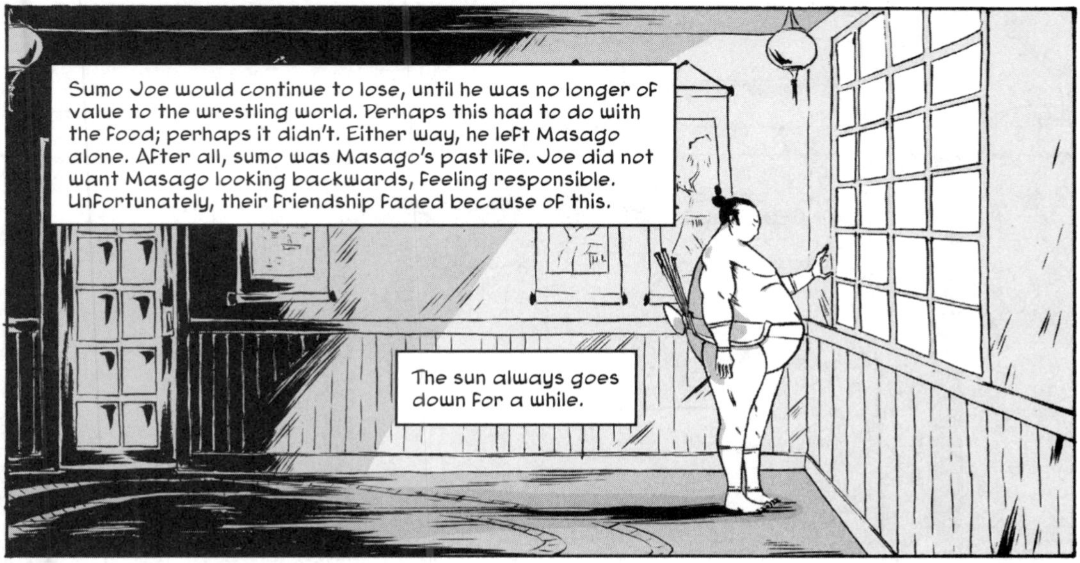
Sumo Joe would continue to lose, until he was no longer of value to the wrestling world. Perhaps this had to do with the food; perhaps it didn't. Either way, he left Masago alone. After all, sumo was Masago's past life. Joe did not want Masago looking backwards, feeling responsible. Unfortunately, their friendship faded because of this.
The sun always goes down for a while.

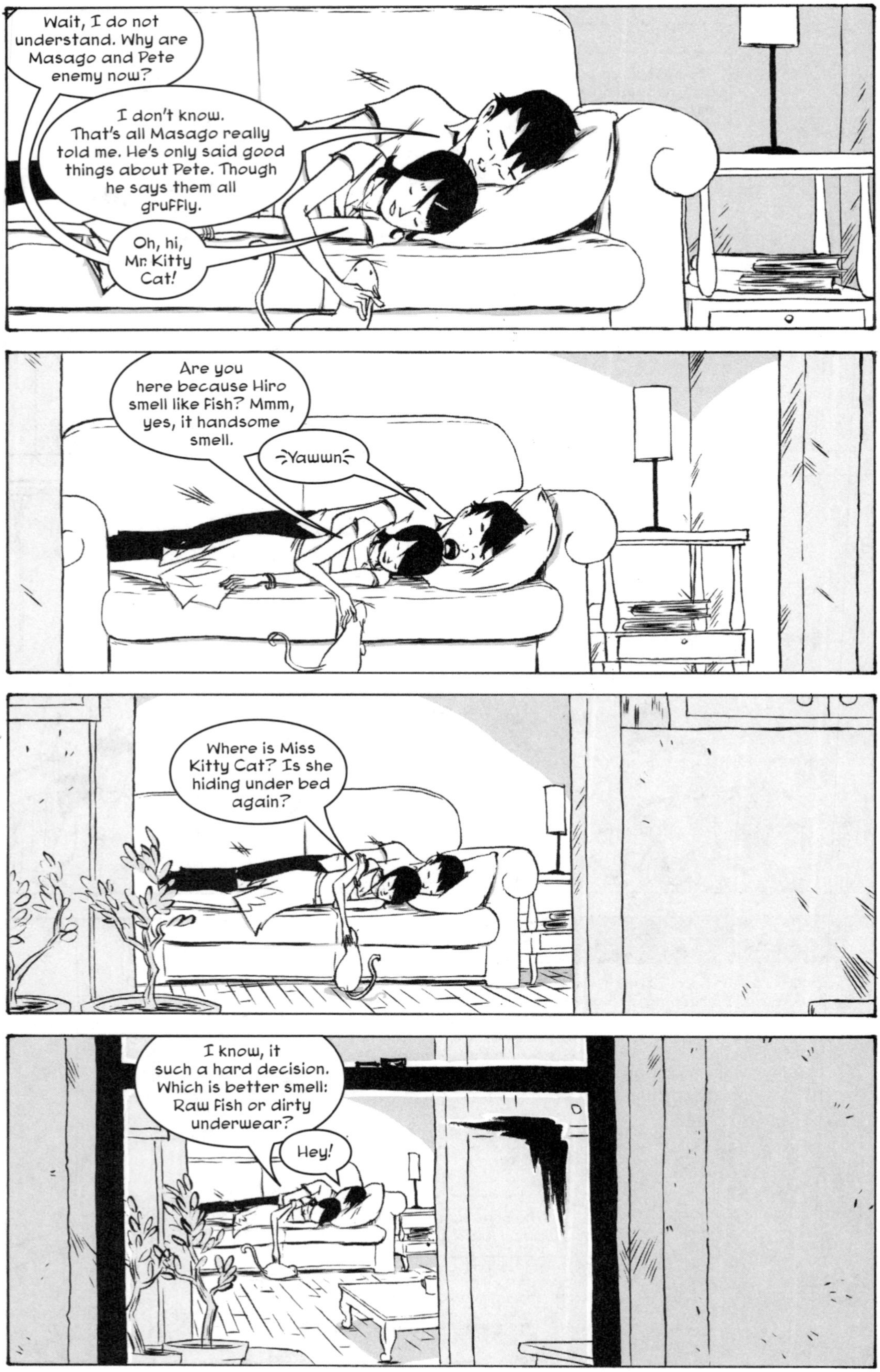
Wait, I do not understand. Why are Masago and Pete enemy now?
I don't know. That's all Masago really told me. He's only said good things about Pete. Though he says them all gruffly.
Oh, hi, Mr. Kitty Cat!
Are you here because Hiro smell like fish? Mmm, yes, it handsome smell.
Yawwn
Where is Miss Kitty Cat? Is she hiding under bed again?
I know, it such a hard decision. Which is better smell: Raw fish or dirty underwear?
Hey!

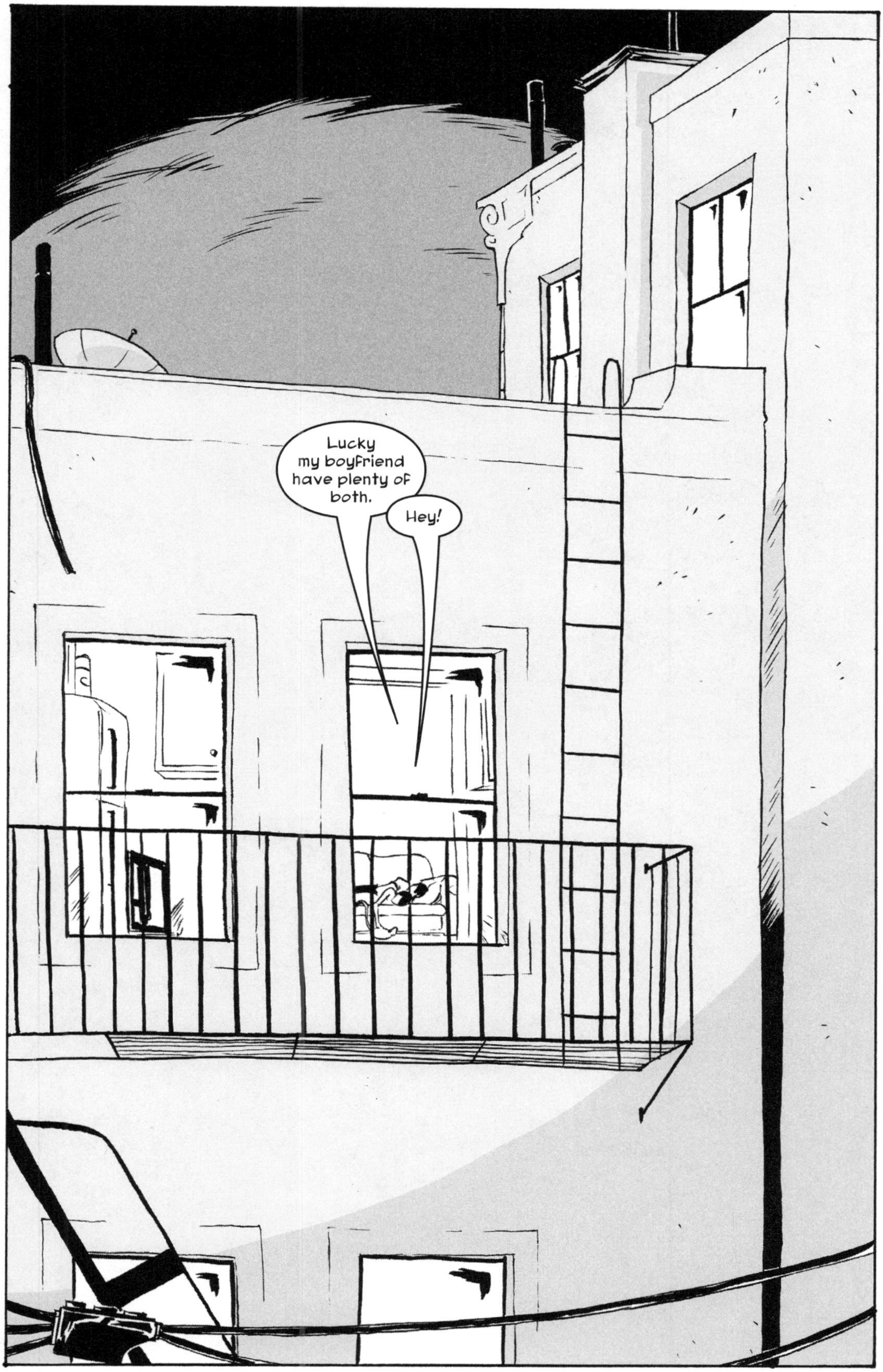
Lucky my boyfriend have plenty of both.
Hey!

こきゅうけい 2

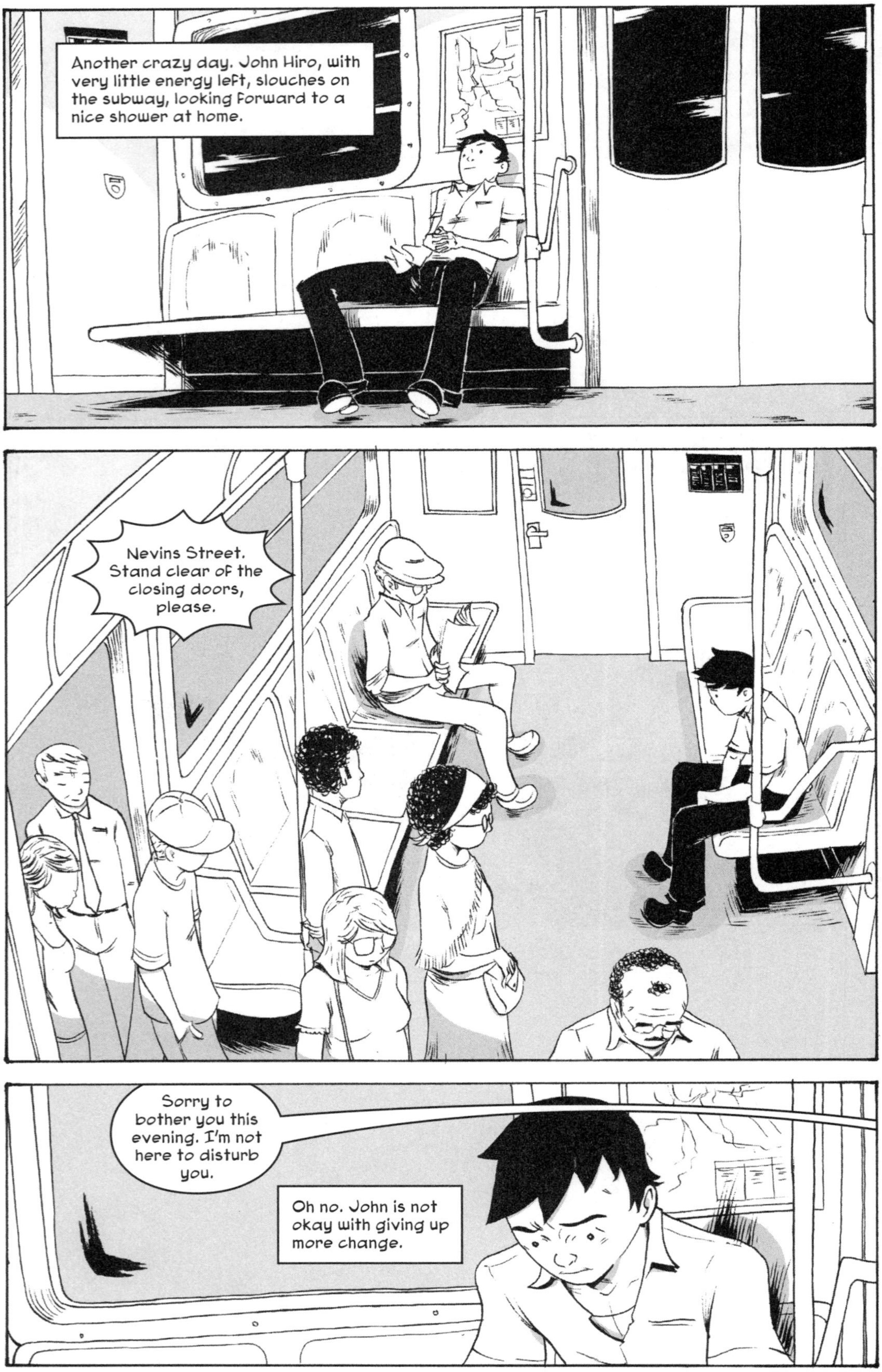
Another crazy day. John Hiro, with very little energy left, slouches on the subway, looking forward to a nice shower at home.
Nevins Street. Stand clear of the closing doors, please.
Sorry to bother you this evening. I'm not here to disturb you.
Oh no. John is not okay with giving up more change.

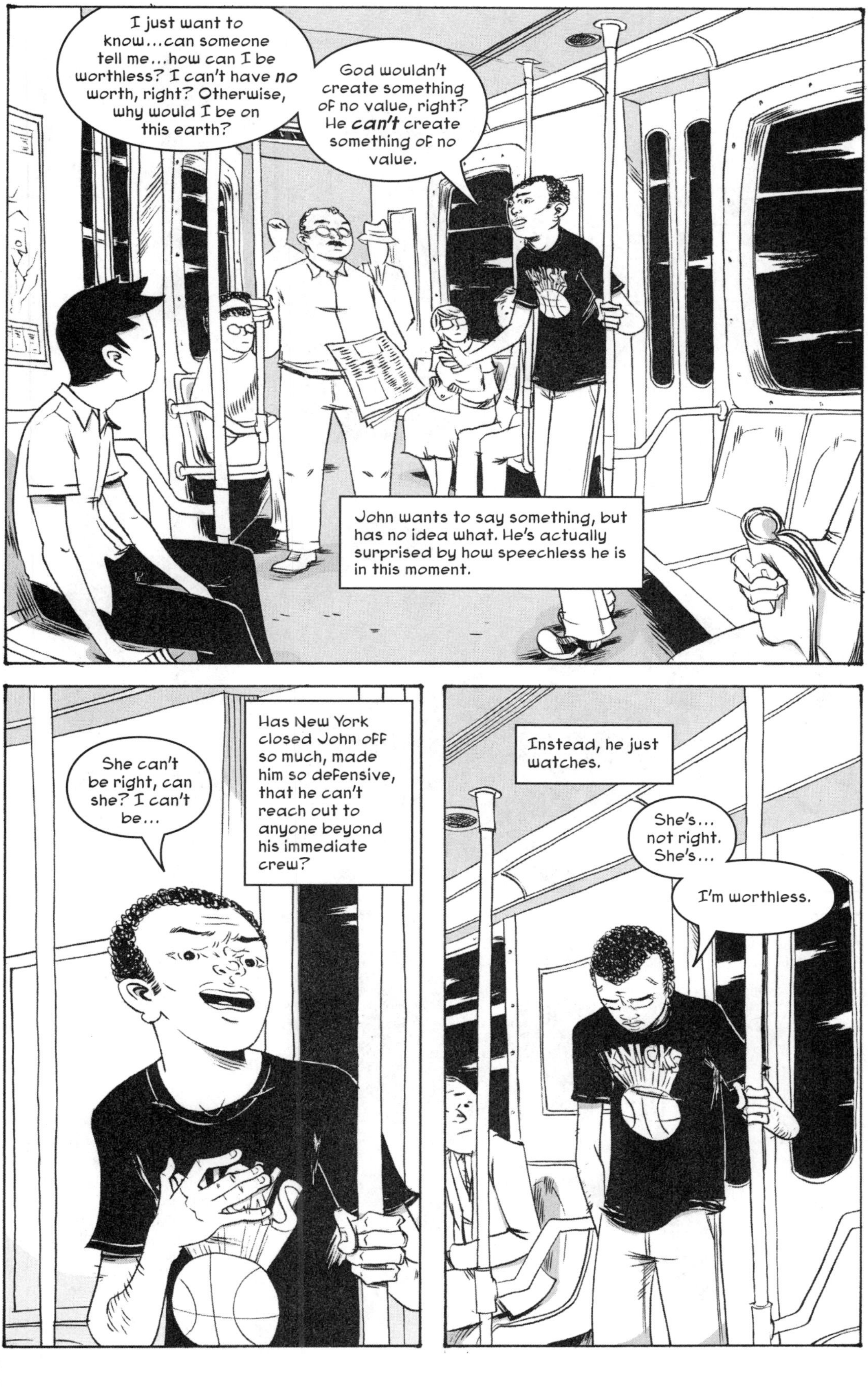
I just want to know...can someone tell me...how can I be worthless? I can't have *no* worth, right? Otherwise, why would I be on this earth?
God wouldn't create something of no value, right? He *can't* create something of no value.
John wants to say something, but has no idea what. He's actually surprised by how speechless he is in this moment.
She can't be right, can she? I can't be...
Has New York closed John off so much, made him so defensive, that he can't reach out to anyone beyond his immediate crew?
Instead, he just watches.
She's... not right. She's...
I'm worthless.

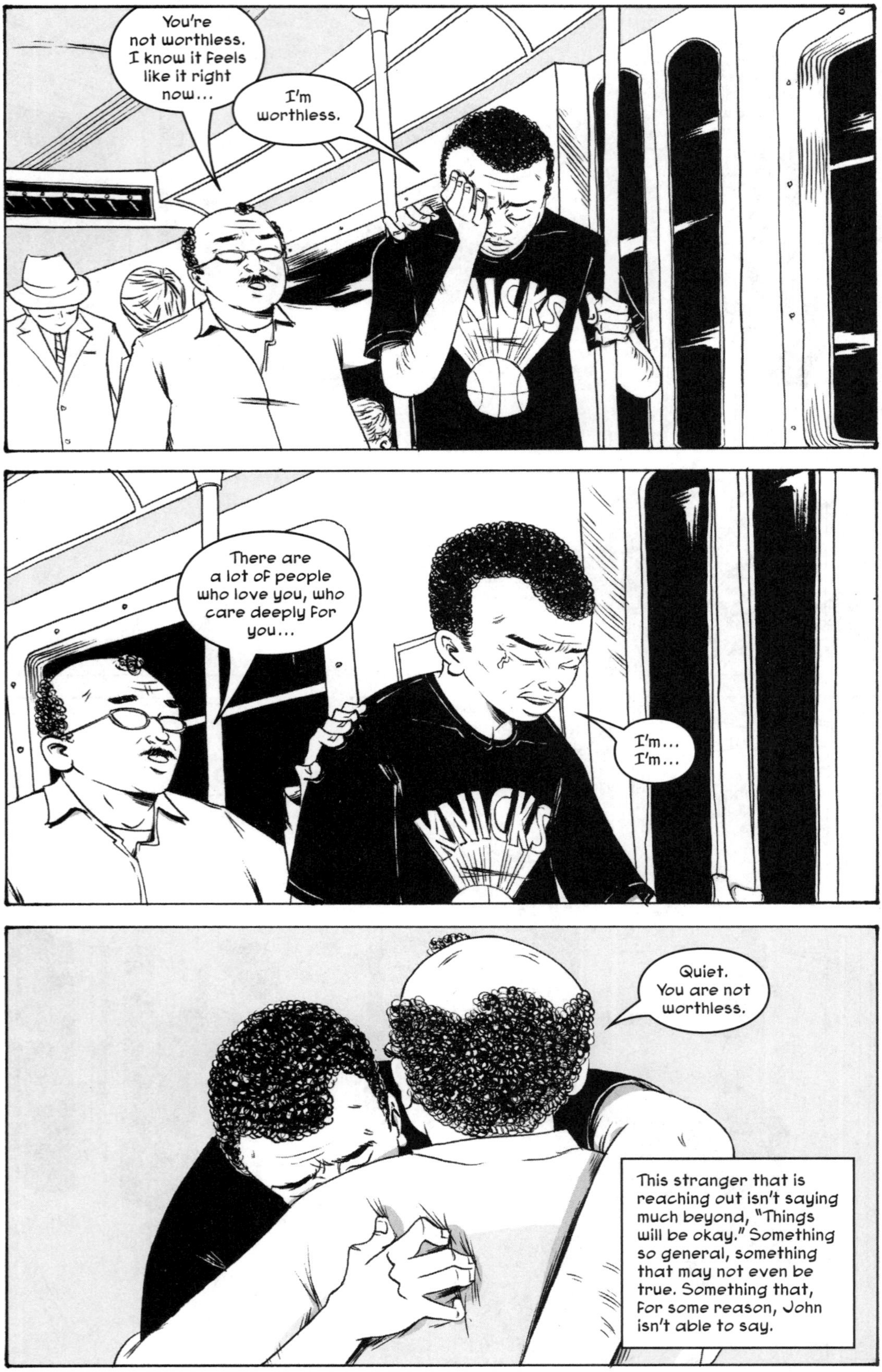
You're not worthless. I know it feels like it right now...
I'm worthless.
There are a lot of people who love you, who care deeply for you...
I'm... I'm...
Quiet. You are not worthless.
This stranger that is reaching out isn't saying much beyond, "Things will be okay." Something so general, something that may not even be true. Something that, for some reason, John isn't able to say.

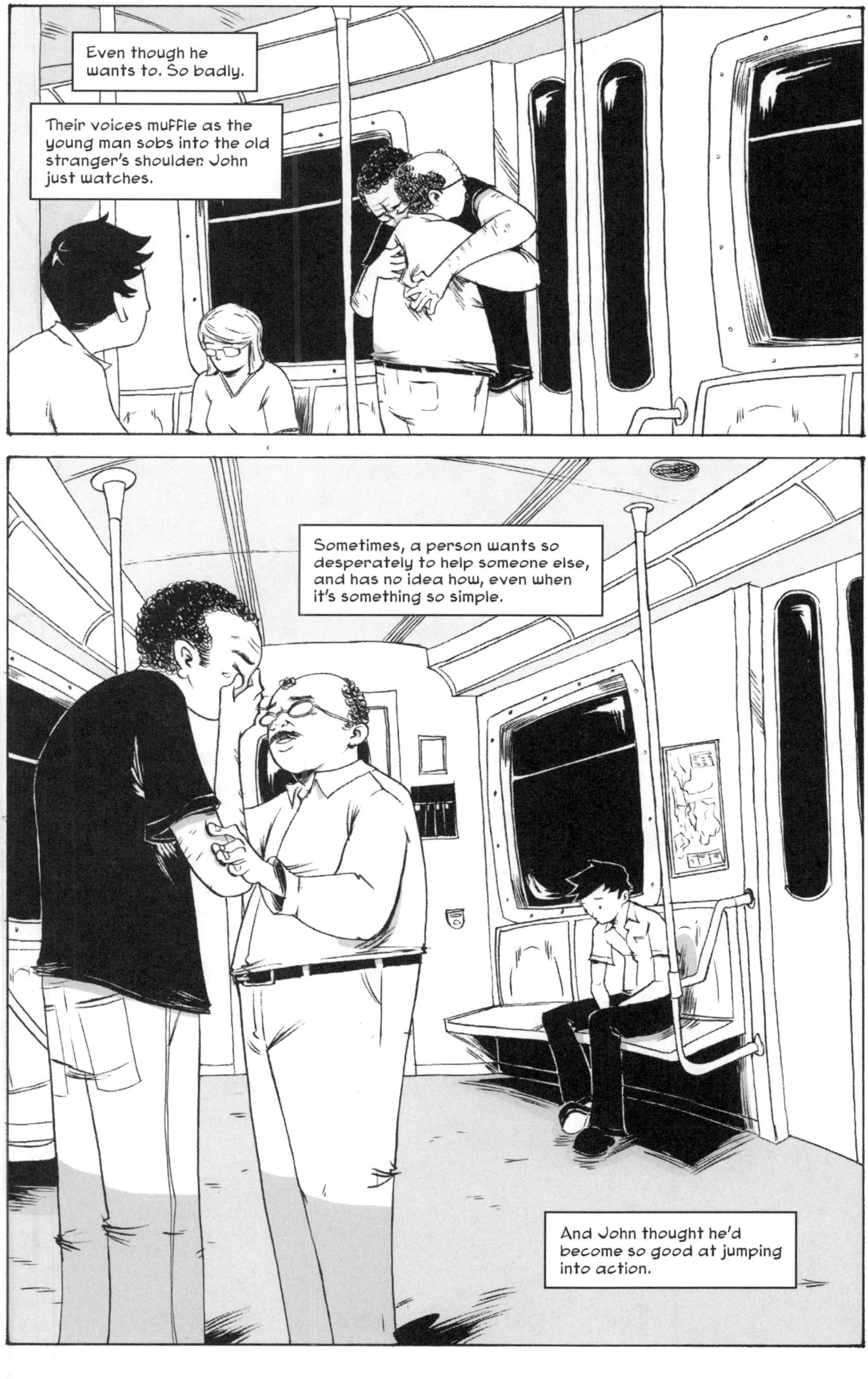
Even though he wants to. So badly.
Their voices muffle as the young man sobs into the old stranger's shoulder. John just watches.
Sometimes, a person wants so desperately to help someone else, and has no idea how, even when it's something so simple.
And John thought he'd become so good at jumping into action.

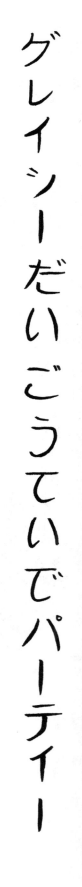

グレイシーだいごうていでパーティー

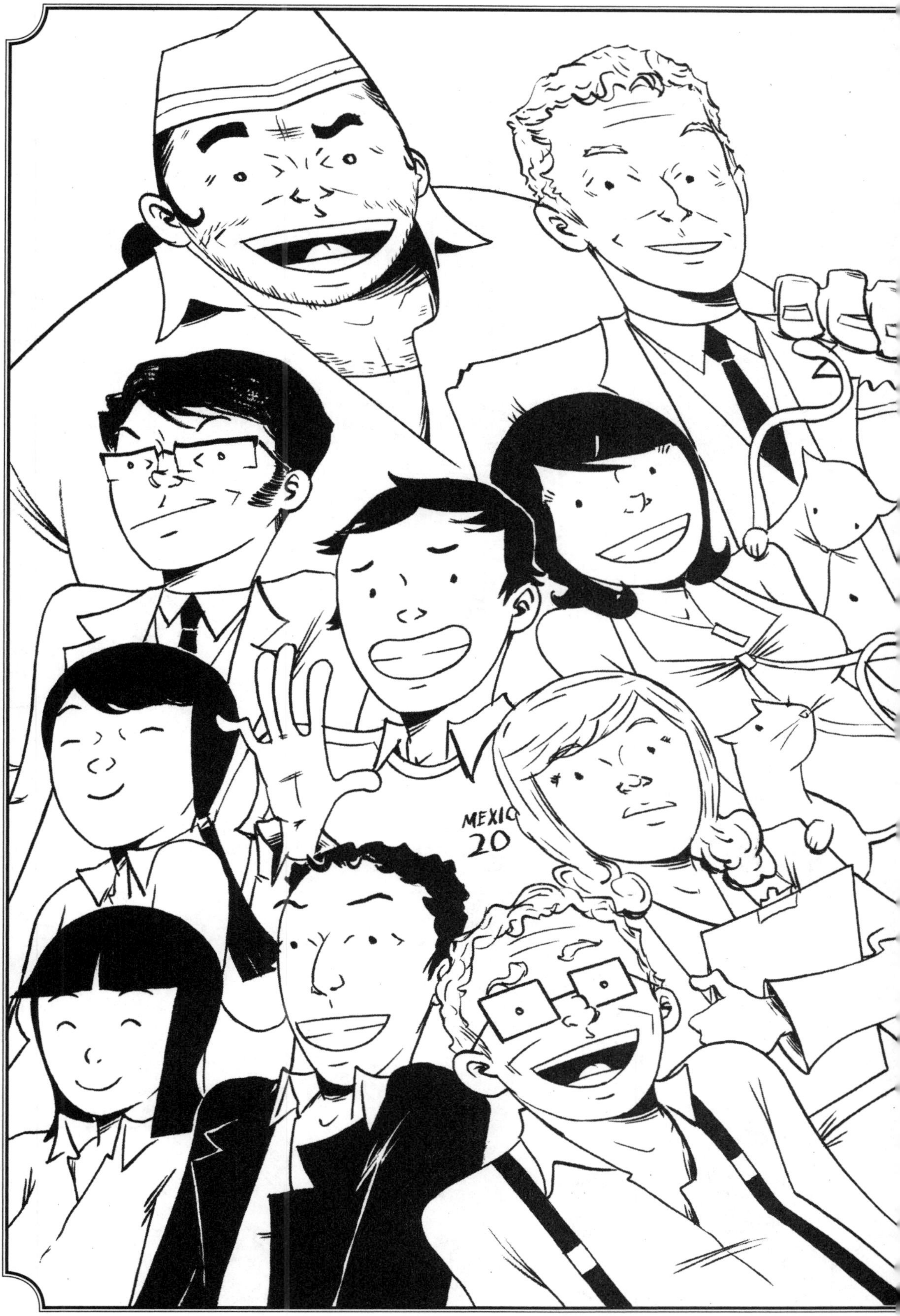
MEXIC
20

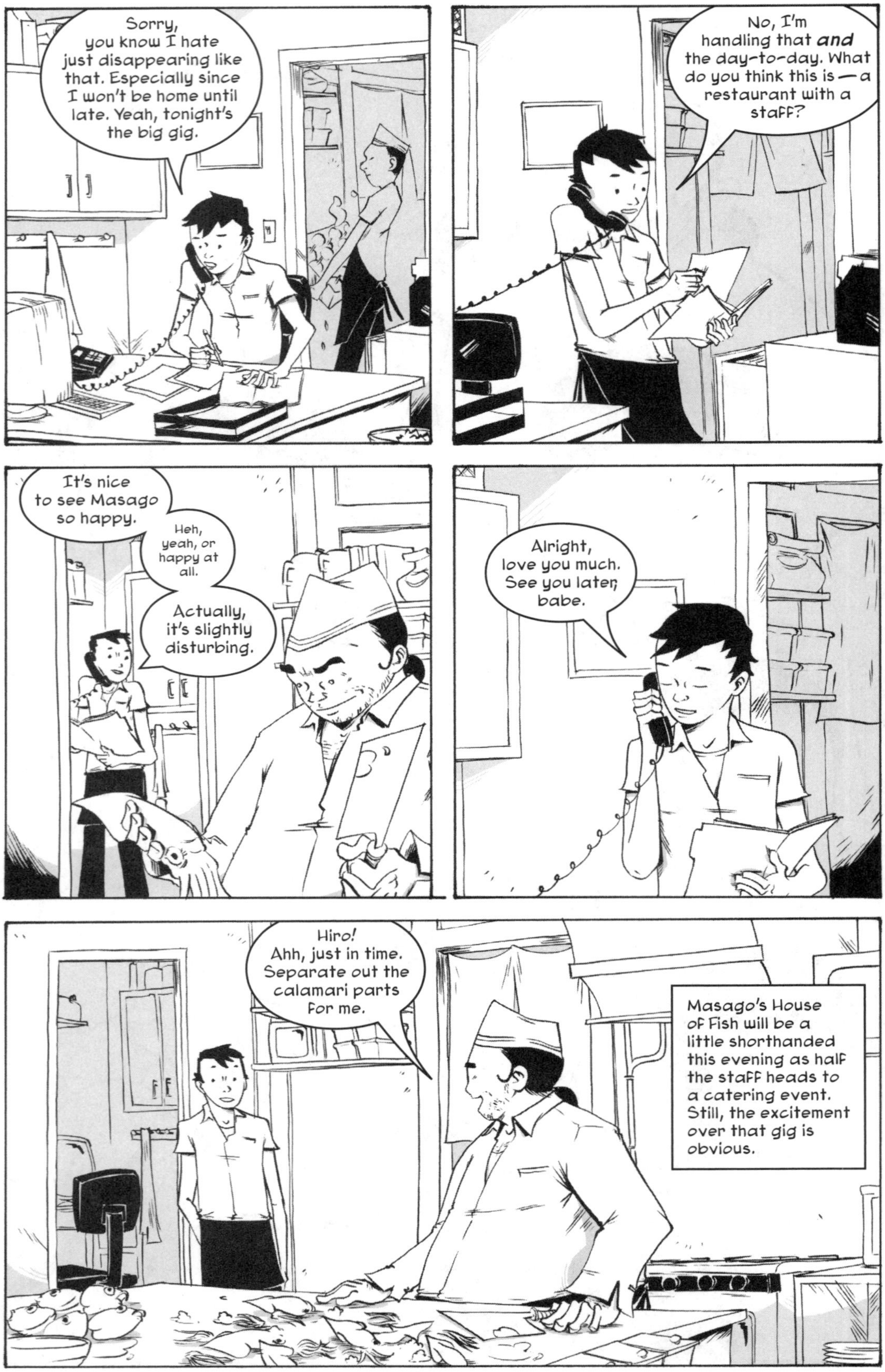
Sorry, you know I hate just disappearing like that. Especially since I won't be home until late. Yeah, tonight's the big gig.
No, I'm handling that ***and*** the day-to-day. What do you think this is — a restaurant with a staff?
It's nice to see Masago so happy.
Heh, yeah, or happy at all.
Actually, it's slightly disturbing.
Alright, love you much. See you later, babe.
Hiro! Ahh, just in time. Separate out the calamari parts for me.
Masago's House of Fish will be a little shorthanded this evening as half the staff heads to a catering event. Still, the excitement over that gig is obvious.

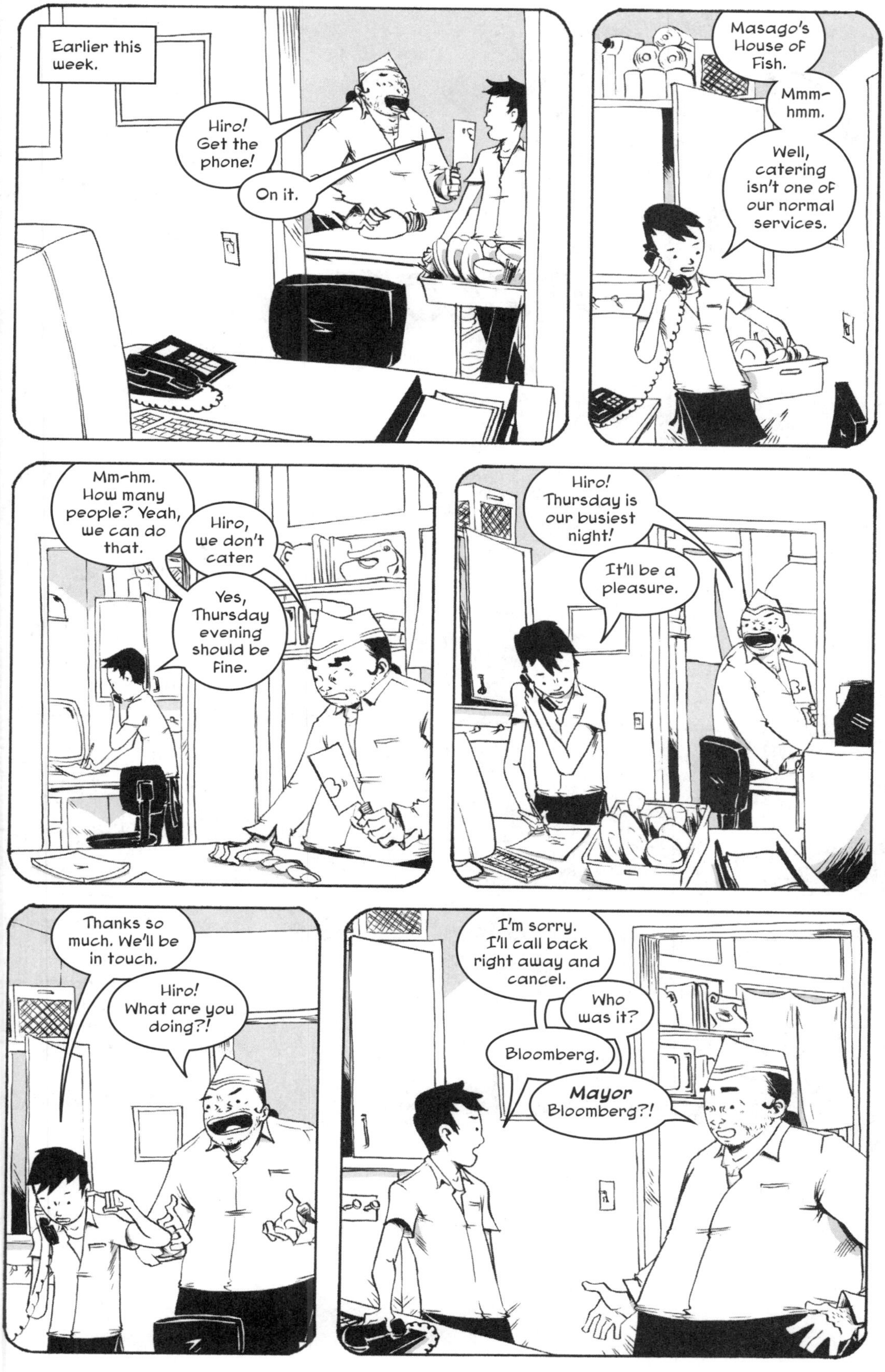
Earlier this week.
Hiro! Get the phone!
On it.
Masago's House of Fish.
Mmm-hmm.
Well, catering isn't one of our normal services.
Mm-hm. How many people? Yeah, we can do that.
Hiro, we don't cater.
Yes, Thursday evening should be fine.
Hiro! Thursday is our busiest night!
It'll be a pleasure.
Thanks so much. We'll be in touch.
Hiro! What are you doing?!
I'm sorry. I'll call back right away and cancel.
Who was it?
Bloomberg.
Mayor Bloomberg?!

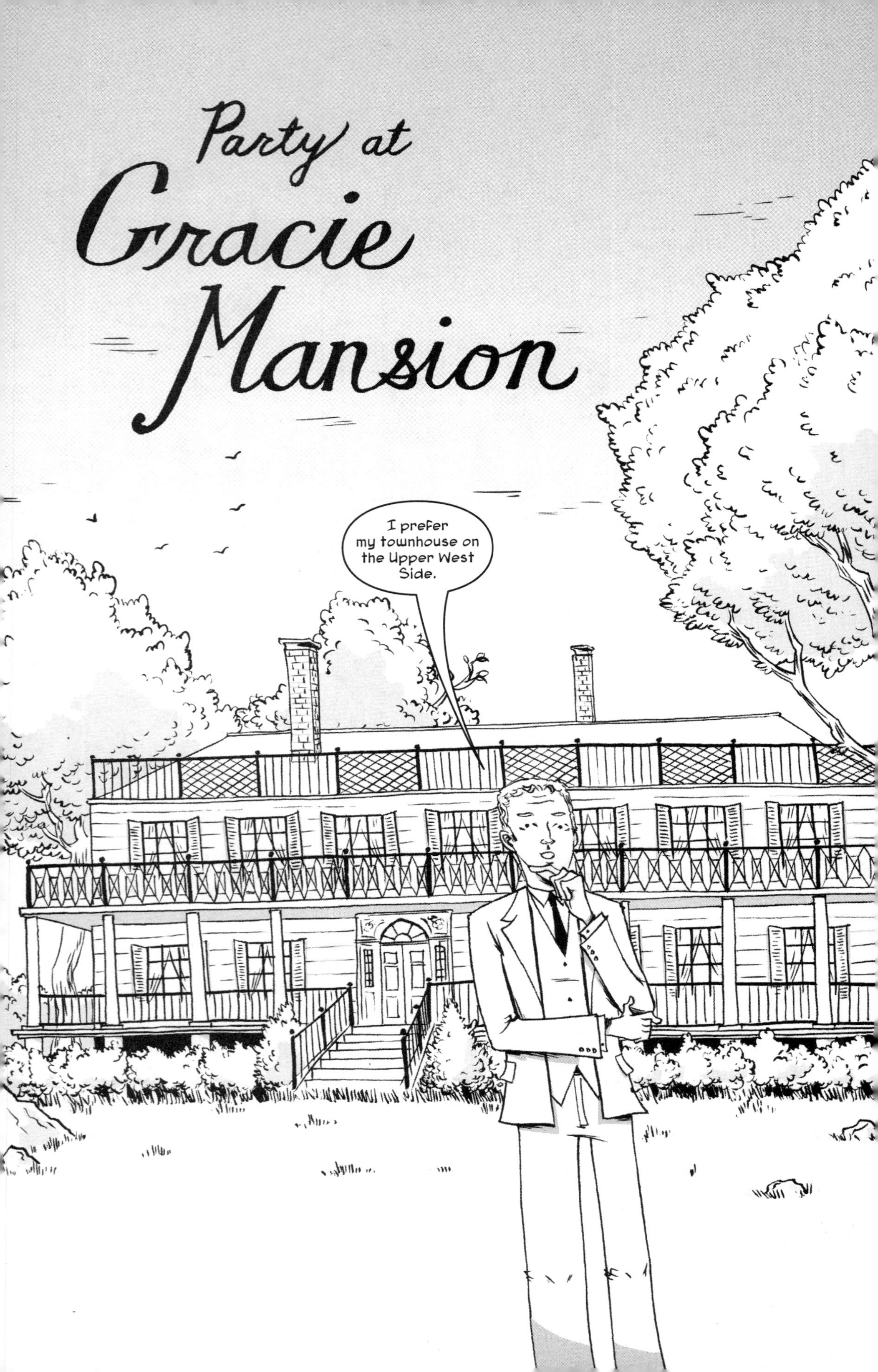
Party at Gracie Mansion
I prefer my townhouse on the Upper West Side.

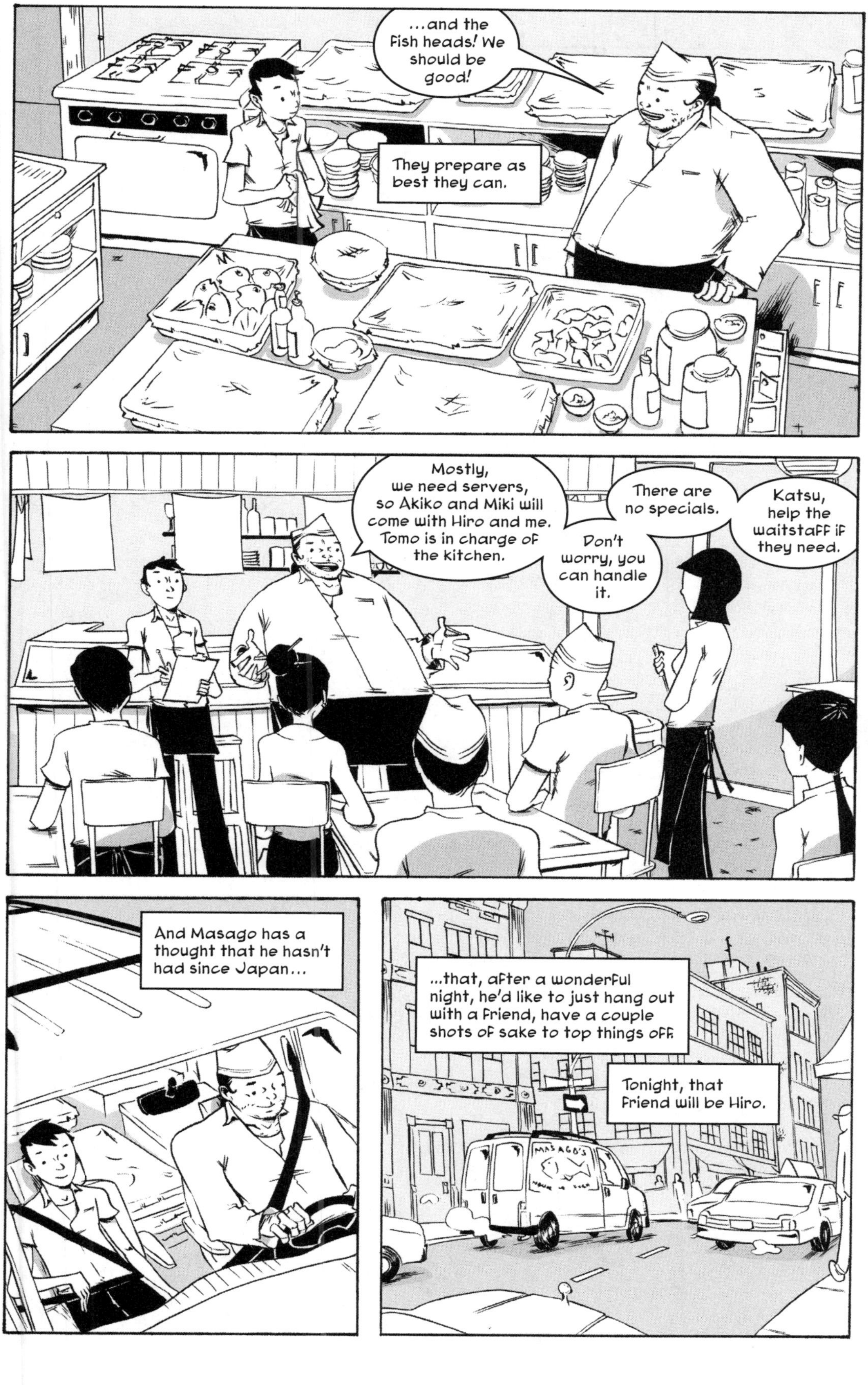
...and the fish heads! We should be good!
They prepare as best they can.
Mostly, we need servers, so Akiko and Miki will come with Hiro and me. Tomo is in charge of the kitchen.
There are no specials.
Don't worry, you can handle it.
Katsu, help the waitstaff if they need.
And Masago has a thought that he hasn't had since Japan...
...that, after a wonderful night, he'd like to just hang out with a friend, have a couple shots of sake to top things off.
Tonight, that friend will be Hiro.

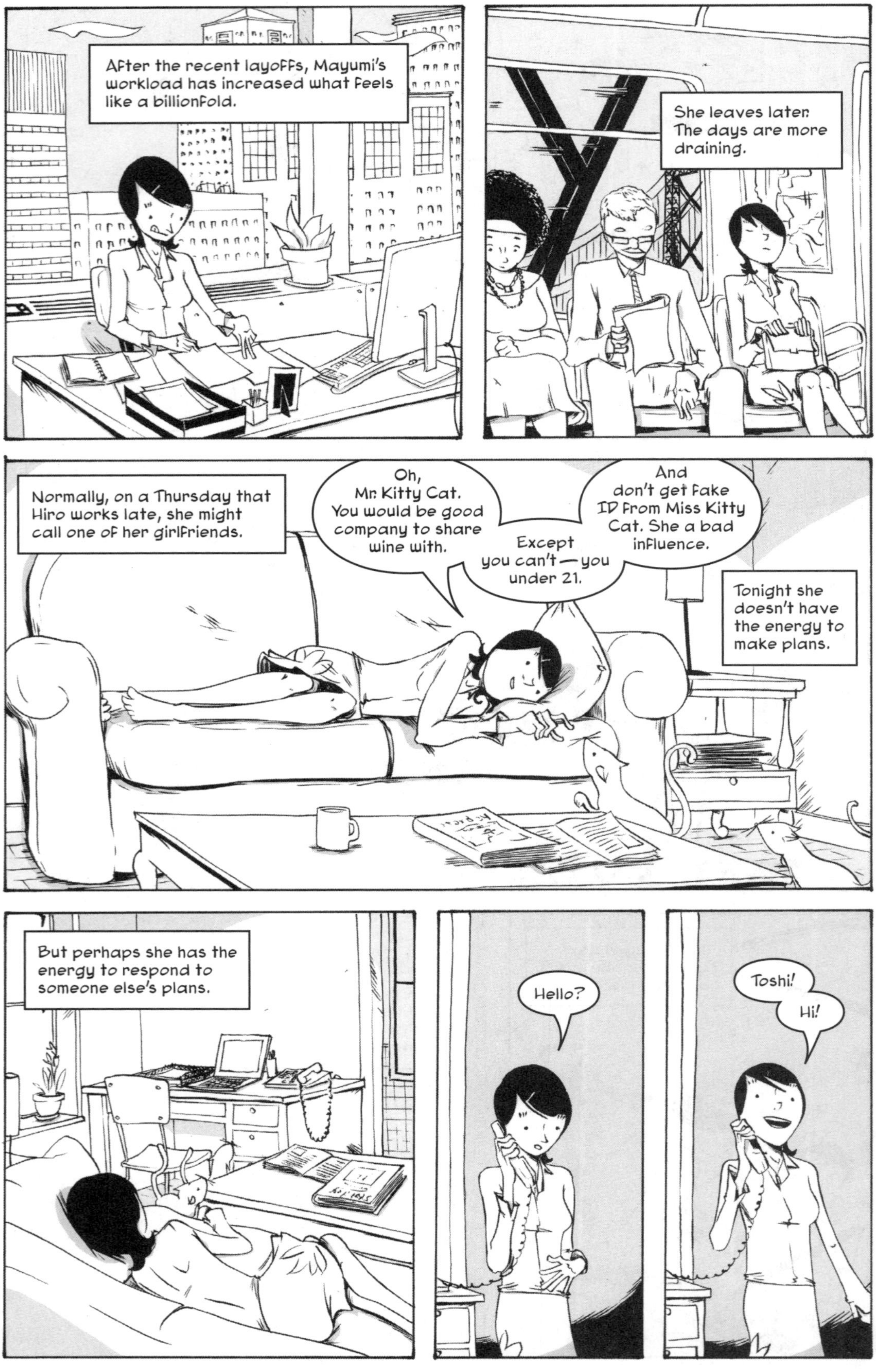
After the recent layoffs, Mayumi's workload has increased what feels like a billionfold.
She leaves later. The days are more draining.
Normally, on a Thursday that Hiro works late, she might call one of her girlfriends.
Oh, Mr. Kitty Cat. You would be good company to share wine with.
Except you can't — you under 21.
And don't get fake ID from Miss Kitty Cat. She a bad influence.
Tonight she doesn't have the energy to make plans.
But perhaps she has the energy to respond to someone else's plans.
Hello?
Toshi!
Hi!

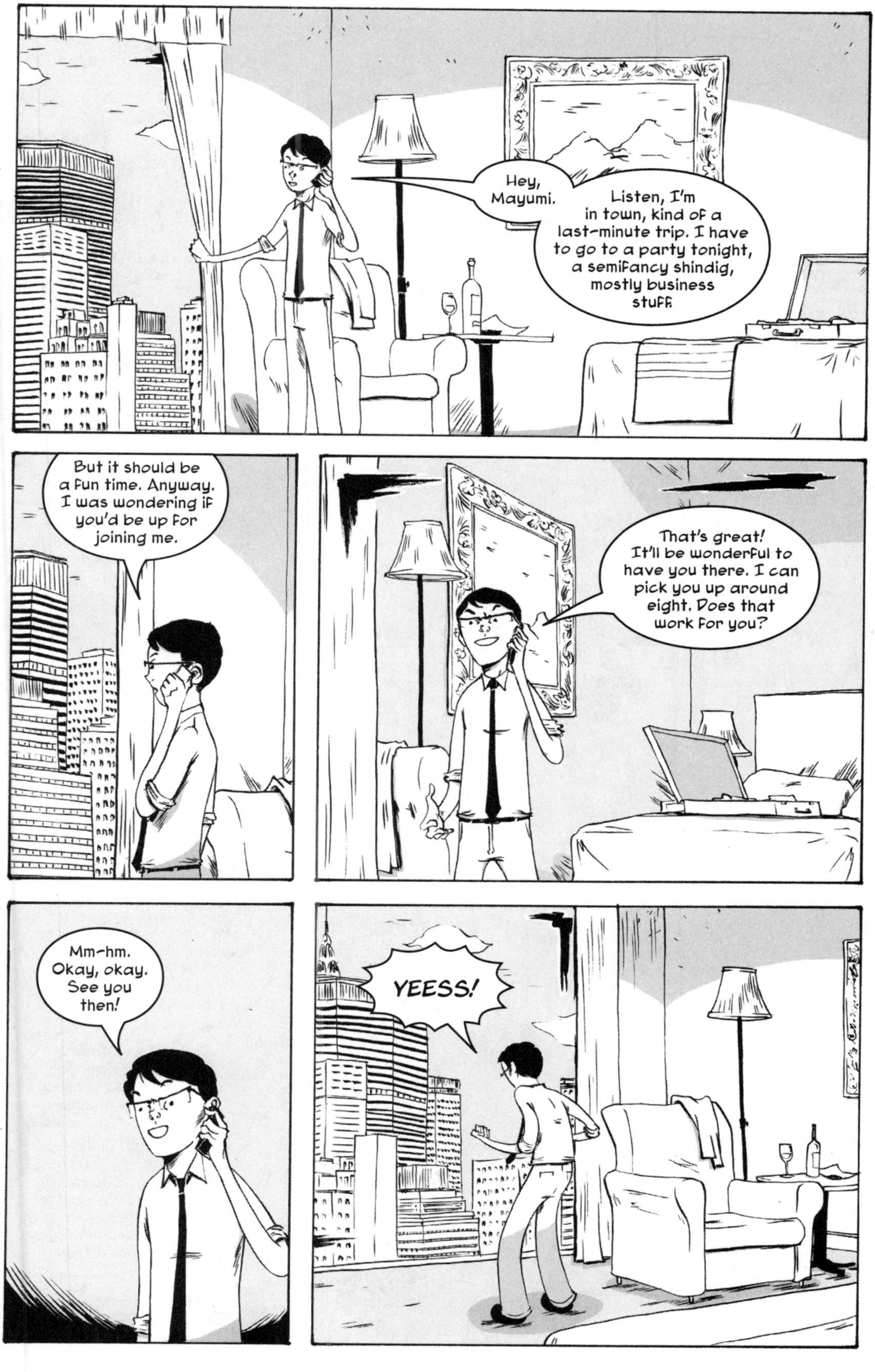
Hey, Mayumi.
Listen, I'm in town, kind of a last-minute trip. I have to go to a party tonight, a semifancy shindig, mostly business stuff.
But it should be a fun time. Anyway. I was wondering if you'd be up for joining me.
That's great! It'll be wonderful to have you there. I can pick you up around eight. Does that work for you?
Mm-hm. Okay, okay. See you then!
YEESS!

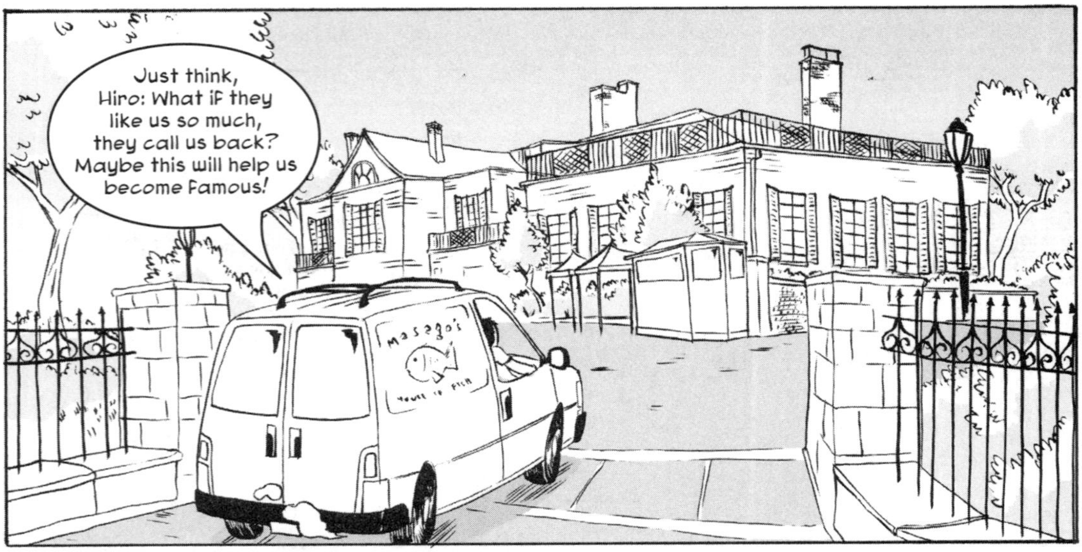
Just think, Hiro: What if they like us so much, they call us back? Maybe this will help us become famous!

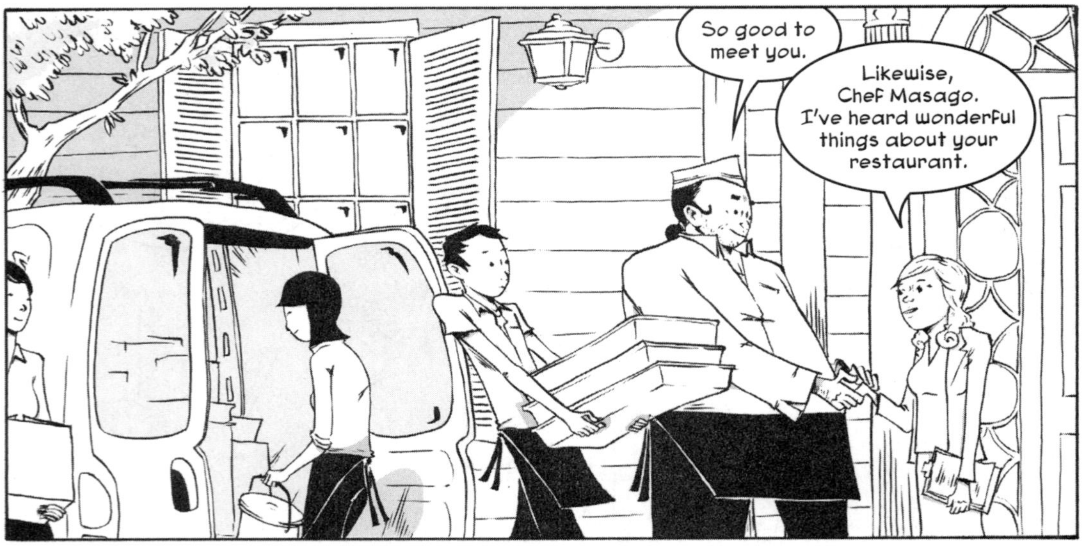
So good to meet you.
Likewise, Chef Masago. I've heard wonderful things about your restaurant.

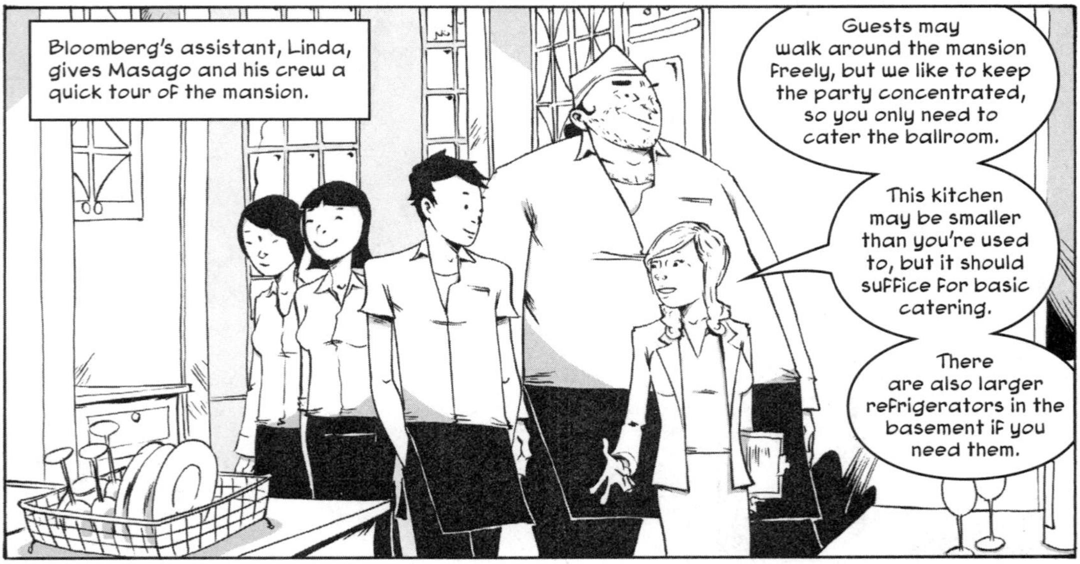
Bloomberg's assistant, Linda, gives Masago and his crew a quick tour of the mansion.
Guests may walk around the mansion freely, but we like to keep the party concentrated, so you only need to cater the ballroom.
This kitchen may be smaller than you're used to, but it should suffice for basic catering.
There are also larger refrigerators in the basement if you need them.

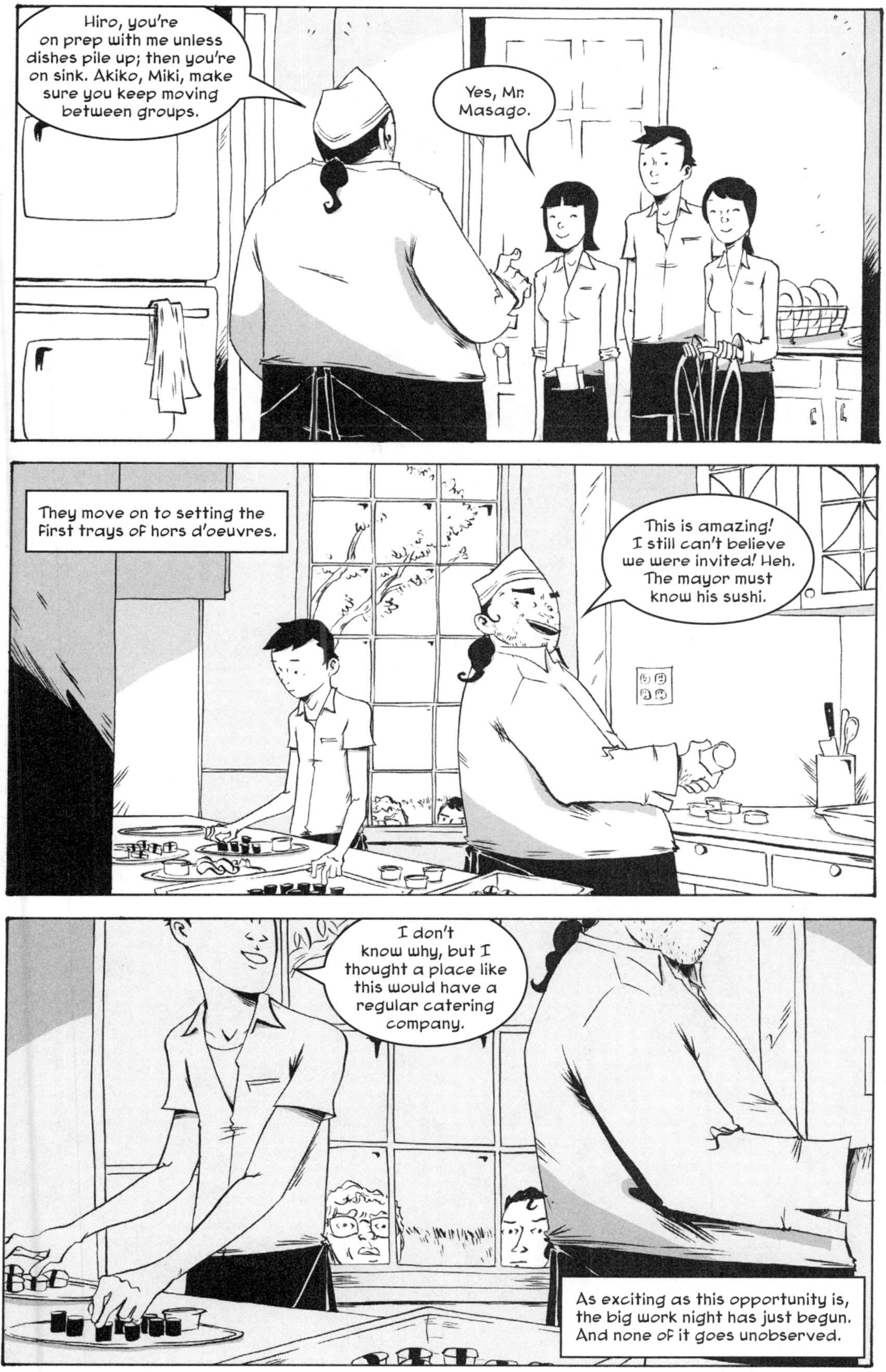
Hiro, you're on prep with me unless dishes pile up; then you're on sink. Akiko, Miki, make sure you keep moving between groups.
Yes, Mr. Masago.
They move on to setting the first trays of hors d'oeuvres.
This is amazing! I still can't believe we were invited! Heh. The mayor must know his sushi.
I don't know why, but I thought a place like this would have a regular catering company.
As exciting as this opportunity is, the big work night has just begun. And none of it goes unobserved.

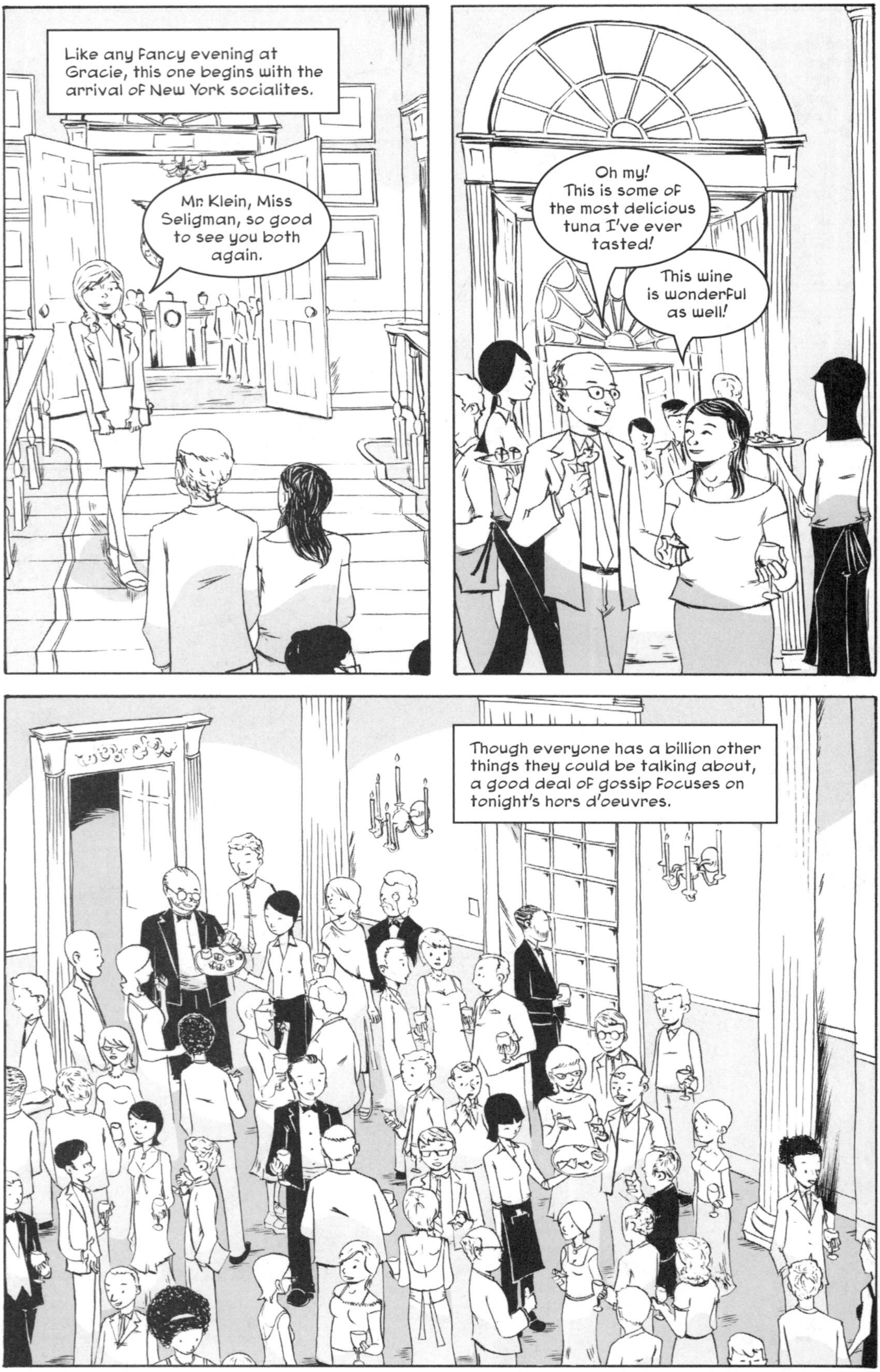
Like any fancy evening at Gracie, this one begins with the arrival of New York socialites.
Mr. Klein, Miss Seligman, so good to see you both again.
Oh my! This is some of the most delicious tuna I've ever tasted!
This wine is wonderful as well!
Though everyone has a billion other things they could be talking about, a good deal of gossip focuses on tonight's hors d'oeuvres.

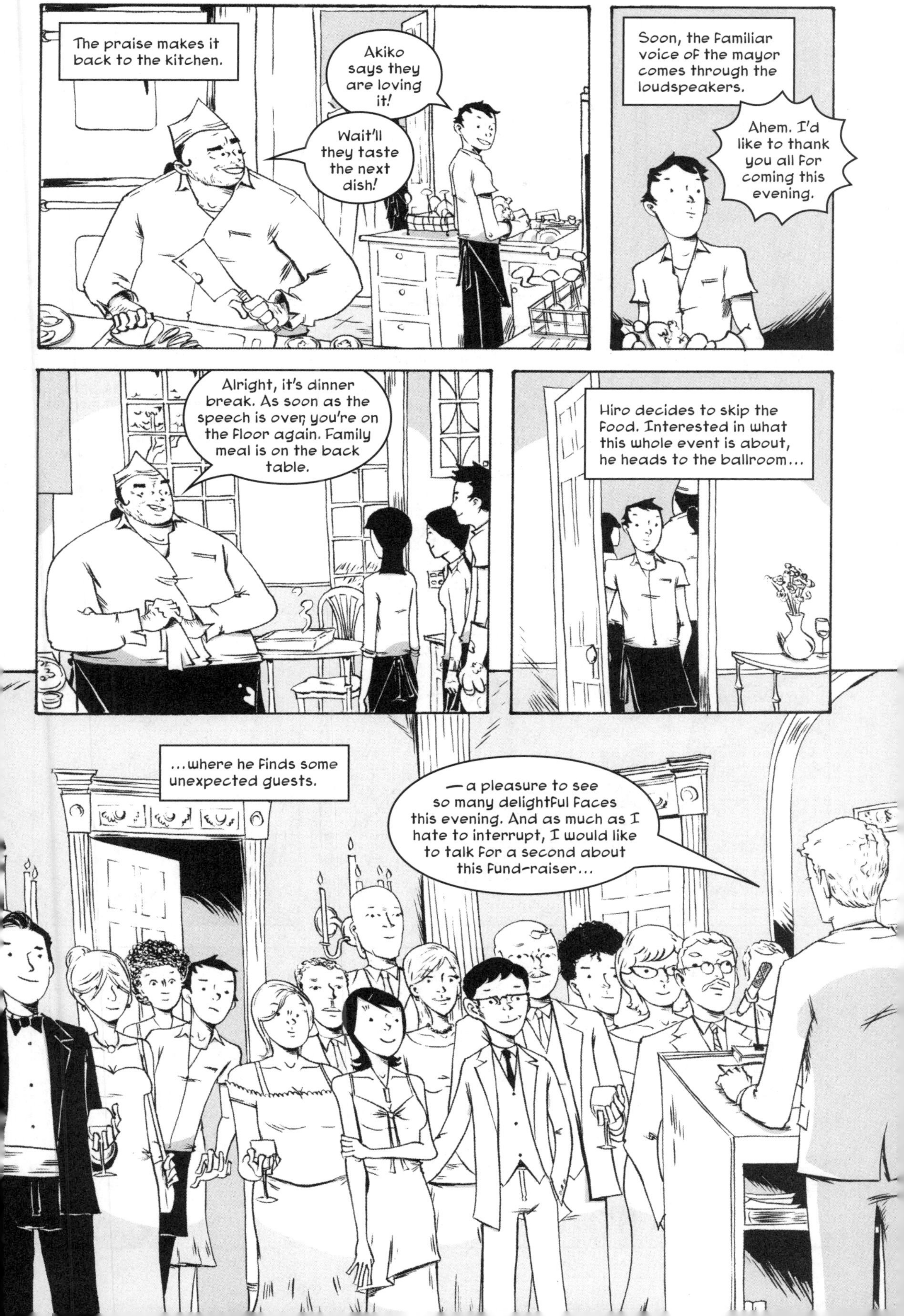
The praise makes it back to the kitchen.
Akiko says they are loving it!
Wait'll they taste the next dish!
Soon, the familiar voice of the mayor comes through the loudspeakers.
Ahem. I'd like to thank you all for coming this evening.
Alright, it's dinner break. As soon as the speech is over, you're on the floor again. Family meal is on the back table.
Hiro decides to skip the food. Interested in what this whole event is about, he heads to the ballroom...
...where he finds some unexpected guests.
—a pleasure to see so many delightful faces this evening. And as much as I hate to interrupt, I would like to talk for a second about this fund-raiser...

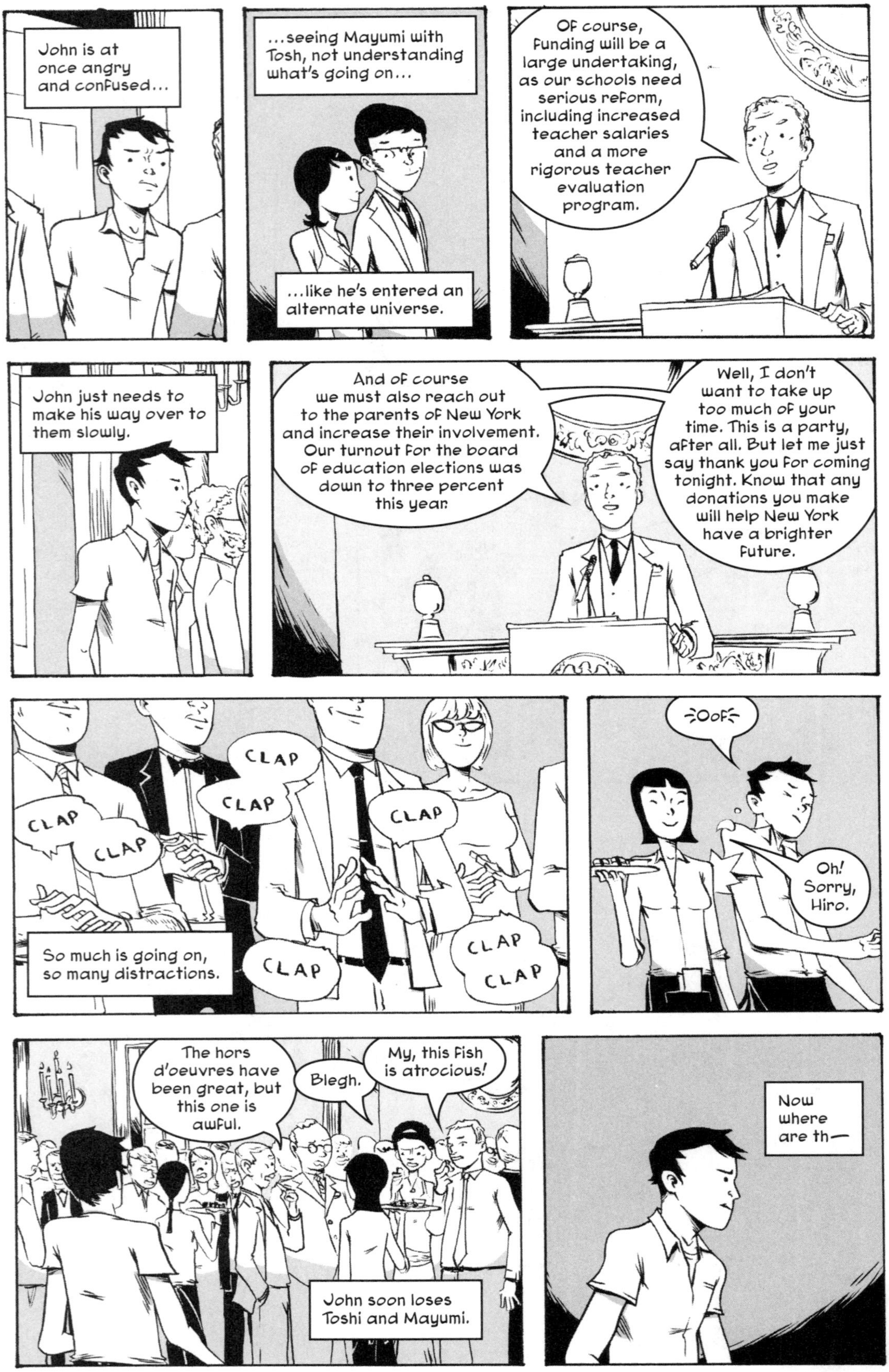
John is at once angry and confused…
…seeing Mayumi with Tosh, not understanding what's going on…
…like he's entered an alternate universe.
Of course, funding will be a large undertaking, as our schools need serious reform, including increased teacher salaries and a more rigorous teacher evaluation program.
John just needs to make his way over to them slowly.
And of course we must also reach out to the parents of New York and increase their involvement. Our turnout for the board of education elections was down to three percent this year.
Well, I don't want to take up too much of your time. This is a party, after all. But let me just say thank you for coming tonight. Know that any donations you make will help New York have a brighter future.
CLAP
CLAP
CLAP
CLAP
CLAP
So much is going on, so many distractions.
CLAP
CLAP
CLAP
Oof
Oh! Sorry, Hiro.
The hors d'oeuvres have been great, but this one is awful.
Blegh.
My, this fish is atrocious!
John soon loses Toshi and Mayumi.
Now where are th—

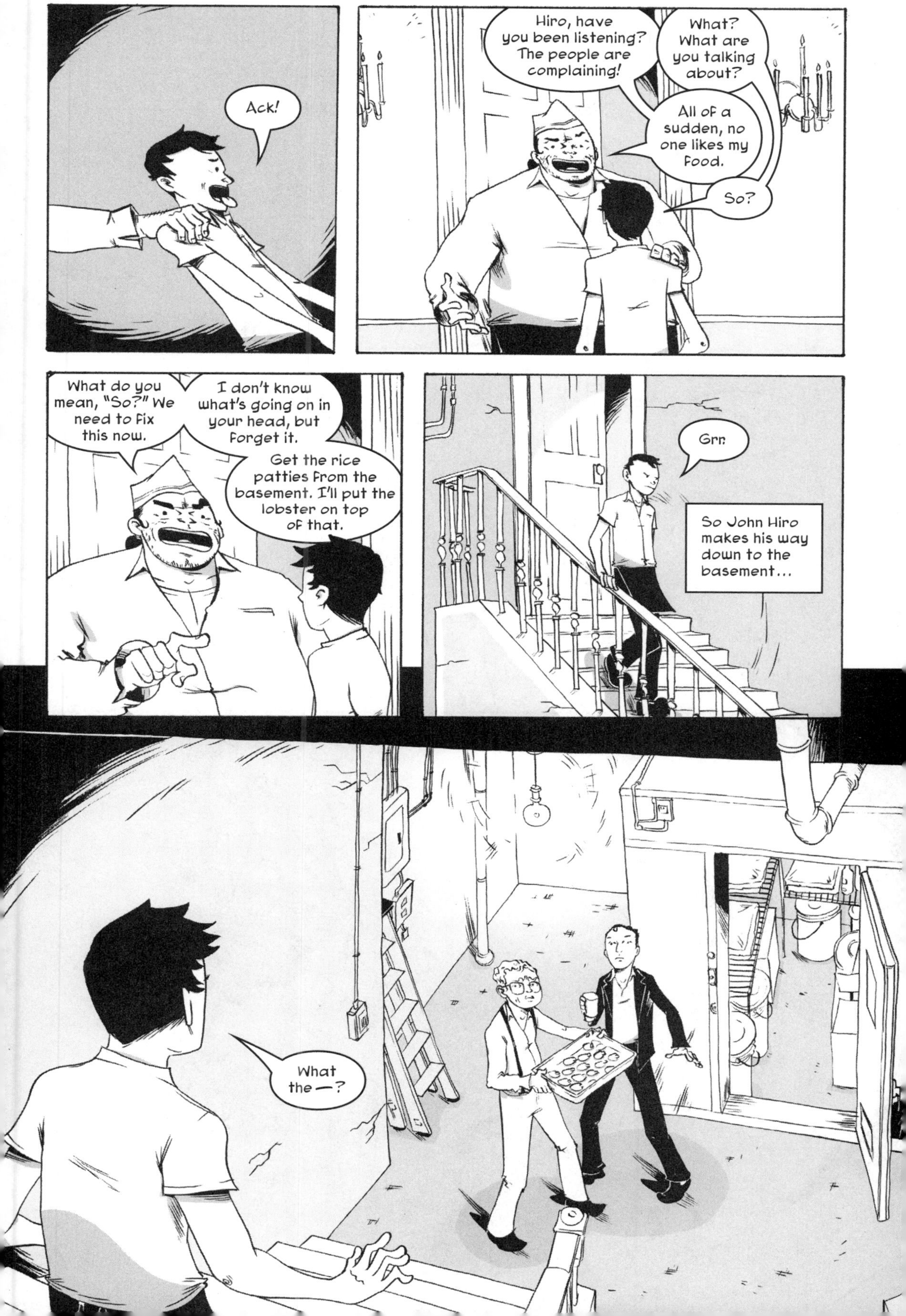
Ack!
Hiro, have you been listening? The people are complaining!
What? What are you talking about?
All of a sudden, no one likes my food.
So?
What do you mean, "So?" We need to fix this now.
I don't know what's going on in your head, but forget it.
Get the rice patties from the basement. I'll put the lobster on top of that.
Grr.
So John Hiro makes his way down to the basement...
What the—?

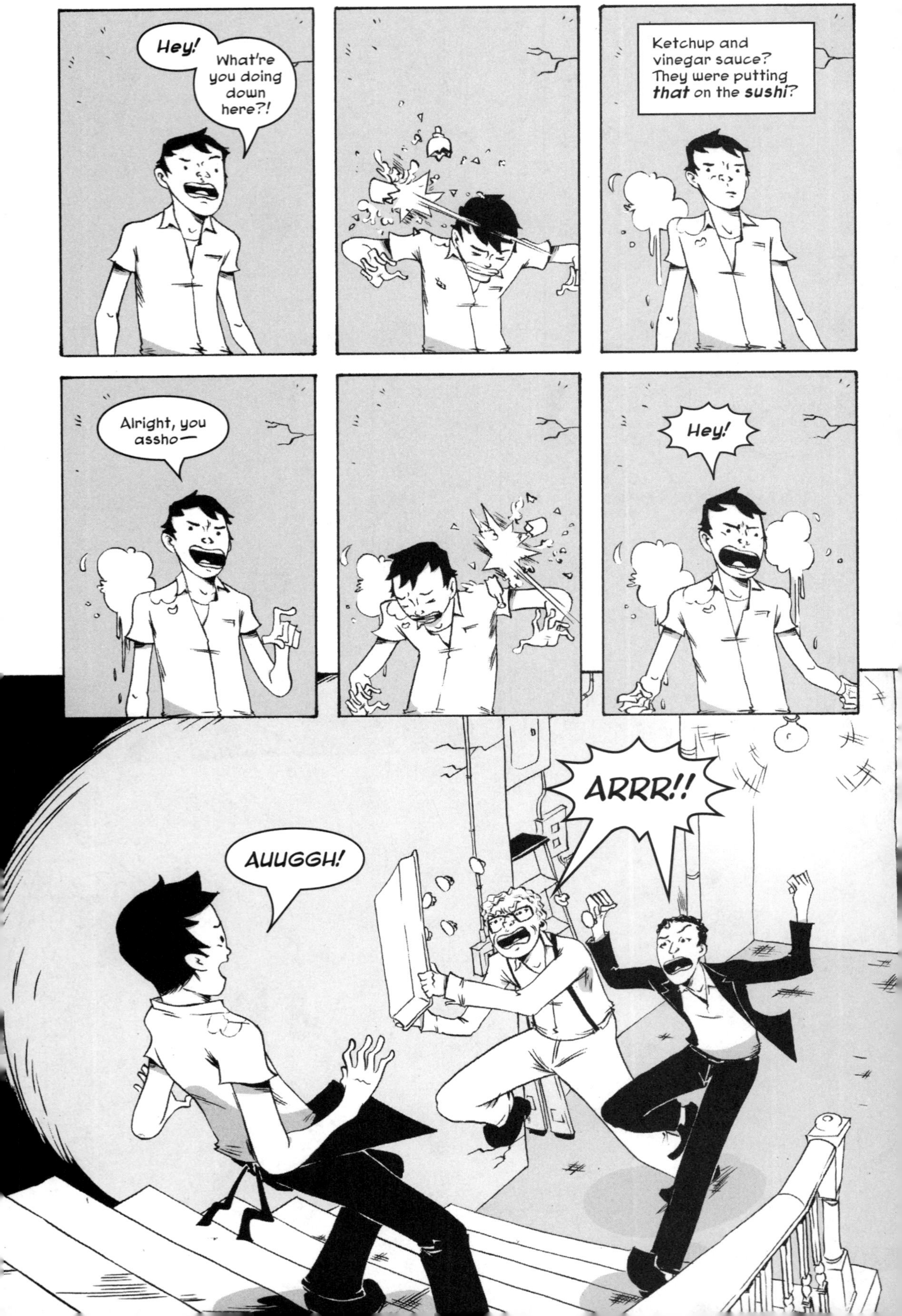
Hey!
What're you doing down here?!
Ketchup and vinegar sauce? They were putting that on the sushi?
Alright, you assho—
Hey!
ARRR!!
AUUGGH!

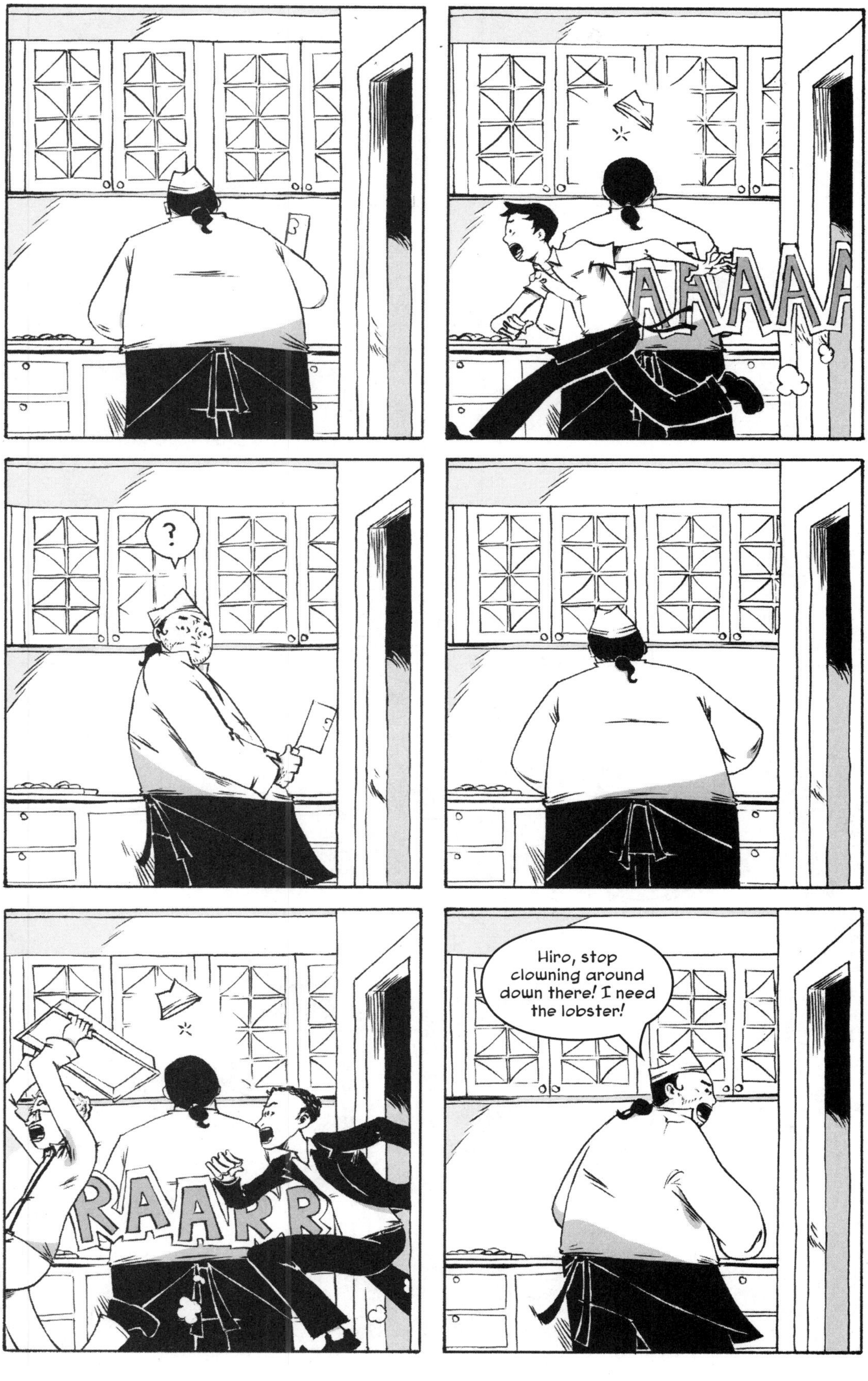
AAAAA
?
RAARR
Hiro, stop clowning around down there! I need the lobster!

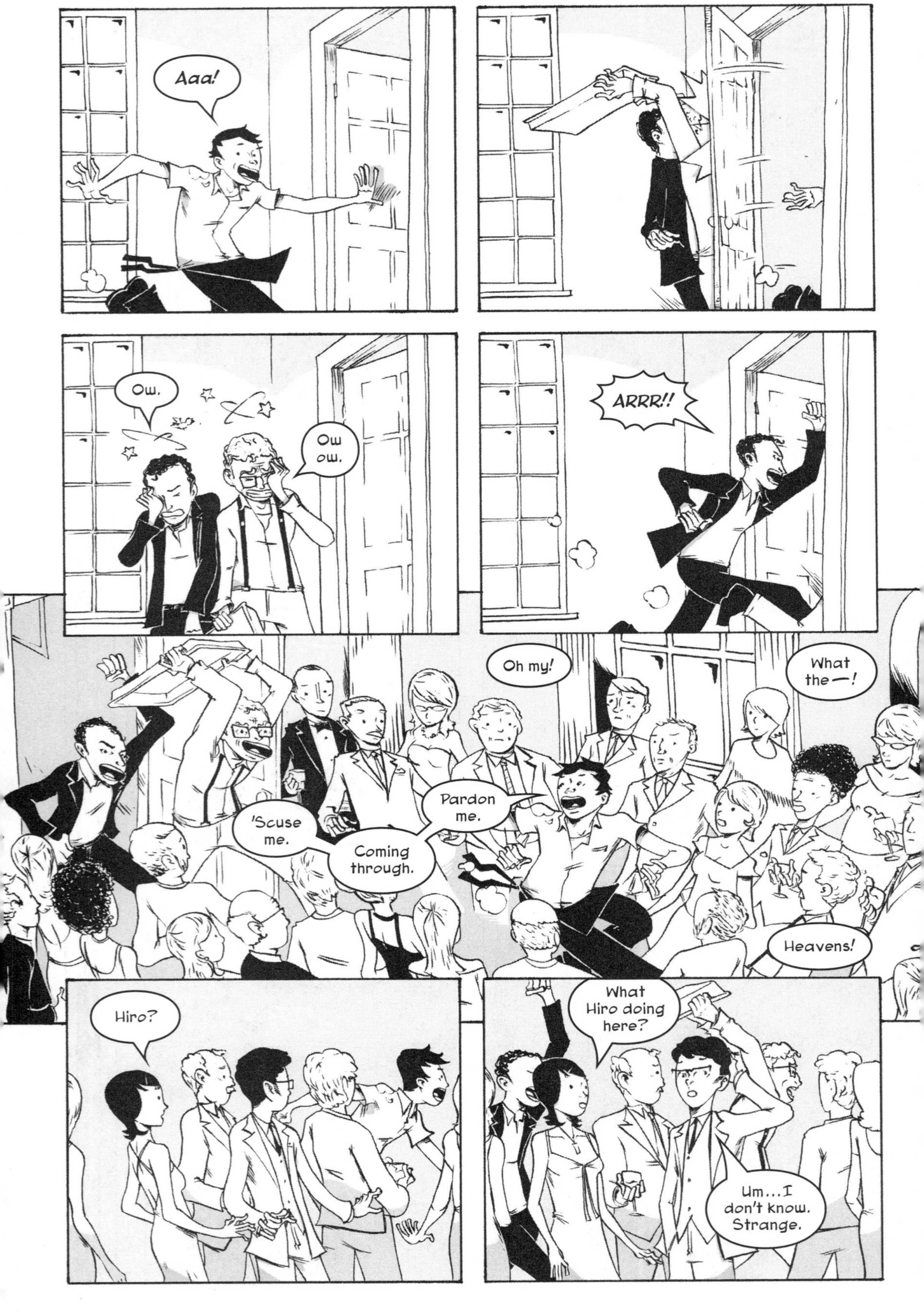
Aaa!
Ow.
Ow ow.
ARRR!!
Oh my!
What the—!
Pardon me.
'Scuse me.
Coming through.
Heavens!
Hiro?
What Hiro doing here?
Um... I don't know. Strange.

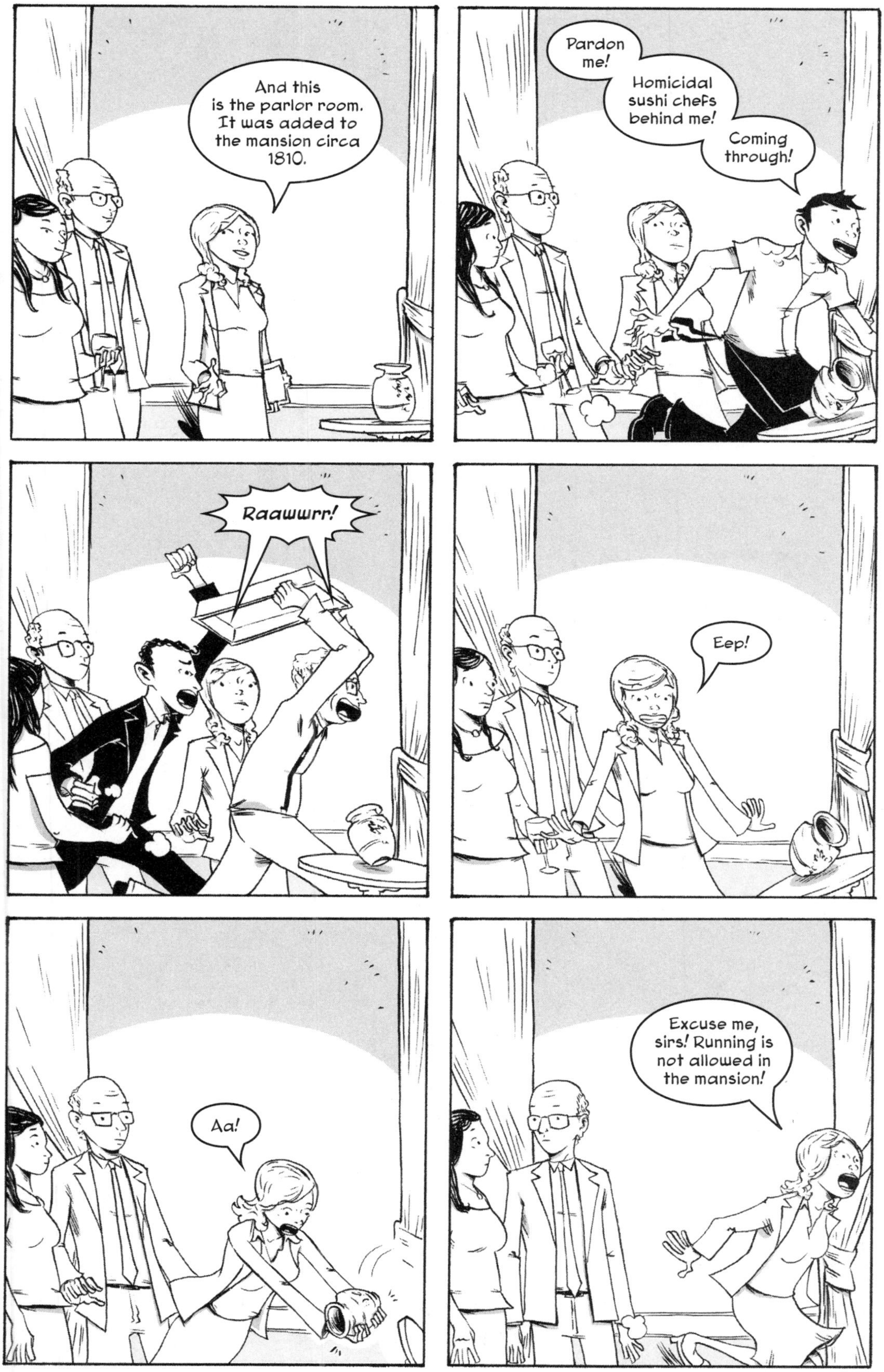
And this is the parlor room. It was added to the mansion circa 1810.
Pardon me!
Homicidal sushi chefs behind me!
Coming through!
Raawwrr!
Eep!
Aa!
Excuse me, sirs! Running is not allowed in the mansion!

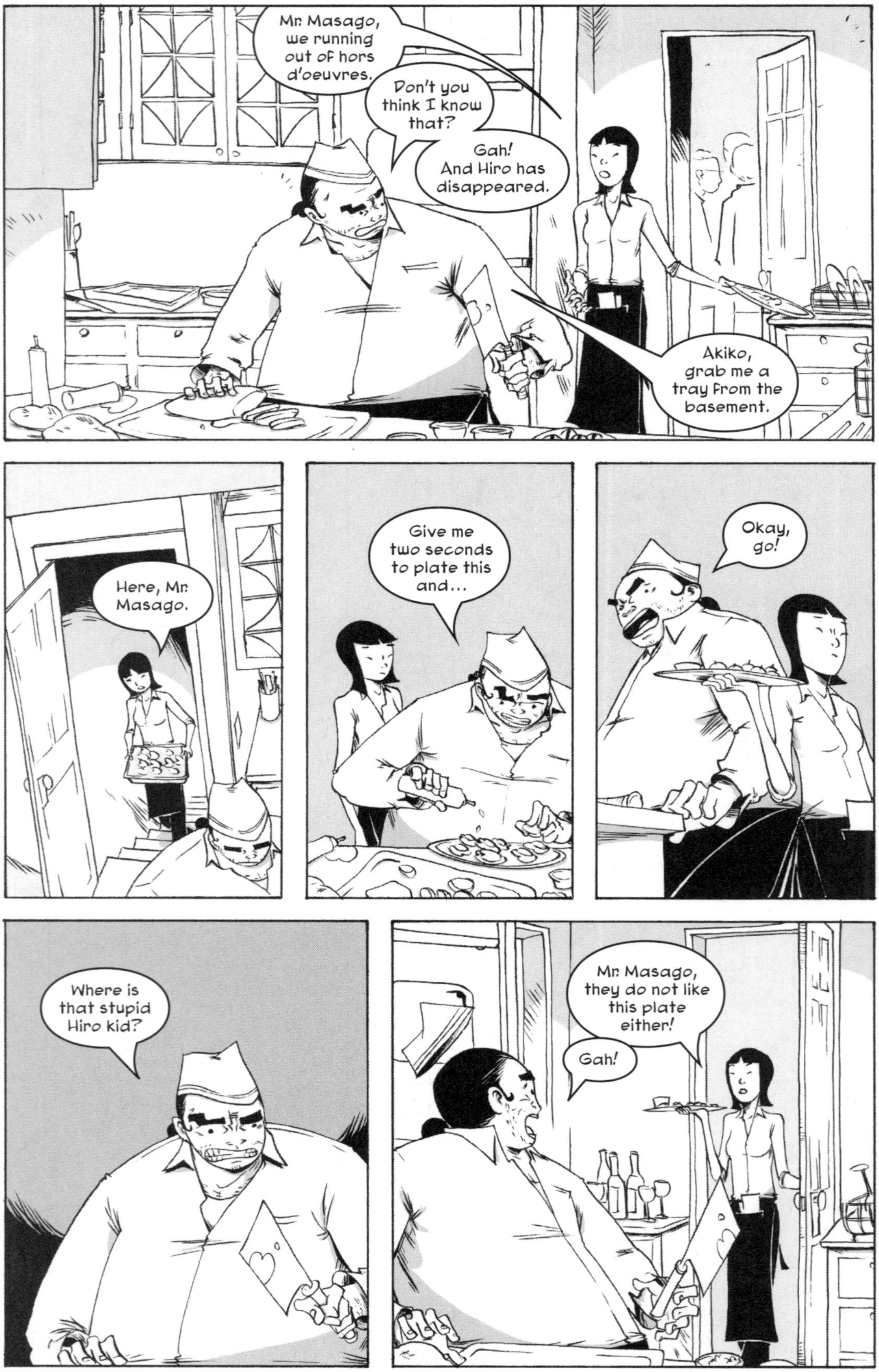
Mr. Masago, we running out of hors d'oeuvres.
Don't you think I know that?
Gah! And Hiro has disappeared.
Akiko, grab me a tray from the basement.
Here, Mr. Masago.
Give me two seconds to plate this and...
Okay, go!
Where is that stupid Hiro kid?
Mr. Masago, they do not like this plate either!
Gah!

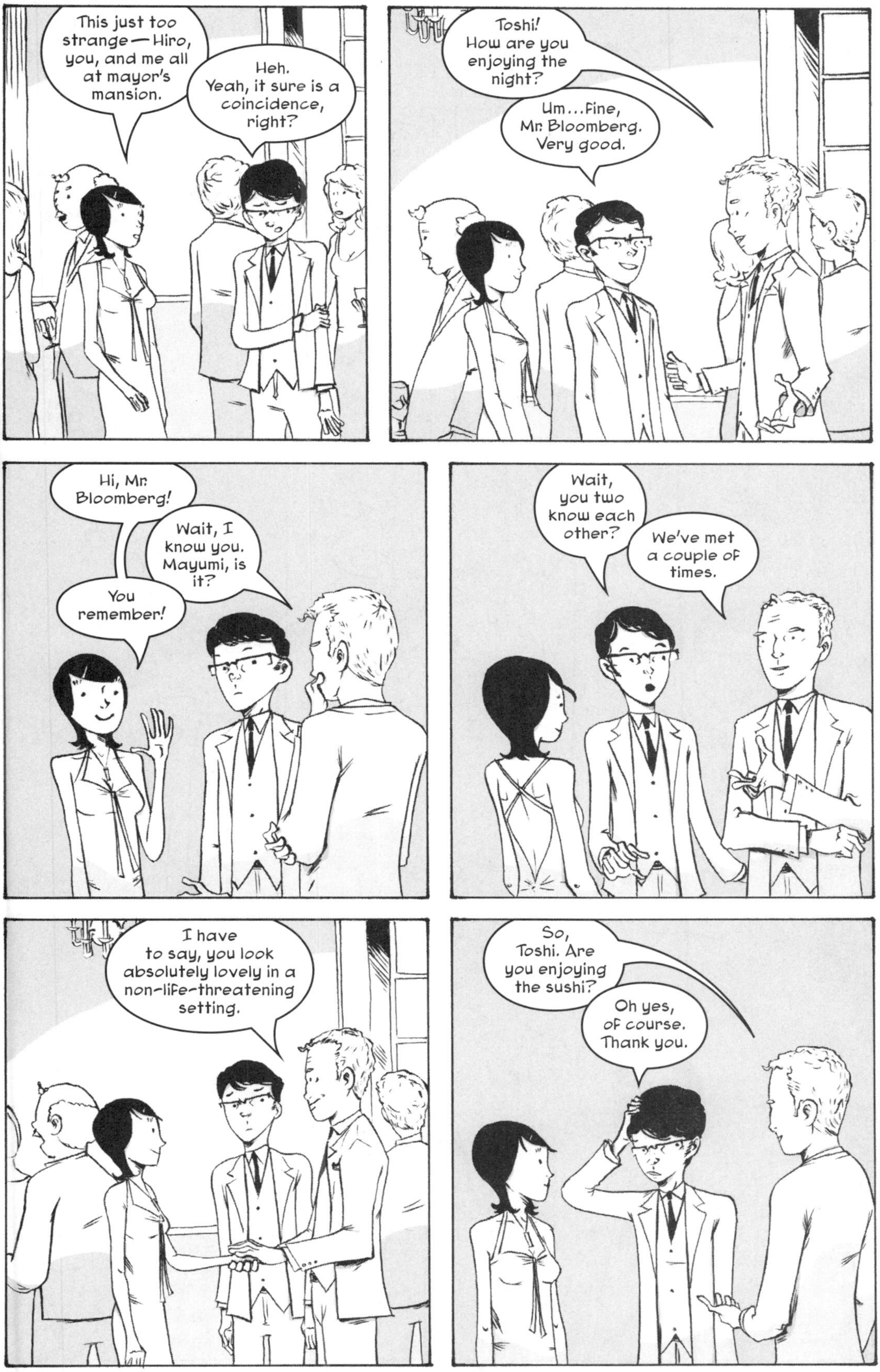
This just too strange—Hiro, you, and me all at mayor's mansion.
Heh. Yeah, it sure is a coincidence, right?
Toshi! How are you enjoying the night?
Um...fine, Mr. Bloomberg. Very good.
Hi, Mr. Bloomberg!
Wait, I know you. Mayumi, is it?
You remember!
Wait, you two know each other?
We've met a couple of times.
I have to say, you look absolutely lovely in a non-life-threatening setting.
So, Toshi. Are you enjoying the sushi?
Oh yes, of course. Thank you.

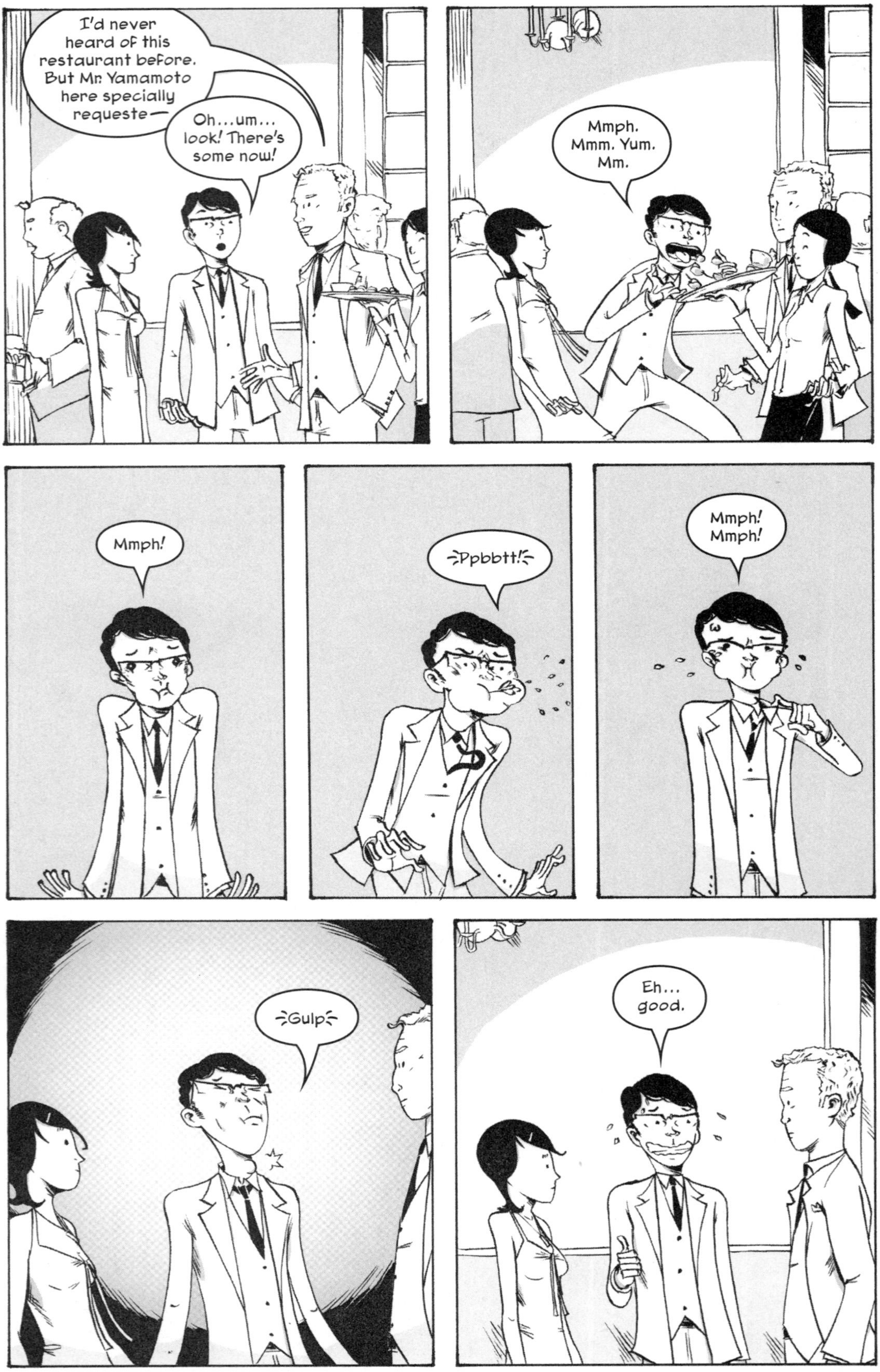
I'd never heard of this restaurant before. But Mr. Yamamoto here specially requeste—
Oh...um... look! There's some now!
Mmph. Mmm. Yum. Mm.
Mmph!
Ppbbtt!
Mmph! Mmph!
Gulp
Eh... good.

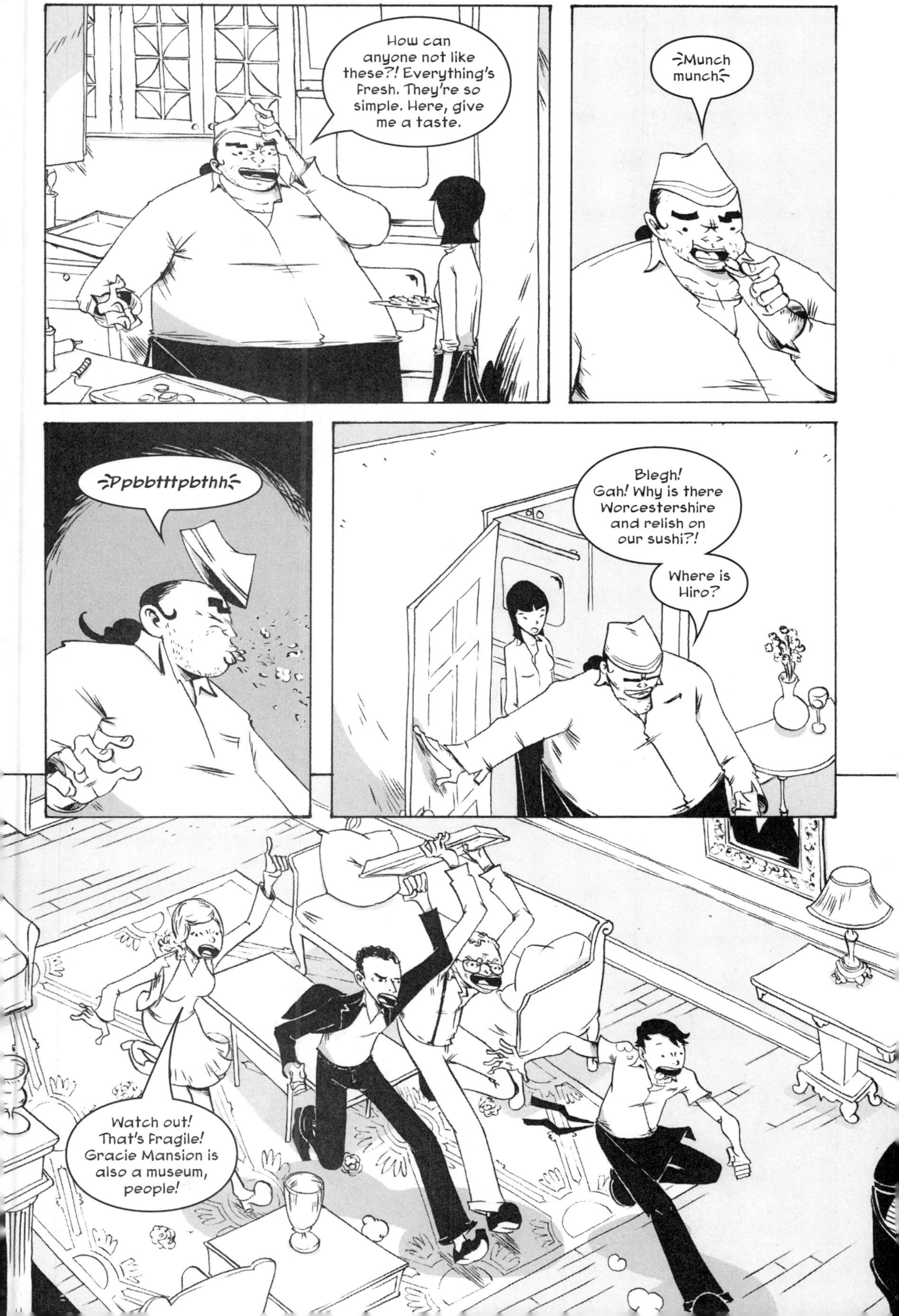
How can anyone not like these?! Everything's fresh. They're so simple. Here, give me a taste.
Munch munch
Ppbbtttpbthh
Blegh! Gah! Why is there Worcestershire and relish on our sushi?!
Where is Hiro?
Watch out! That's fragile! Gracie Mansion is also a museum, people!

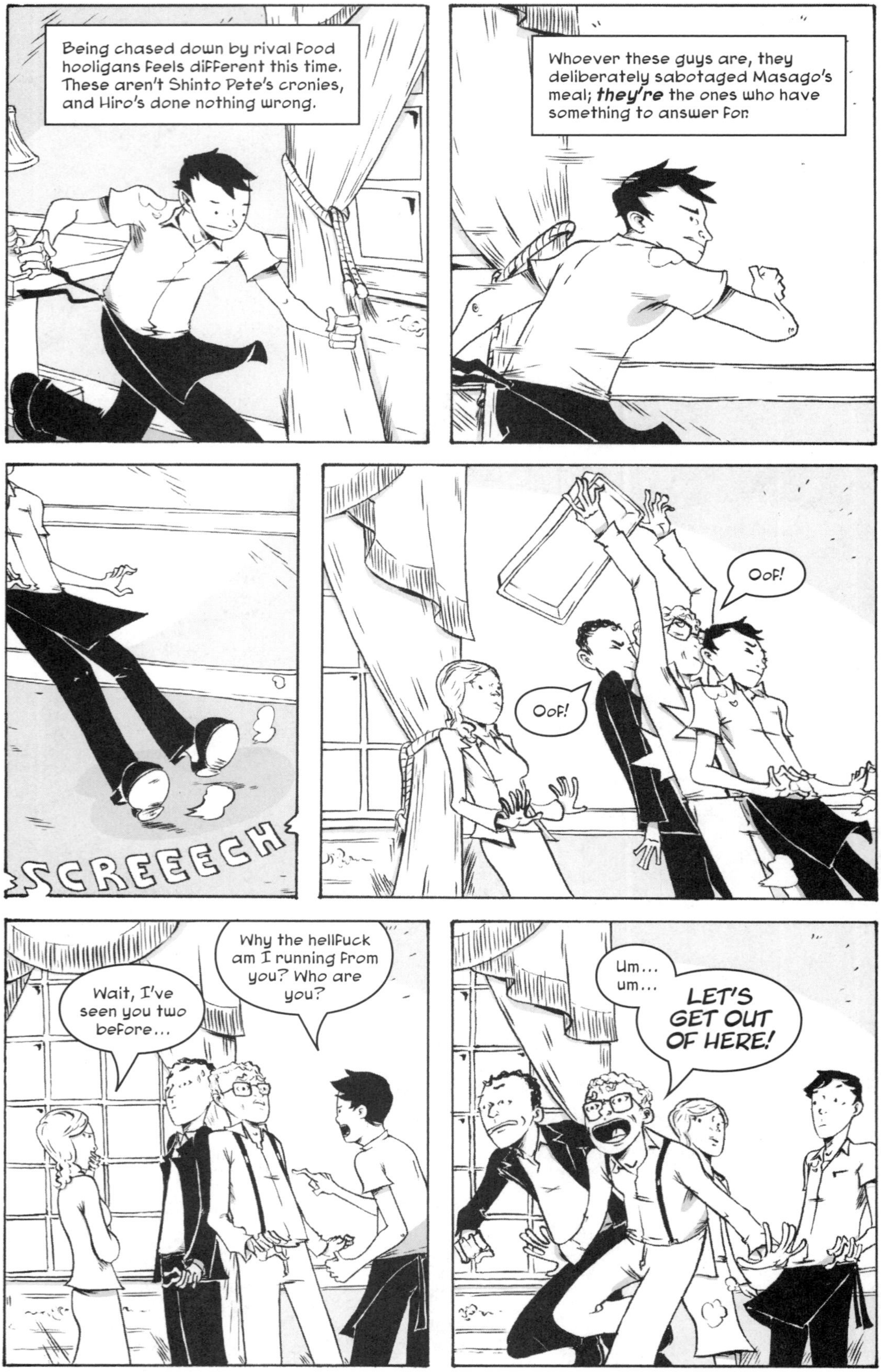
Being chased down by rival food hooligans feels different this time. These aren't Shinto Pete's cronies, and Hiro's done nothing wrong.
Whoever these guys are, they deliberately sabotaged Masago's meal; *they're* the ones who have something to answer for.
SCREEECH
Oof!
Oof!
Wait, I've seen you two before...
Why the hellfuck am I running from you? Who are you?
Um... um...
LET'S GET OUT OF HERE!

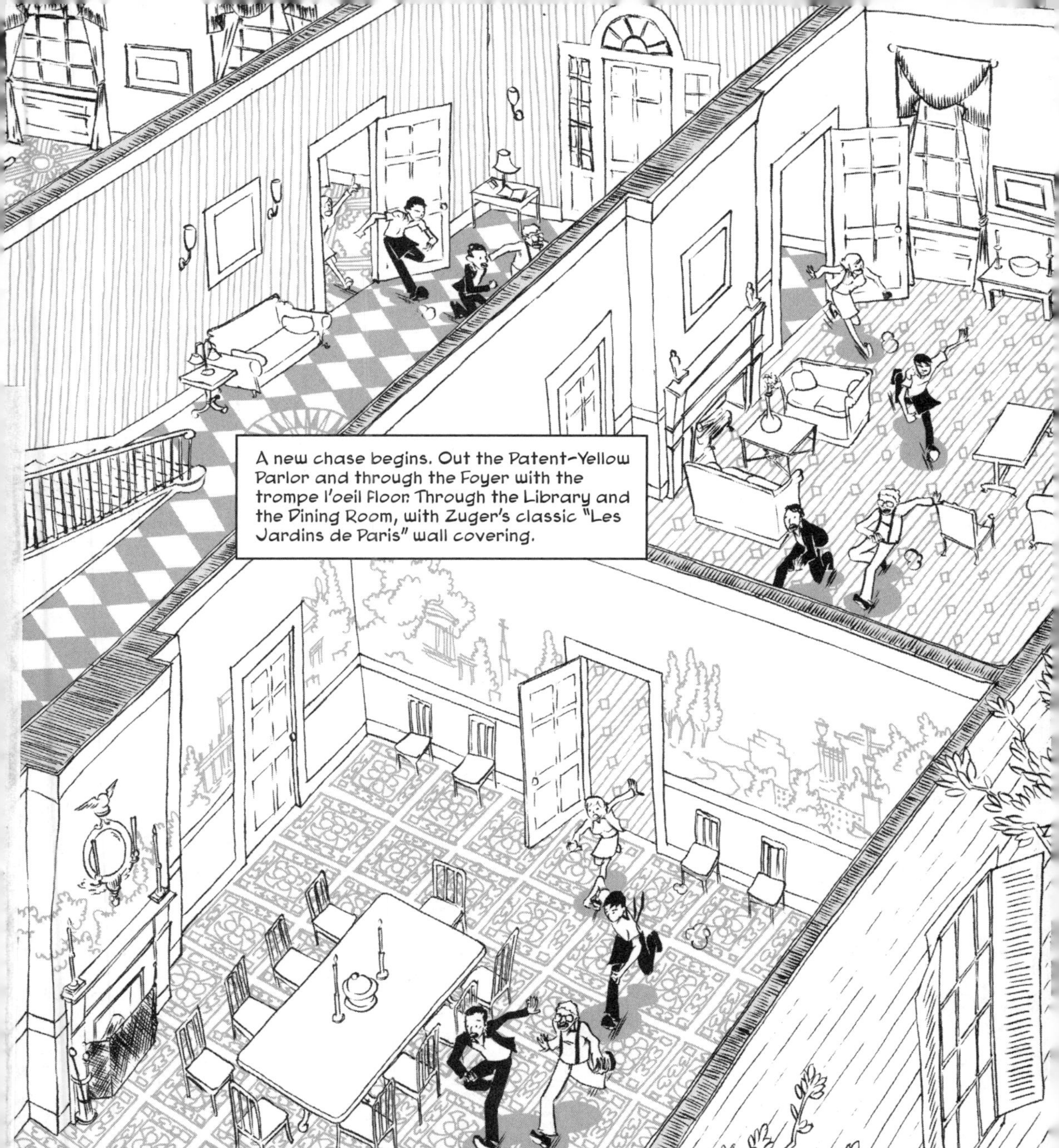
A new chase begins. Out the Patent-Yellow Parlor and through the Foyer with the trompe l'oeil floor. Through the Library and the Dining Room, with Zuger's classic "Les Jardins de Paris" wall covering.

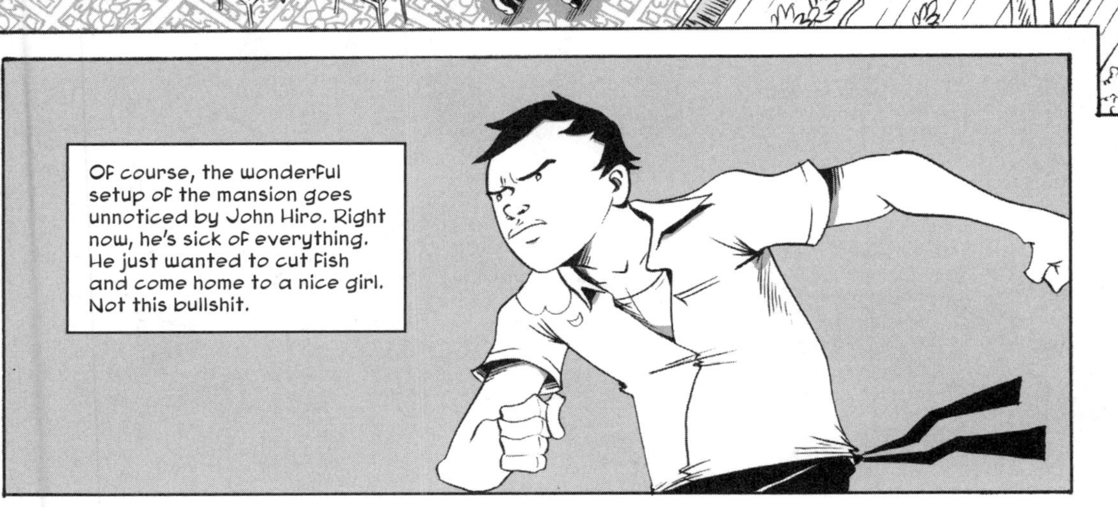
Of course, the wonderful setup of the mansion goes unnoticed by John Hiro. Right now, he's sick of everything. He just wanted to cut fish and come home to a nice girl. Not this bullshit.

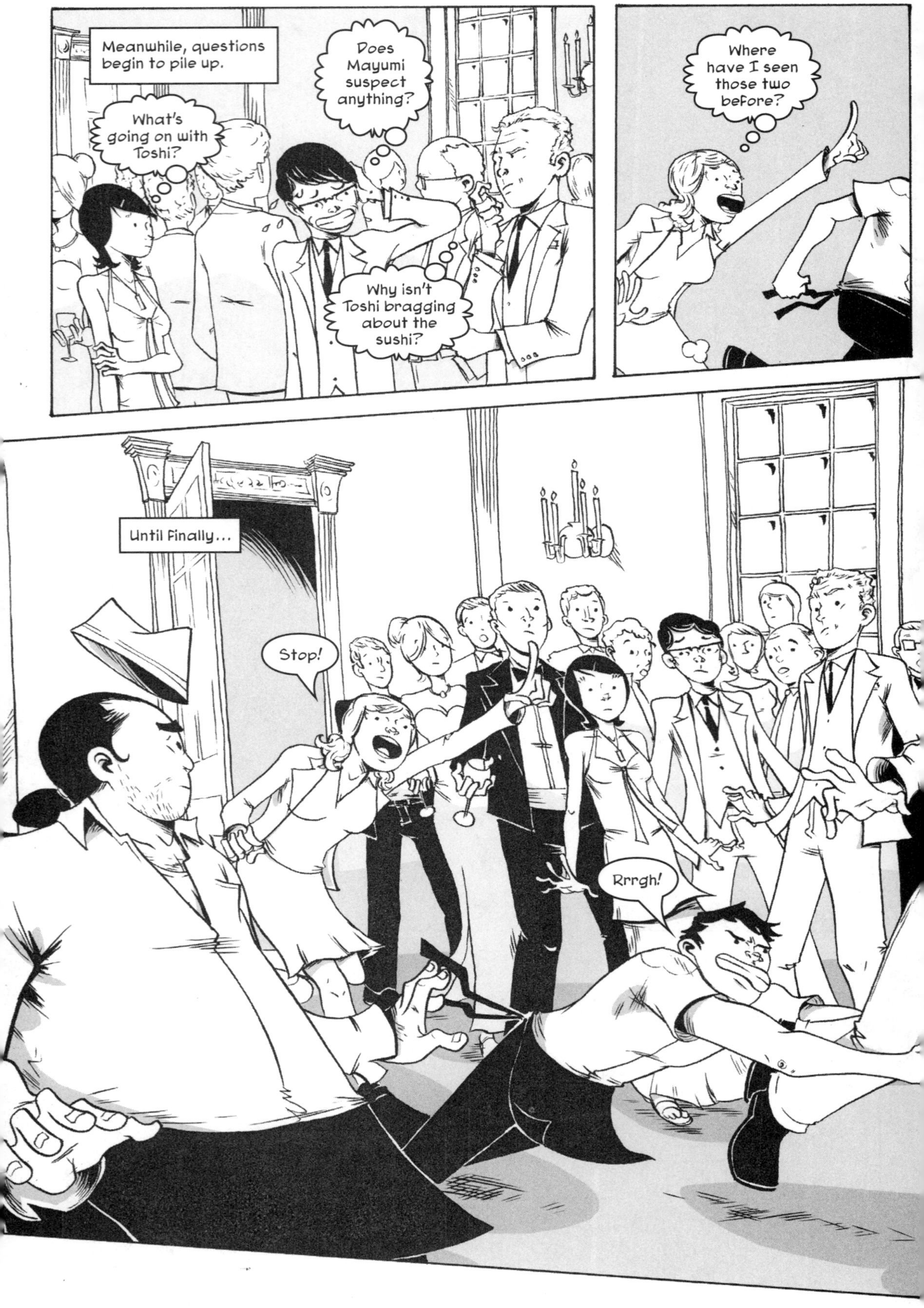
Meanwhile, questions begin to pile up.
What's going on with Toshi?
Does Mayumi suspect anything?
Why isn't Toshi bragging about the sushi?
Where have I seen those two before?
Until finally...
Stop!
Rrrgh!

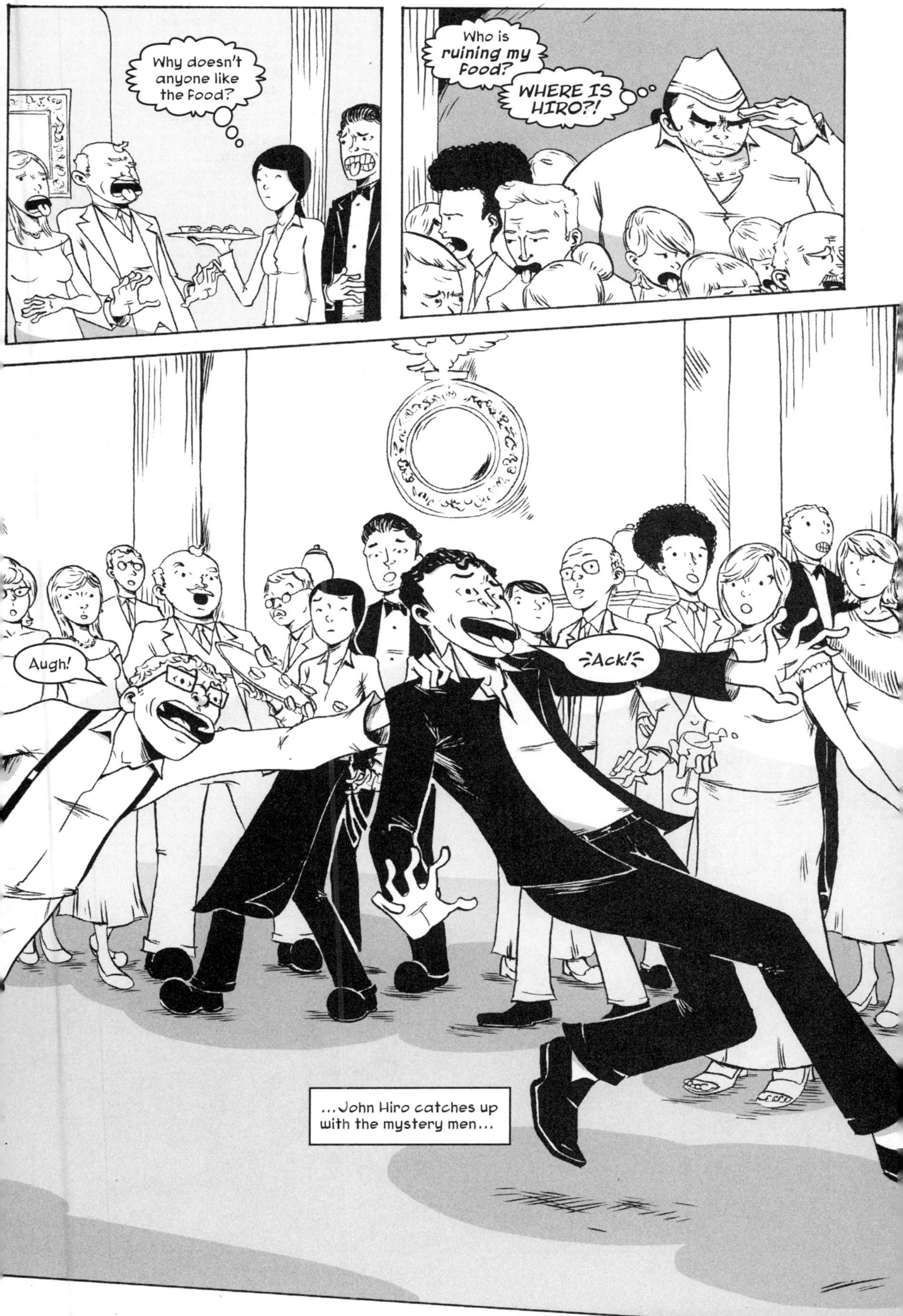
Why doesn't anyone like the food?
Who is ruining my food?
WHERE IS HIRO?!
Augh!
Ack!
...John Hiro catches up with the mystery men...

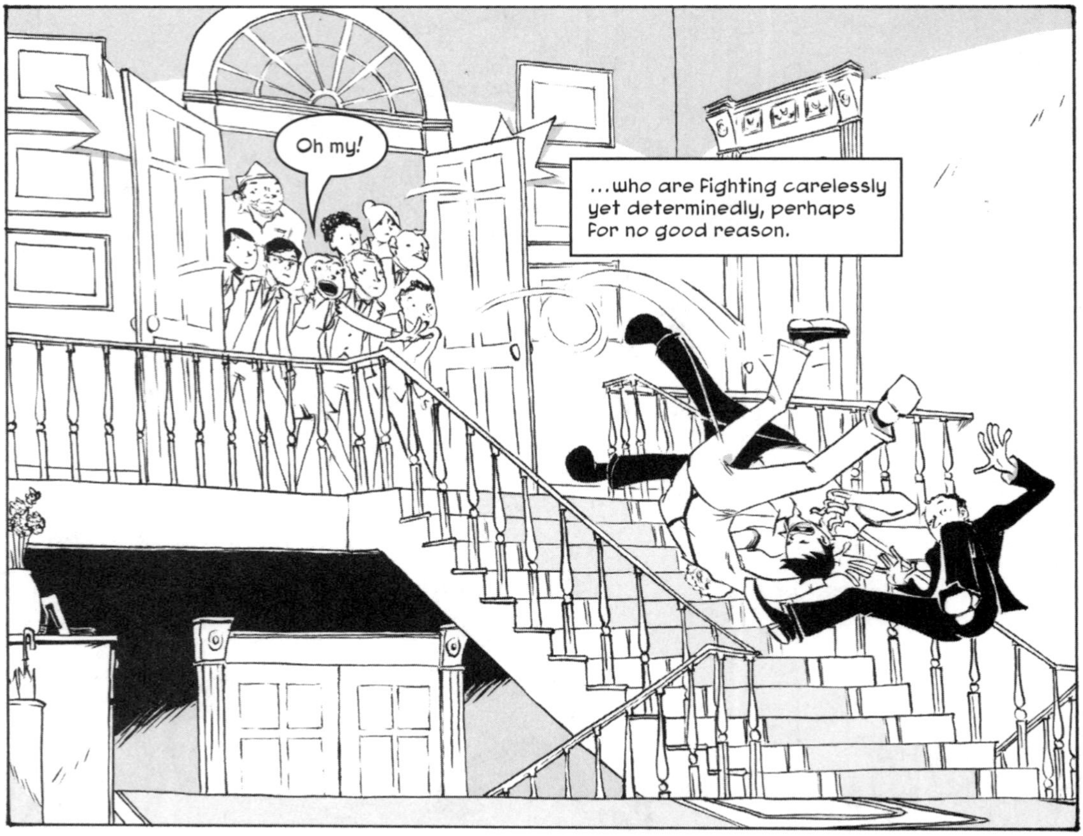
Oh my!
...who are fighting carelessly yet determinedly, perhaps for no good reason.

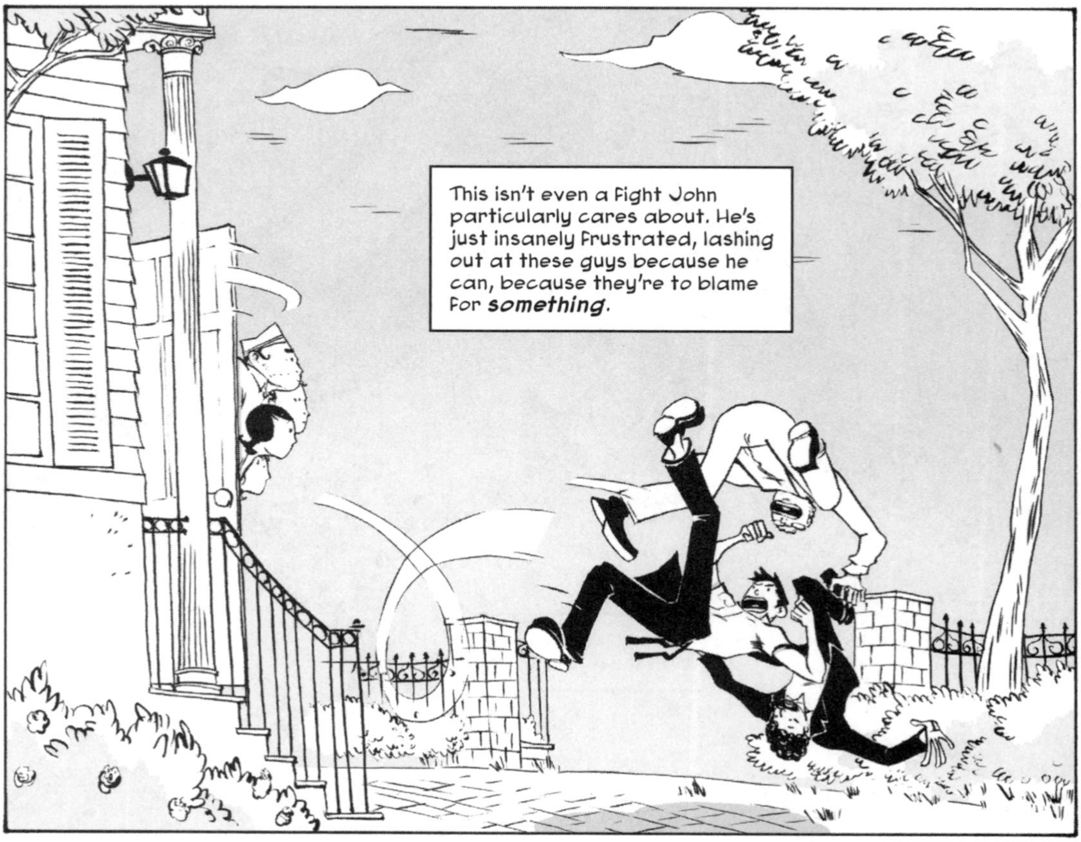
This isn't even a fight John particularly cares about. He's just insanely frustrated, lashing out at these guys because he can, because they're to blame for *something*.

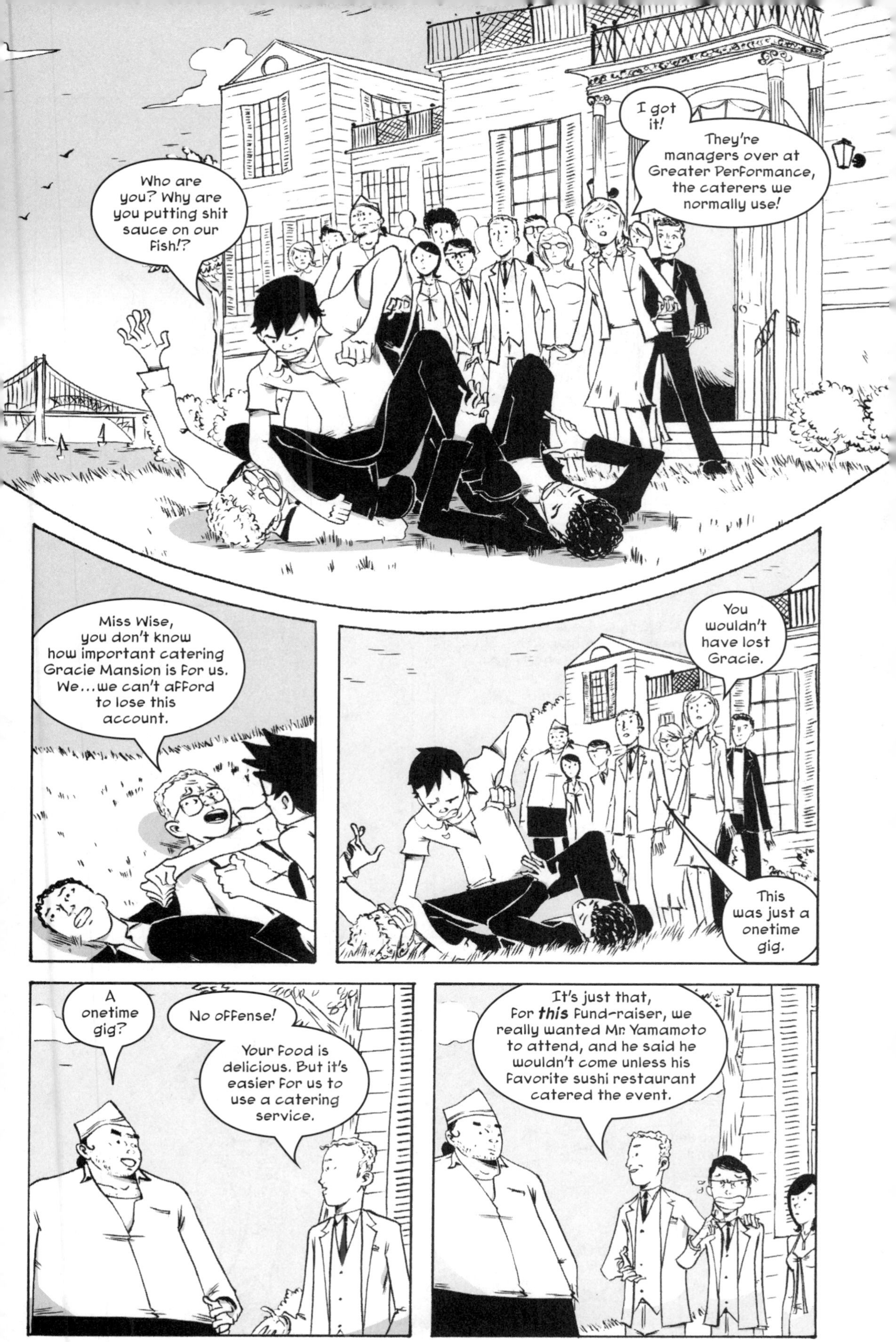
Who are you? Why are you putting shit sauce on our fish!?
I got it!
They're managers over at Greater Performance, the caterers we normally use!
Miss Wise, you don't know how important catering Gracie Mansion is for us. We...we can't afford to lose this account.
You wouldn't have lost Gracie.
This was just a onetime gig.
A onetime gig?
No offense!
Your food is delicious. But it's easier for us to use a catering service.
It's just that, for **this** fund-raiser, we really wanted Mr. Yamamoto to attend, and he said he wouldn't come unless his favorite sushi restaurant catered the event.

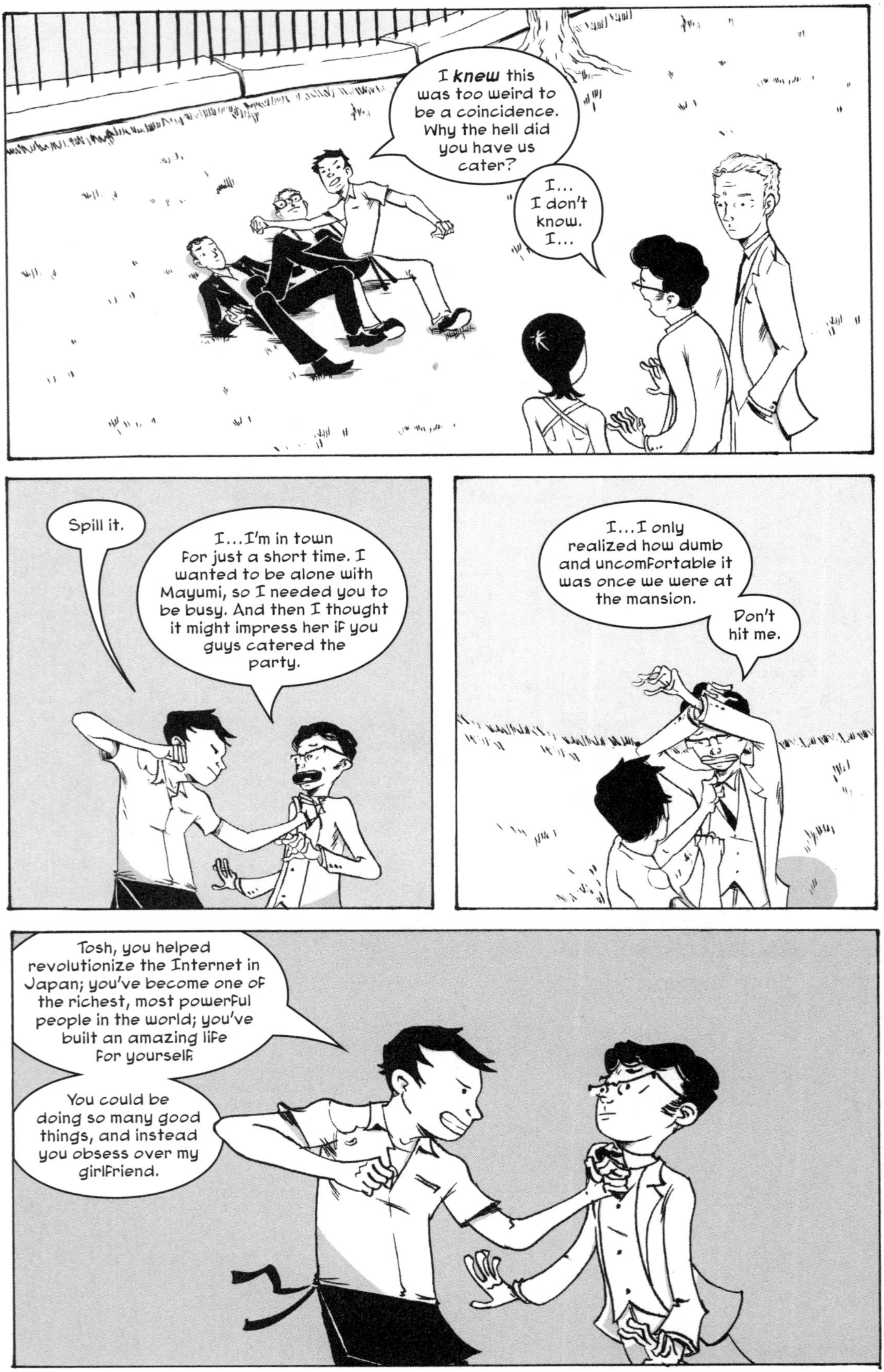
I knew this was too weird to be a coincidence. Why the hell did you have us cater?
I... I don't know. I...
Spill it.
I...I'm in town for just a short time. I wanted to be alone with Mayumi, so I needed you to be busy. And then I thought it might impress her if you guys catered the party.
I...I only realized how dumb and uncomfortable it was once we were at the mansion.
Don't hit me.
Tosh, you helped revolutionize the Internet in Japan; you've become one of the richest, most powerful people in the world; you've built an amazing life for yourself.
You could be doing so many good things, and instead you obsess over my girlfriend.

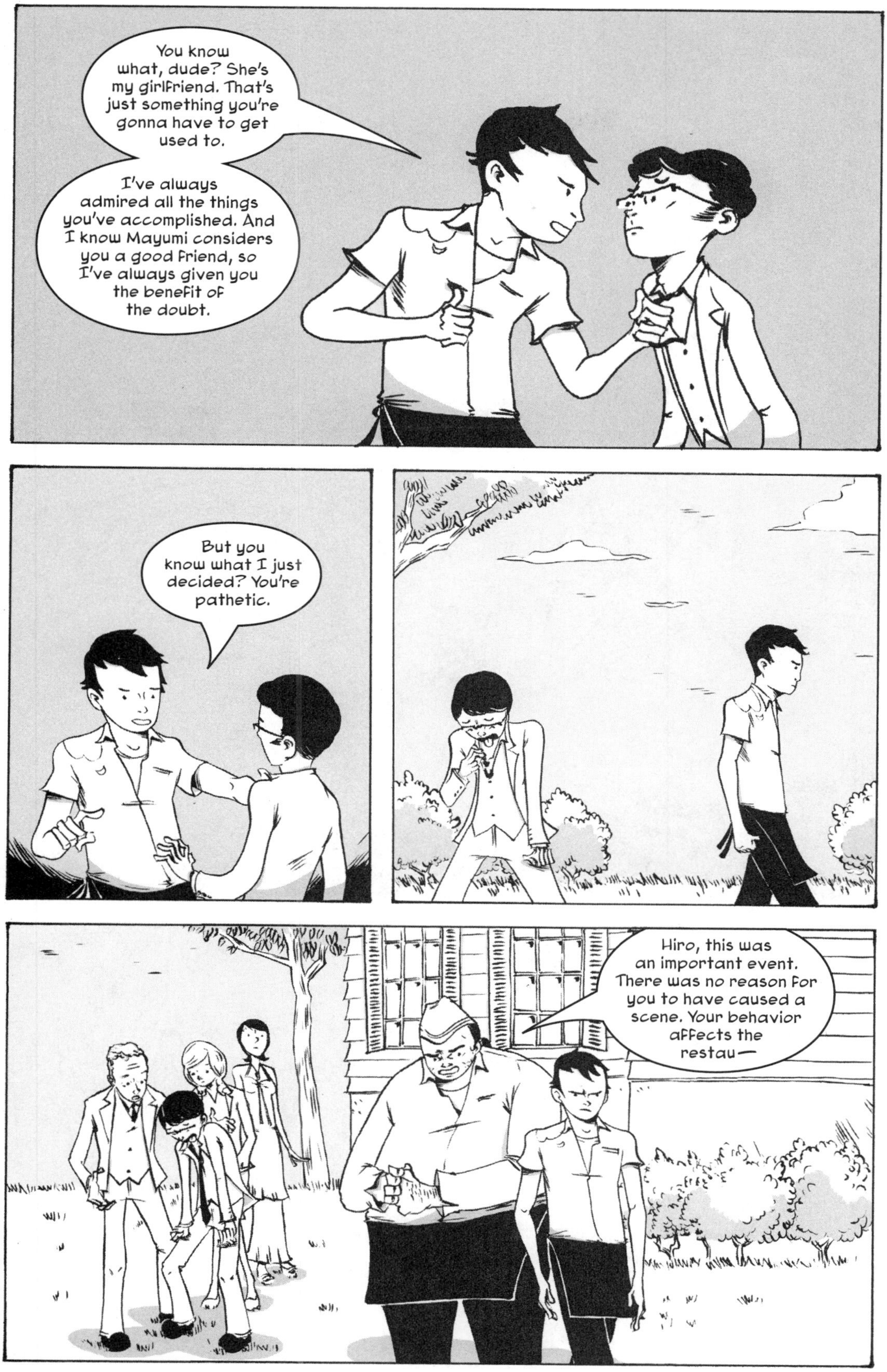
You know what, dude? She's my girlfriend. That's just something you're gonna have to get used to.
I've always admired all the things you've accomplished. And I know Mayumi considers you a good friend, so I've always given you the benefit of the doubt.
But you know what I just decided? You're pathetic.
Hiro, this was an important event. There was no reason for you to have caused a scene. Your behavior affects the restau—

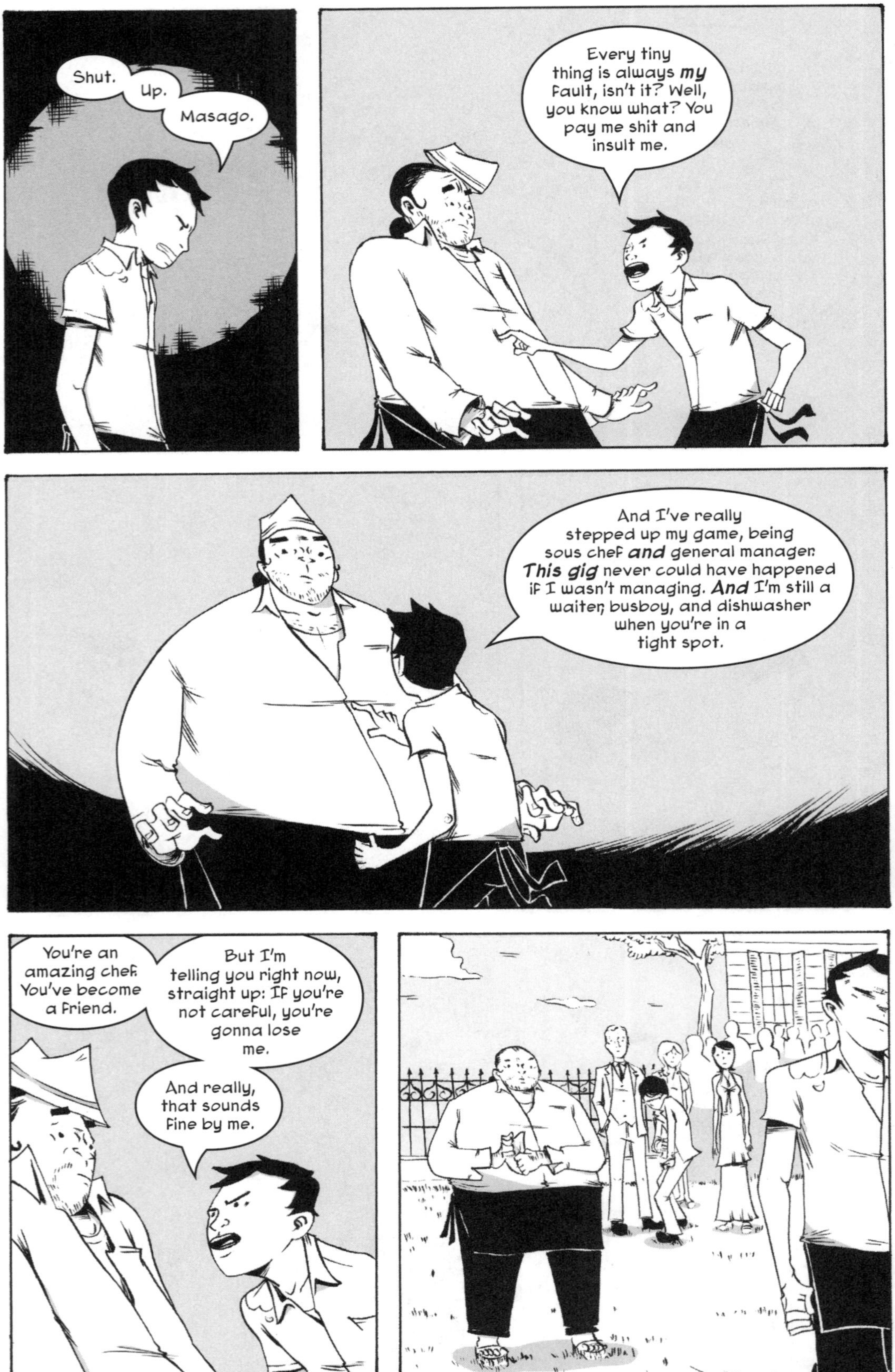
Shut.
Up.
Masago.
Every tiny thing is always my fault, isn't it? Well, you know what? You pay me shit and insult me.
And I've really stepped up my game, being sous chef and general manager. This gig never could have happened if I wasn't managing. And I'm still a waiter, busboy, and dishwasher when you're in a tight spot.
You're an amazing chef. You've become a friend.
But I'm telling you right now, straight up: If you're not careful, you're gonna lose me.
And really, that sounds fine by me.

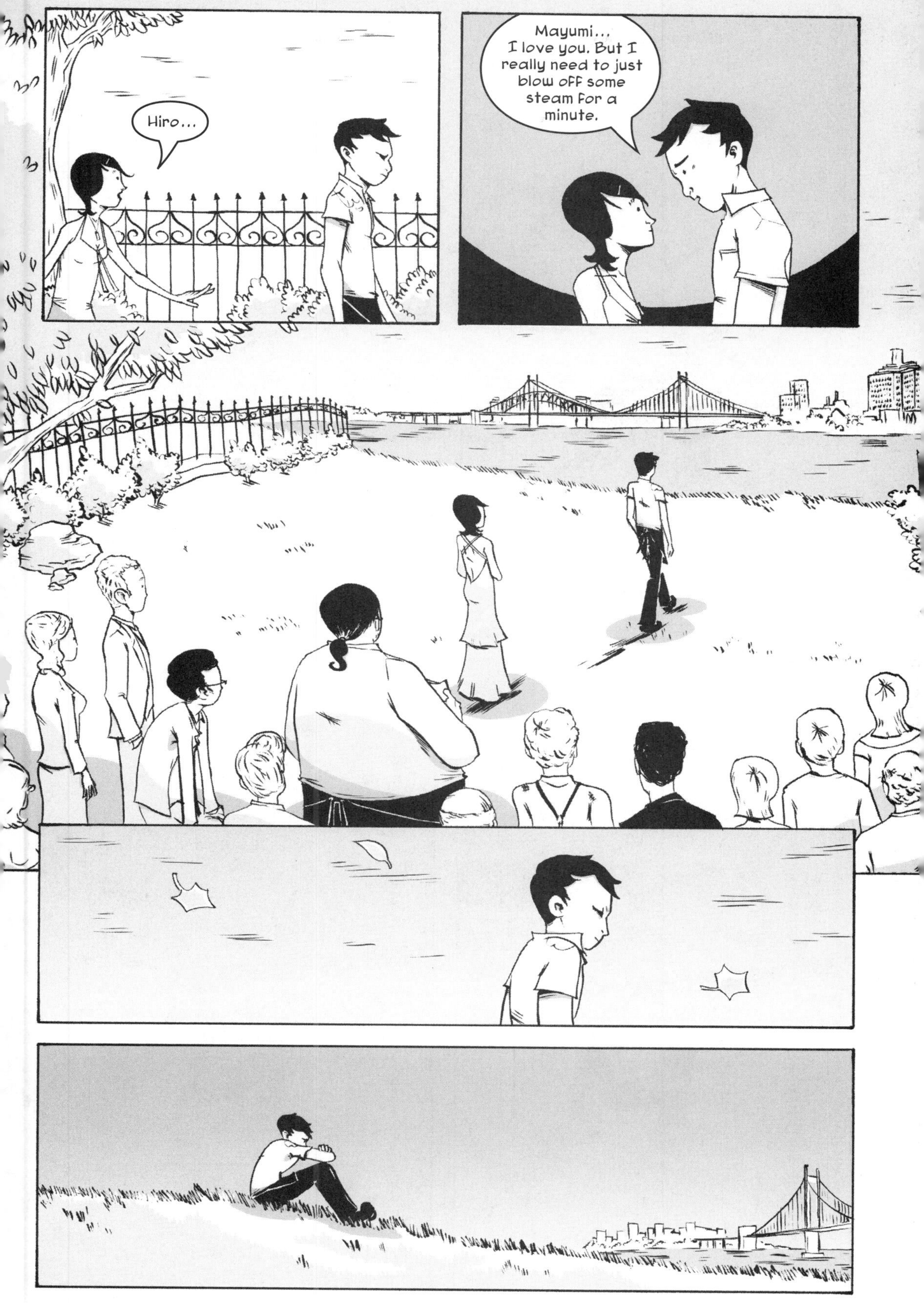
Hiro...
Mayumi... I love you. But I really need to just blow off some steam for a minute.

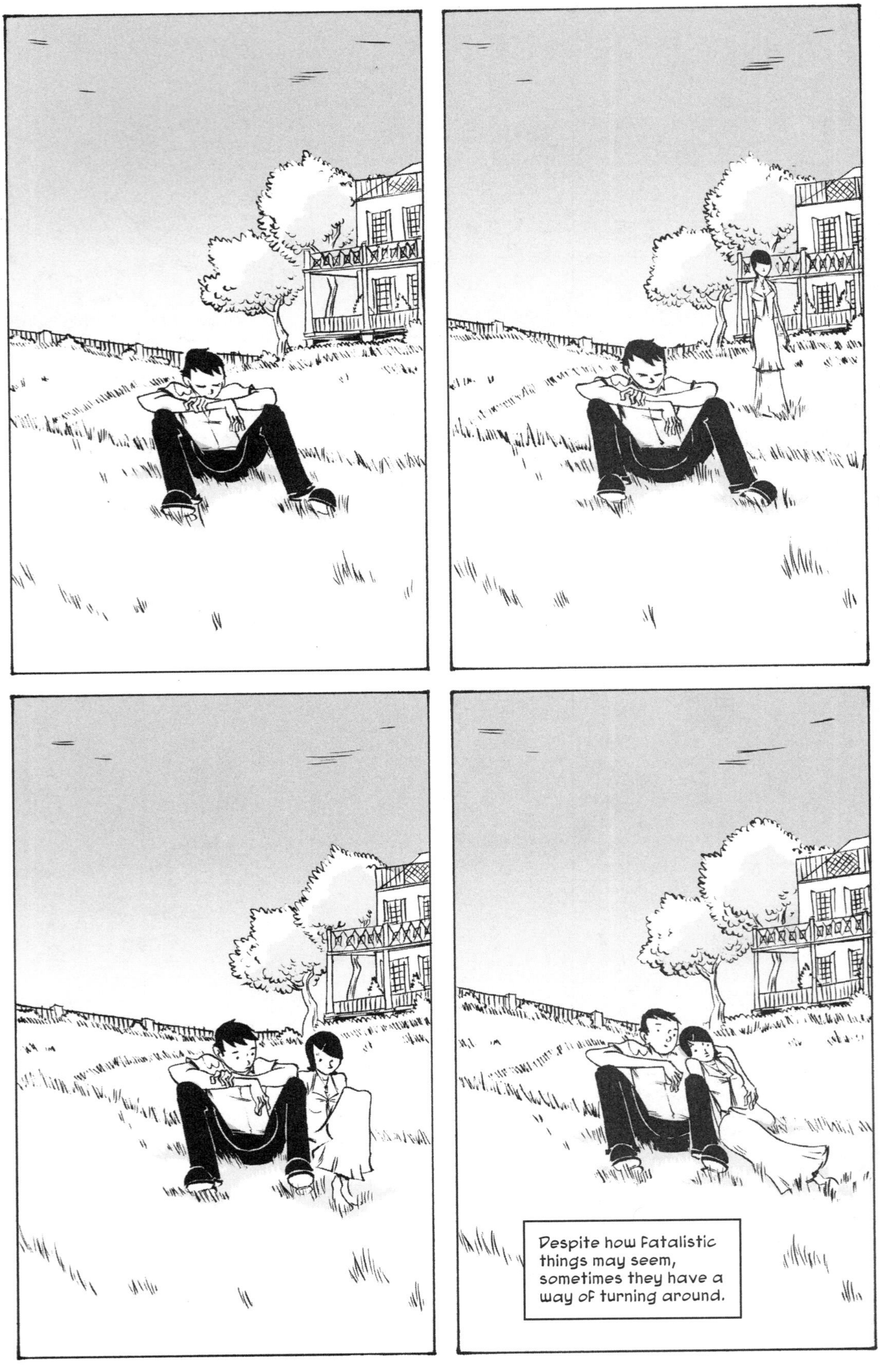
Despite how fatalistic things may seem, sometimes they have a way of turning around.

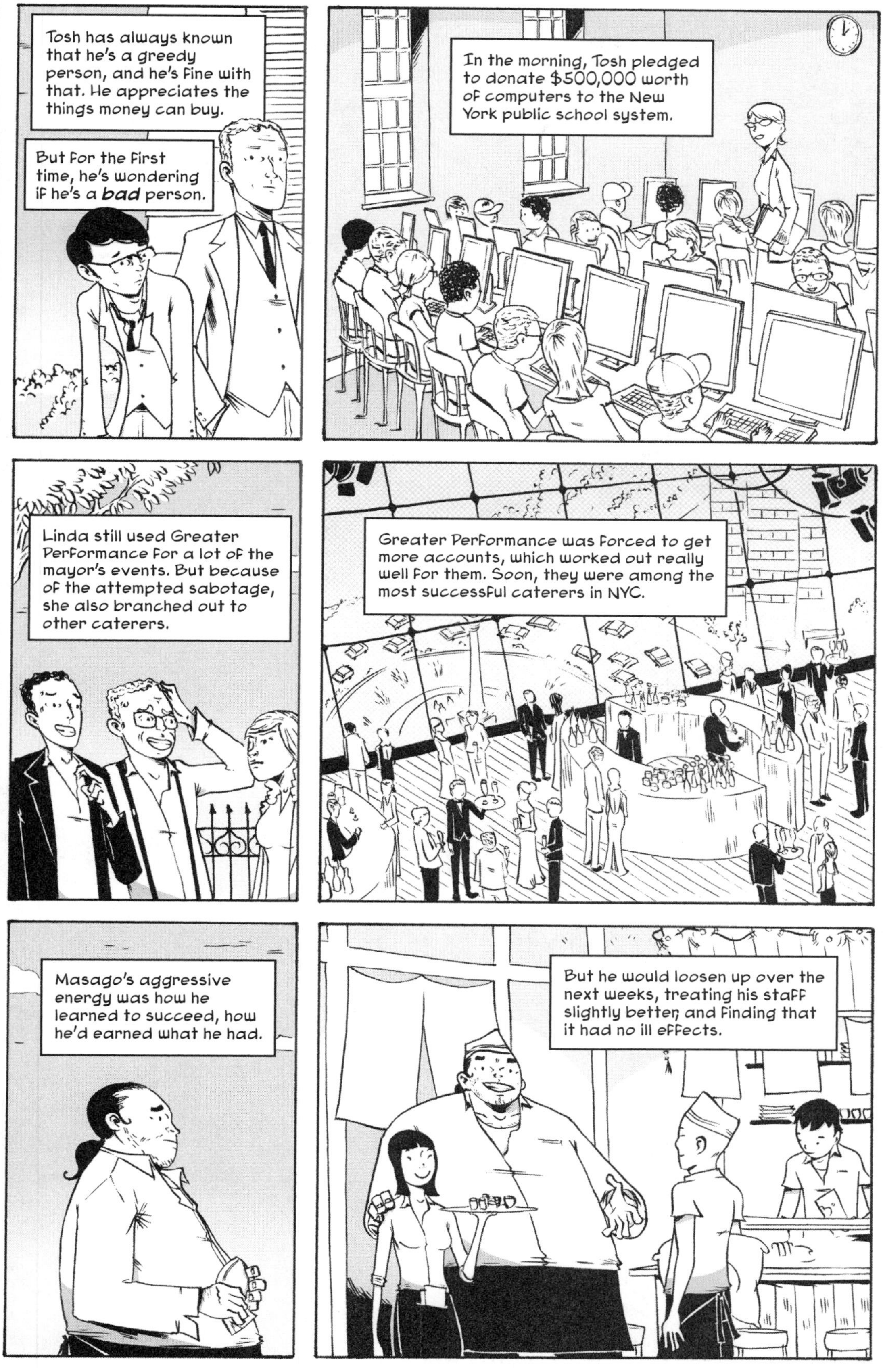
Tosh has always known that he's a greedy person, and he's fine with that. He appreciates the things money can buy.
But for the first time, he's wondering if he's a **bad** person.
In the morning, Tosh pledged to donate $500,000 worth of computers to the New York public school system.
Linda still used Greater Performance for a lot of the mayor's events. But because of the attempted sabotage, she also branched out to other caterers.
Greater Performance was forced to get more accounts, which worked out really well for them. Soon, they were among the most successful caterers in NYC.
Masago's aggressive energy was how he learned to succeed, how he'd earned what he had.
But he would loosen up over the next weeks, treating his staff slightly better, and finding that it had no ill effects.

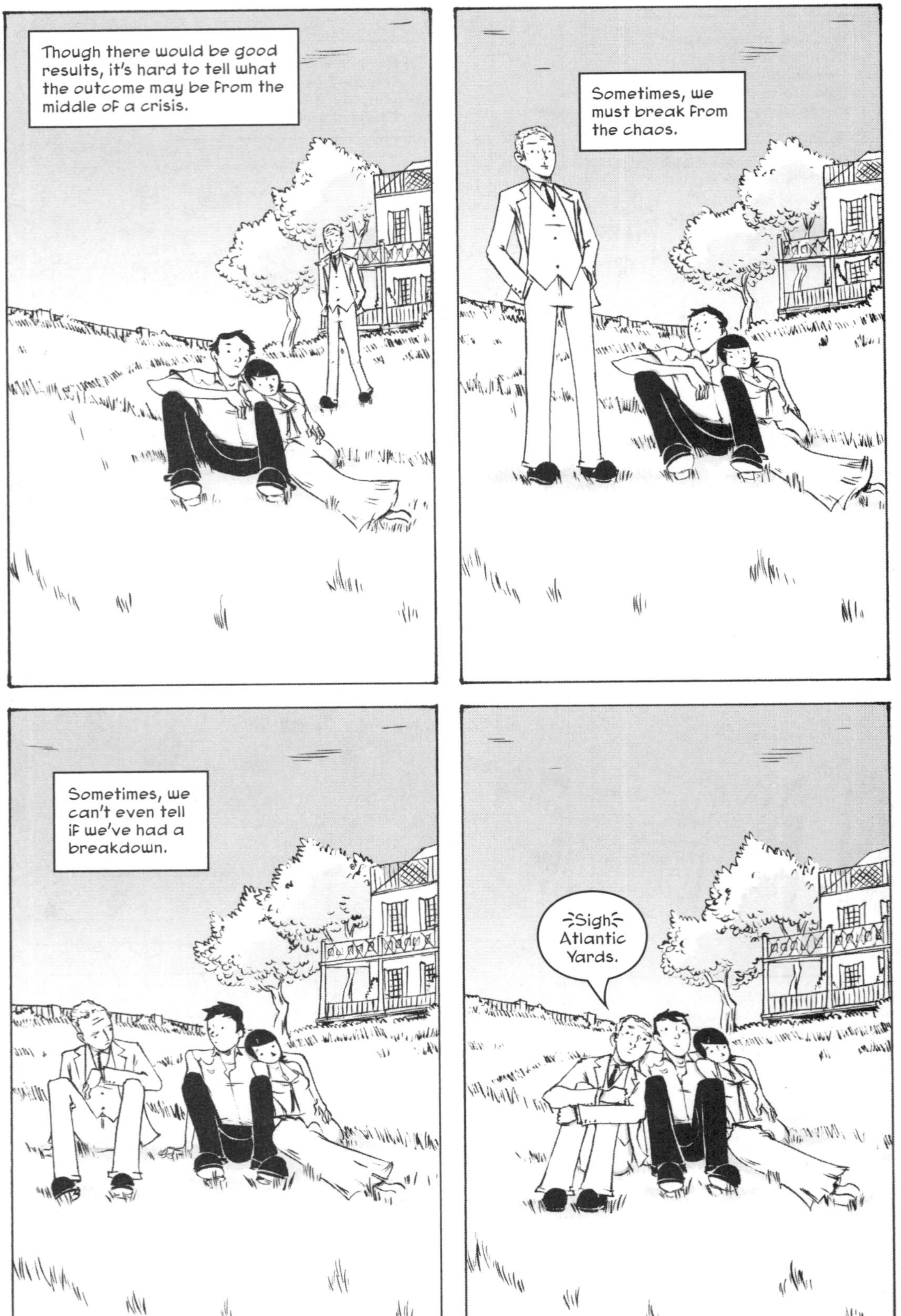
Though there would be good results, it's hard to tell what the outcome may be from the middle of a crisis.
Sometimes, we must break from the chaos.
Sometimes, we can't even tell if we've had a breakdown.
Sigh
Atlantic Yards.

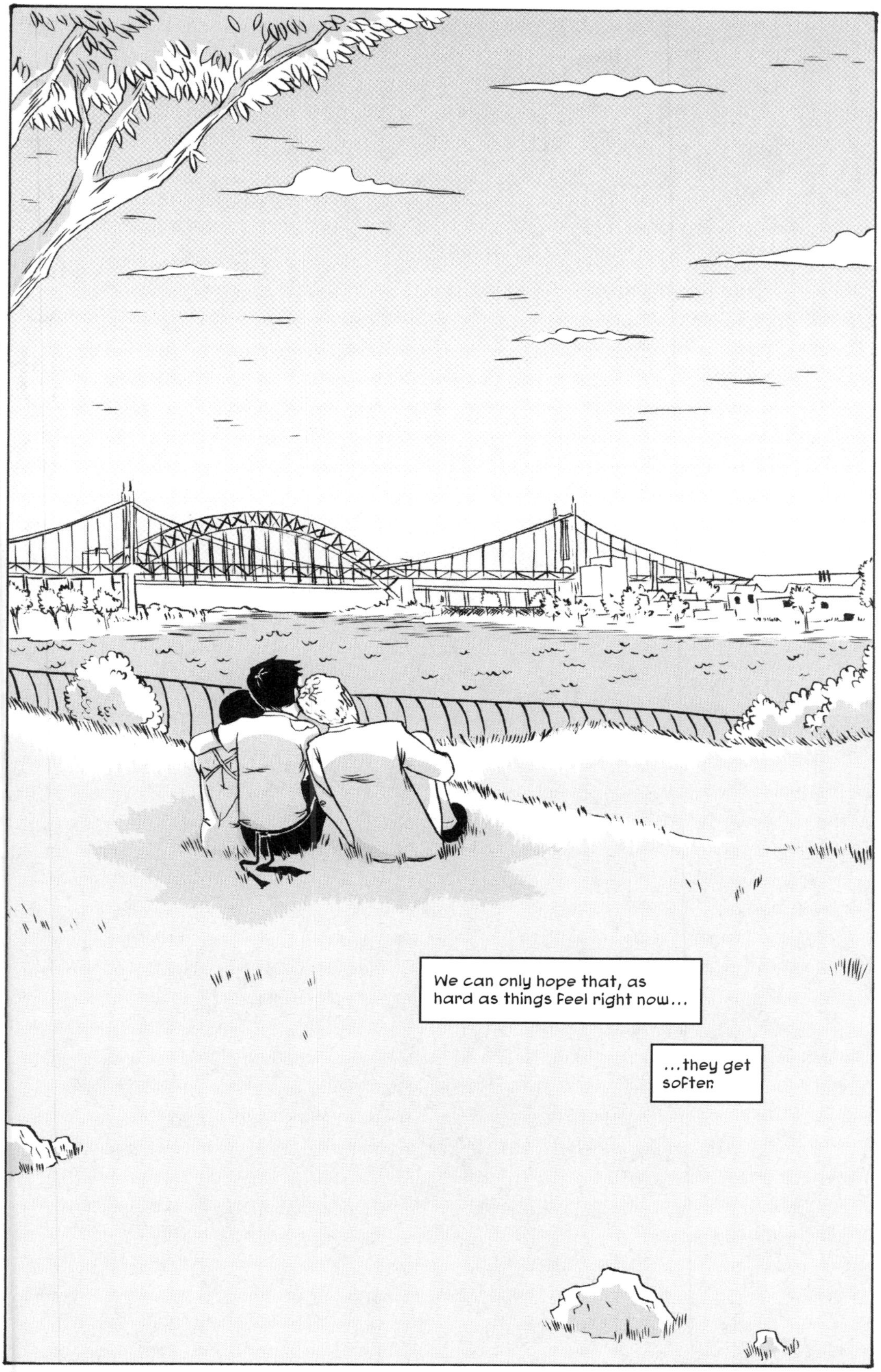
We can only hope that, as hard as things feel right now...
...they get softer.

こきゅうけい 3

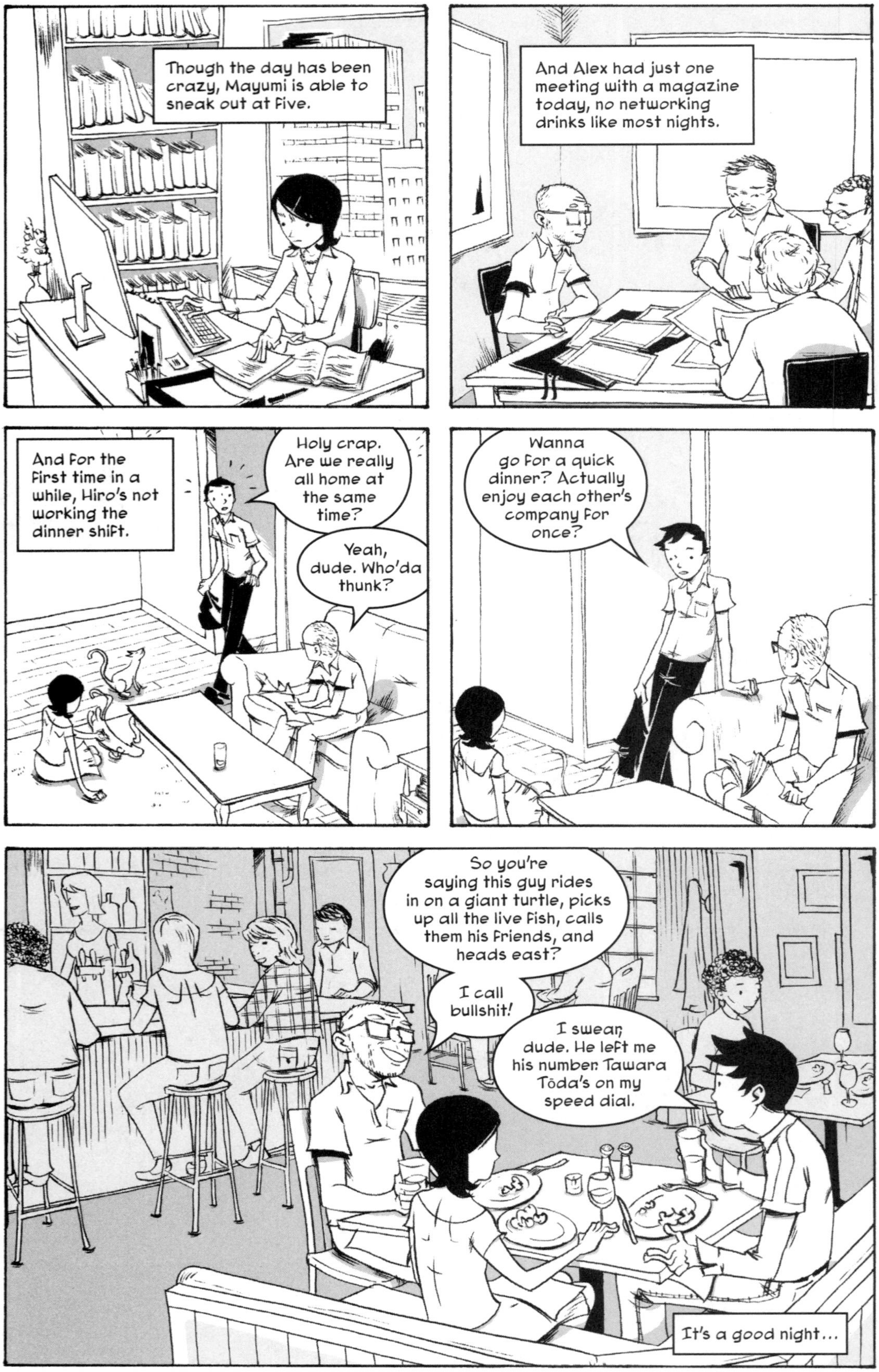
Though the day has been crazy, Mayumi is able to sneak out at five.
And Alex had just one meeting with a magazine today, no networking drinks like most nights.
And for the first time in a while, Hiro's not working the dinner shift.
Holy crap. Are we really all home at the same time?
Yeah, dude. Who'da thunk?
Wanna go for a quick dinner? Actually enjoy each other's company for once?
So you're saying this guy rides in on a giant turtle, picks up all the live fish, calls them his friends, and heads east?
I call bullshit!
I swear, dude. He left me his number. Tawara Tōda's on my speed dial.
It's a good night...

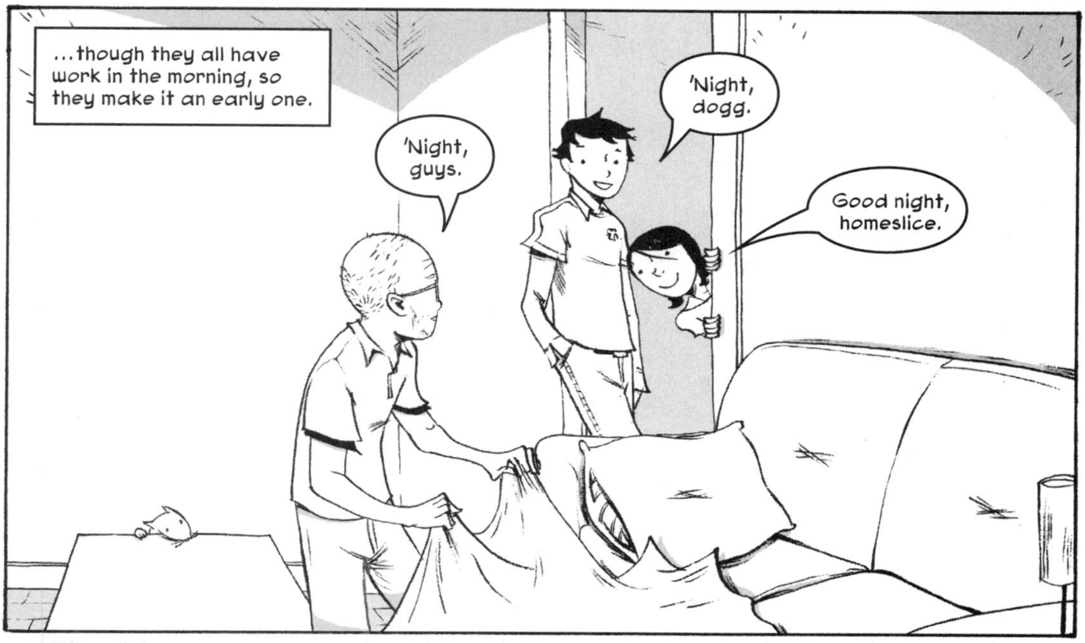
...though they all have work in the morning, so they make it an early one.
'Night, guys.
'Night, dogg.
Good night, homeslice.

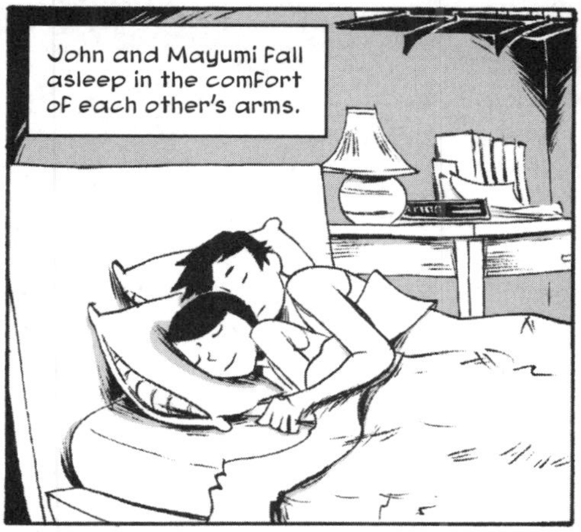
John and Mayumi fall asleep in the comfort of each other's arms.

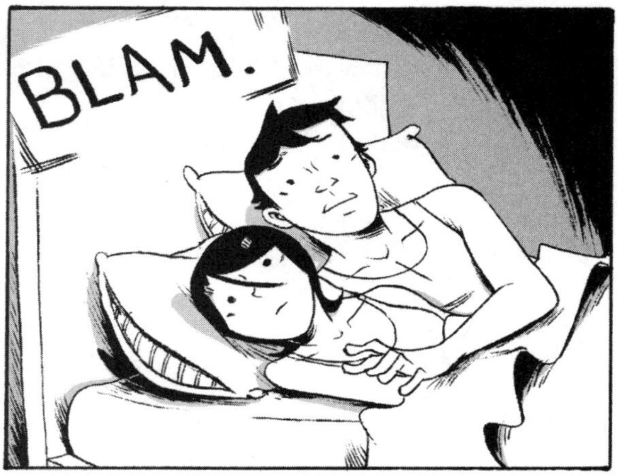
BLAM.

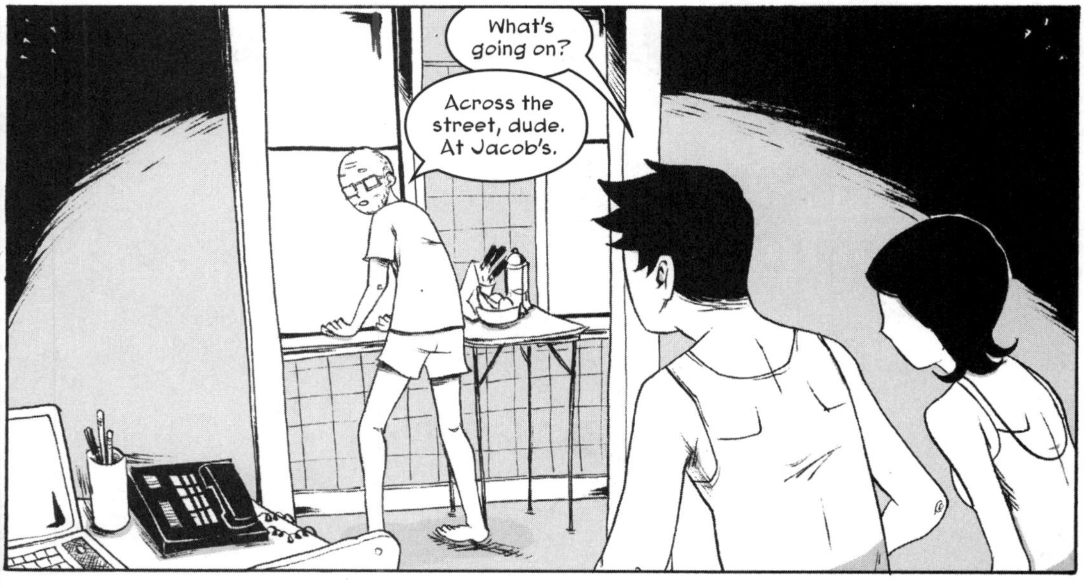
What's going on?
Across the street, dude. At Jacob's.

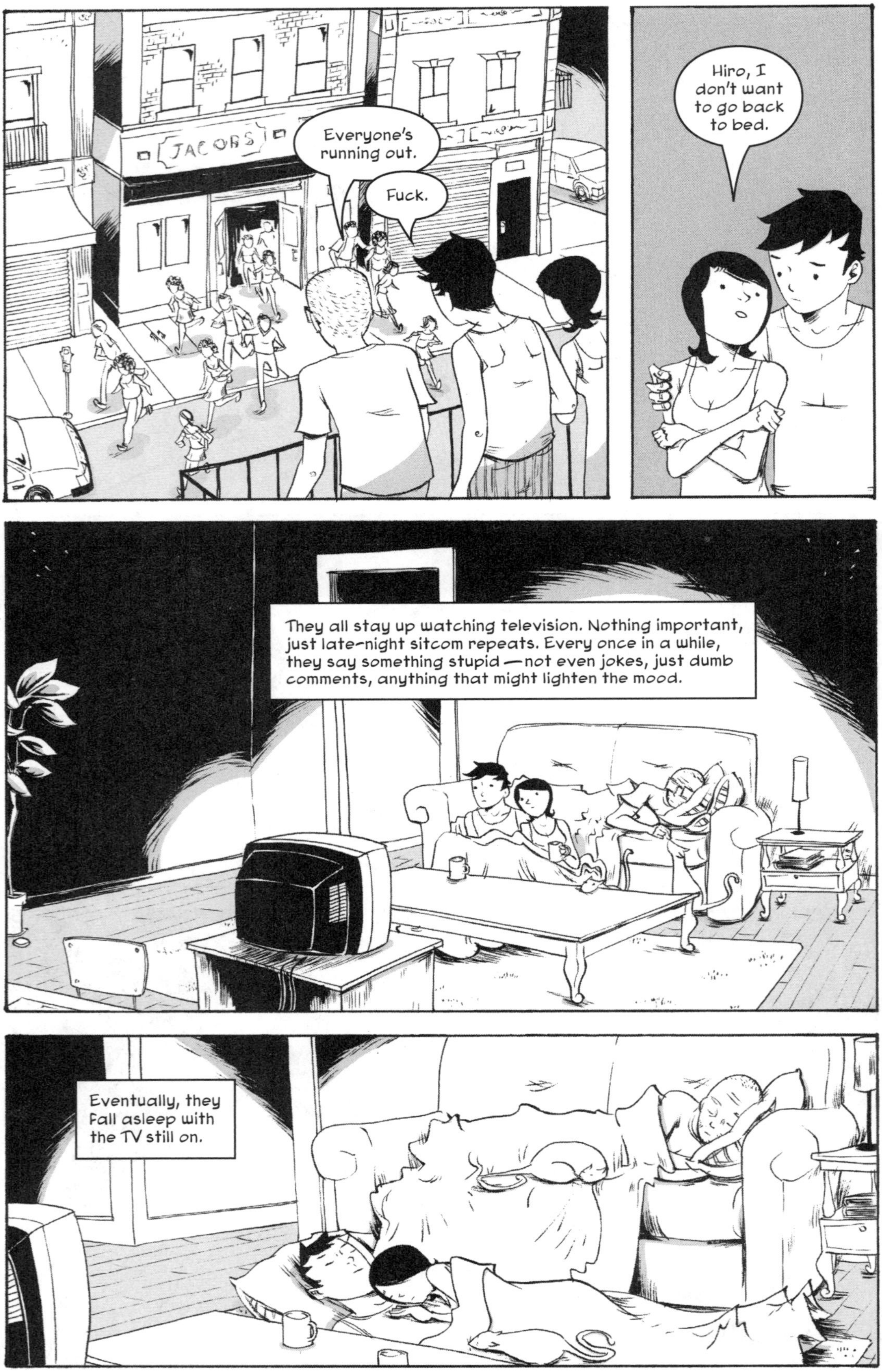
JACOBS
Everyone's running out.
Fuck.
Hiro, I don't want to go back to bed.
They all stay up watching television. Nothing important, just late-night sitcom repeats. Every once in a while, they say something stupid—not even jokes, just dumb comments, anything that might lighten the mood.
Eventually, they fall asleep with the TV still on.

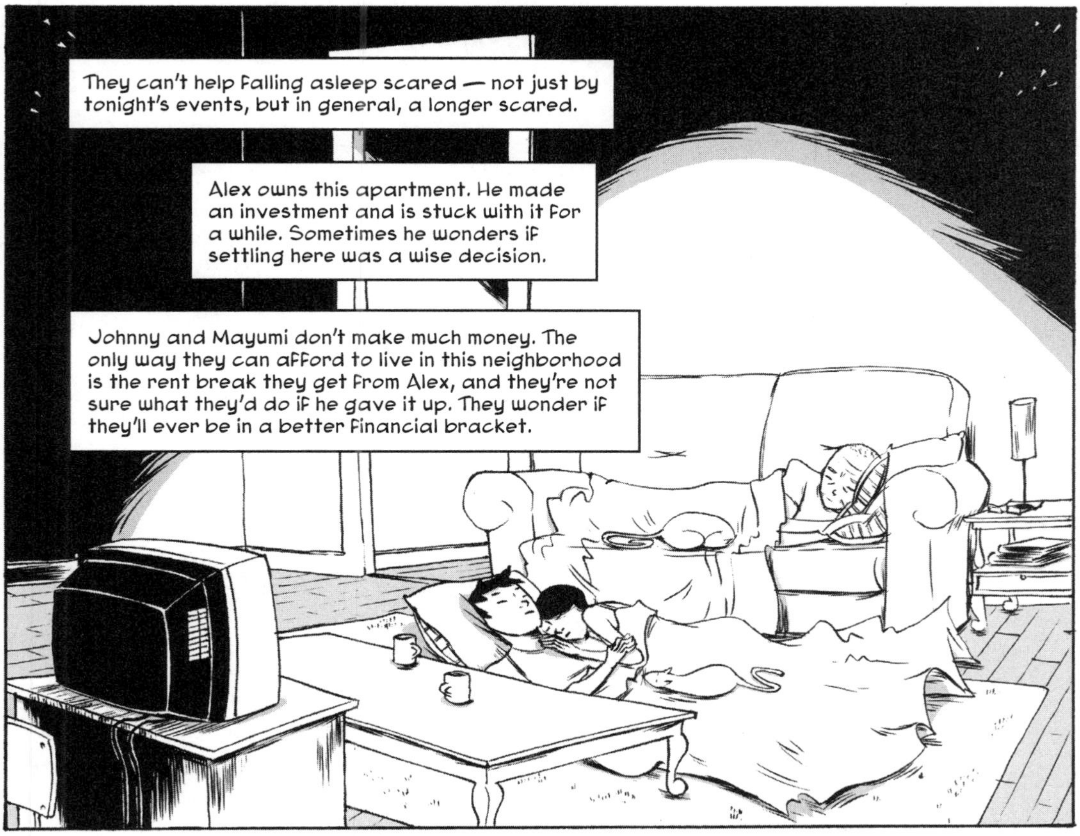
They can't help falling asleep scared — not just by tonight's events, but in general, a longer scared.
Alex owns this apartment. He made an investment and is stuck with it for a while. Sometimes he wonders if settling here was a wise decision.
Johnny and Mayumi don't make much money. The only way they can afford to live in this neighborhood is the rent break they get from Alex, and they're not sure what they'd do if he gave it up. They wonder if they'll ever be in a better financial bracket.

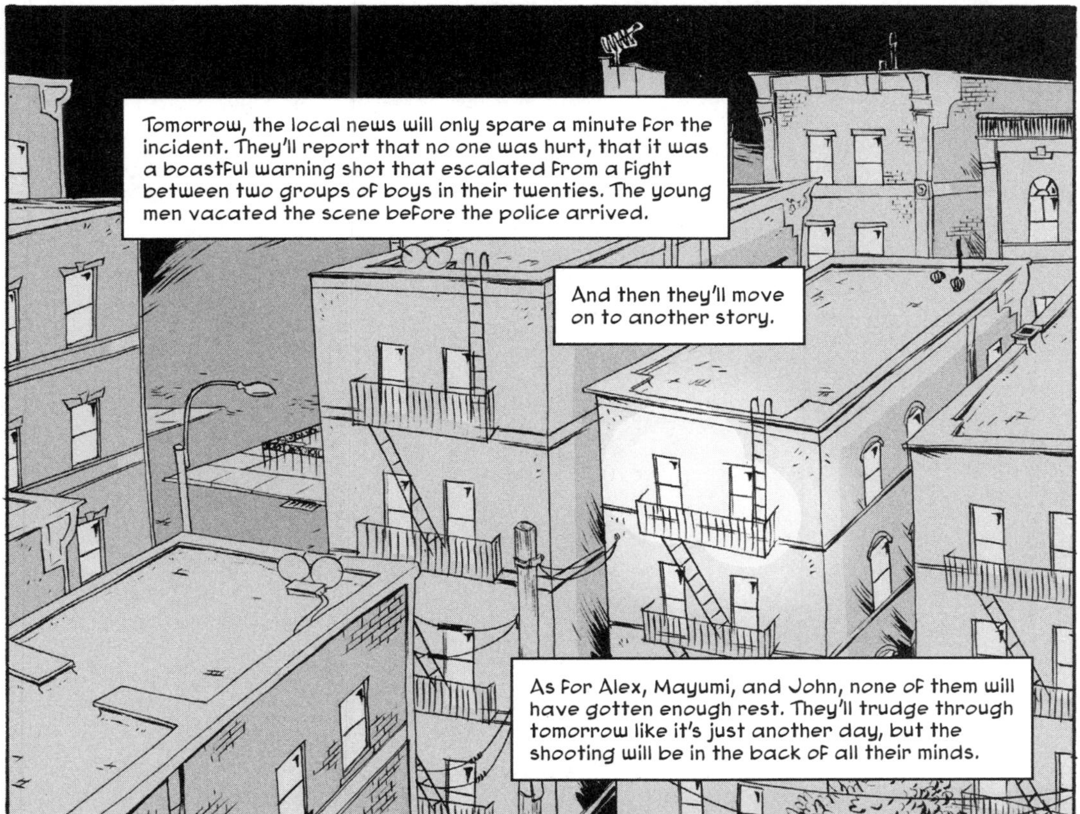
Tomorrow, the local news will only spare a minute for the incident. They'll report that no one was hurt, that it was a boastful warning shot that escalated from a fight between two groups of boys in their twenties. The young men vacated the scene before the police arrived.
And then they'll move on to another story.
As for Alex, Mayumi, and John, none of them will have gotten enough rest. They'll trudge through tomorrow like it's just another day, but the shooting will be in the back of all their minds.

かわにつれていって

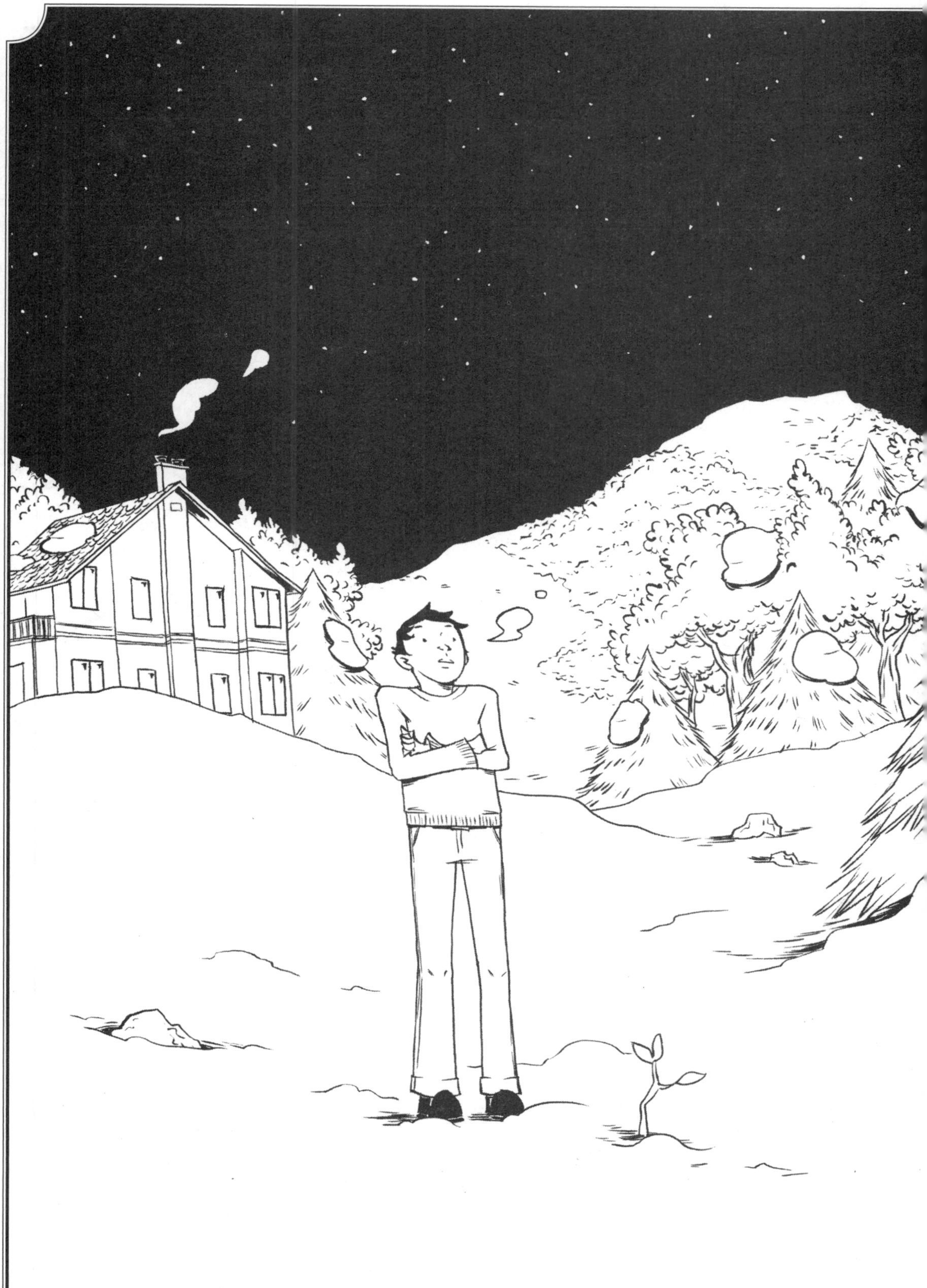

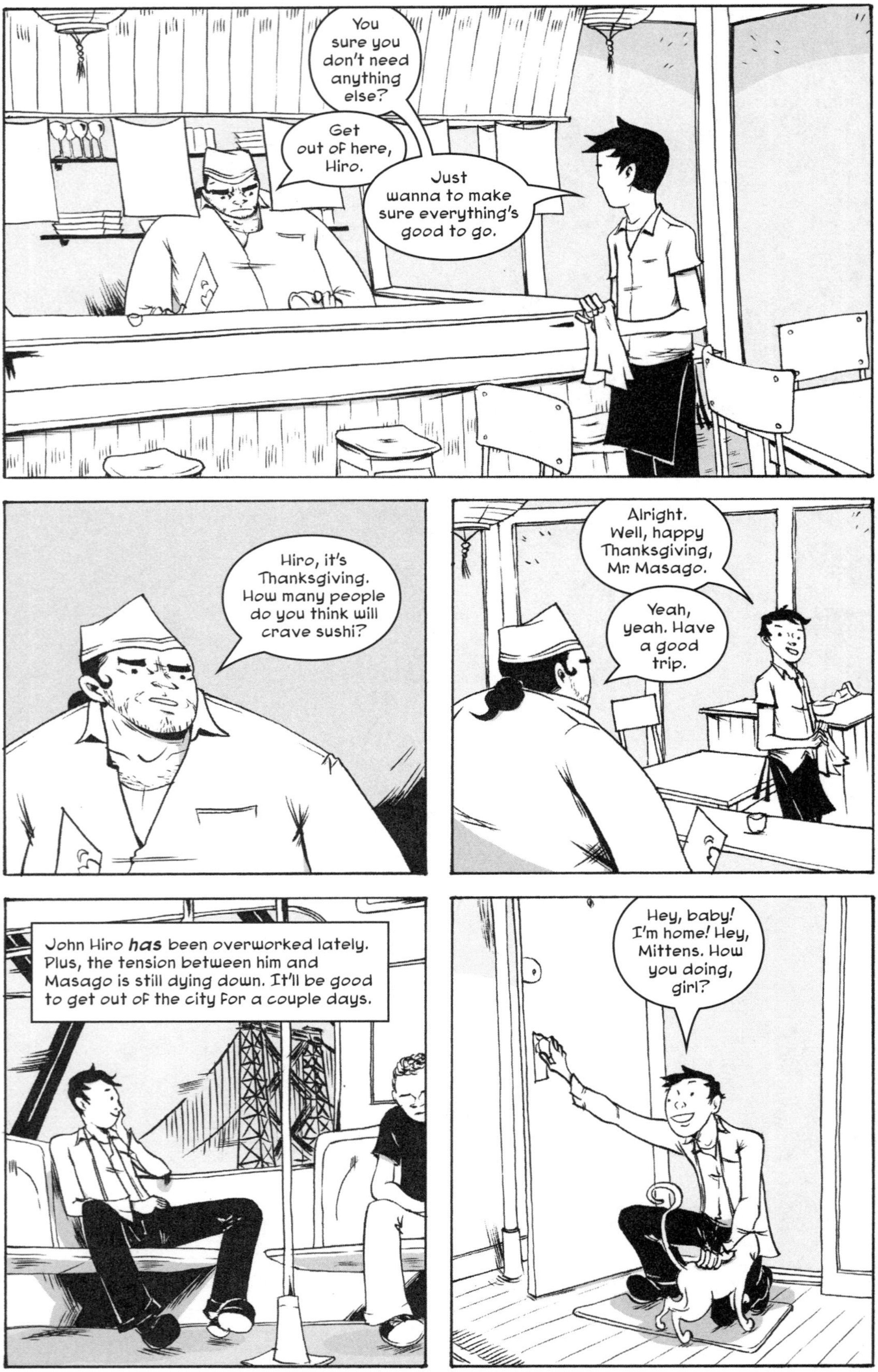
You sure you don't need anything else?
Get out of here, Hiro.
Just wanna to make sure everything's good to go.
Hiro, it's Thanksgiving. How many people do you think will crave sushi?
Alright. Well, happy Thanksgiving, Mr. Masago.
Yeah, yeah. Have a good trip.
John Hiro **has** been overworked lately. Plus, the tension between him and Masago is still dying down. It'll be good to get out of the city for a couple days.
Hey, baby! I'm home! Hey, Mittens. How you doing, girl?

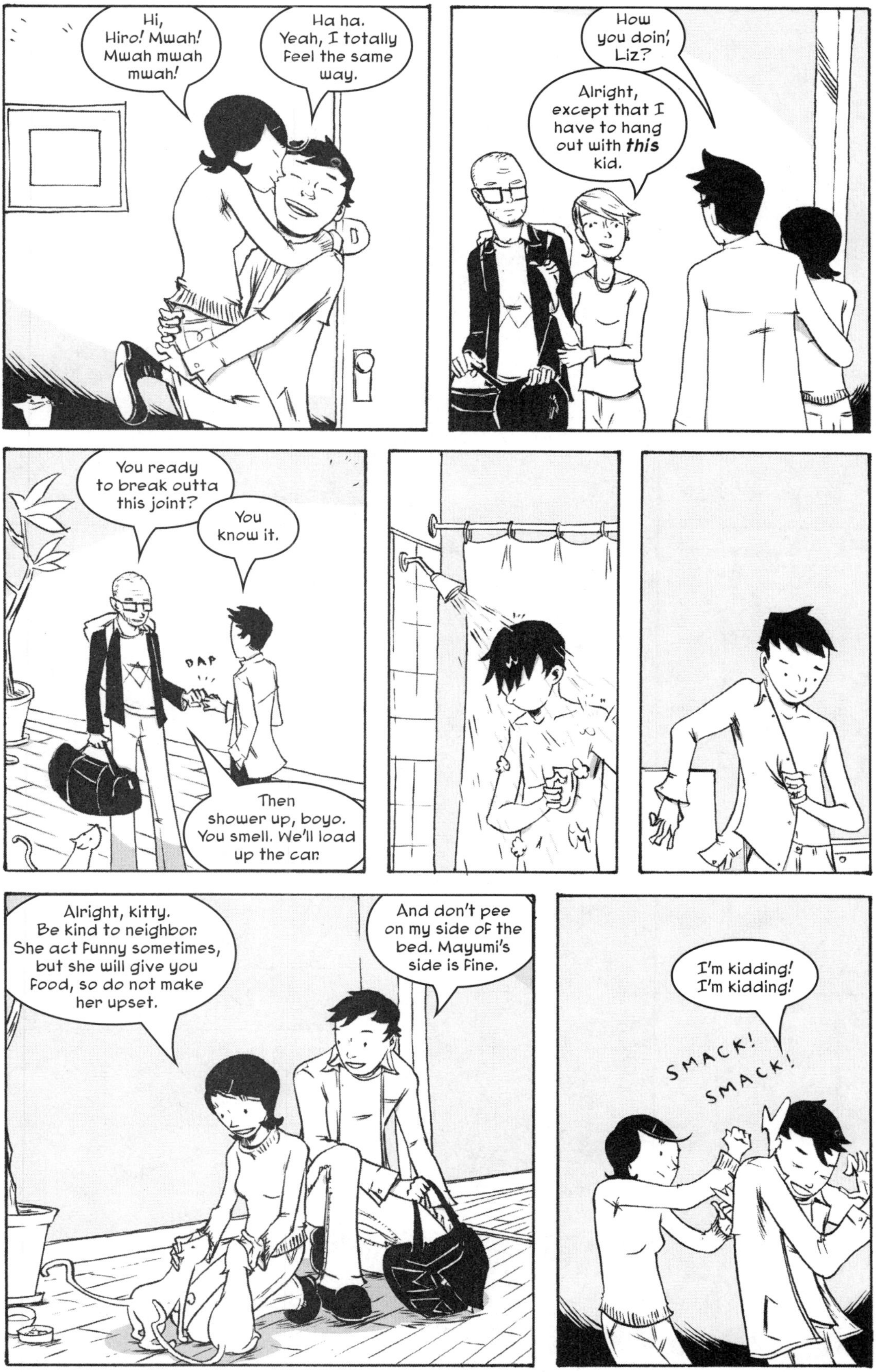
Hi, Hiro! Mwah! Mwah mwah mwah!
Ha ha. Yeah, I totally feel the same way.
How you doin', Liz?
Alright, except that I have to hang out with **this** kid.
You ready to break outta this joint?
You know it.
DAP
Then shower up, boyo. You smell. We'll load up the car.
Alright, kitty. Be kind to neighbor. She act funny sometimes, but she will give you food, so do not make her upset.
And don't pee on my side of the bed. Mayumi's side is fine.
I'm kidding! I'm kidding!
SMACK!
SMACK!

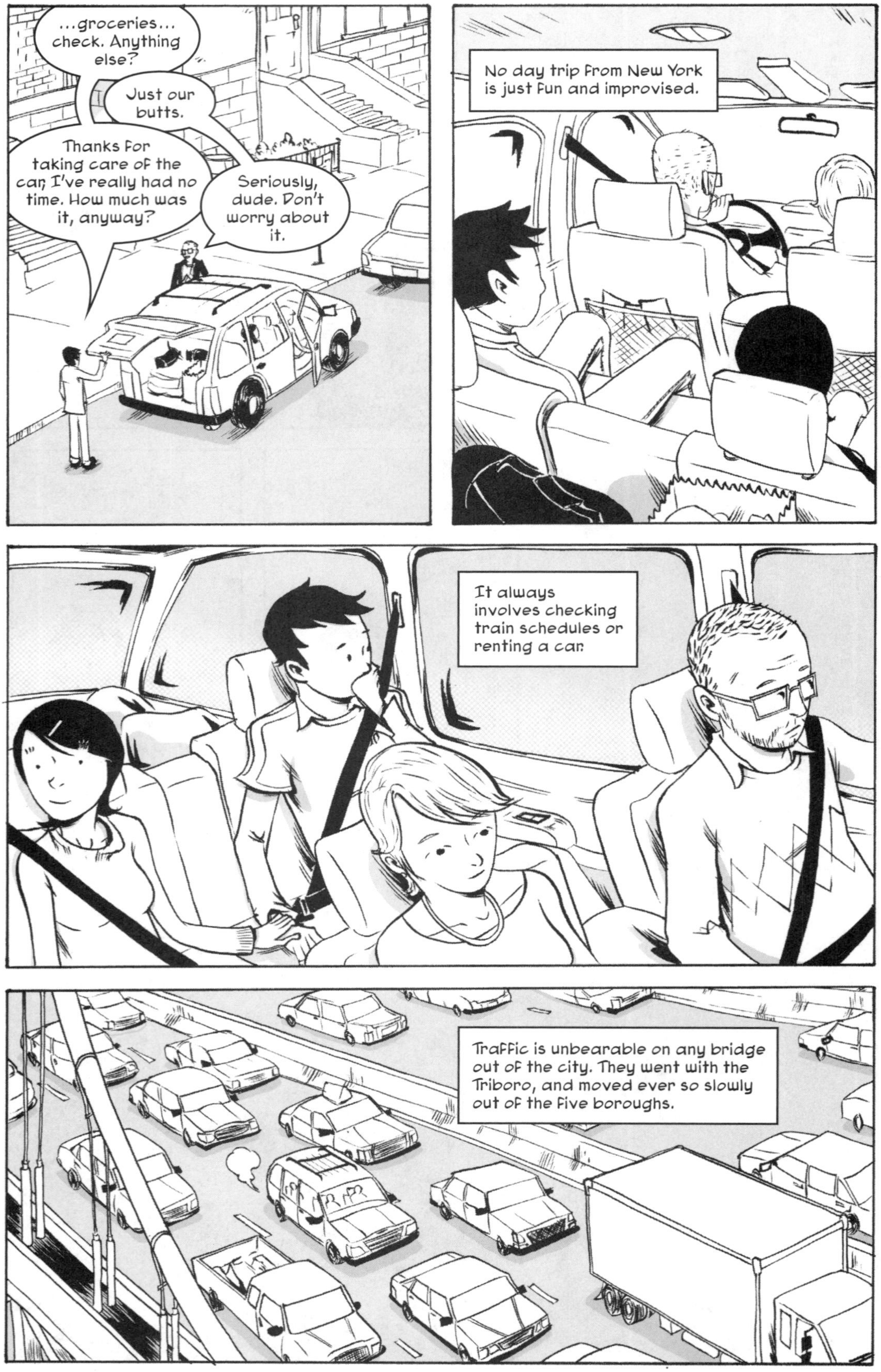
...groceries... check. Anything else?
Just our butts.
Thanks for taking care of the car, I've really had no time. How much was it, anyway?
Seriously, dude. Don't worry about it.
No day trip from New York is just fun and improvised.
It always involves checking train schedules or renting a car.
Traffic is unbearable on any bridge out of the city. They went with the Triboro, and moved ever so slowly out of the five boroughs.

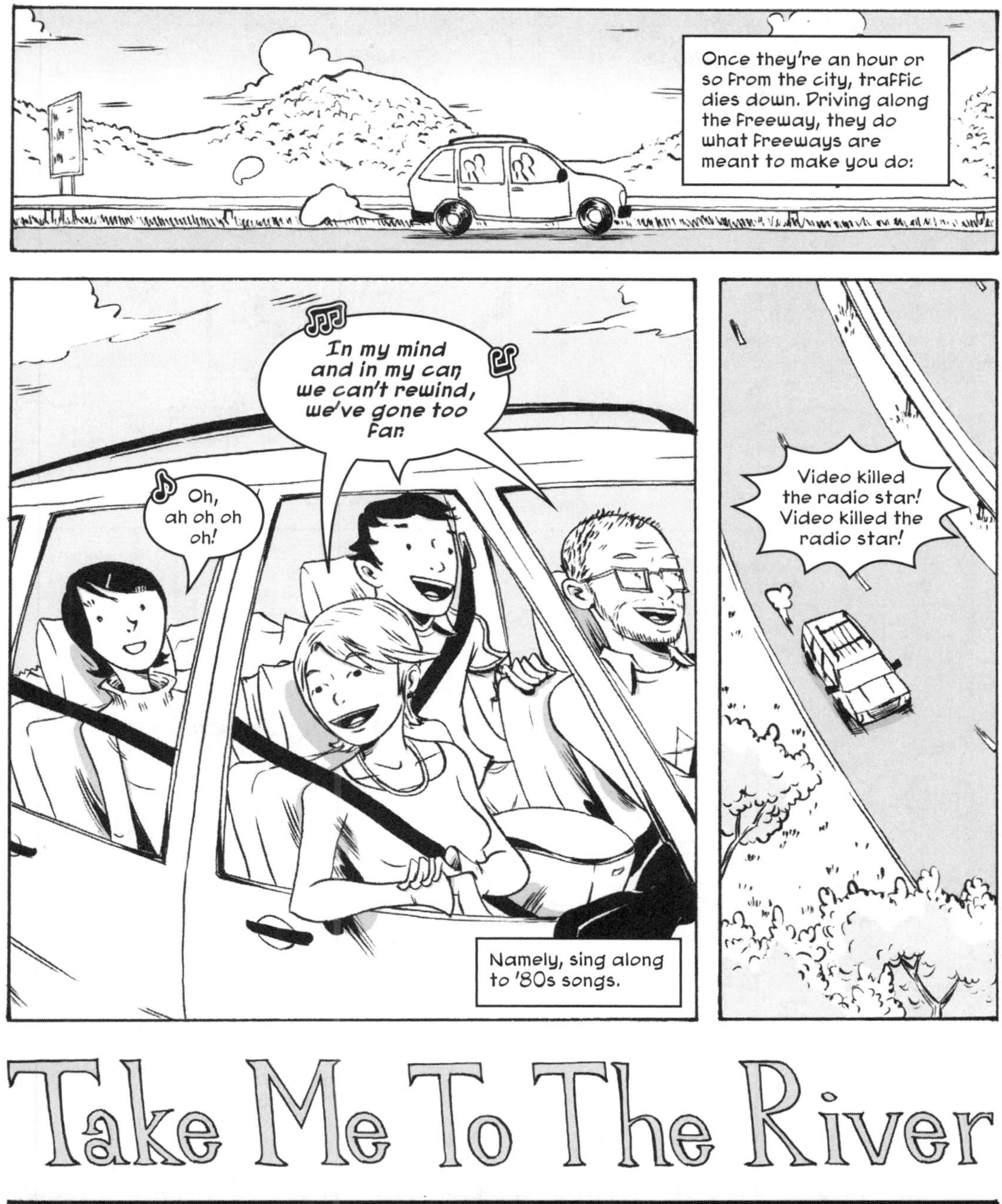
Once they're an hour or so from the city, traffic dies down. Driving along the freeway, they do what freeways are meant to make you do:
In my mind and in my car, we can't rewind, we've gone too far.
Oh, ah oh oh oh!
Namely, sing along to '80s songs.
Video killed the radio star! Video killed the radio star!

Take Me To The River

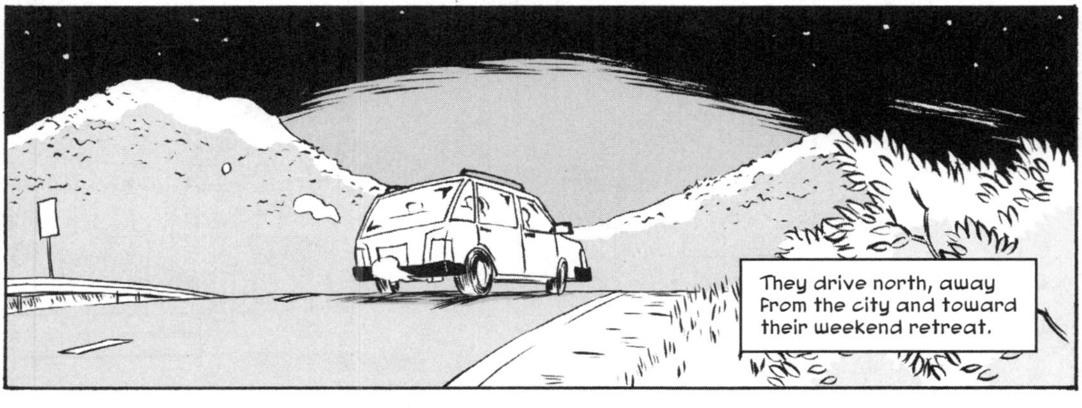
They drive north, away from the city and toward their weekend retreat.

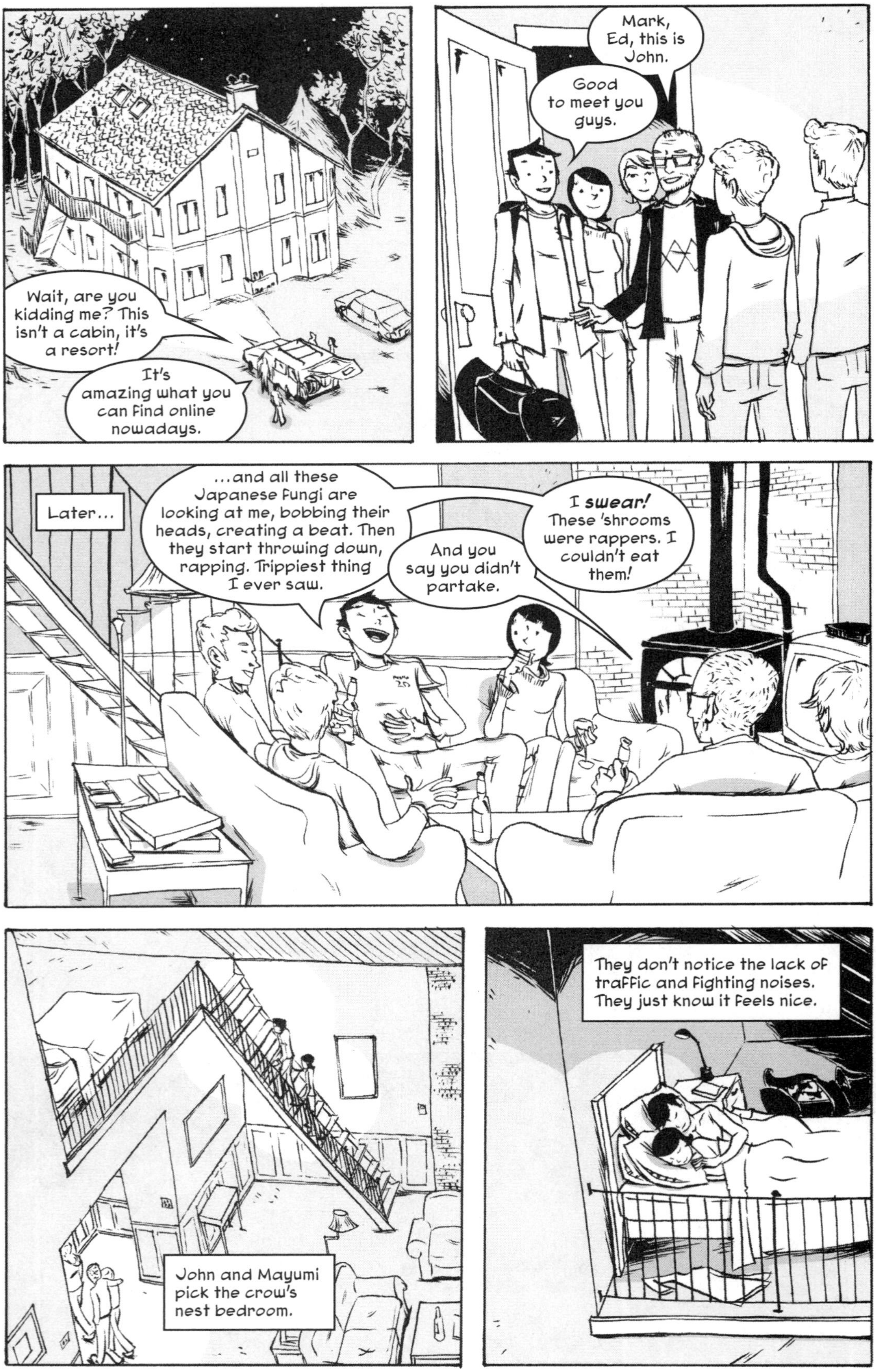
Wait, are you kidding me? This isn't a cabin, it's a resort!
It's amazing what you can find online nowadays.
Mark, Ed, this is John.
Good to meet you guys.
Later...
...and all these Japanese fungi are looking at me, bobbing their heads, creating a beat. Then they start throwing down, rapping. Trippiest thing I ever saw.
And you say you didn't partake.
I swear! These 'shrooms were rappers. I couldn't eat them!
John and Mayumi pick the crow's nest bedroom.
They don't notice the lack of traffic and fighting noises. They just know it feels nice.

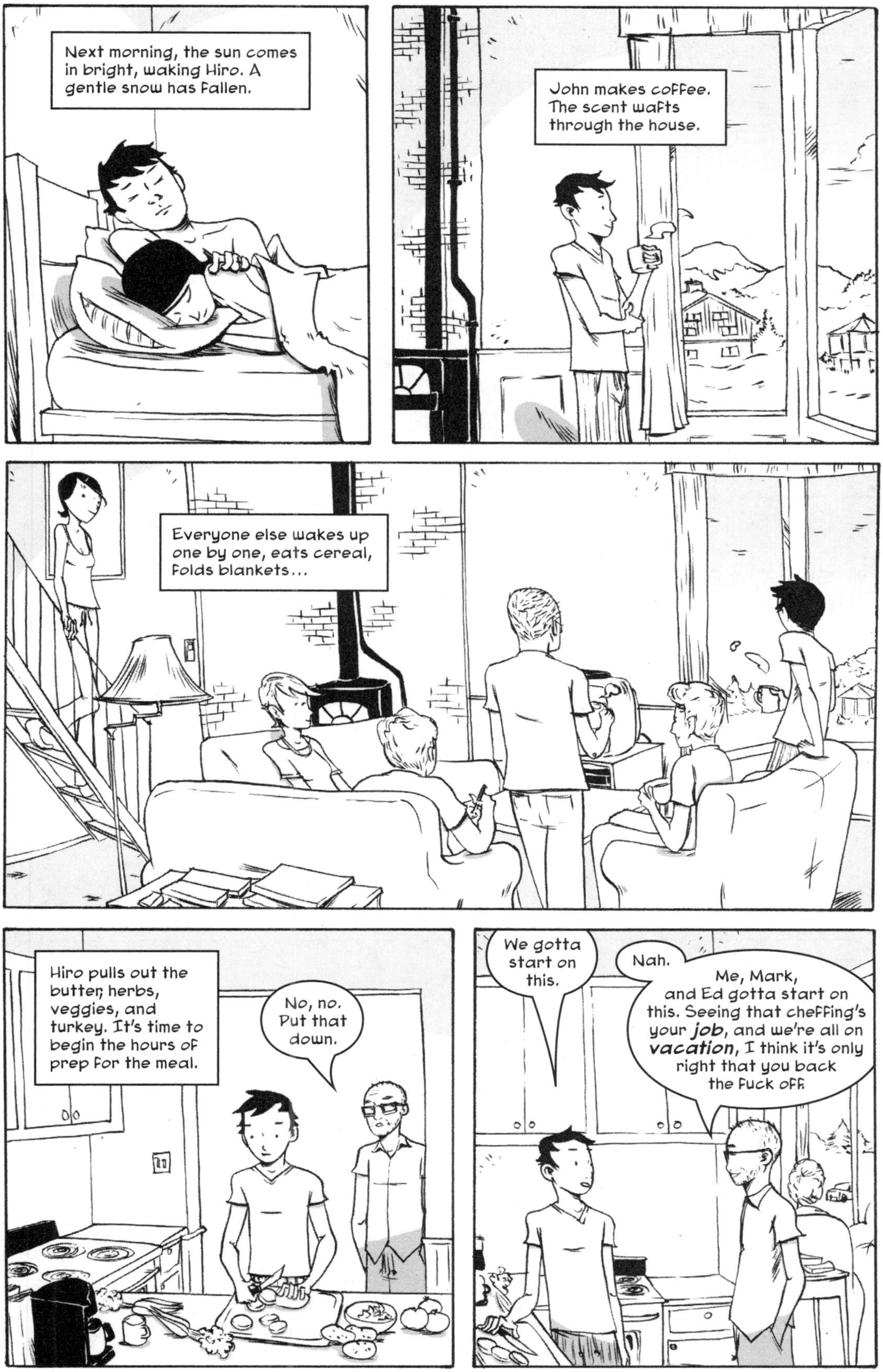
Next morning, the sun comes in bright, waking Hiro. A gentle snow has fallen.
John makes coffee. The scent wafts through the house.
Everyone else wakes up one by one, eats cereal, folds blankets…
Hiro pulls out the butter, herbs, veggies, and turkey. It's time to begin the hours of prep for the meal.
No, no. Put that down.
We gotta start on this.
Nah.
Me, Mark, and Ed gotta start on this. Seeing that cheffing's your job, and we're all on vacation, I think it's only right that you back the fuck off.

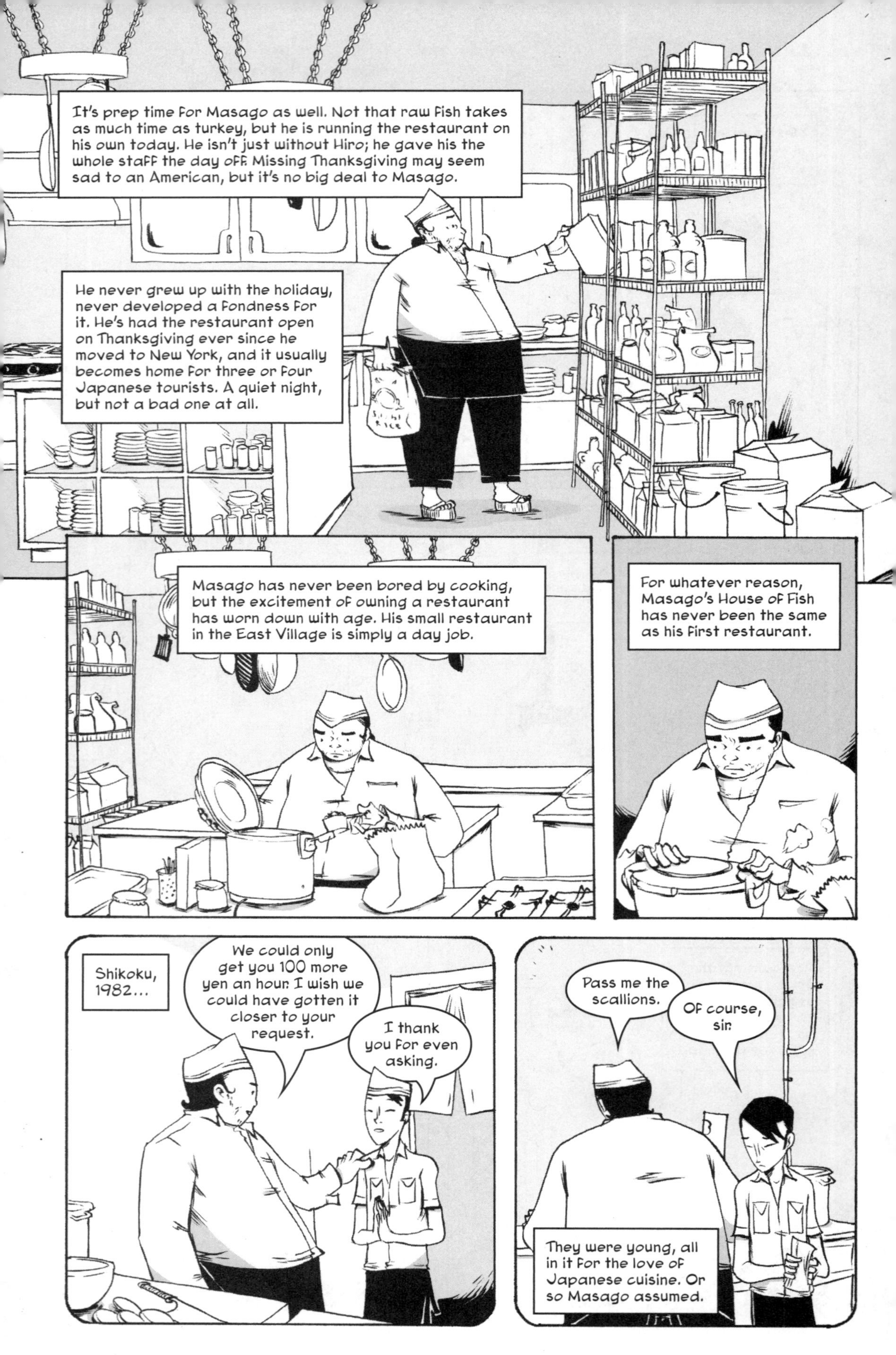
It's prep time for Masago as well. Not that raw fish takes as much time as turkey, but he is running the restaurant on his own today. He isn't just without Hiro; he gave his the whole staff the day off. Missing Thanksgiving may seem sad to an American, but it's no big deal to Masago.
He never grew up with the holiday, never developed a fondness for it. He's had the restaurant open on Thanksgiving ever since he moved to New York, and it usually becomes home for three or four Japanese tourists. A quiet night, but not a bad one at all.
Masago has never been bored by cooking, but the excitement of owning a restaurant has worn down with age. His small restaurant in the East Village is simply a day job.
For whatever reason, Masago's House of Fish has never been the same as his first restaurant.
Shikoku, 1982...
We could only get you 100 more yen an hour. I wish we could have gotten it closer to your request.
I thank you for even asking.
Pass me the scallions.
Of course, sir.
They were young, all in it for the love of Japanese cuisine. Or so Masago assumed.

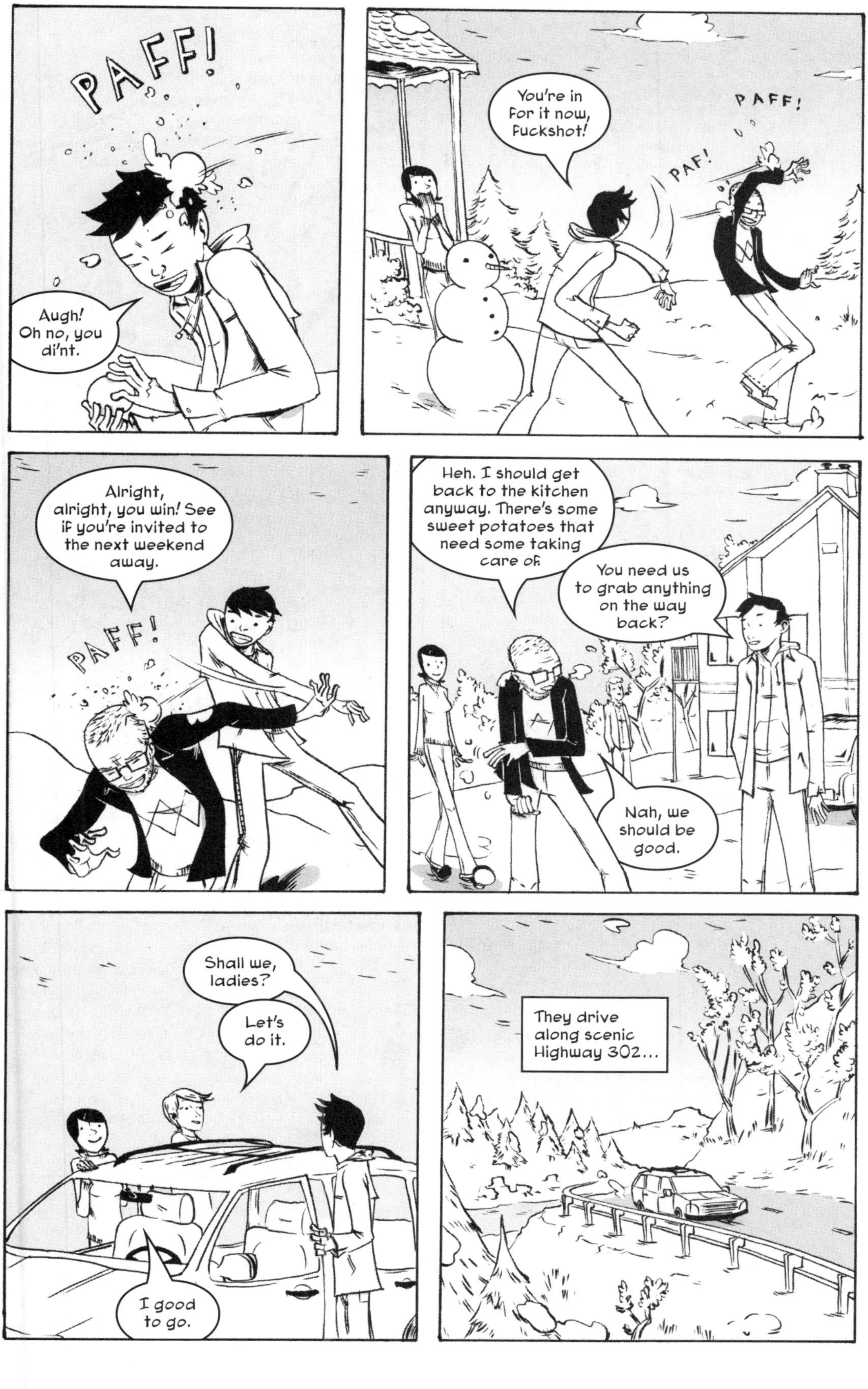
PAFF!
Augh! Oh no, you di'nt.
You're in for it now, Fuckshot!
PAF!
PAFF!
Alright, alright, you win! See if you're invited to the next weekend away.
PAFF!
Heh. I should get back to the kitchen anyway. There's some sweet potatoes that need some taking care of.
You need us to grab anything on the way back?
Nah, we should be good.
Shall we, ladies?
Let's do it.
I good to go.
They drive along scenic Highway 302...

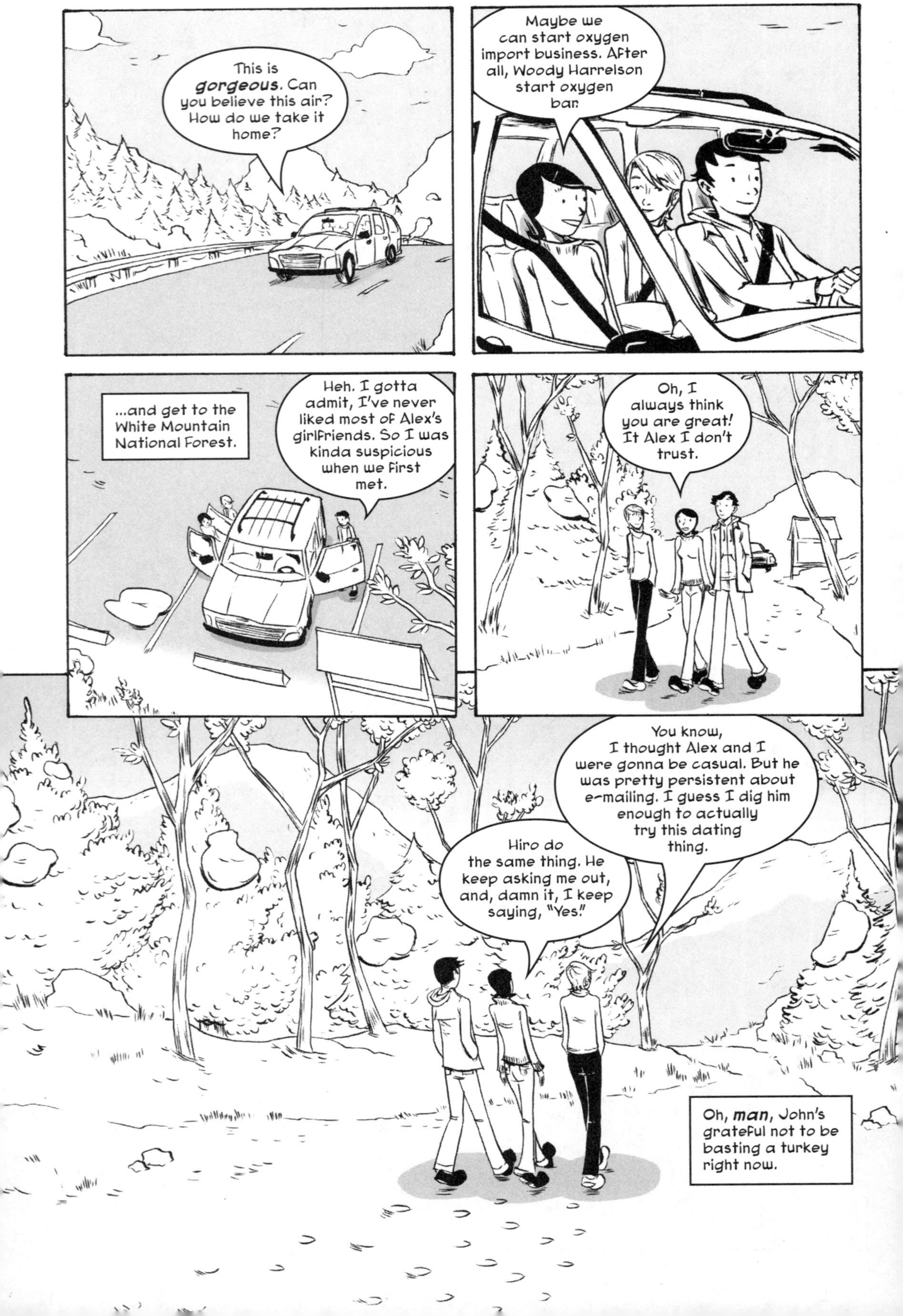
This is *gorgeous*. Can you believe this air? How do we take it home?
Maybe we can start oxygen import business. After all, Woody Harrelson start oxygen bar.
...and get to the White Mountain National Forest.
Heh. I gotta admit, I've never liked most of Alex's girlfriends. So I was kinda suspicious when we first met.
Oh, I always think you are great! It Alex I don't trust.
You know, I thought Alex and I were gonna be casual. But he was pretty persistent about e-mailing. I guess I dig him enough to actually try this dating thing.
Hiro do the same thing. He keep asking me out, and, damn it, I keep saying, "Yes."
Oh, *man*, John's grateful not to be basting a turkey right now.

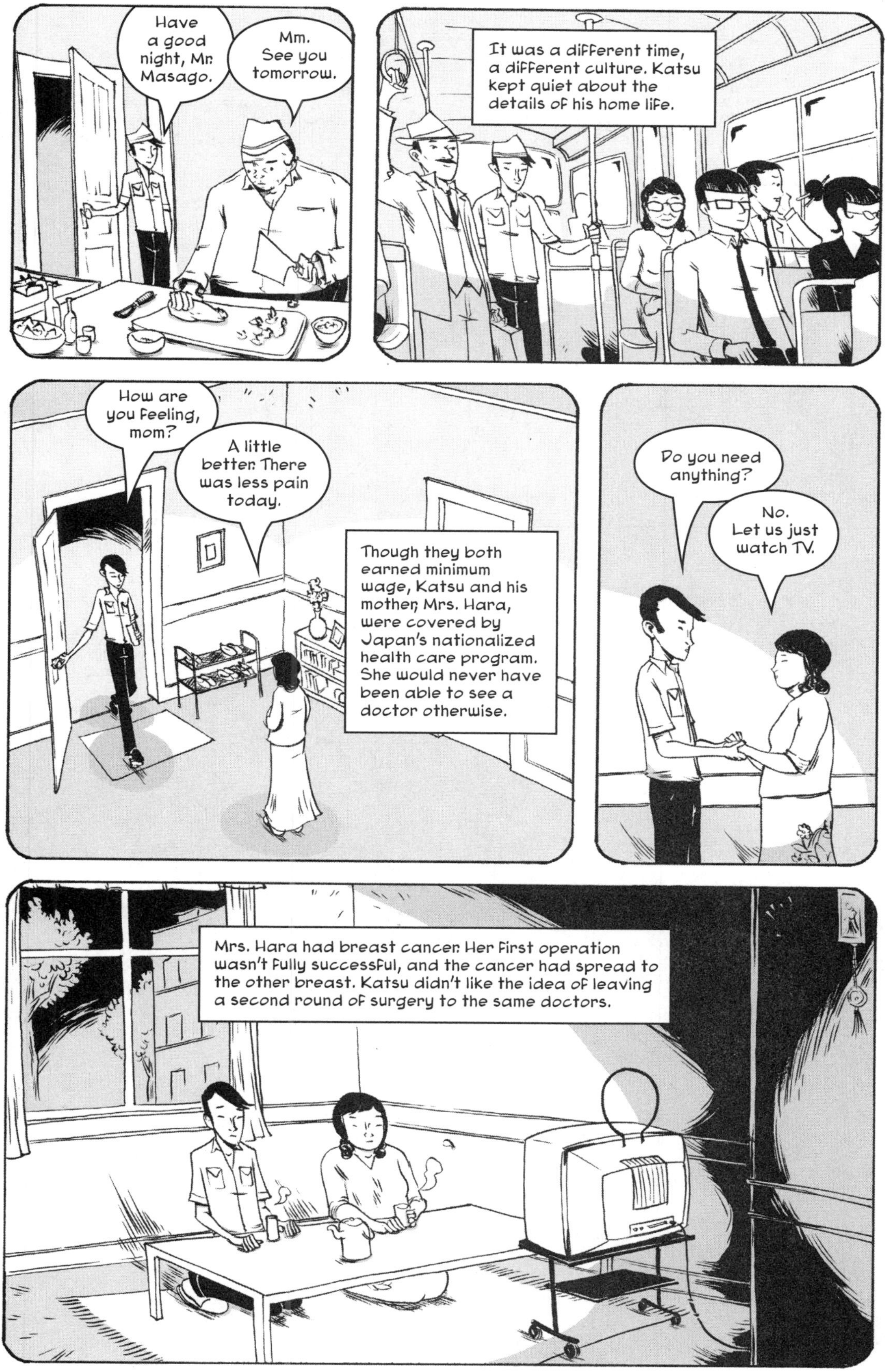
Have a good night, Mr. Masago.
Mm. See you tomorrow.
It was a different time, a different culture. Katsu kept quiet about the details of his home life.
How are you feeling, mom?
A little better. There was less pain today.
Though they both earned minimum wage, Katsu and his mother, Mrs. Hara, were covered by Japan's nationalized health care program. She would never have been able to see a doctor otherwise.
Do you need anything?
No. Let us just watch TV.
Mrs. Hara had breast cancer. Her first operation wasn't fully successful, and the cancer had spread to the other breast. Katsu didn't like the idea of leaving a second round of surgery to the same doctors.

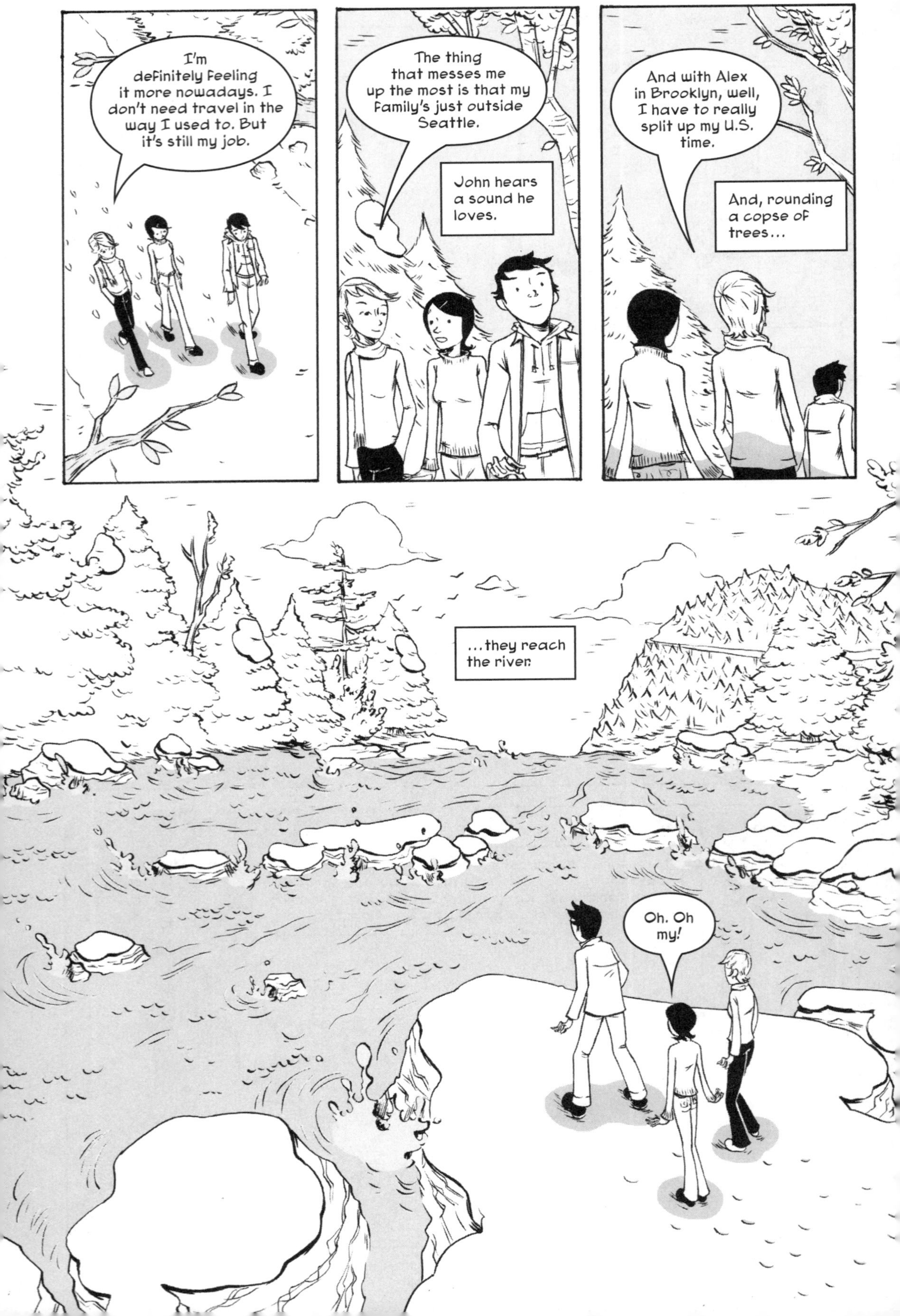
I'm definitely feeling it more nowadays. I don't need travel in the way I used to. But it's still my job.
The thing that messes me up the most is that my family's just outside Seattle.
John hears a sound he loves.
And with Alex in Brooklyn, well, I have to really split up my U.S. time.
And, rounding a copse of trees...
...they reach the river.
Oh. Oh my!

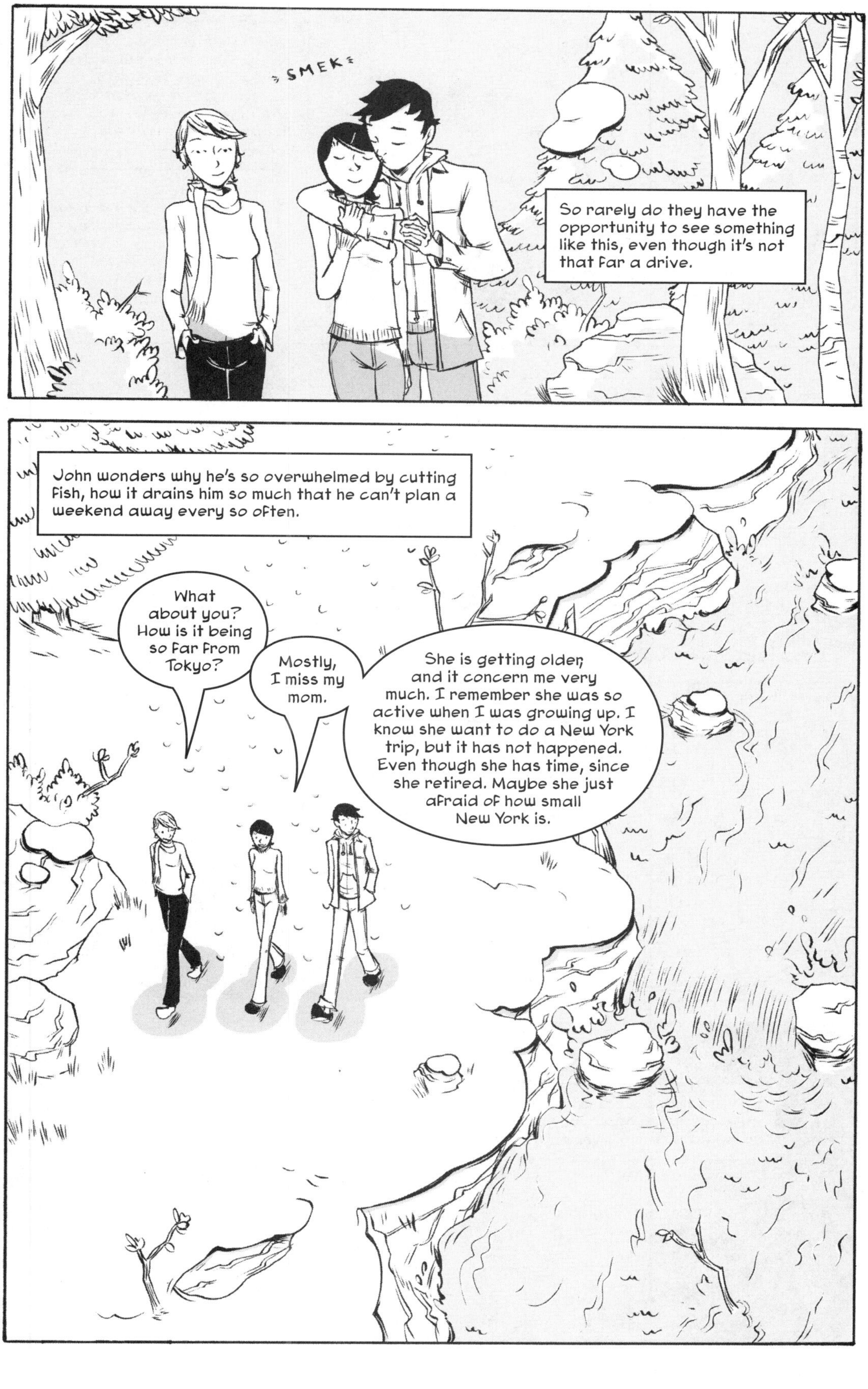
SMEK
So rarely do they have the opportunity to see something like this, even though it's not that far a drive.
John wonders why he's so overwhelmed by cutting fish, how it drains him so much that he can't plan a weekend away every so often.
What about you? How is it being so far from Tokyo?
Mostly, I miss my mom.
She is getting older, and it concern me very much. I remember she was so active when I was growing up. I know she want to do a New York trip, but it has not happened. Even though she has time, since she retired. Maybe she just afraid of how small New York is.

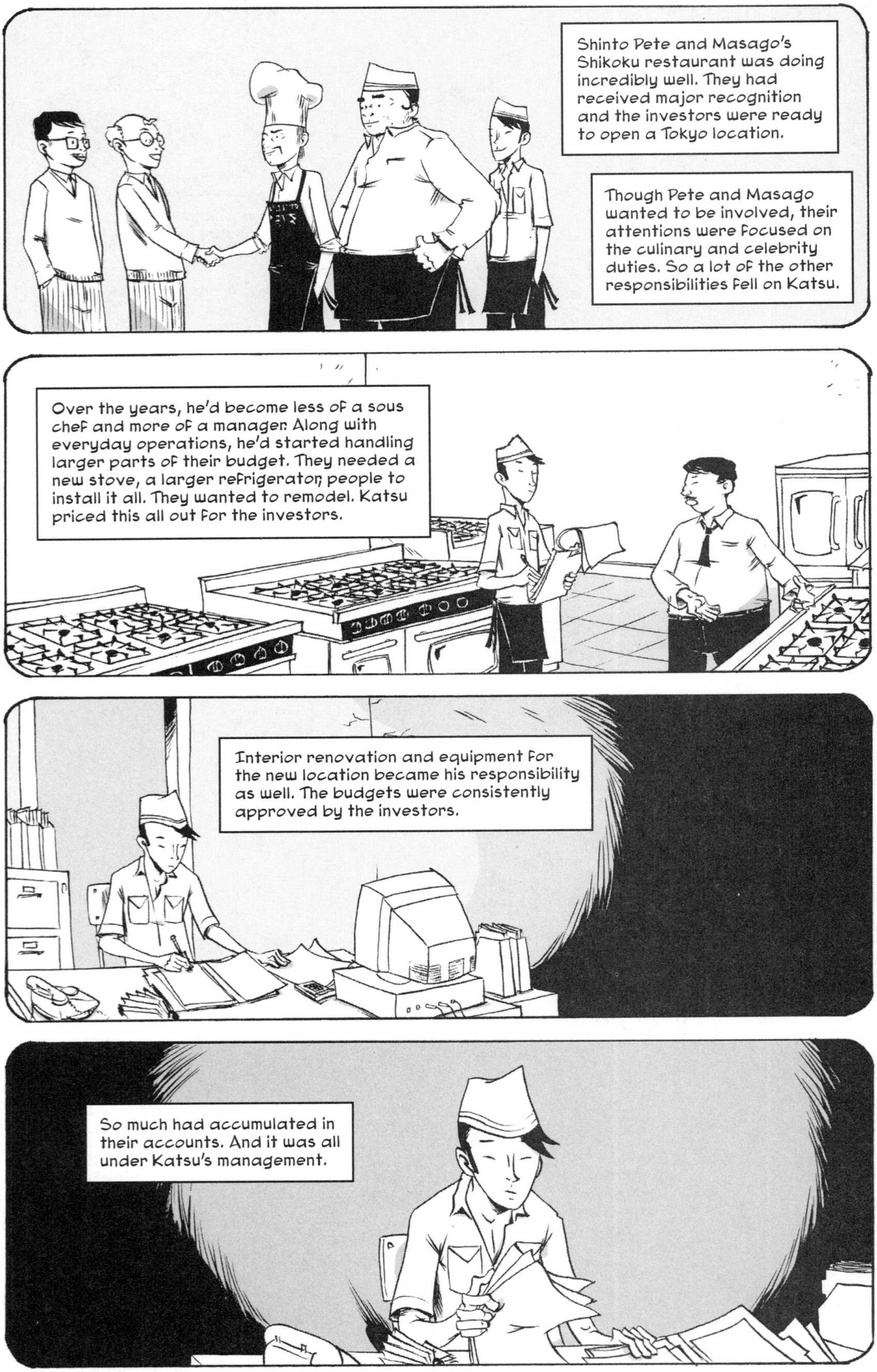
Shinto Pete and Masago's Shikoku restaurant was doing incredibly well. They had received major recognition and the investors were ready to open a Tokyo location.
Though Pete and Masago wanted to be involved, their attentions were focused on the culinary and celebrity duties. So a lot of the other responsibilities fell on Katsu.
Over the years, he'd become less of a sous chef and more of a manager. Along with everyday operations, he'd started handling larger parts of their budget. They needed a new stove, a larger refrigerator, people to install it all. They wanted to remodel. Katsu priced this all out for the investors.
Interior renovation and equipment for the new location became his responsibility as well. The budgets were consistently approved by the investors.
So much had accumulated in their accounts. And it was all under Katsu's management.

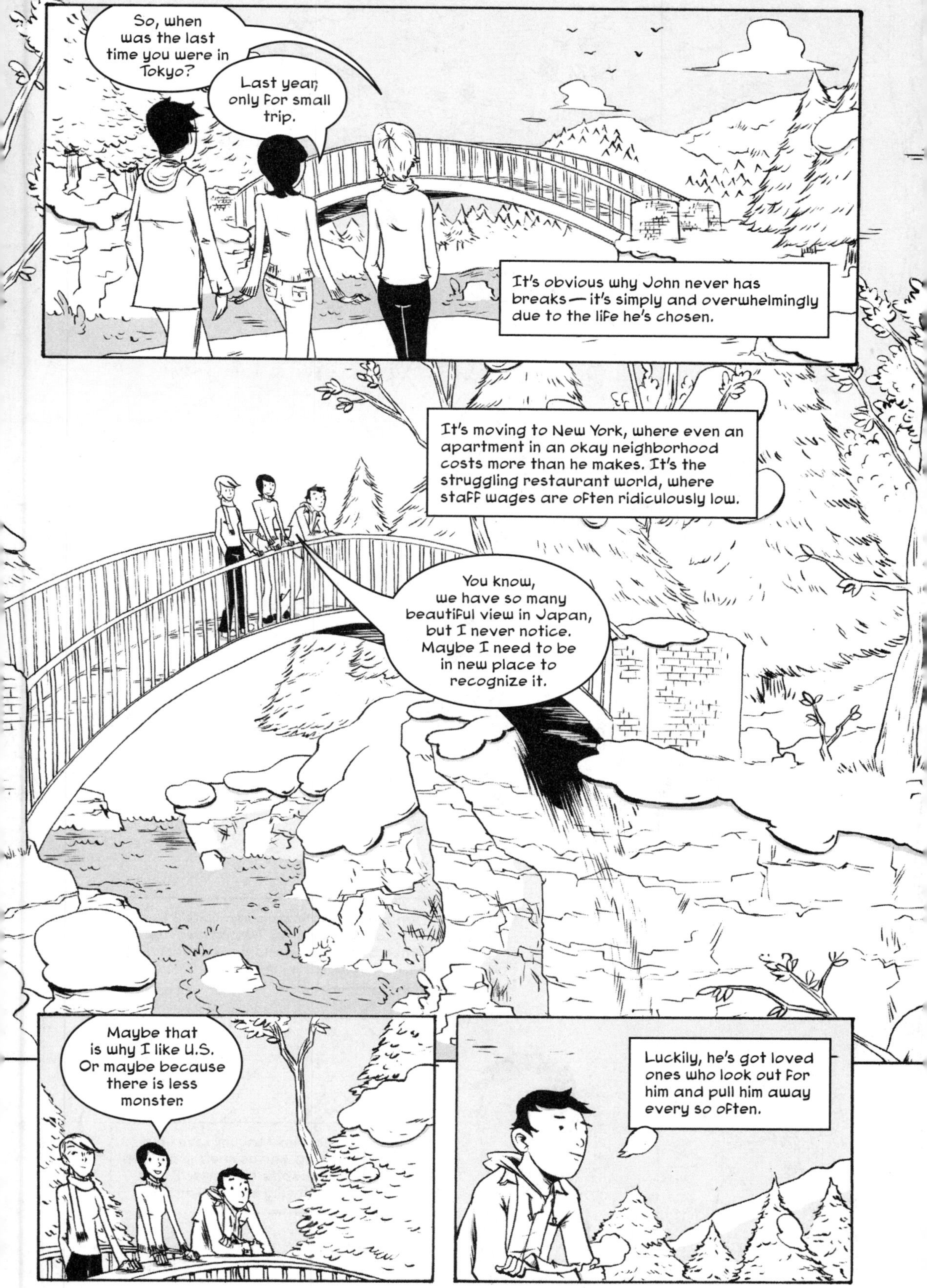
So, when was the last time you were in Tokyo?
Last year, only for small trip.
It's obvious why John never has breaks—it's simply and overwhelmingly due to the life he's chosen.
It's moving to New York, where even an apartment in an okay neighborhood costs more than he makes. It's the struggling restaurant world, where staff wages are often ridiculously low.
You know, we have so many beautiful view in Japan, but I never notice. Maybe I need to be in new place to recognize it.
Maybe that is why I like U.S. Or maybe because there is less monster.
Luckily, he's got loved ones who look out for him and pull him away every so often.

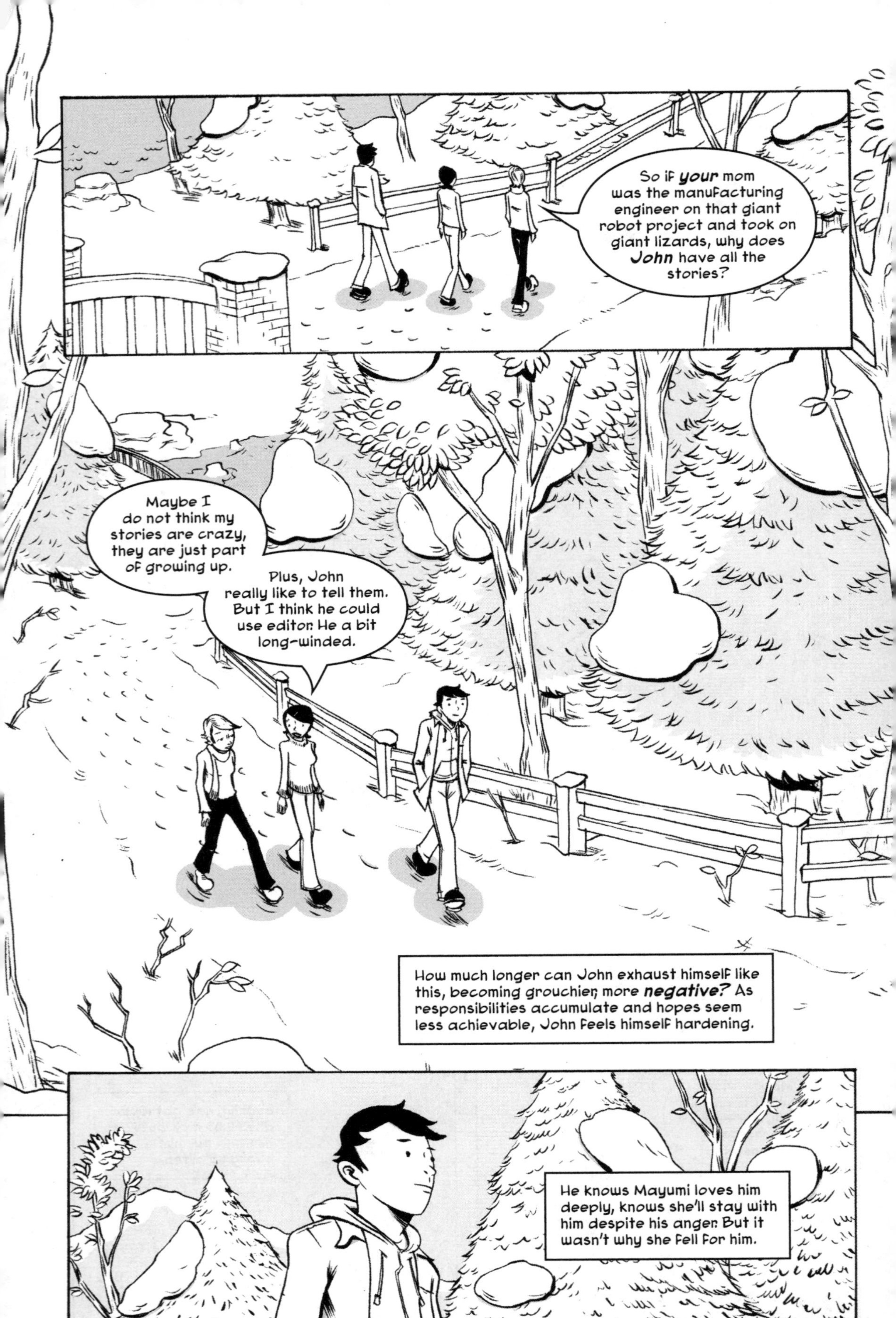
So if *your* mom was the manufacturing engineer on that giant robot project and took on giant lizards, why does *John* have all the stories?
Maybe I do not think my stories are crazy, they are just part of growing up.
Plus, John really like to tell them. But I think he could use editor. He a bit long-winded.
How much longer can John exhaust himself like this, becoming grouchier, more *negative?* As responsibilities accumulate and hopes seem less achievable, John feels himself hardening.
He knows Mayumi loves him deeply, knows she'll stay with him despite his anger. But it wasn't why she fell for him.

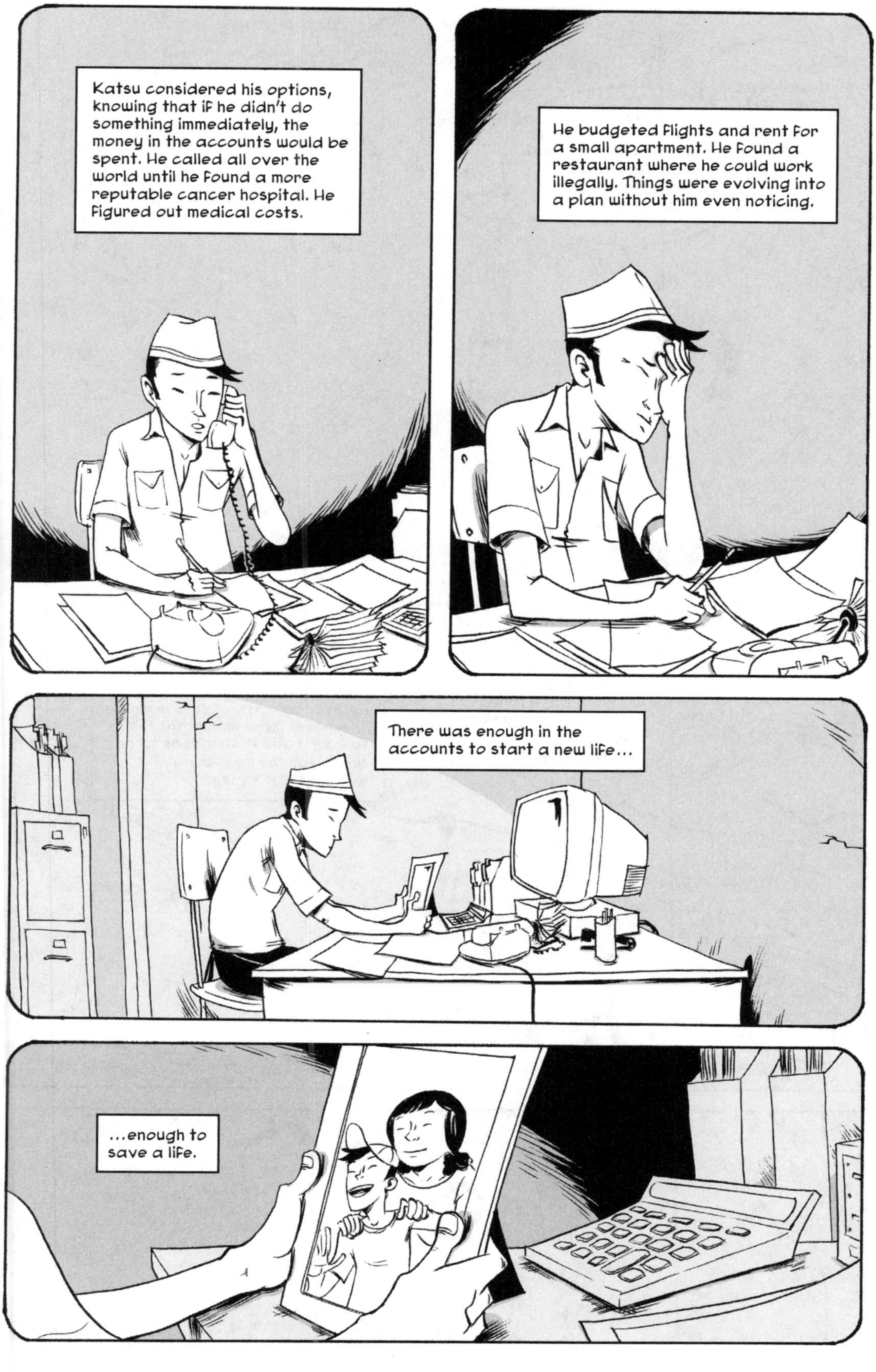
Katsu considered his options, knowing that if he didn't do something immediately, the money in the accounts would be spent. He called all over the world until he found a more reputable cancer hospital. He figured out medical costs.
He budgeted flights and rent for a small apartment. He found a restaurant where he could work illegally. Things were evolving into a plan without him even noticing.
There was enough in the accounts to start a new life...
...enough to save a life.

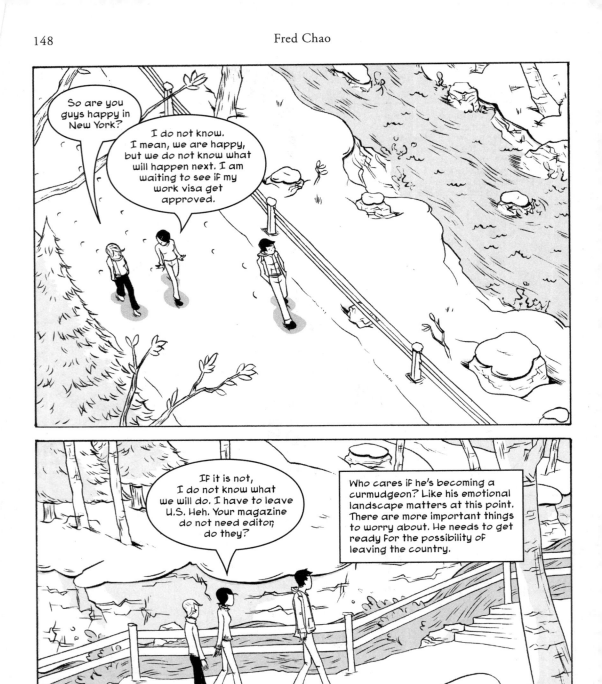

So are you guys happy in New York?

I do not know. I mean, we are happy, but we do not know what will happen next. I am waiting to see if my work visa get approved.

If it is not, I do not know what we will do. I have to leave U.S. Heh. Your magazine do not need editor, do they?

Who cares if he's becoming a curmudgeon? Like his emotional landscape matters at this point. There are more important things to worry about. He needs to get ready for the possibility of leaving the country.

Oh wow.

That so beautiful.

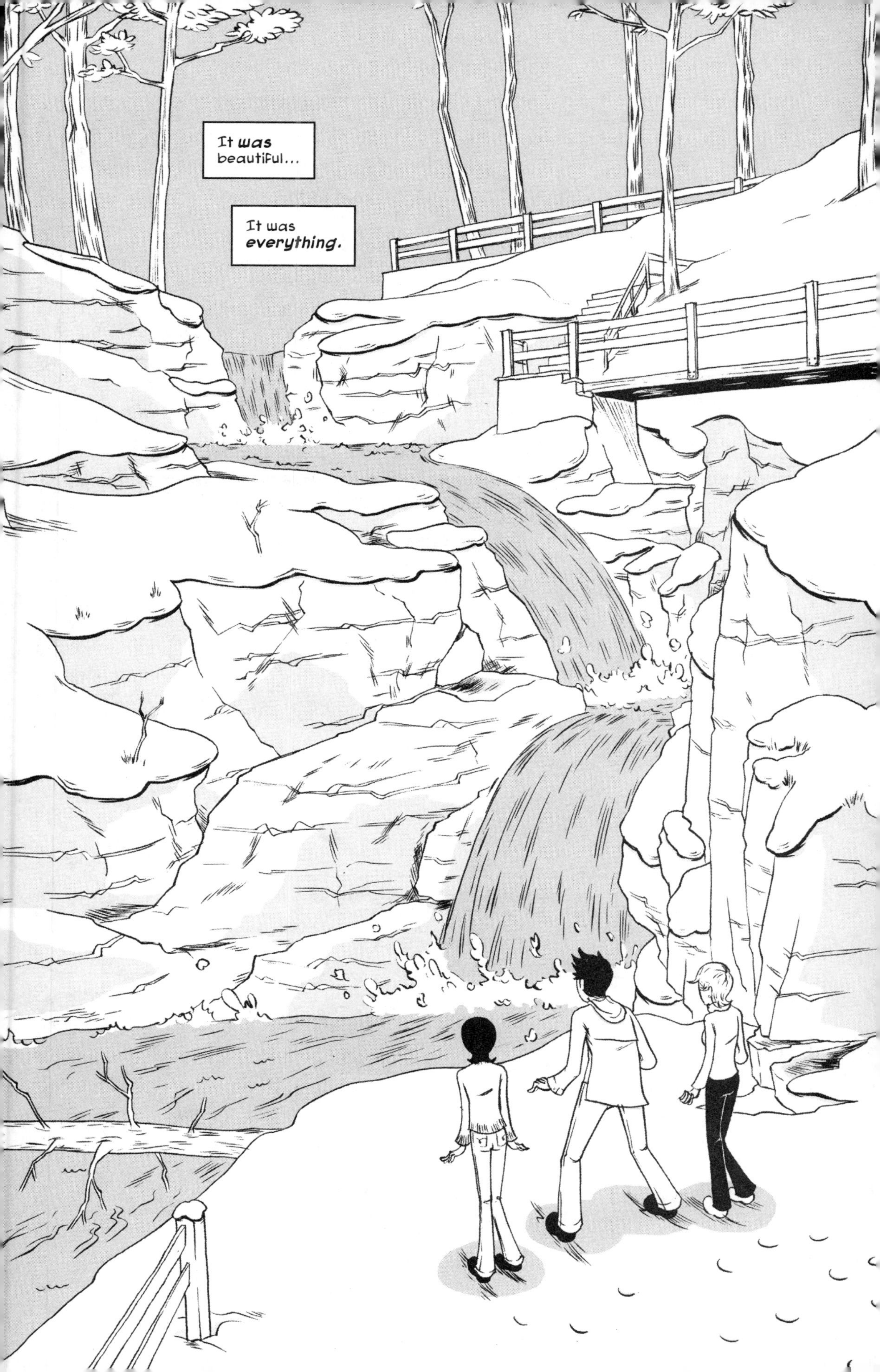
It *was* beautiful...
It was *everything.*

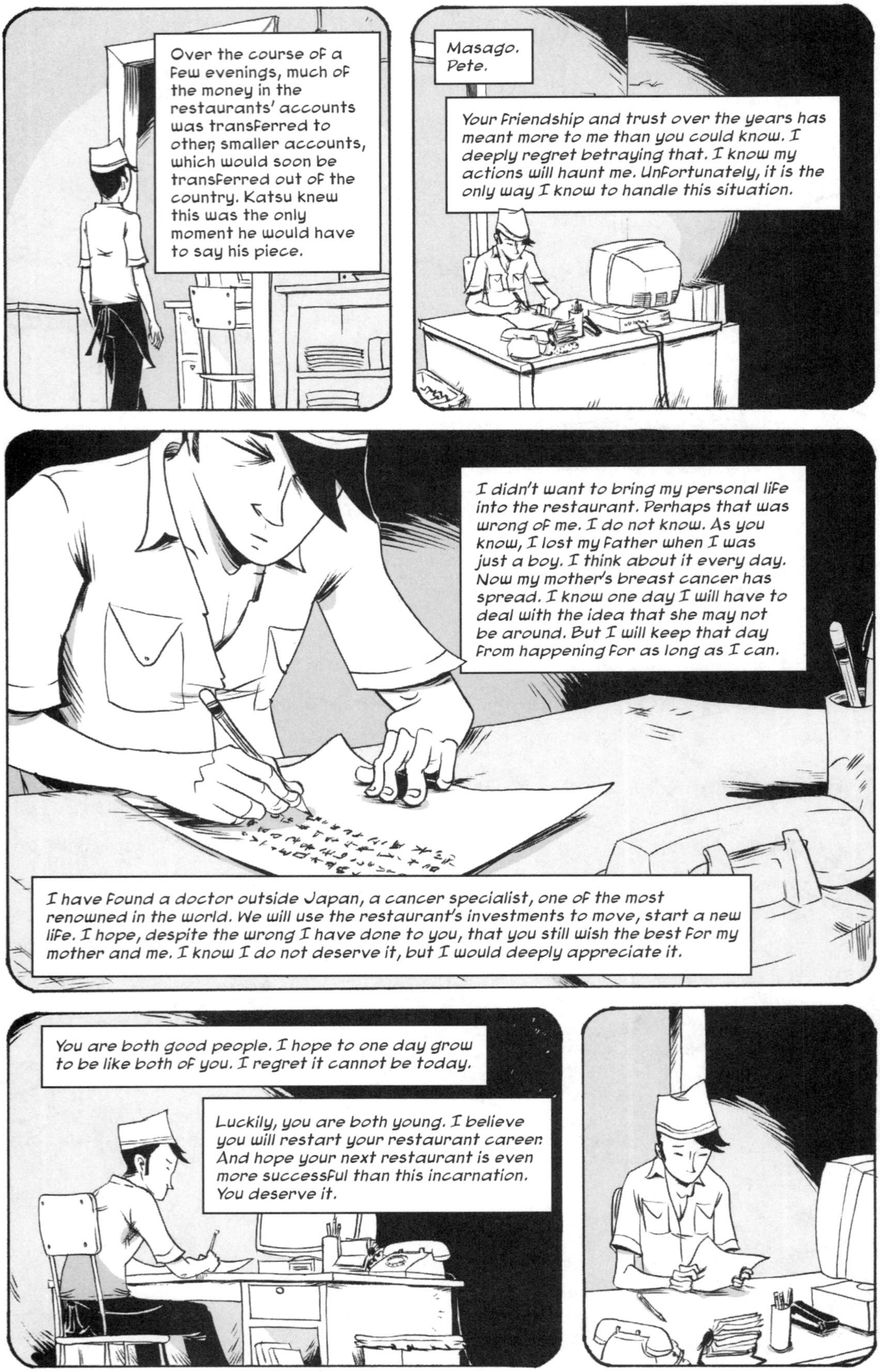
Over the course of a few evenings, much of the money in the restaurants' accounts was transferred to other, smaller accounts, which would soon be transferred out of the country. Katsu knew this was the only moment he would have to say his piece.
Masago. Pete.
Your friendship and trust over the years has meant more to me than you could know. I deeply regret betraying that. I know my actions will haunt me. Unfortunately, it is the only way I know to handle this situation.
I didn't want to bring my personal life into the restaurant. Perhaps that was wrong of me. I do not know. As you know, I lost my father when I was just a boy. I think about it every day. Now my mother's breast cancer has spread. I know one day I will have to deal with the idea that she may not be around. But I will keep that day from happening for as long as I can.
I have found a doctor outside Japan, a cancer specialist, one of the most renowned in the world. We will use the restaurant's investments to move, start a new life. I hope, despite the wrong I have done to you, that you still wish the best for my mother and me. I know I do not deserve it, but I would deeply appreciate it.
You are both good people. I hope to one day grow to be like both of you. I regret it cannot be today.
Luckily, you are both young. I believe you will restart your restaurant career. And hope your next restaurant is even more successful than this incarnation. You deserve it.

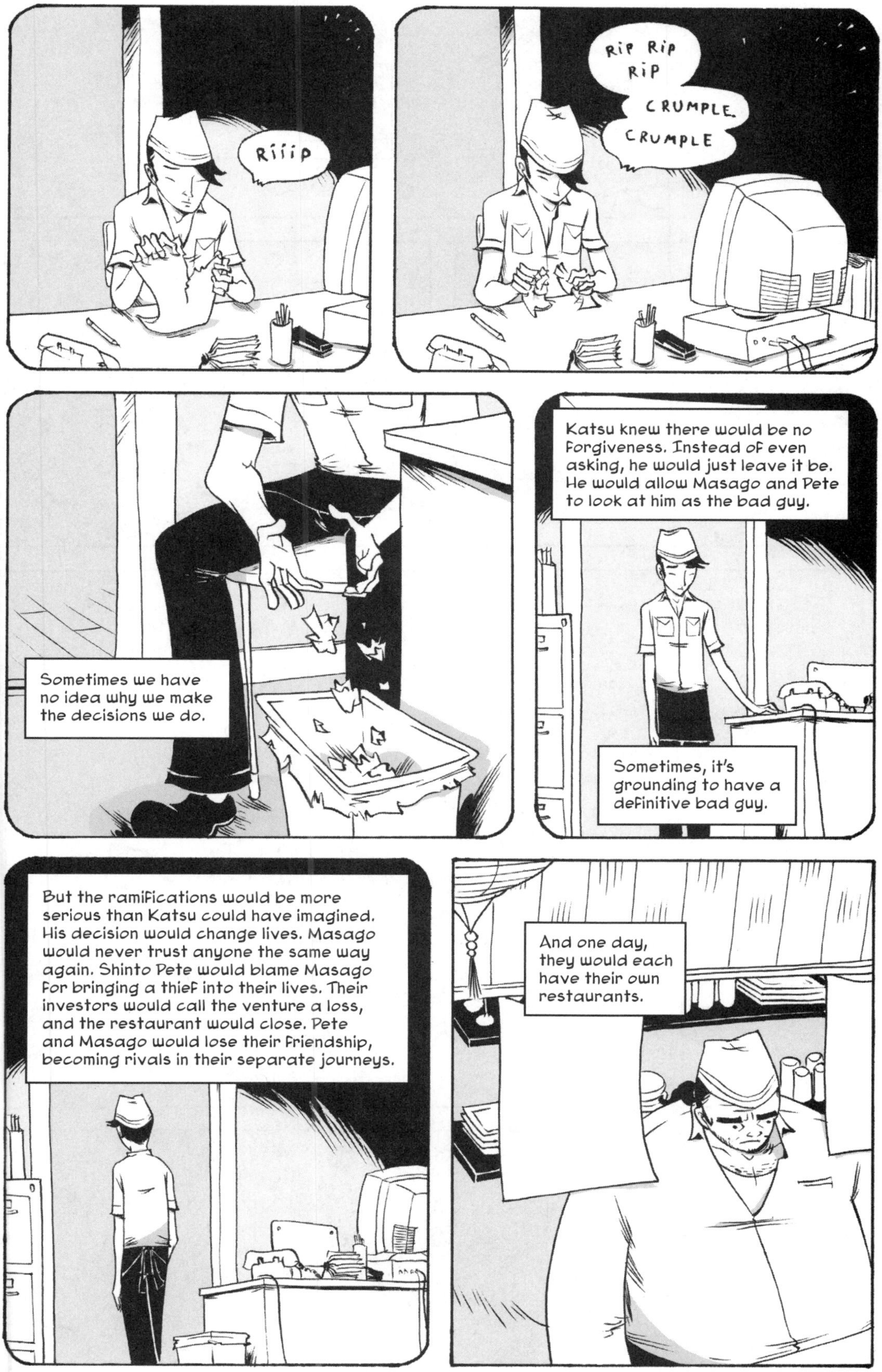
Riiip
Rip Rip
Rip
CRUMPLE
CRUMPLE
Sometimes we have no idea why we make the decisions we do.
Katsu knew there would be no forgiveness. Instead of even asking, he would just leave it be. He would allow Masago and Pete to look at him as the bad guy.
Sometimes, it's grounding to have a definitive bad guy.
But the ramifications would be more serious than Katsu could have imagined. His decision would change lives. Masago would never trust anyone the same way again. Shinto Pete would blame Masago for bringing a thief into their lives. Their investors would call the venture a loss, and the restaurant would close. Pete and Masago would lose their friendship, becoming rivals in their separate journeys.
And one day, they would each have their own restaurants.

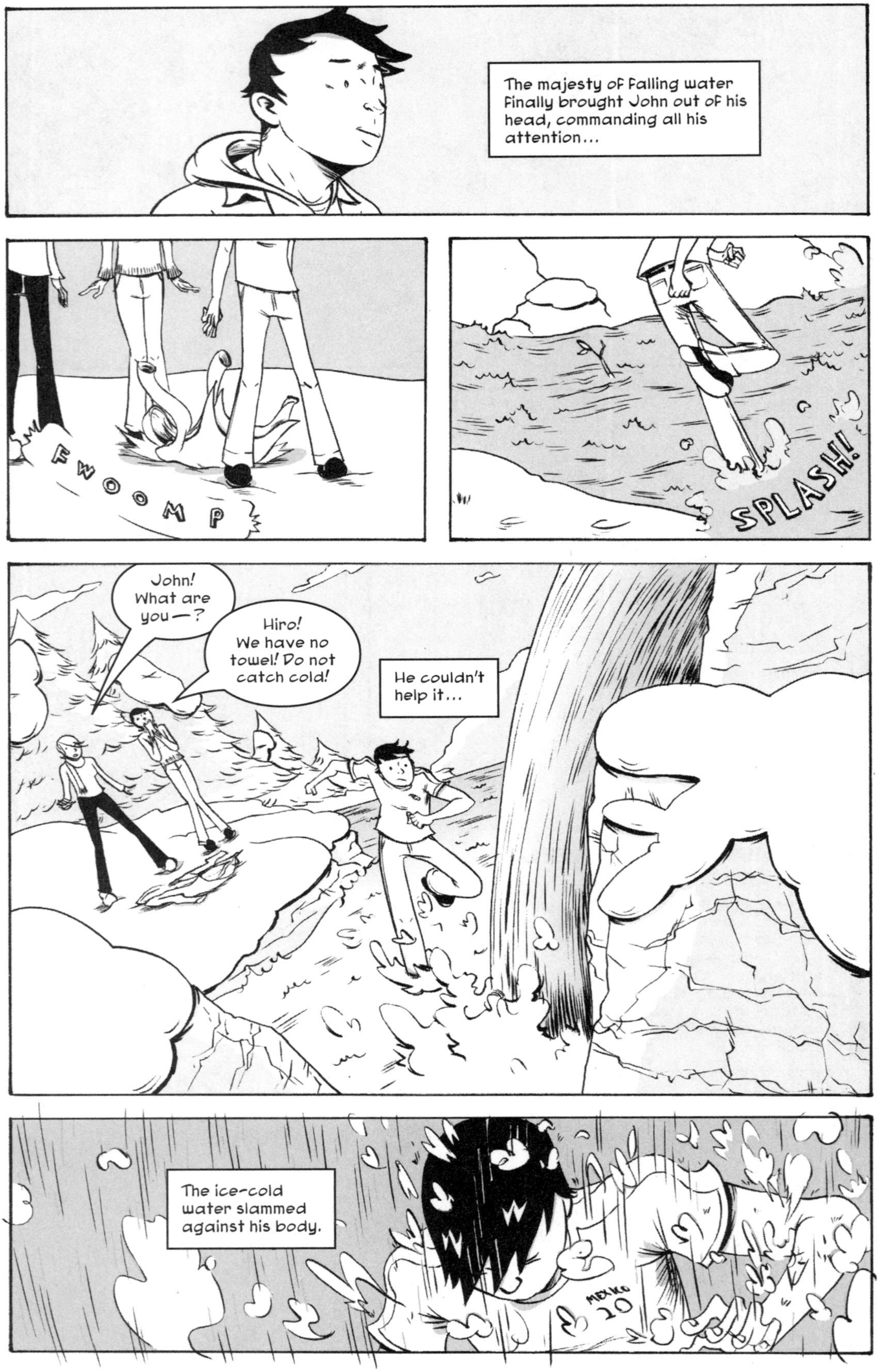
The majesty of falling water finally brought John out of his head, commanding all his attention…
FWOOMP
SPLASH!
John! What are you—?
Hiro! We have no towel! Do not catch cold!
He couldn't help it…
The ice-cold water slammed against his body.
MEXICO 20

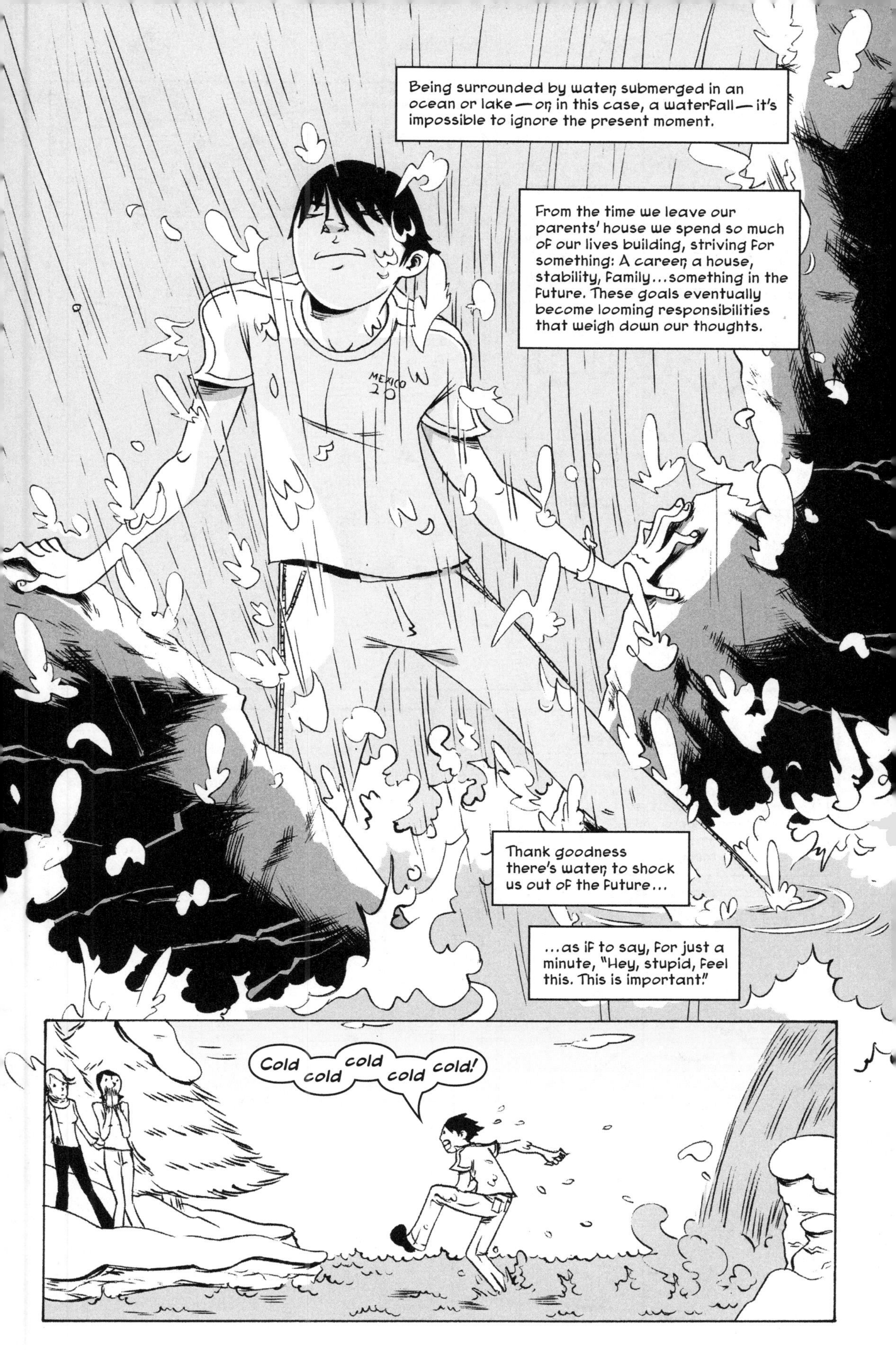
Being surrounded by water, submerged in an ocean or lake — or, in this case, a waterfall — it's impossible to ignore the present moment.
From the time we leave our parents' house we spend so much of our lives building, striving for something: A career, a house, stability, family... something in the future. These goals eventually become looming responsibilities that weigh down our thoughts.
MEXICO 20
Thank goodness there's water, to shock us out of the future...
...as if to say, for just a minute, "Hey, stupid, feel this. This is important."
Cold cold cold cold cold!

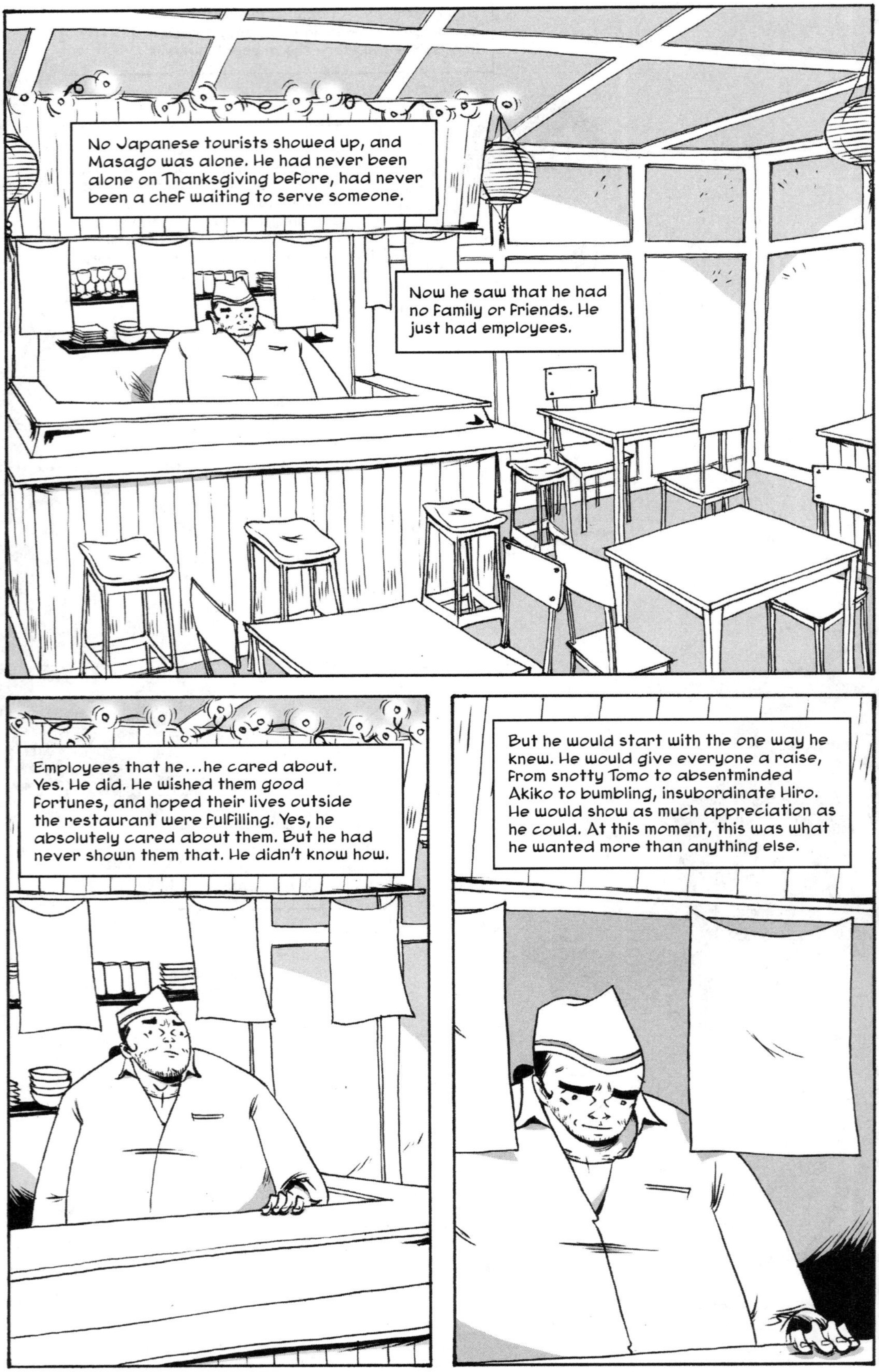
No Japanese tourists showed up, and Masago was alone. He had never been alone on Thanksgiving before, had never been a chef waiting to serve someone.
Now he saw that he had no family or friends. He just had employees.
Employees that he...he cared about. Yes. He did. He wished them good fortunes, and hoped their lives outside the restaurant were fulfilling. Yes, he absolutely cared about them. But he had never shown them that. He didn't know how.
But he would start with the one way he knew. He would give everyone a raise, from snotty Tomo to absentminded Akiko to bumbling, insubordinate Hiro. He would show as much appreciation as he could. At this moment, this was what he wanted more than anything else.

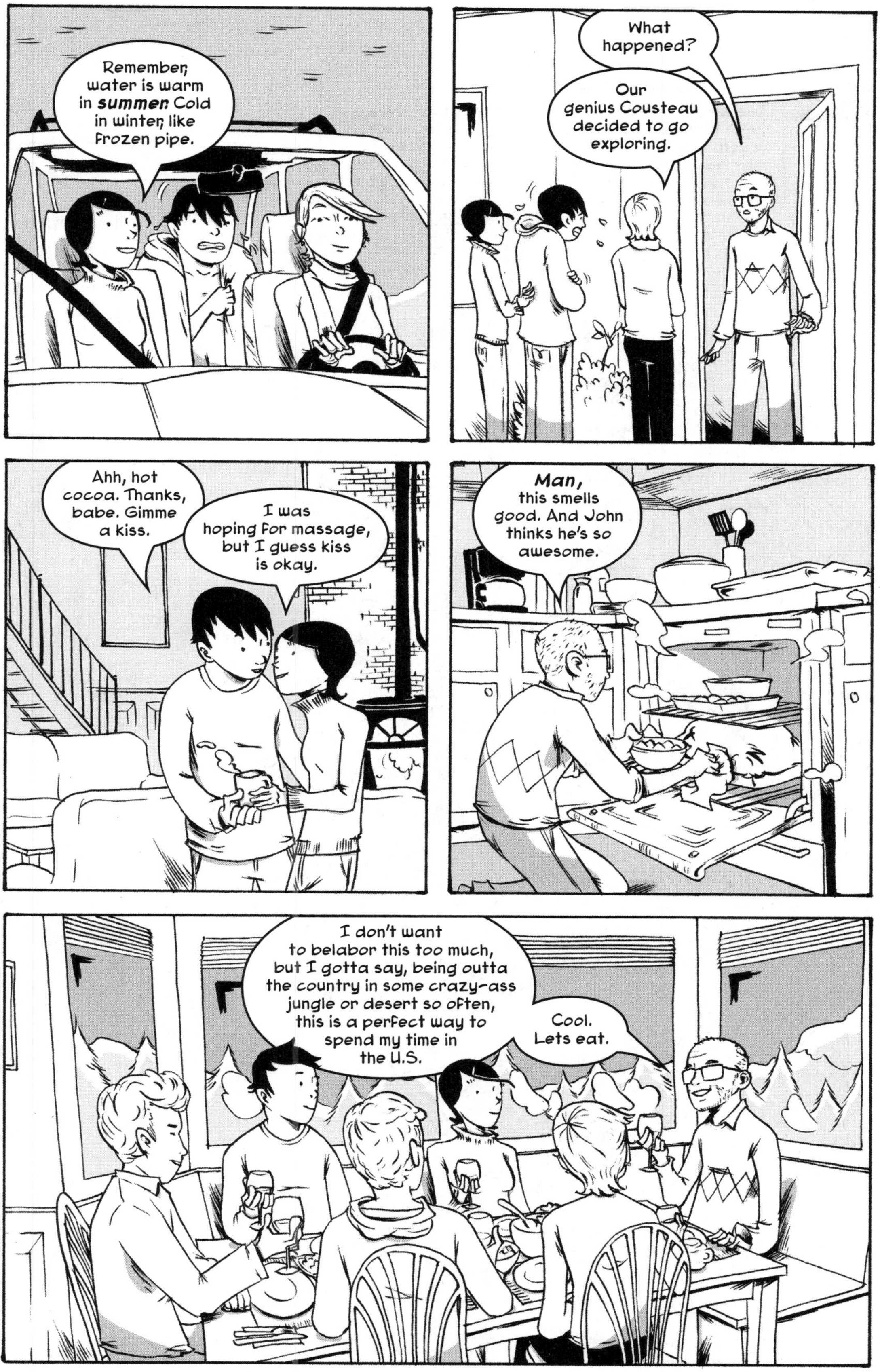
Remember, water is warm in **summer**. Cold in winter, like frozen pipe.
What happened?
Our genius Cousteau decided to go exploring.
Ahh, hot cocoa. Thanks, babe. Gimme a kiss.
I was hoping for massage, but I guess kiss is okay.
Man, this smells good. And John thinks he's so awesome.
I don't want to belabor this too much, but I gotta say, being outta the country in some crazy-ass jungle or desert so often, this is a perfect way to spend my time in the U.S.
Cool. Lets eat.

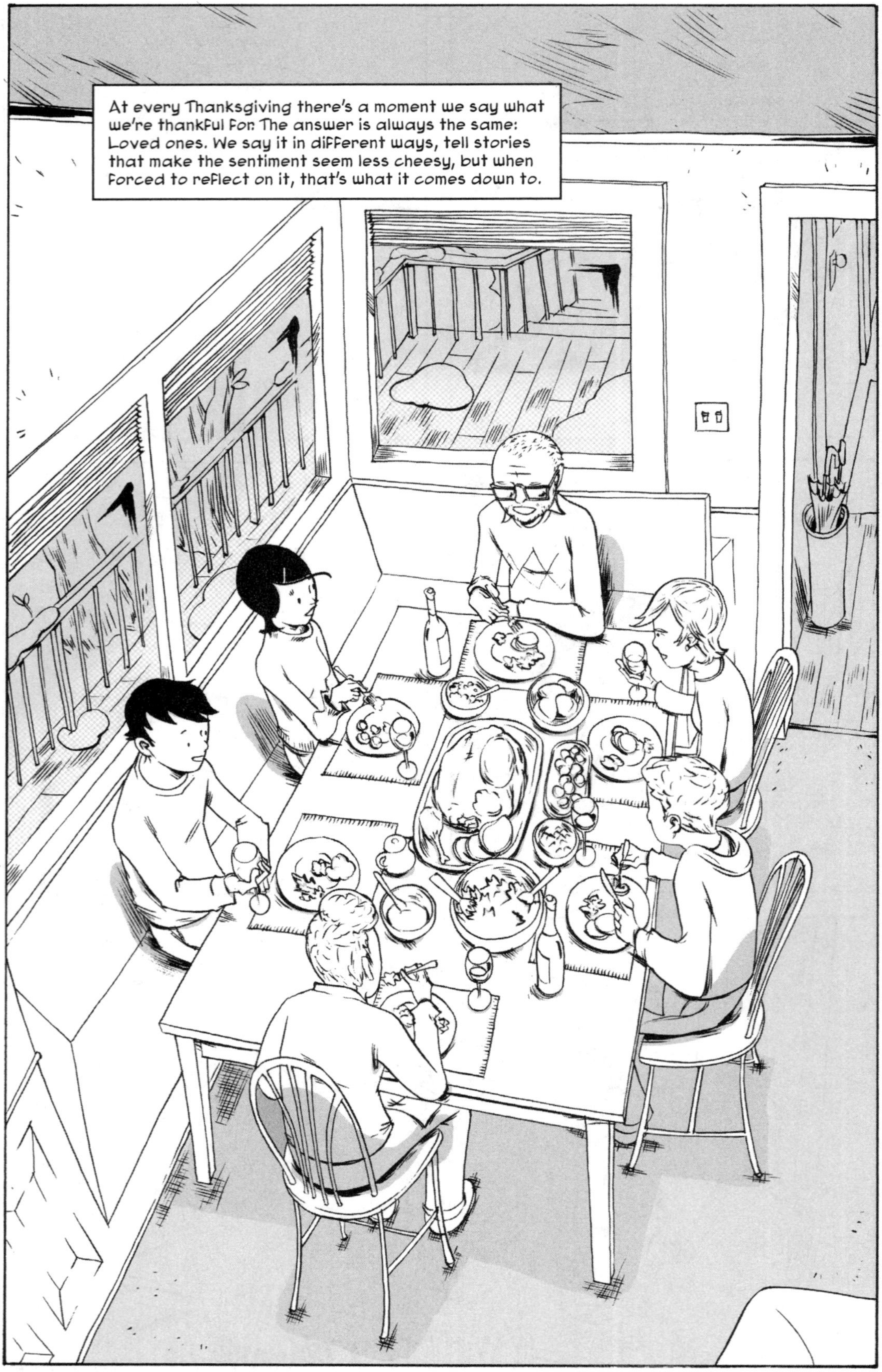
At every Thanksgiving there's a moment we say what we're thankful for. The answer is always the same: Loved ones. We say it in different ways, tell stories that make the sentiment seem less cheesy, but when forced to reflect on it, that's what it comes down to.

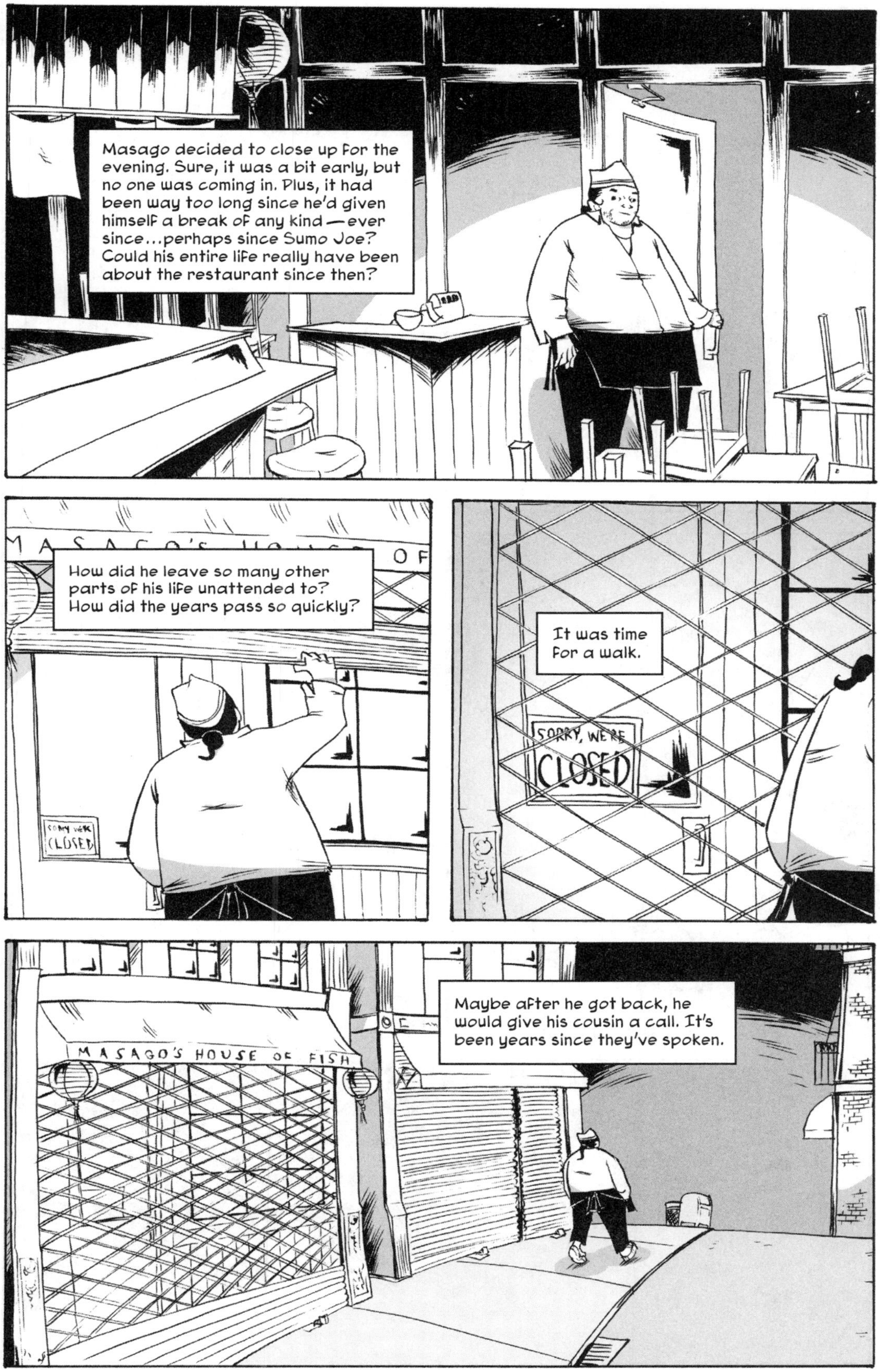
Masago decided to close up for the evening. Sure, it was a bit early, but no one was coming in. Plus, it had been way too long since he'd given himself a break of any kind — ever since...perhaps since Sumo Joe? Could his entire life really have been about the restaurant since then?
How did he leave so many other parts of his life unattended to? How did the years pass so quickly?
SORRY, WE'RE CLOSED
It was time for a walk.
SORRY, WE'RE CLOSED
MASAGO'S HOUSE OF FISH
Maybe after he got back, he would give his cousin a call. It's been years since they've spoken.

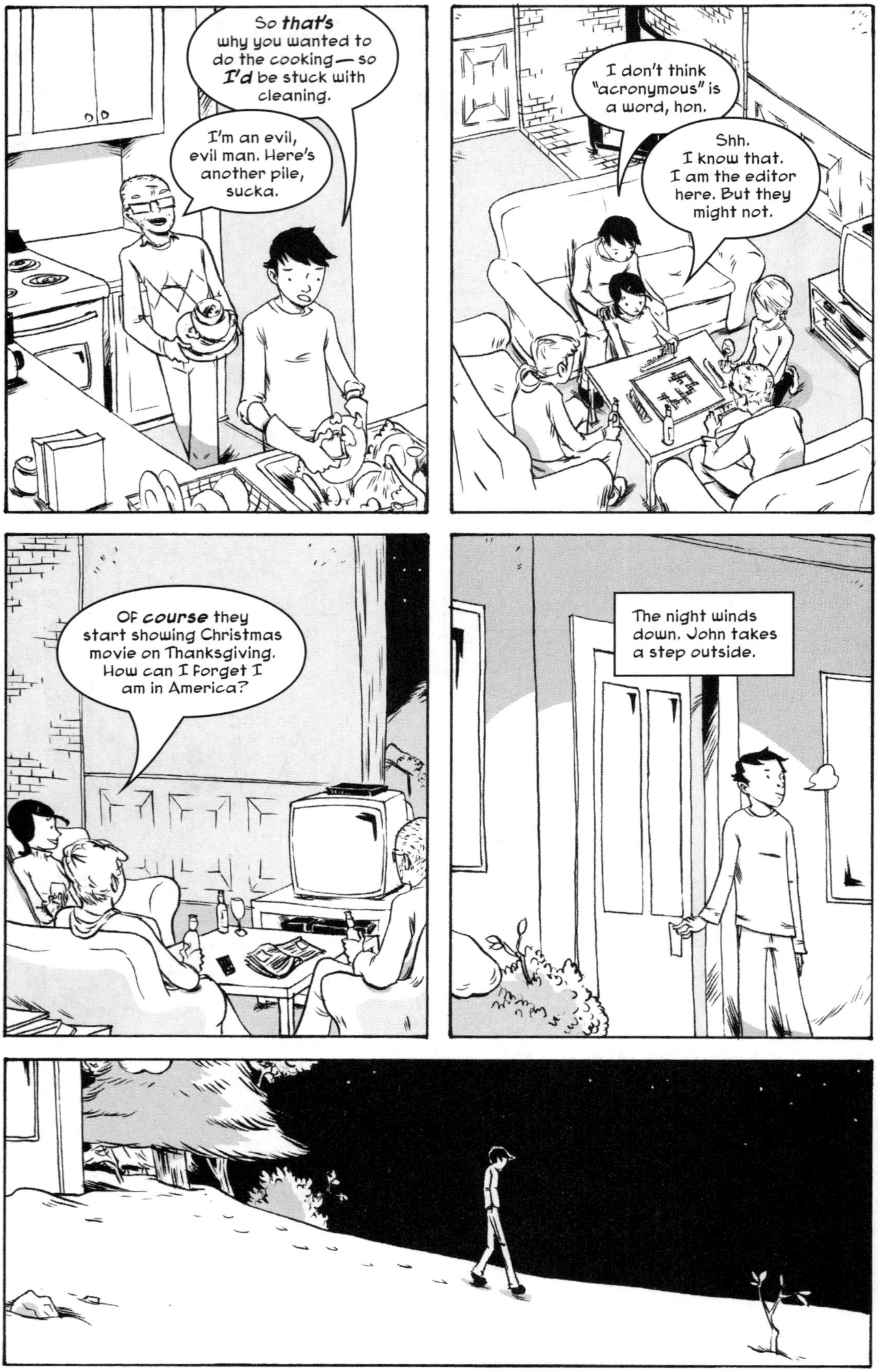
So *that's* why you wanted to do the cooking—so *I'd* be stuck with cleaning.
I'm an evil, evil man. Here's another pile, sucka.
I don't think "acronymous" is a word, hon.
Shh. I know that. I am the editor here. But they might not.
Of *course* they start showing Christmas movie on Thanksgiving. How can I forget I am in America?
The night winds down. John takes a step outside.

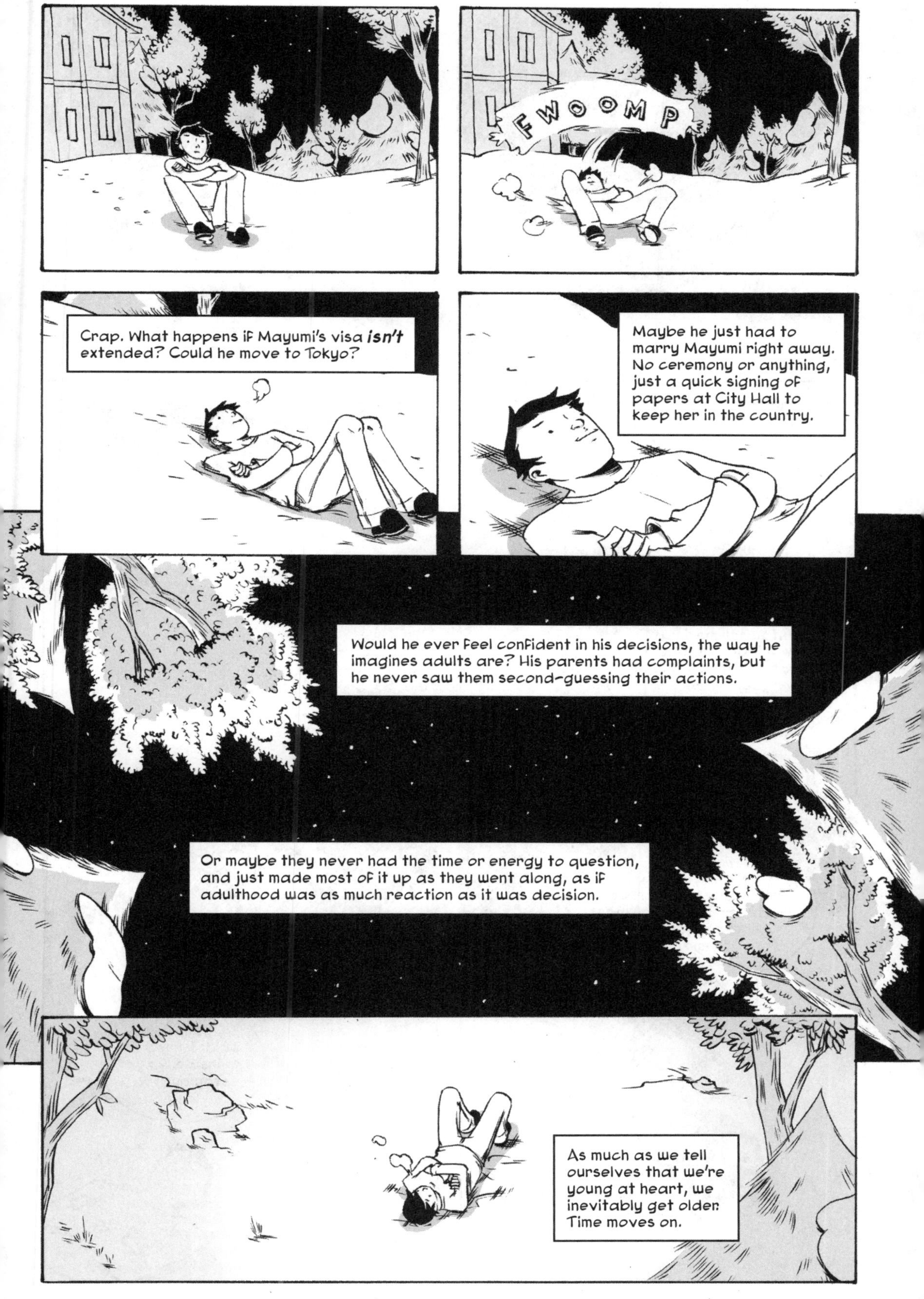

Crap. What happens if Mayumi's visa *isn't* extended? Could he move to Tokyo?

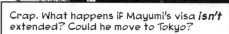

Maybe he just had to marry Mayumi right away. No ceremony or anything, just a quick signing of papers at City Hall to keep her in the country.

Would he ever feel confident in his decisions, the way he imagines adults are? His parents had complaints, but he never saw them second-guessing their actions.

Or maybe they never had the time or energy to question, and just made most of it up as they went along, as if adulthood was as much reaction as it was decision.

As much as we tell ourselves that we're young at heart, we inevitably get older. Time moves on.

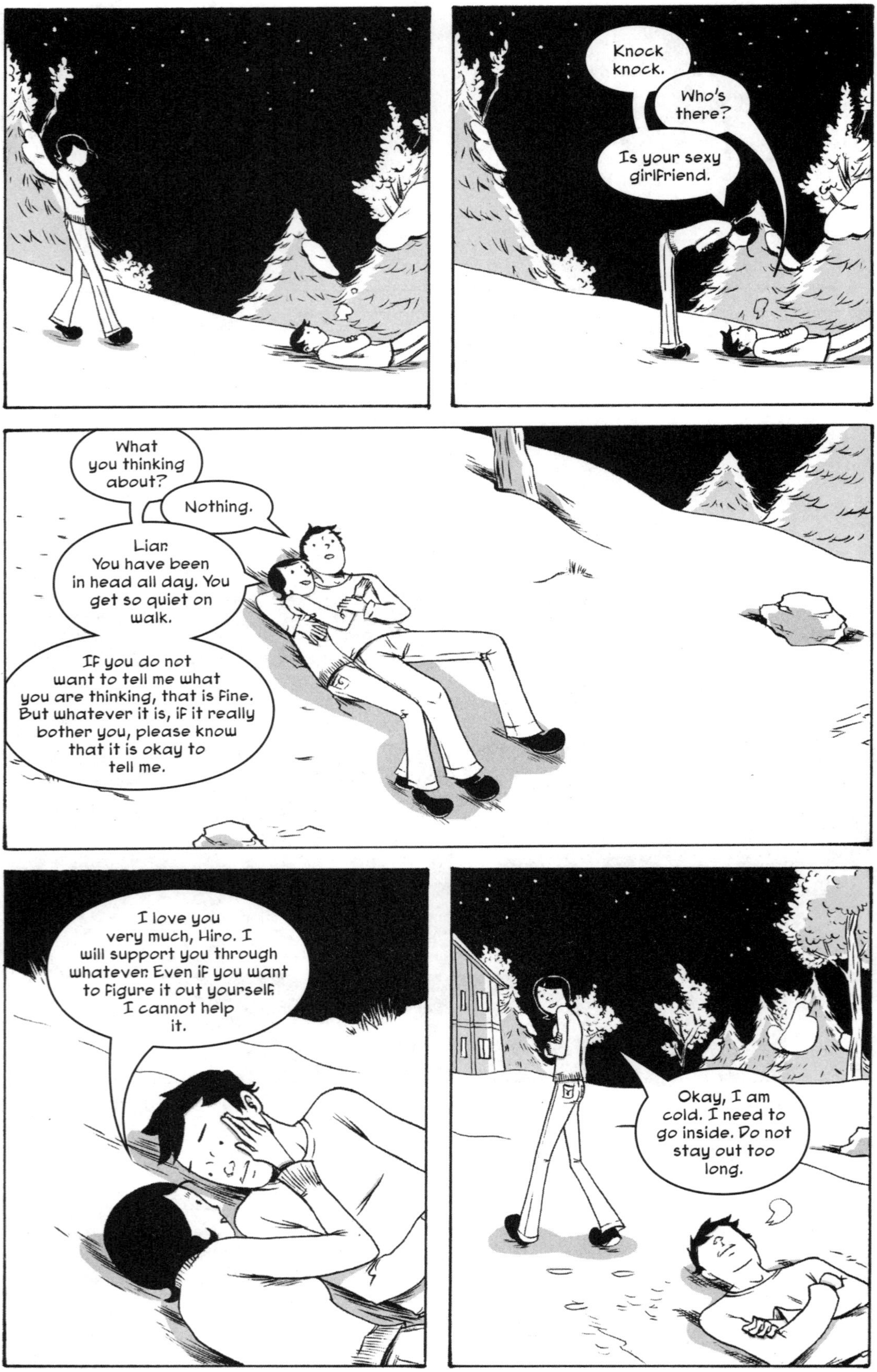
Knock knock.
Who's there?
Is your sexy girlfriend.
What you thinking about?
Nothing.
Liar. You have been in head all day. You get so quiet on walk.
If you do not want to tell me what you are thinking, that is fine. But whatever it is, if it really bother you, please know that it is okay to tell me.
I love you very much, Hiro. I will support you through whatever. Even if you want to figure it out yourself. I cannot help it.
Okay, I am cold. I need to go inside. Do not stay out too long.

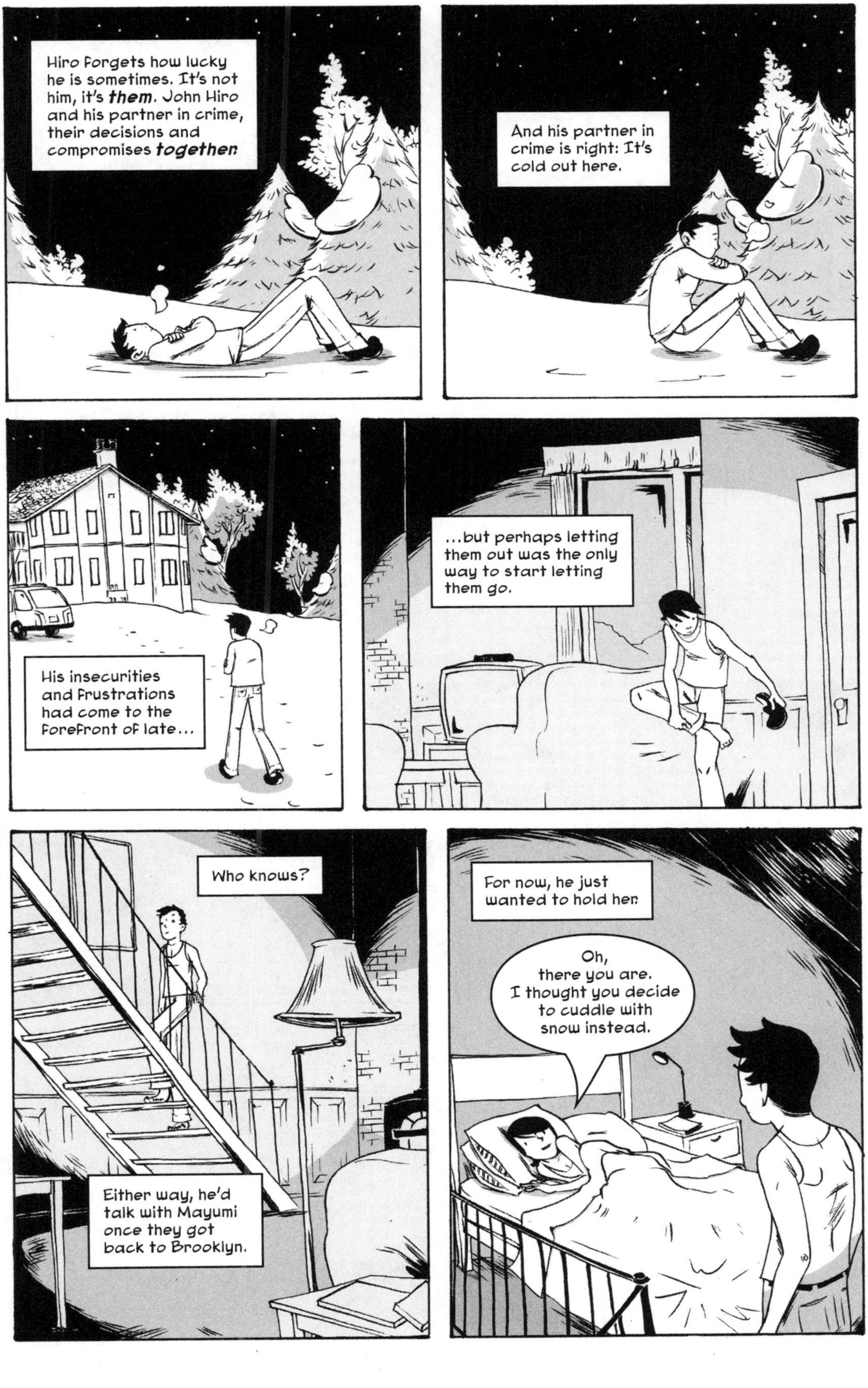
Hiro forgets how lucky he is sometimes. It's not him, it's **them**. John Hiro and his partner in crime, their decisions and compromises **together**.
And his partner in crime is right: It's cold out here.
His insecurities and frustrations had come to the forefront of late...
...but perhaps letting them out was the only way to start letting them go.
Who knows?
Either way, he'd talk with Mayumi once they got back to Brooklyn.
For now, he just wanted to hold her.
Oh, there you are. I thought you decide to cuddle with snow instead.

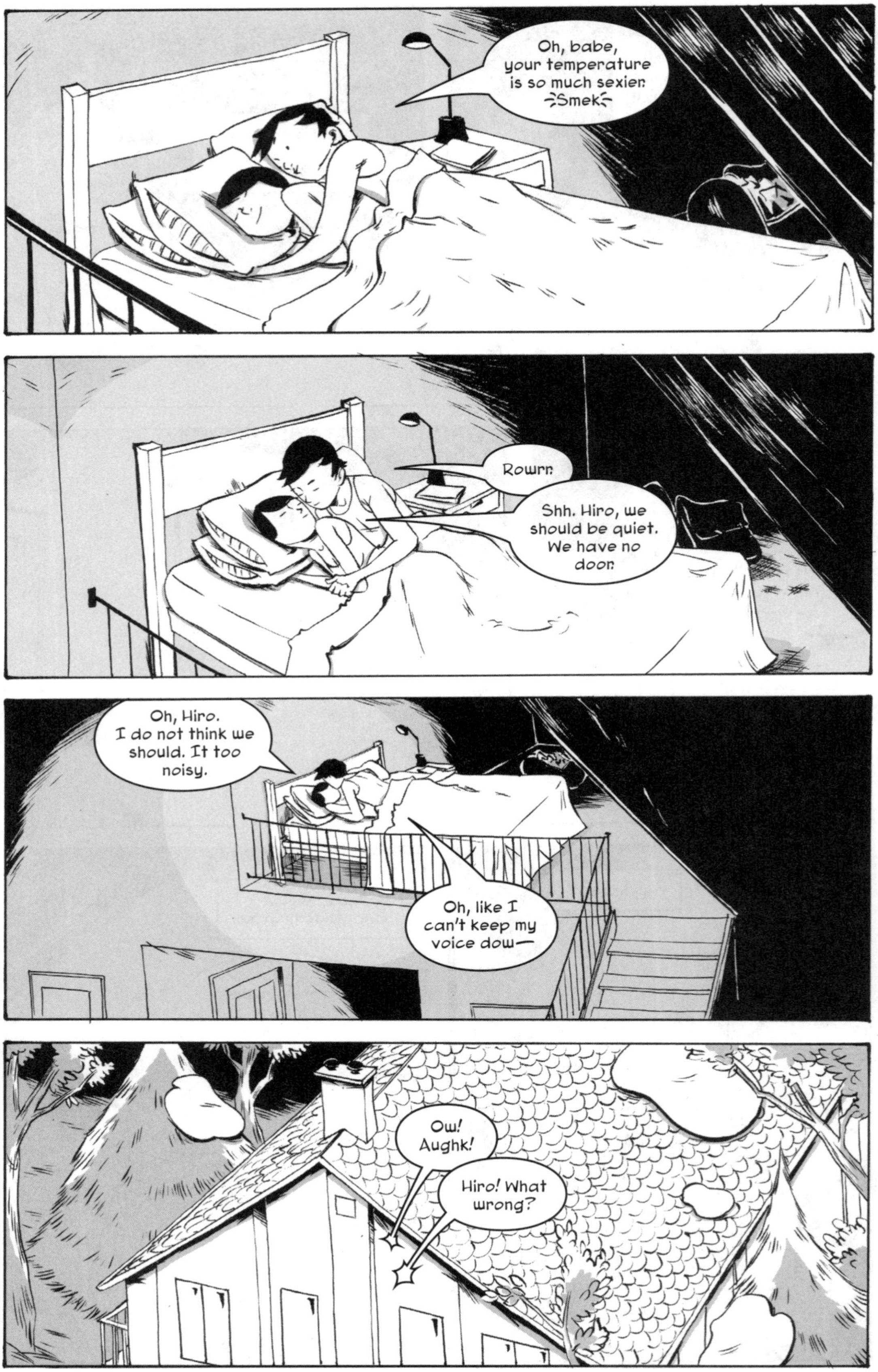
Oh, babe, your temperature is so much sexier. Smek
Rowrr.
Shh. Hiro, we should be quiet. We have no door.
Oh, Hiro. I do not think we should. It too noisy.
Oh, like I can't keep my voice dow—
Ow! Aughk!
Hiro! What wrong?

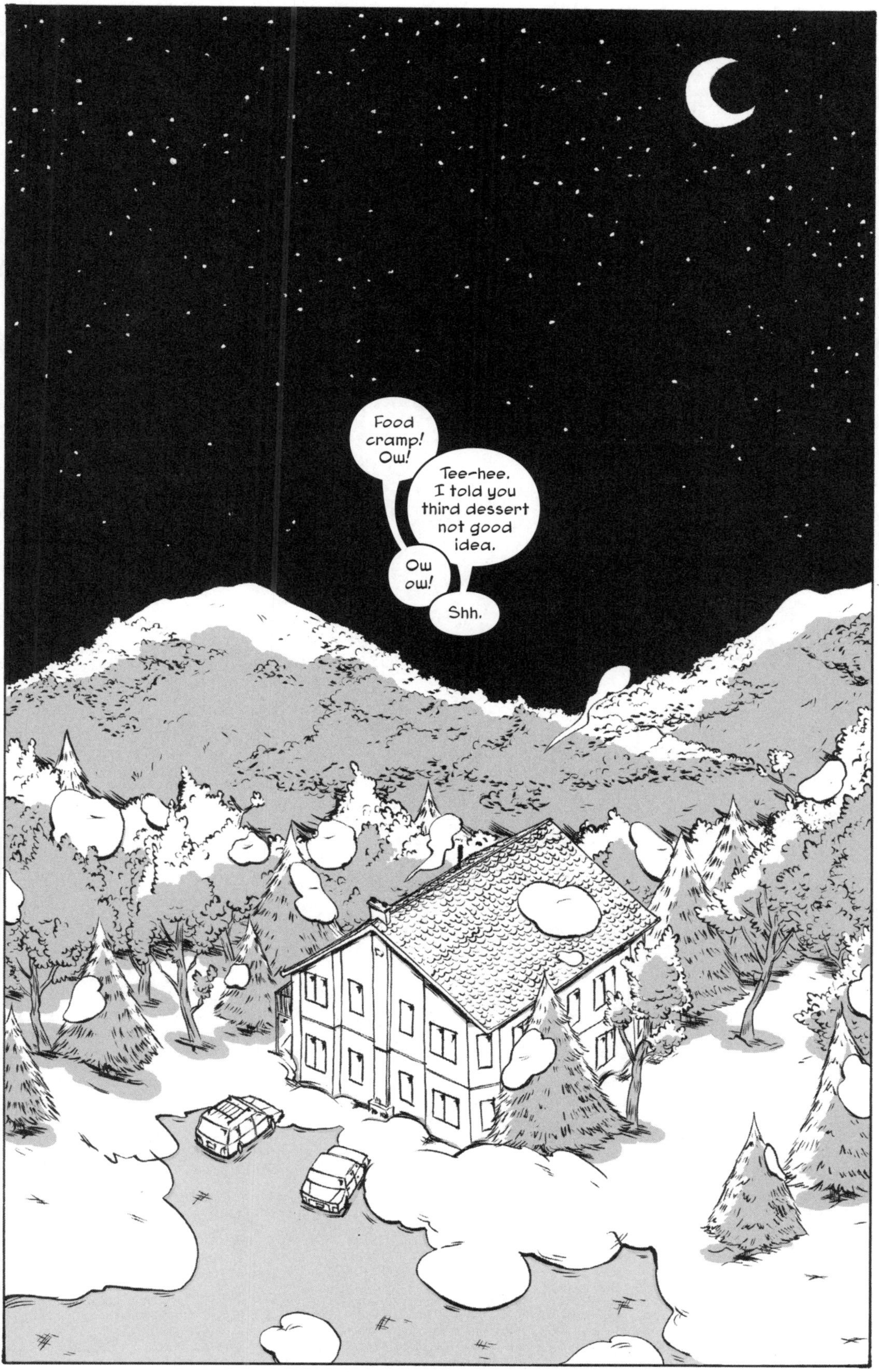
Food cramp! Ow!
Tee-hee. I told you third dessert not good idea.
Ow ow!
Shh.

こきゅうけい4

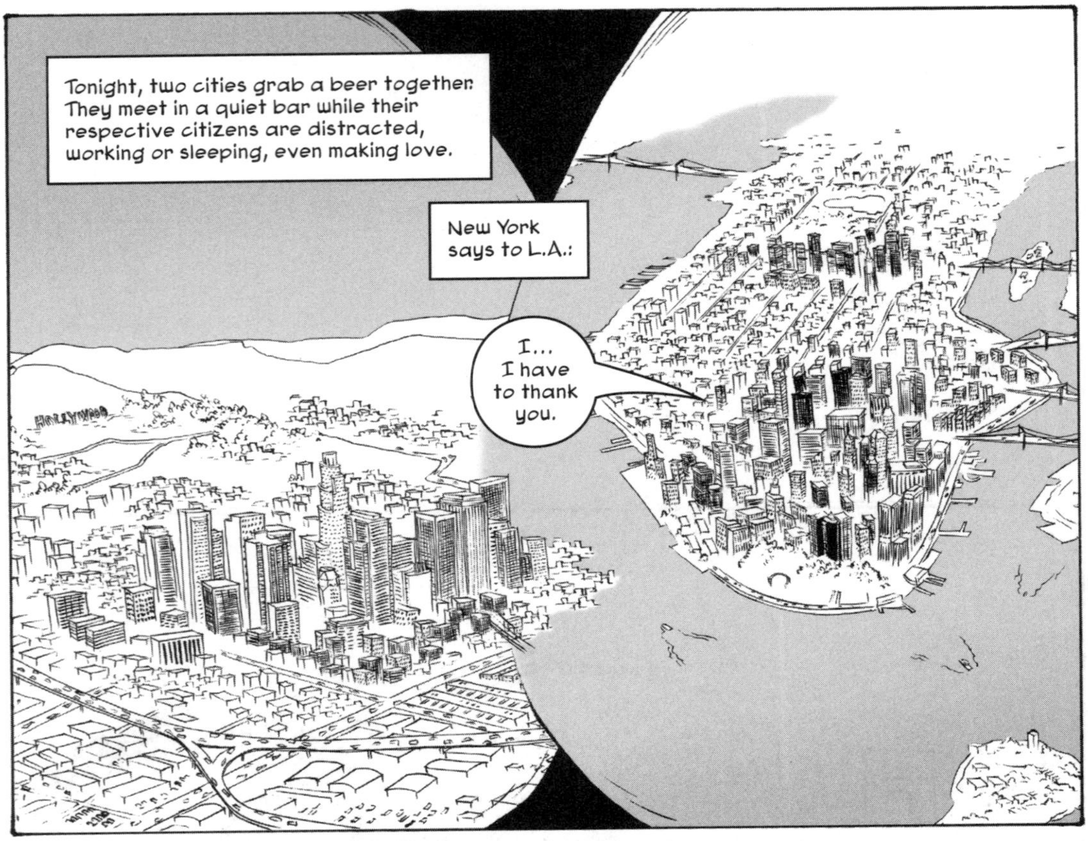
Tonight, two cities grab a beer together. They meet in a quiet bar while their respective citizens are distracted, working or sleeping, even making love.
New York says to L.A.:
I... I have to thank you.

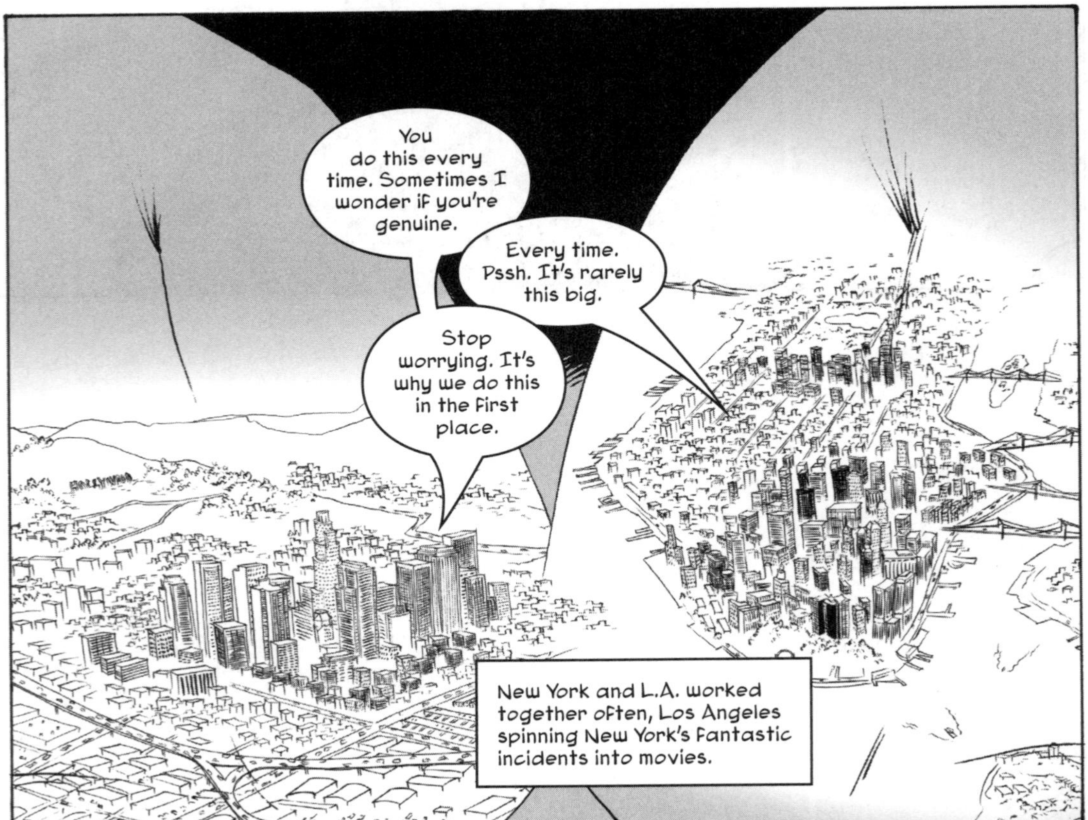
You do this every time. Sometimes I wonder if you're genuine.
Every time. Pssh. It's rarely this big.
Stop worrying. It's why we do this in the first place.
New York and L.A. worked together often, Los Angeles spinning New York's fantastic incidents into movies.

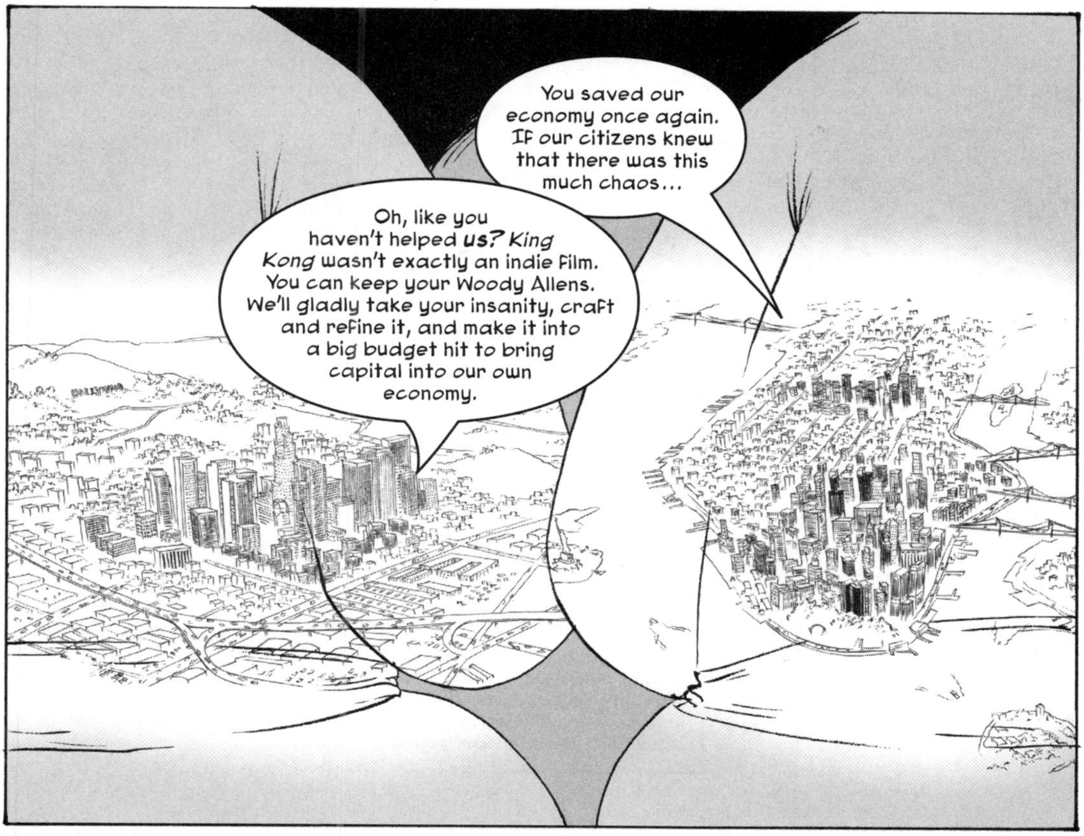
You saved our economy once again. If our citizens knew that there was this much chaos...
Oh, like you haven't helped **us?** *King Kong* wasn't exactly an indie film. You can keep your Woody Allens. We'll gladly take your insanity, craft and refine it, and make it into a big budget hit to bring capital into our own economy.

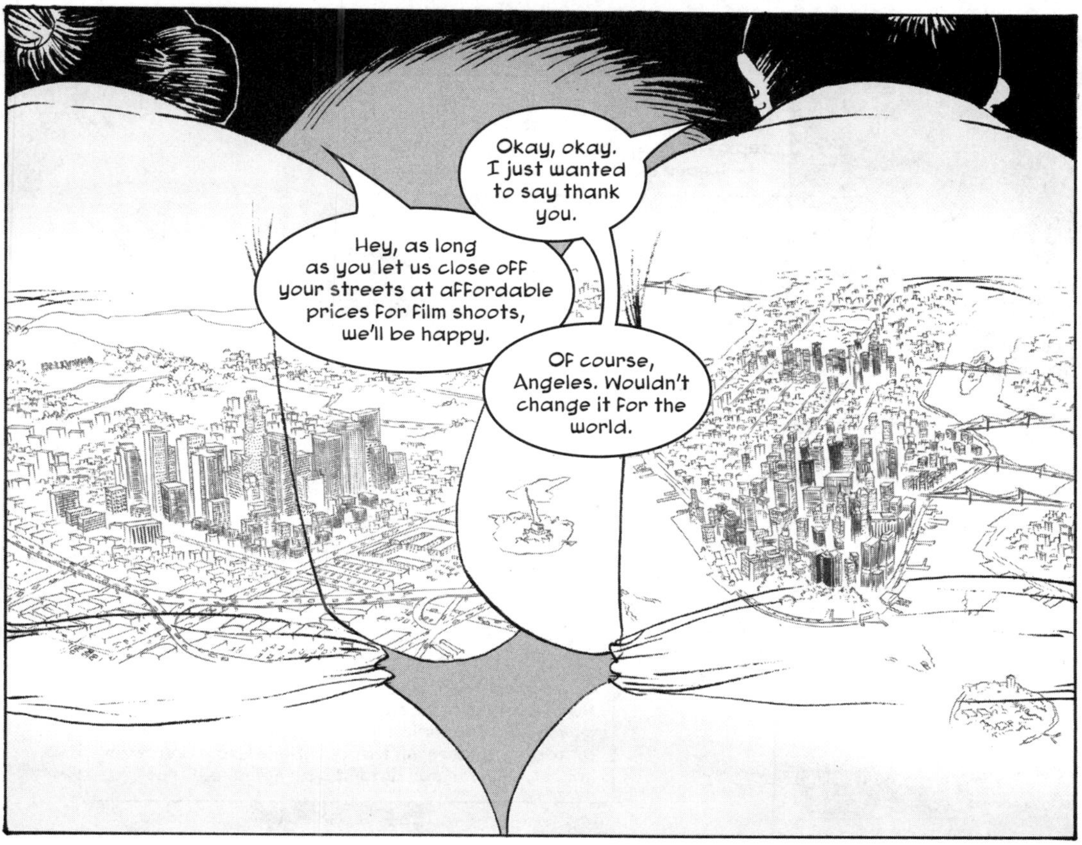
Okay, okay. I just wanted to say thank you.
Hey, as long as you let us close off your streets at affordable prices for film shoots, we'll be happy.
Of course, Angeles. Wouldn't change it for the world.

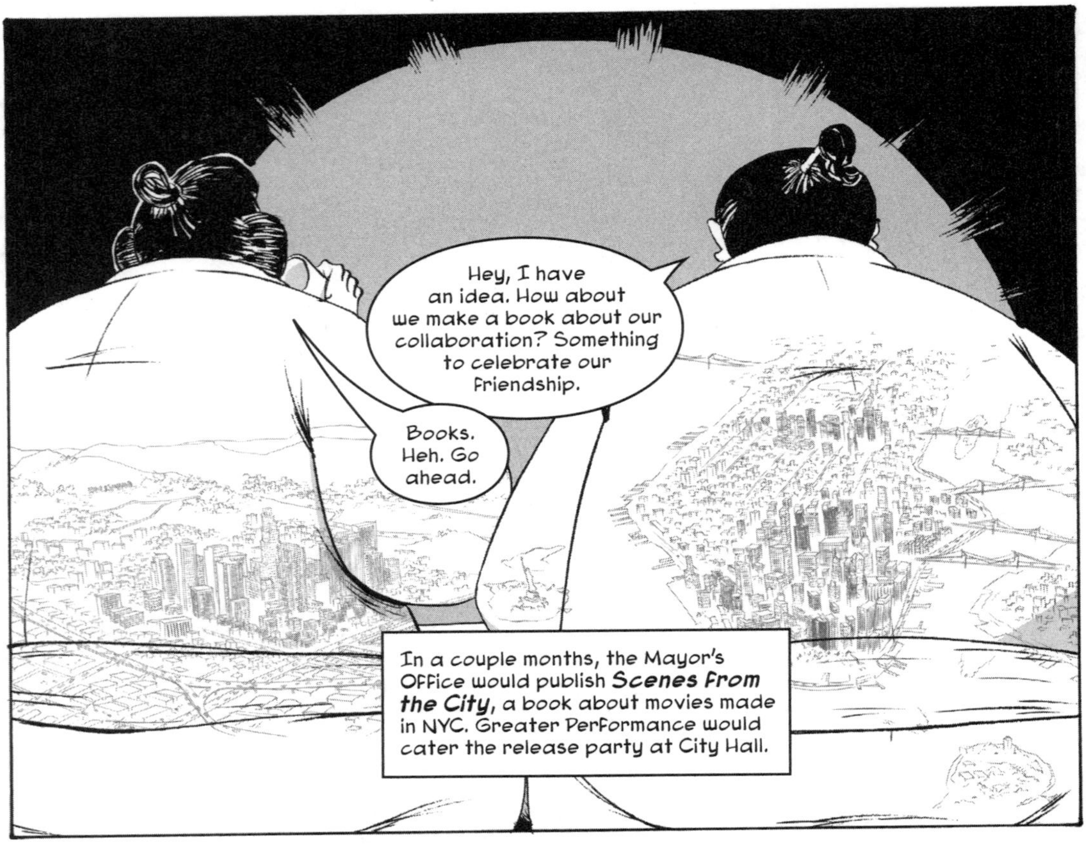
Hey, I have an idea. How about we make a book about our collaboration? Something to celebrate our friendship.
Books. Heh. Go ahead.
In a couple months, the Mayor's Office would publish ***Scenes From the City***, a book about movies made in NYC. Greater Performance would cater the release party at City Hall.

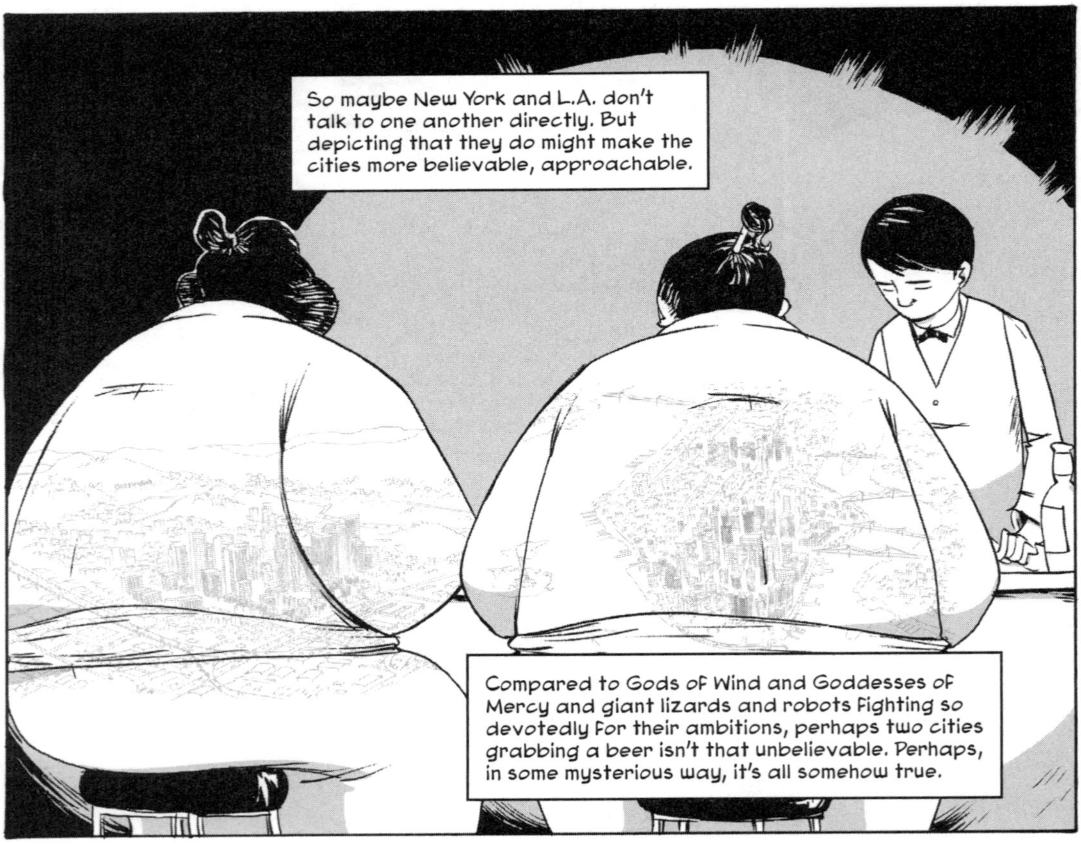
So maybe New York and L.A. don't talk to one another directly. But depicting that they do might make the cities more believable, approachable.
Compared to Gods of Wind and Goddesses of Mercy and giant lizards and robots fighting so devotedly for their ambitions, perhaps two cities grabbing a beer isn't that unbelievable. Perhaps, in some mysterious way, it's all somehow true.

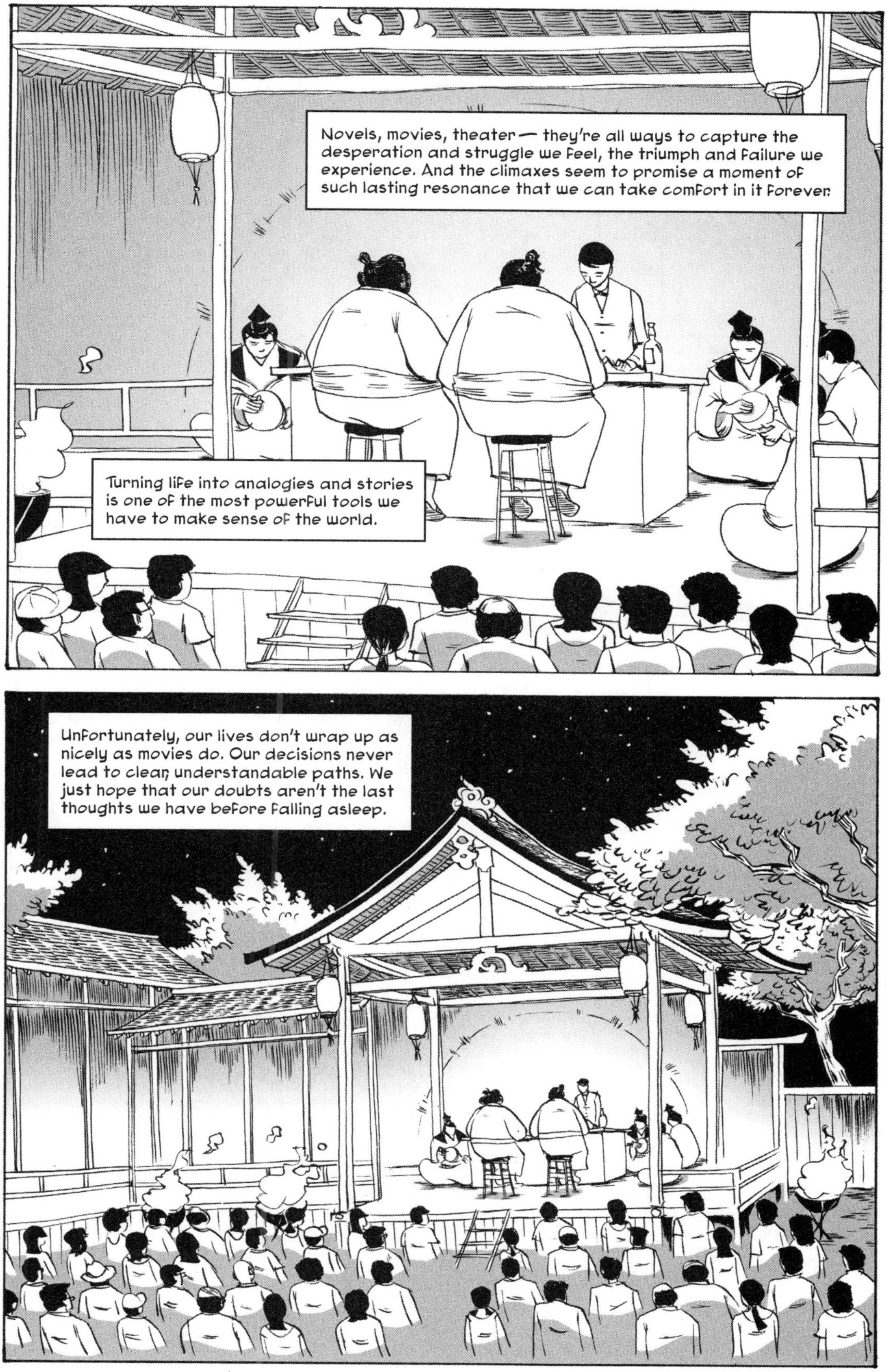
Novels, movies, theater— they're all ways to capture the desperation and struggle we feel, the triumph and failure we experience. And the climaxes seem to promise a moment of such lasting resonance that we can take comfort in it forever.
Turning life into analogies and stories is one of the most powerful tools we have to make sense of the world.
Unfortunately, our lives don't wrap up as nicely as movies do. Our decisions never lead to clear, understandable paths. We just hope that our doubts aren't the last thoughts we have before falling asleep.

チェック、チェック、いち、に

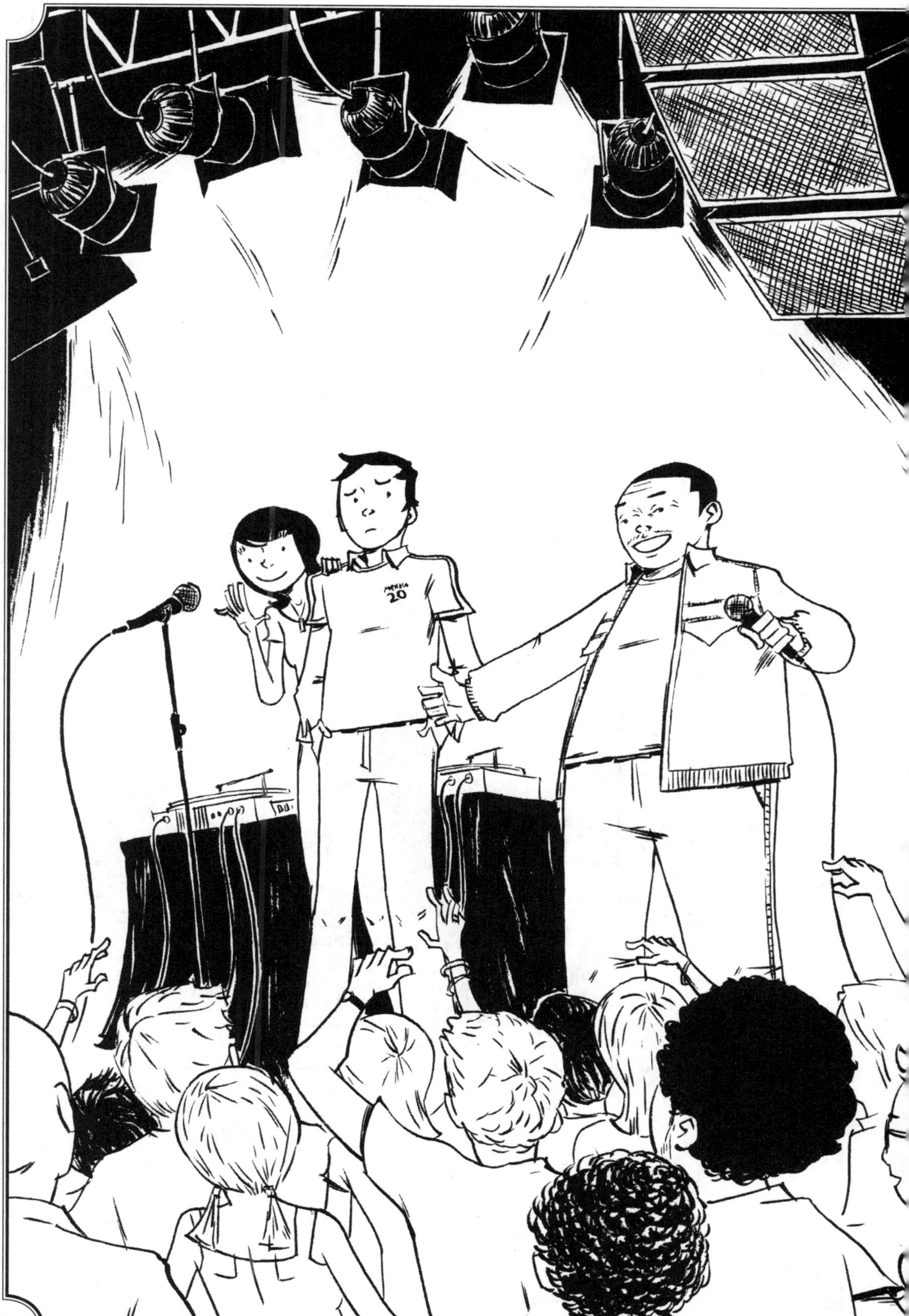
20

There was something different about John Hiro these days.

Masago couldn't quite tell what it was. Perhaps he looked less fearful?

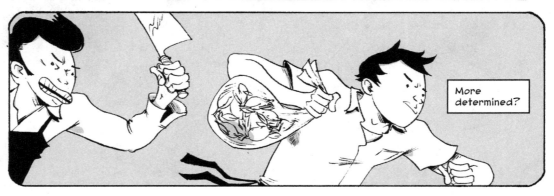

More determined?

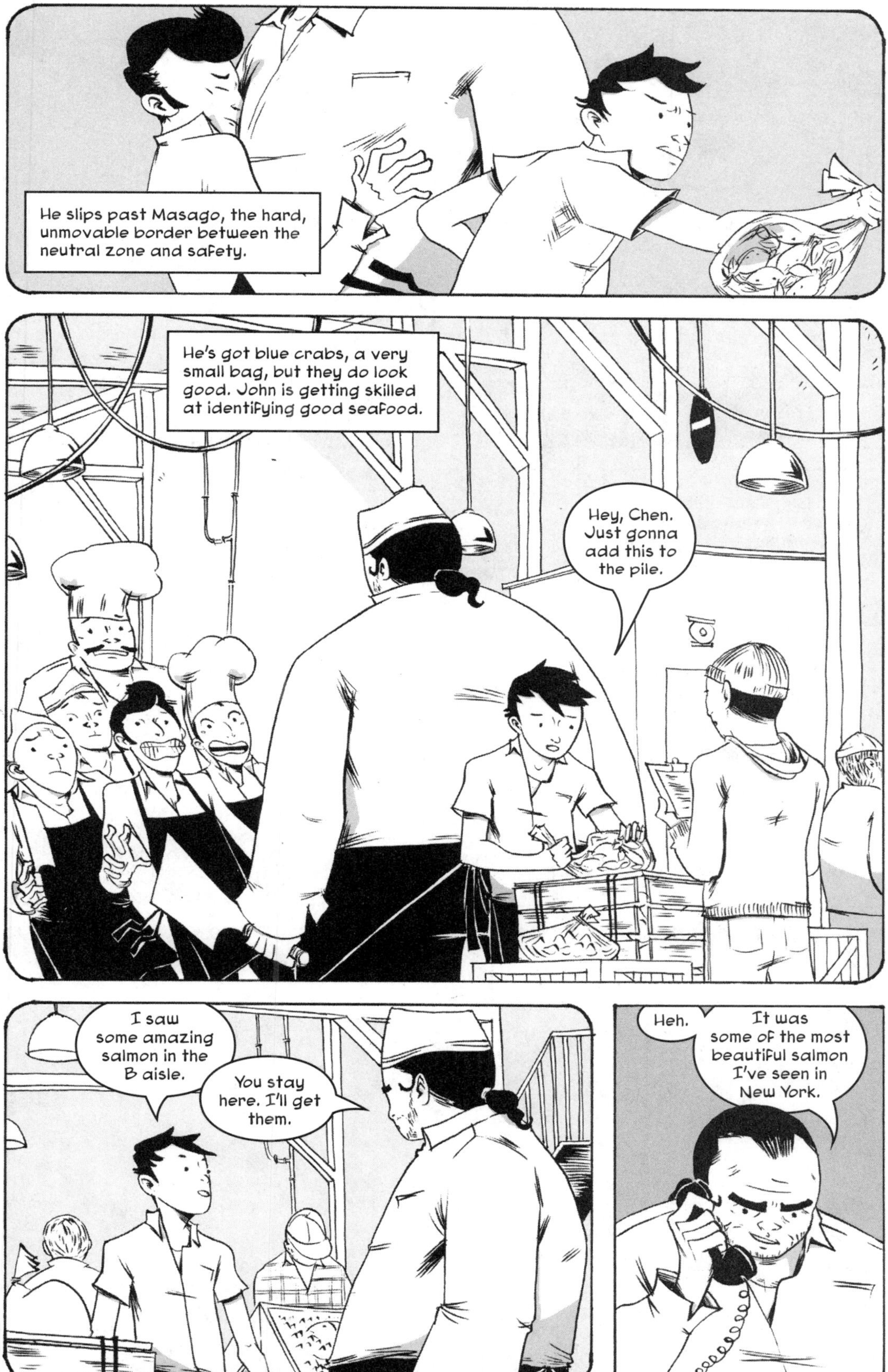
He slips past Masago, the hard, unmovable border between the neutral zone and safety.
He's got blue crabs, a very small bag, but they do look good. John is getting skilled at identifying good seafood.
Hey, Chen. Just gonna add this to the pile.
I saw some amazing salmon in the B aisle.
You stay here. I'll get them.
Heh.
It was some of the most beautiful salmon I've seen in New York.

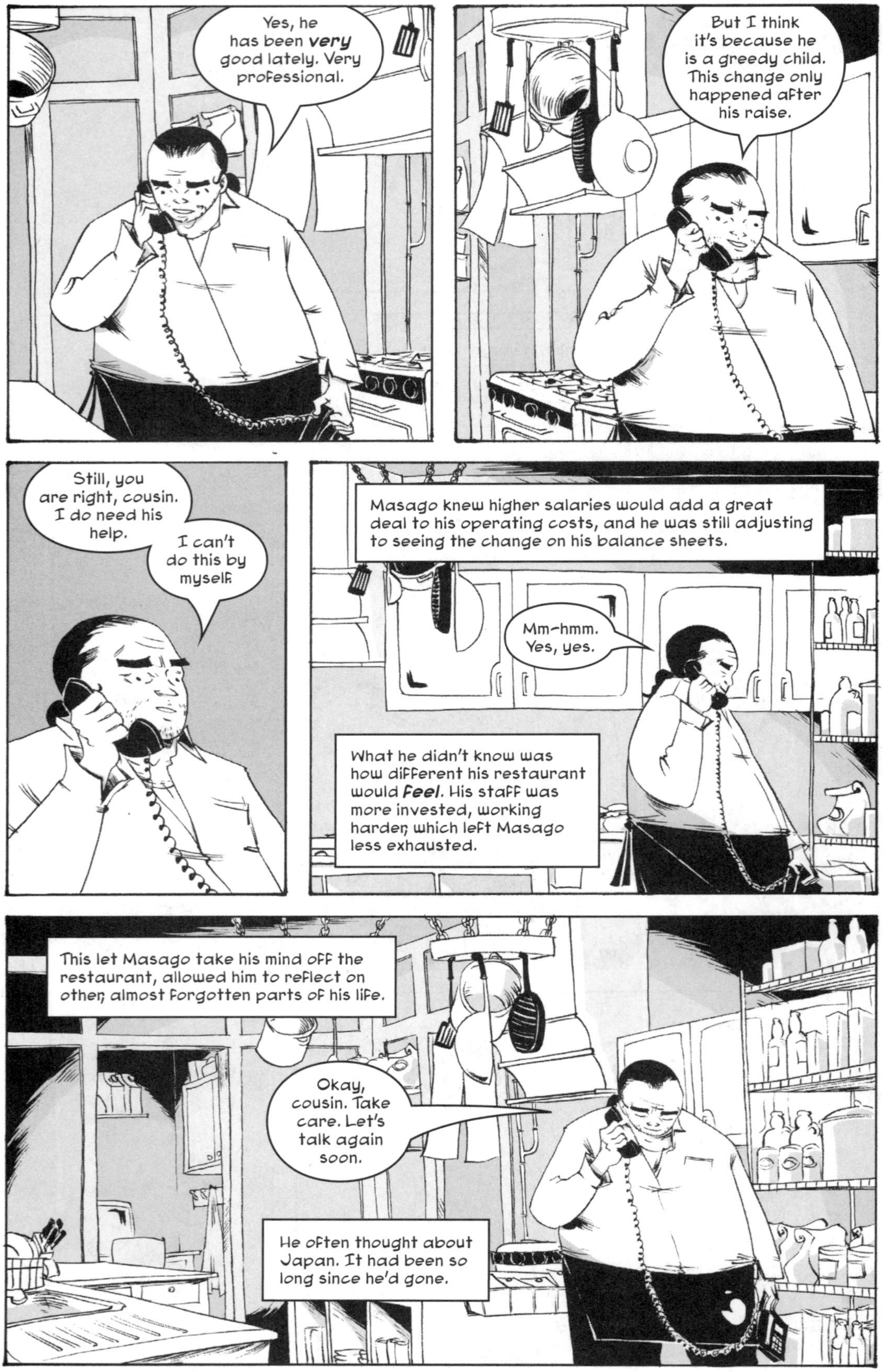
Yes, he has been **very** good lately. Very professional.
But I think it's because he is a greedy child. This change only happened after his raise.
Still, you are right, cousin. I do need his help.
I can't do this by myself.
Masago knew higher salaries would add a great deal to his operating costs, and he was still adjusting to seeing the change on his balance sheets.
Mm-hmm. Yes, yes.
What he didn't know was how different his restaurant would ***feel***. His staff was more invested, working harder, which left Masago less exhausted.
This let Masago take his mind off the restaurant, allowed him to reflect on other, almost forgotten parts of his life.
Okay, cousin. Take care. Let's talk again soon.
He often thought about Japan. It had been so long since he'd gone.

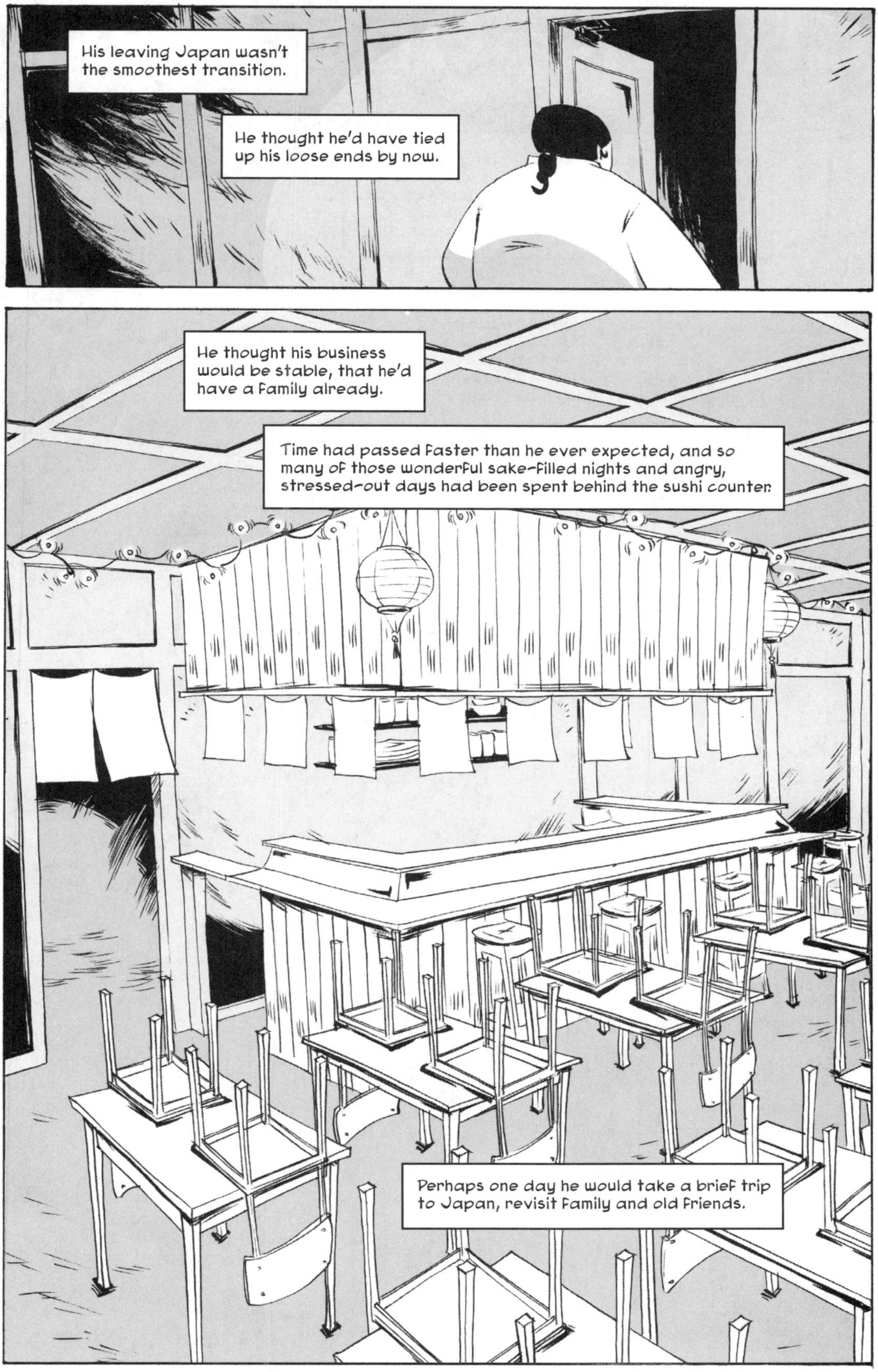
His leaving Japan wasn't the smoothest transition.
He thought he'd have tied up his loose ends by now.
He thought his business would be stable, that he'd have a family already.
Time had passed faster than he ever expected, and so many of those wonderful sake-filled nights and angry, stressed-out days had been spent behind the sushi counter.
Perhaps one day he would take a brief trip to Japan, revisit family and old friends.

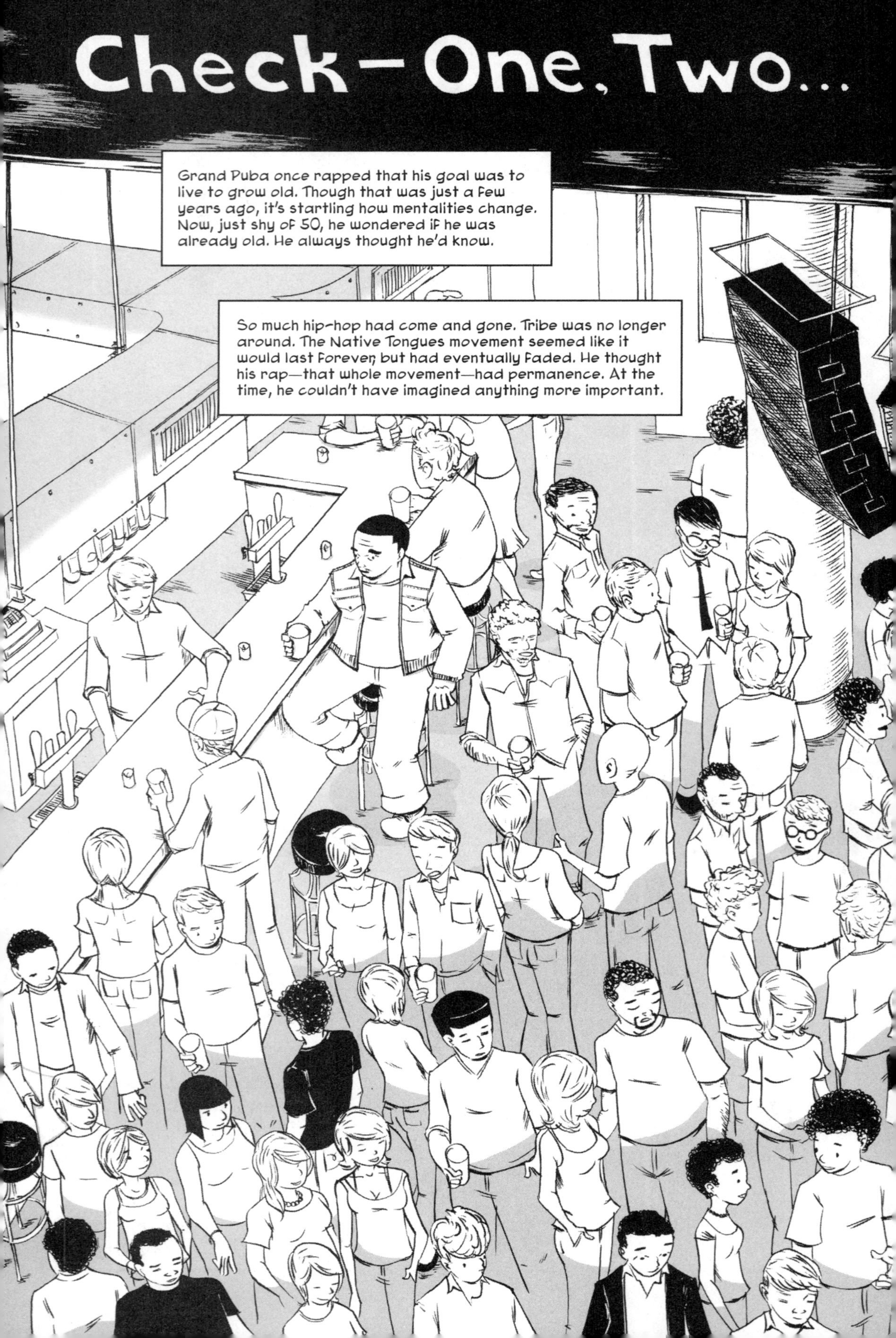
Check-One, Two...
Grand Puba once rapped that his goal was to live to grow old. Though that was just a few years ago, it's startling how mentalities change. Now, just shy of 50, he wondered if he was already old. He always thought he'd know.
So much hip-hop had come and gone. Tribe was no longer around. The Native Tongues movement seemed like it would last forever, but had eventually faded. He thought his rap—that whole movement—had permanence. At the time, he couldn't have imagined anything more important.

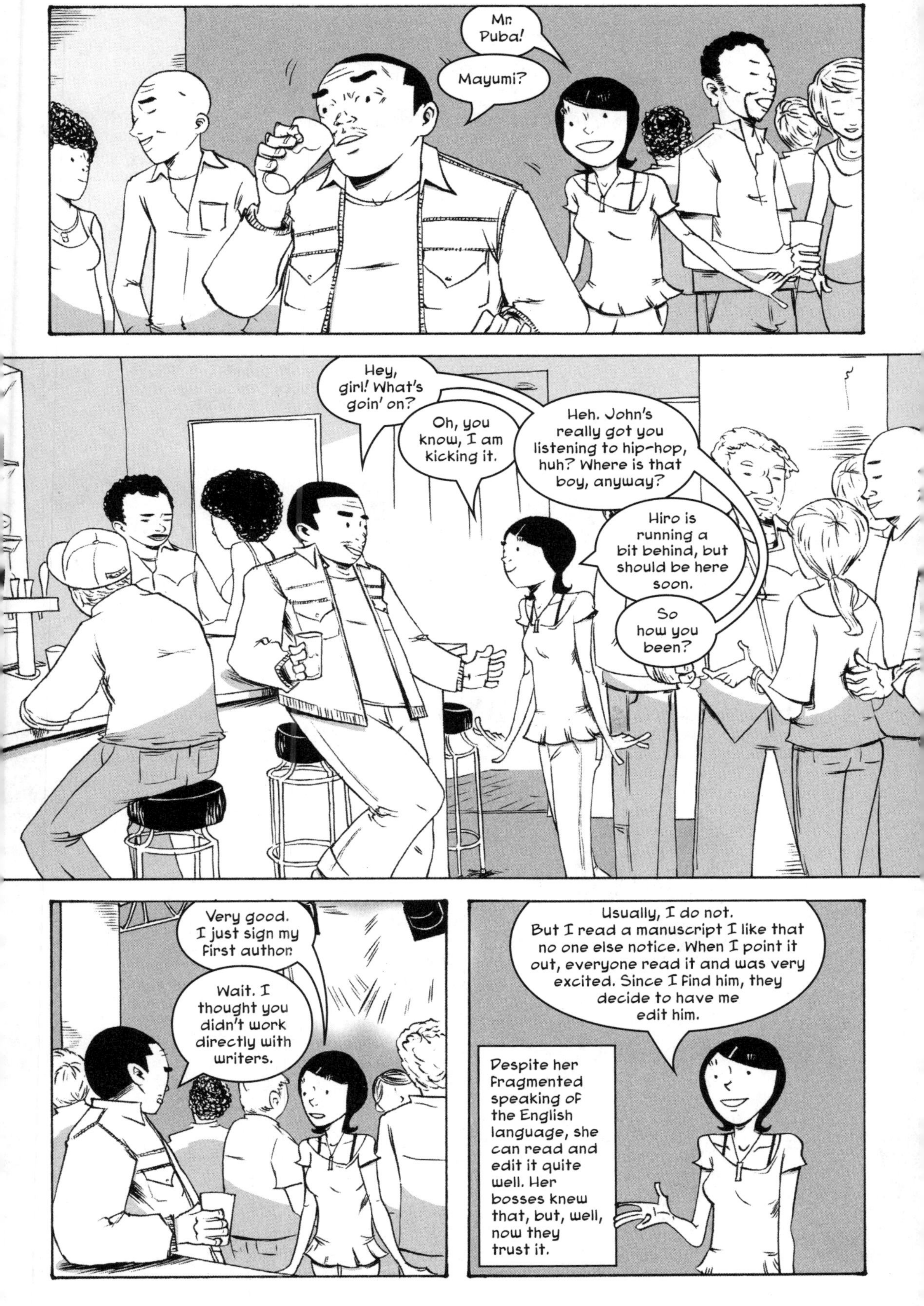
Mr. Puba!
Mayumi?
Hey, girl! What's goin' on?
Oh, you know, I am kicking it.
Heh. John's really got you listening to hip-hop, huh? Where is that boy, anyway?
Hiro is running a bit behind, but should be here soon.
So how you been?
Very good. I just sign my first author.
Wait. I thought you didn't work directly with writers.
Usually, I do not. But I read a manuscript I like that no one else notice. When I point it out, everyone read it and was very excited. Since I find him, they decide to have me edit him.
Despite her fragmented speaking of the English language, she can read and edit it quite well. Her bosses knew that, but, well, now they trust it.

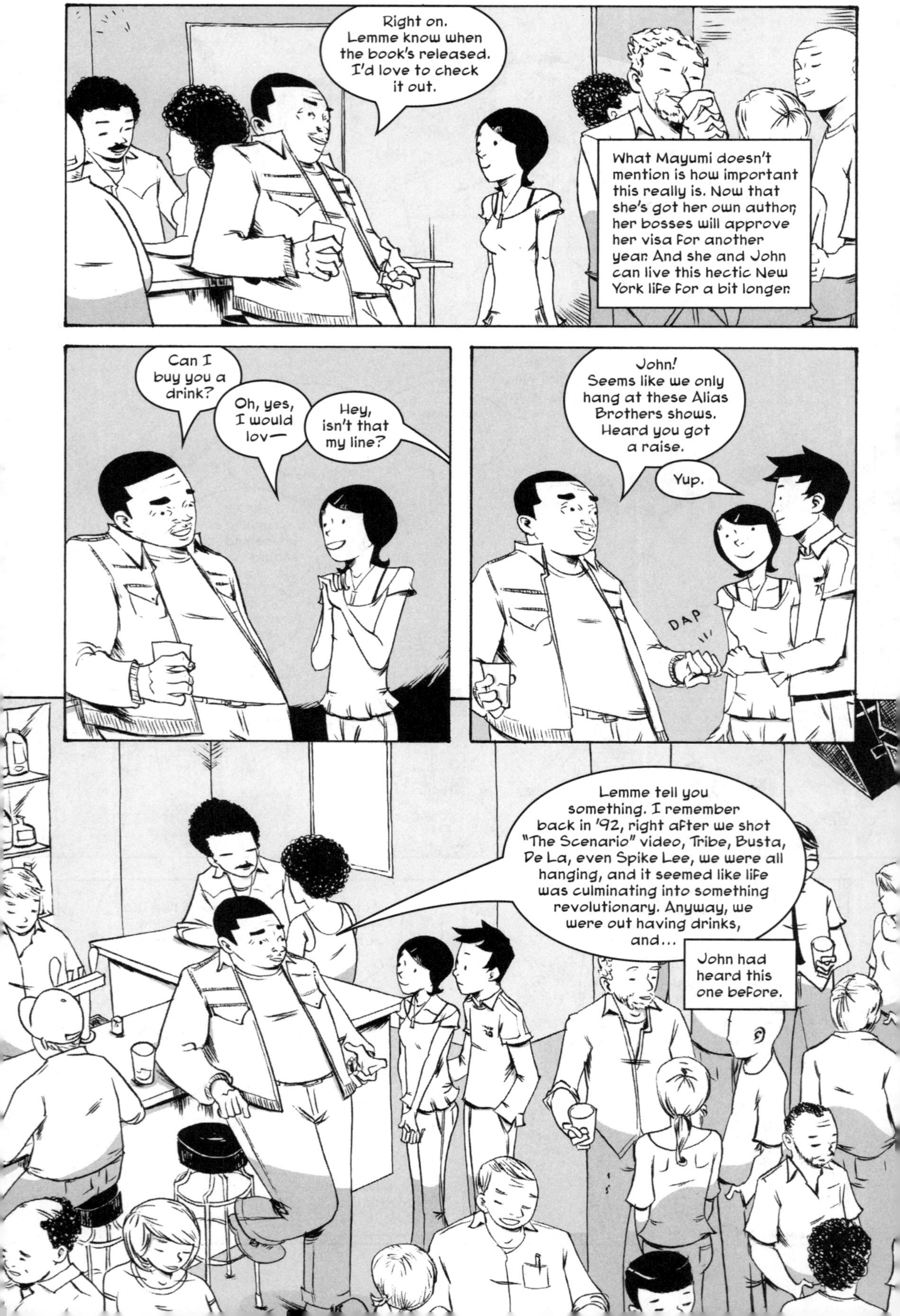
Right on. Lemme know when the book's released. I'd love to check it out.
What Mayumi doesn't mention is how important this really is. Now that she's got her own author, her bosses will approve her visa for another year. And she and John can live this hectic New York life for a bit longer.
Can I buy you a drink?
Oh, yes, I would lov—
Hey, isn't that my line?
John! Seems like we only hang at these Alias Brothers shows. Heard you got a raise.
Yup.
DAP
Lemme tell you something. I remember back in '92, right after we shot "The Scenario" video, Tribe, Busta, De La, even Spike Lee, we were all hanging, and it seemed like life was culminating into something revolutionary. Anyway, we were out having drinks, and...
John had heard this one before.

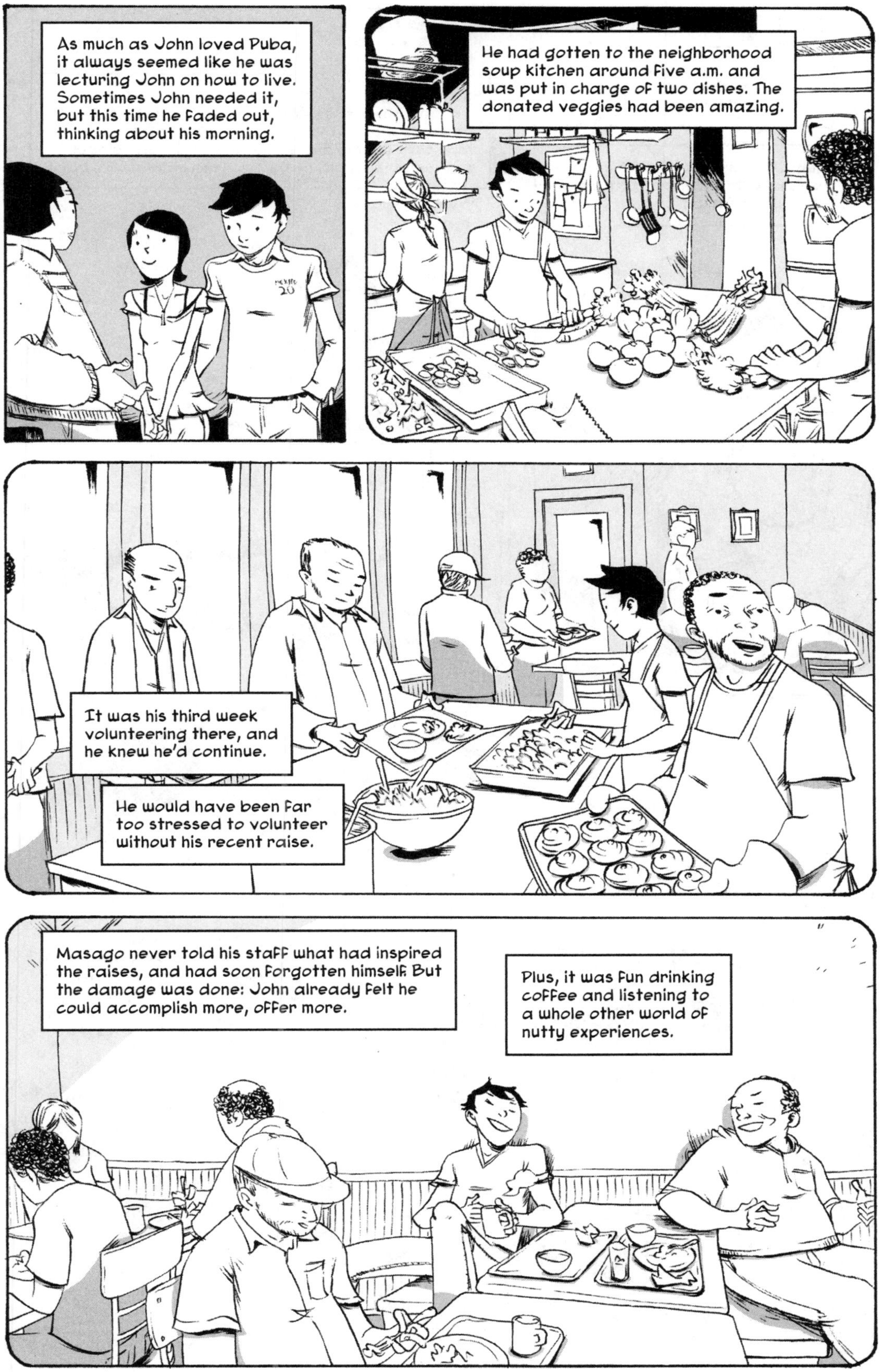
As much as John loved Puba, it always seemed like he was lecturing John on how to live. Sometimes John needed it, but this time he faded out, thinking about his morning.
MEXICO 20
He had gotten to the neighborhood soup kitchen around five a.m. and was put in charge of two dishes. The donated veggies had been amazing.
It was his third week volunteering there, and he knew he'd continue.
He would have been far too stressed to volunteer without his recent raise.
Masago never told his staff what had inspired the raises, and had soon forgotten himself. But the damage was done: John already felt he could accomplish more, offer more.
Plus, it was fun drinking coffee and listening to a whole other world of nutty experiences.

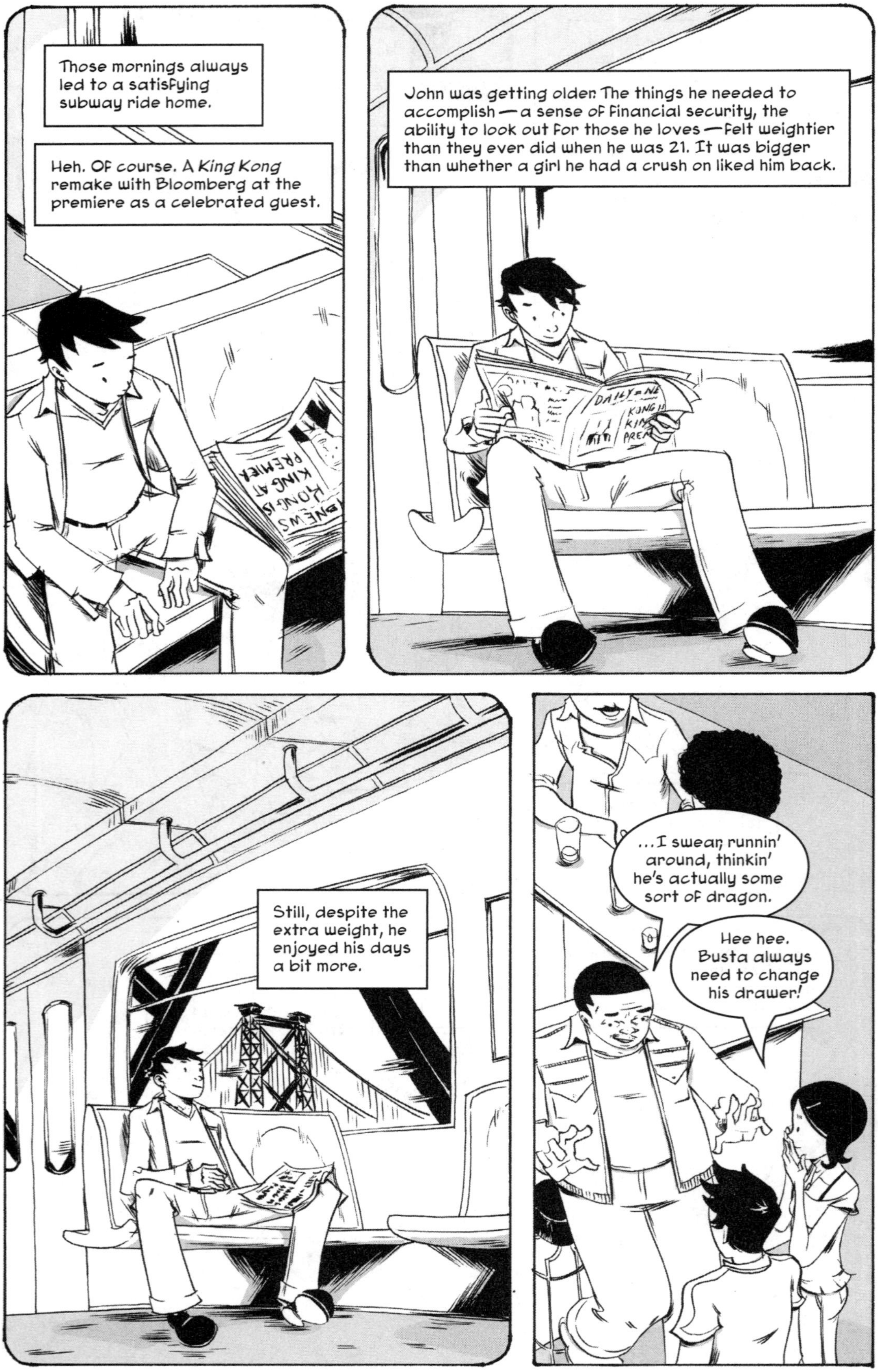
Those mornings always led to a satisfying subway ride home.
Heh. Of course. A *King Kong* remake with Bloomberg at the premiere as a celebrated guest.
John was getting older. The things he needed to accomplish—a sense of financial security, the ability to look out for those he loves—felt weightier than they ever did when he was 21. It was bigger than whether a girl he had a crush on liked him back.
Still, despite the extra weight, he enjoyed his days a bit more.
...I swear, runnin' around, thinkin' he's actually some sort of dragon.
Hee hee. Busta always need to change his drawer!

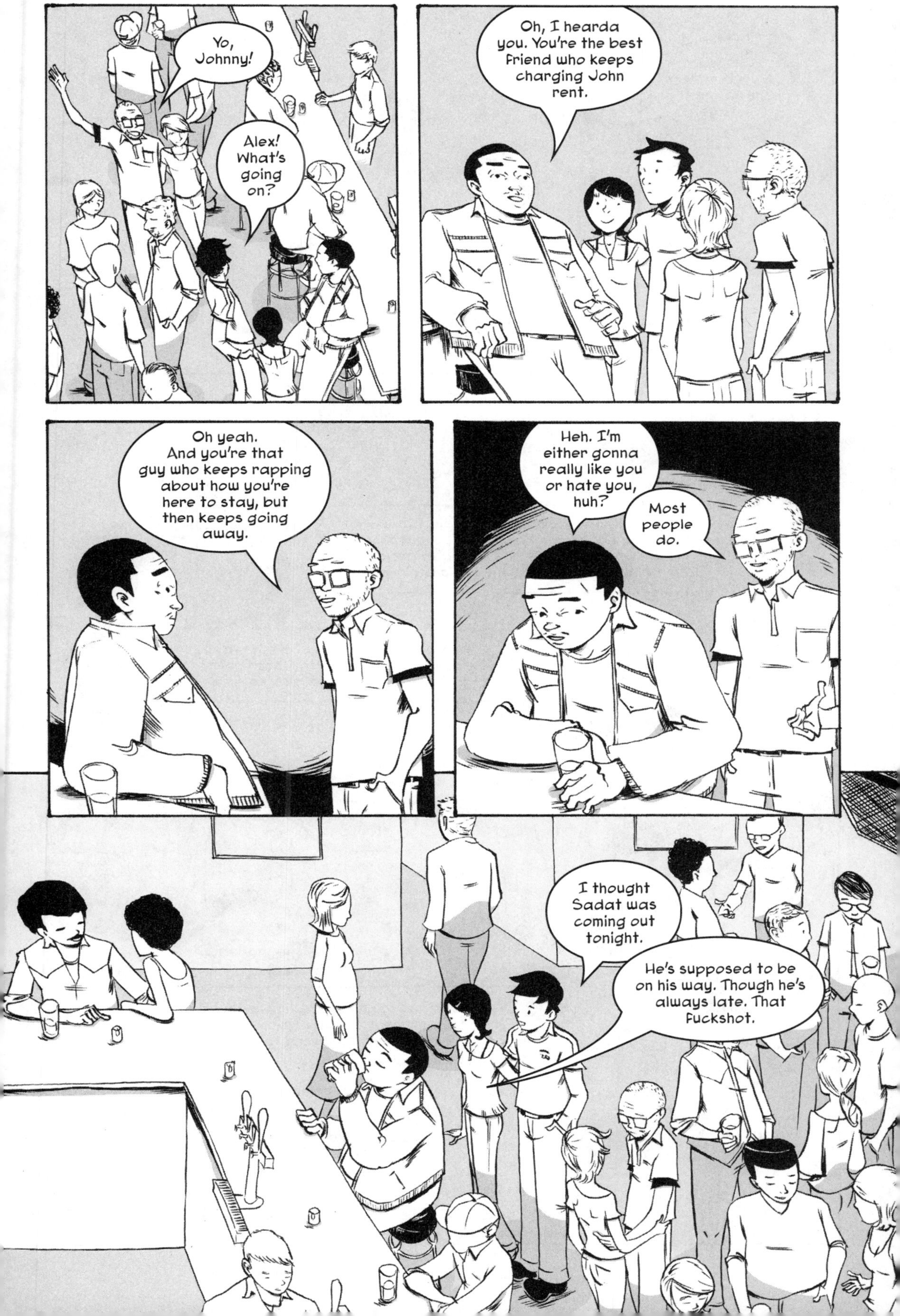
Yo, Johnny!
Alex! What's going on?
Oh, I hearda you. You're the best friend who keeps charging John rent.
Oh yeah. And you're that guy who keeps rapping about how you're here to stay, but then keeps going away.
Heh. I'm either gonna really like you or hate you, huh?
Most people do.
I thought Sadat was coming out tonight.
He's supposed to be on his way. Though he's always late. That fuckshot.

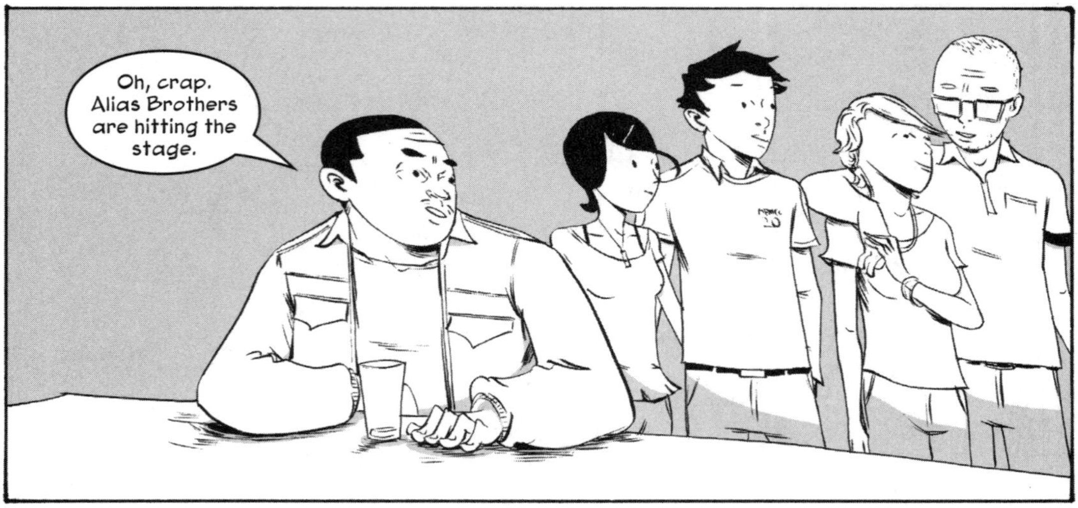
Oh, crap. Alias Brothers are hitting the stage.

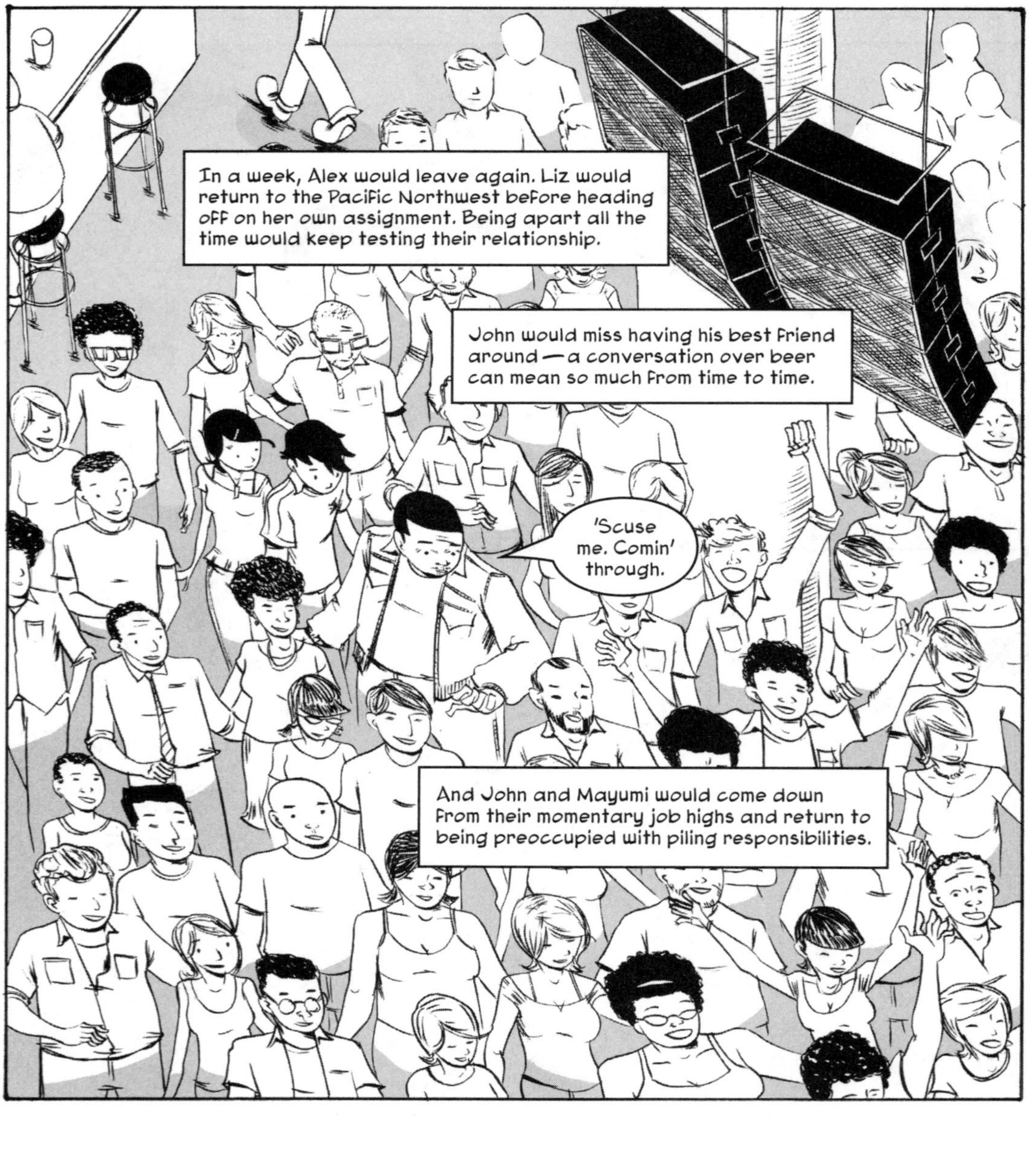
In a week, Alex would leave again. Liz would return to the Pacific Northwest before heading off on her own assignment. Being apart all the time would keep testing their relationship.
John would miss having his best friend around—a conversation over beer can mean so much from time to time.
'Scuse me. Comin' through.
And John and Mayumi would come down from their momentary job highs and return to being preoccupied with piling responsibilities.

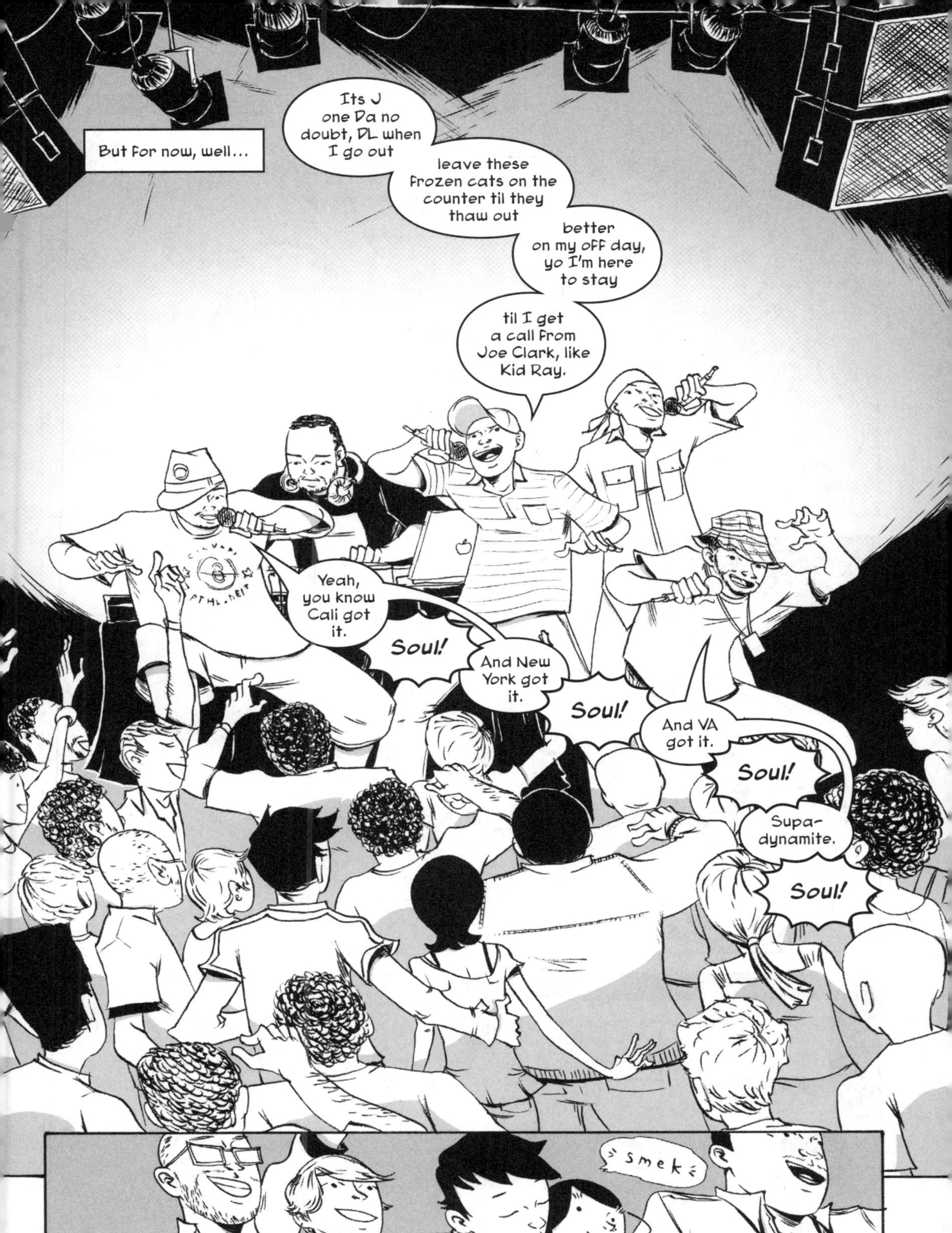
But for now, well...
Its J one Da no doubt, DL when I go out
leave these frozen cats on the counter til they thaw out
better on my off day, yo I'm here to stay
til I get a call from Joe Clark, like Kid Ray.
Yeah, you know Cali got it.
Soul!
And New York got it.
Soul!
And VA got it.
Soul!
Supa-dynamite.
Soul!

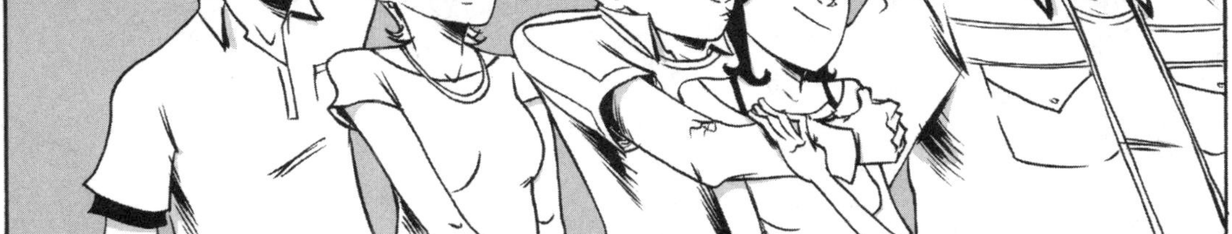
smek

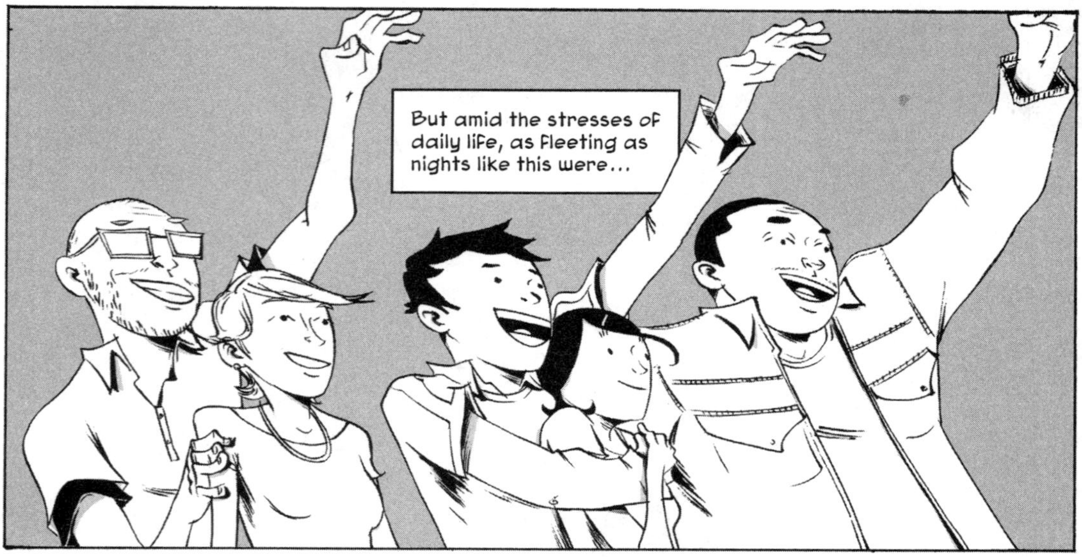
But amid the stresses of daily life, as fleeting as nights like this were...

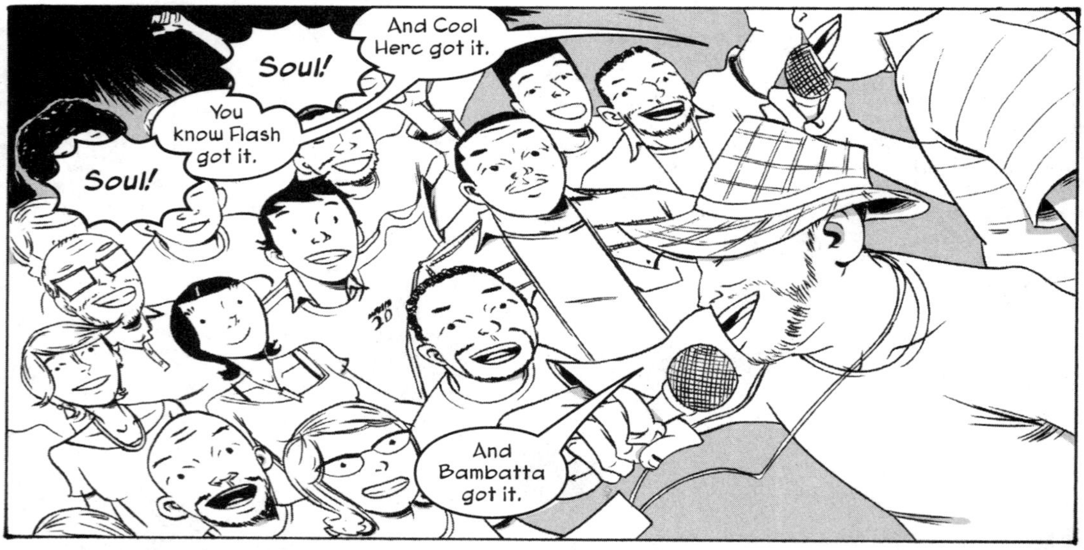
Soul!
You know Flash got it.
Soul!
And Cool Herc got it.
And Bambatta got it.

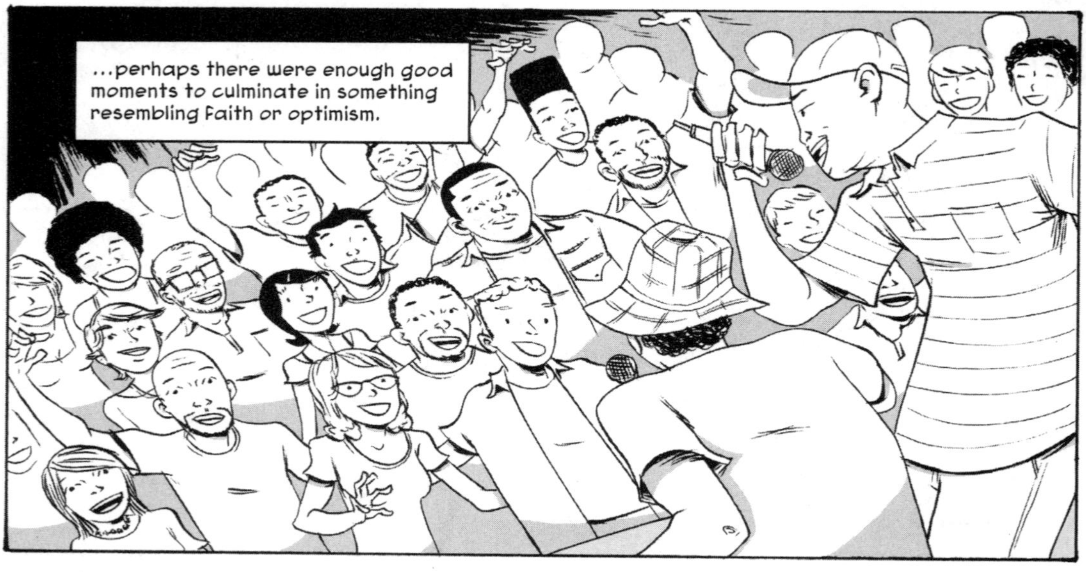
...perhaps there were enough good moments to culminate in something resembling faith or optimism.

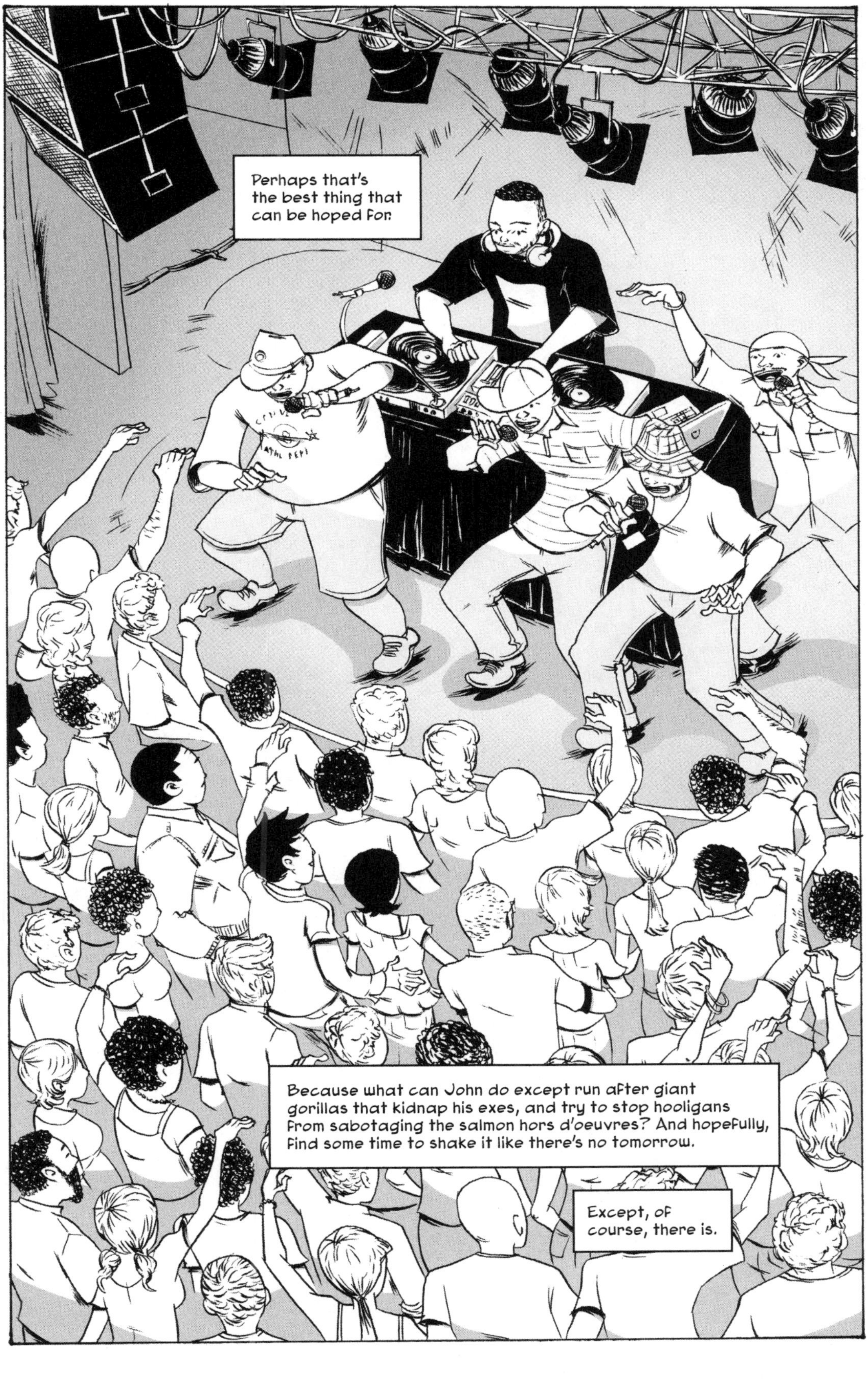
Perhaps that's the best thing that can be hoped for.
Because what can John do except run after giant gorillas that kidnap his exes, and try to stop hooligans from sabotaging the salmon hors d'oeuvres? And hopefully, find some time to shake it like there's no tomorrow.
Except, of course, there is.

Acknowledgments

The support of my family has meant so incredibly much. Mom, Dad, Shirley, and Katherine—if I could hug you all until you broke, I would, so you better watch out.

And of course, appreciation goes out to my extended family—San shu gong, Jiu jiu, Gu po, Gong gong, and everyone else in the Chao and Wang families. And Ye ye and Nai nai, who would have loved this.

Thanks for being just as confused as me in the attempt to figure things out—Sean Boggs, Rick Farley, Nate Gibson, Tracey Long, Kathe McKenna, Joe Merkel, Peter Meulenbroek, Jesse Post, Matthue Roth, Davy Rothbart, Michelle Sarrat, John Sazaklis, Stephen Shipps, Tom Starace, and Thomas Turnbull.

So many thanks to Liz Gorinsky, who I really believe was the perfect editor for this book, David Hopkins, and Seth Fishman.

And Dylan Babb, who's made my life far richer in so many ways.

Ballard C. Boyd

FRED CHAO wrote and illustrated the first book in this series, *Johnny Hiro {Half Asian, All Hero}*, parts of which appeared in *The Best American Comics 2010*.

His comics have also appeared in the anthology *Found: Requiem for a Paper Bag*. And he wrote and illustrated the children's comic book *Alison and Her Rainy Day Robot*.

He was born in 1978 in San Francisco, California, and recently moved back to the Bay Area. He misses Brooklyn terribly.

———— ✑ ————